SURE TO RISE

THE EDMONDS STORY

PETER ALSOP
KATE PARSONSON
RICHARD WOLFE

CANTERBURY UNIVERSITY PRESS

CONTENTS

EDMO
59 YEARS
1879
SURE
SOLD EVERYWHERE
EDMONDS
ESTD
PRIZE
BAKING · POWD
SURE TO RISE
TRADE
REGISTERED

ONDS
PROGRESS
1938
POWDER
VANILLA
EDMONDS
CUSTARD
POWDER
VANILLA
VANILLA
VANILLA
RISE
EDMONDS
CUSTARD

SOLD EVERYWHERE
EDMONDS'
PRIZE
ESTD 1879
BAKING • POWDER
SURE TO RISE
TRADE MARK
(REGISTERED)
N.Z. JUBILEE
1900-1
AWARDED FIRST PRIZE
FOR
BAKING POWDER
AND
CUSTARD POWDER
T.J. EDMONDS
NEW ZEALAND INTERNATIONAL EXHIBITION
1906
CHRISTCHURCH
EXHIBITION DUNEDIN
1889-90

THE STORY

PROLOGUE

It's one of the best-known and most recognised brands and slogans in New Zealand: Edmonds Sure to Rise, with its radiant sun. The man behind the company, Thomas John Edmonds, came to New Zealand with his wife Jane in 1879. Young and resourceful, but not financially secure, he was determined to make a go of life in a land far from his birthplace in London's East End. While running a modest corner grocery store in a working-class Christchurch suburb, where he and his family also lived, he expanded into making baking powder, experimenting until he got the mixture just right. His product, initially packed in bags and then in tins, took off, and before long he needed a store beside the shop, then land for a wooden factory and finally, in the 1920s, he built the Art Deco factory that became a Christchurch landmark, with its saw-tooth roof, proud rising sun symbol and nationally admired gardens.

Thomas Edmonds was also a benefactor, a man who had grown up with little and who helped others, a man interested in chemistry and plants and alternative beliefs, a man who loved music and gave his daughters every opportunity to express their talents, while his sons worked in the ever-growing business, a man who gave his city some of its best-known buildings. He embraced imaginative advertising and marketing techniques and ensured progressive working conditions for his loyal and long-serving staff.

Thomas and Jane Edmonds, photographed about 1920. In the photo overleaf, Thomas is seated at the Edmonds factory around 1906 with his eldest son Will on the right.

After his death in 1932, the company continued to flourish for some time but eventually the family connections faded and takeover became inevitable. However, the Edmonds name, and that rising sun, remain on the baking powder and other essential products that thousands of New Zealanders use every day, and on the best-selling cookery book they still purchase in impressive numbers.

This is the story of a man from humble beginnings who, thanks to hard work, creativity and persistence, and with considerable support from his wife, created an iconic business.

FAMILY TREES

EDMONDS FAMILY

James Edmonds
1814–1880

m. 1839

Jane Elizabeth Darley
c.1814–1892

- + 7 Others
- Edwin Edmonds b. 1851 *m.* Sarah Irvine b. 1852
- **THOMAS JOHN EDMONDS** 1858–1932 *m.* 1879 **JANE ELIZABETH MIDDLETON IRVINE** 1860–1938
  - Thomas William (Will) b. 1880 *m.* Alice Hart b. 1879
    - Rita b. 1905
    - Nelma b. 1908
    - Keith b. 1909
    - Brenda b. 1914
  - Ernest b. 1881 *m.* Ethel McCausland b. 1880
    - Eileen (Lily) b. 1905
    - Edna b. 1911
  - Lilian b. 1883 *m.* Albert (Bert) Cropp b. 1880
    - David b. 1914
    - Elaine b. 1920
  - George b. 1886 *m.* 1 Clara Thomson b. 1888; *m.* 2 Dorothy Welsh
    - Thelma b. 1910
    - Jack b. 1912
    - Nola b. 1914
    - Ray b. 1917
    - Murray b. 1926
  - James (Jim) b. 1888 *m.* 1 Edith Daniels b. 1892; *m.* 2 Thelma Stone b. 1909
    - Marijean b. 1920
  - Gertrude b. 1891 *m.* Henry (Harry) Williams b. 1880
    - Pamela b. 1922
    - Elizabeth b. 1925
    - John b. 1926
  - Beatrice b. 1895 *m.* 1 Samuel (Peter) Fripp; *m.* 2 Leslie Jauncey
  - Irene (Rene) b. 1898 *m.* Kenneth Ballantyne b. 1898
    - Irene (Day) b. 1927
    - Margaret (Jan) b. 1930
    - John b. 1934

IRVINE FAMILY

David Irvine
d. 1862

- *m.* 1 Susannah
  - Henry
  - Eliza ⚓ b. 1851
- *m.* 2 Eliza Middleton ⚓ b. 1823
  - Sarah ⚓ b. 1852 *m.* Edwin Edmonds ⚓ b. 1851
  - **JANE ELIZABETH MIDDLETON IRVINE** ⚓ b. 1860 *m.* **THOMAS JOHN EDMONDS** ⚓ b. 1858

⚓ Emigrated on the *Waitangi* 1879

GARDNER & SONS

CHRIST CHURCH
ST PAUL
Old Ford
ST JAMES THE LESS
ST BARNABAS
ST STEPHEN
Old Ford
ST JOHN
ST SIMON
Zelotes
ST MARY BOW
BROMLEY ST MARY
or ST LEONARD
HOLY TRINITY
Stepney
ST ANTHONY
Stepney
ST BENET
Stepney
ST PETER
Stepney
ST ANDREW
Bromley St Leonard
IMPERIAL GAS WORKS
ST LUKE
Stepney
ALL HALLOWS
CHRIST CHURCH
Stepney
ST DUNSTAN
Stepney
ST PAUL
Bow Common
ST GABRIEL
ST MICHAEL AND ALL ANGELS
COMMERCIAL GAS WORKS
ST THOMAS
Arbour Sq. Stepney
ST MATTHIAS
Stepney
ST SAVIOUR
ALL HALLOWS
East India Docks
ST FRIDESWIDE
CHRIST CHURCH
Watney Street
ST MARY
Johnson Street
ST JAMES
Ratcliffe
ST ANNE
Limehouse
ST STEPHEN
ST MATTHIAS
ST PAUL
SHADWELL NEW BASIN
ST PETER
London Docks
ST PETER
Limehouse
ALL SAINTS
WEST INDIA DOCKS
ST JOHN
ST MARY
Rotherhithe
HOLY TRINITY
ST LUKE
Millwall
ST JOHN
Cubitt Town
ST ANDREW
ALL SAINTS
ST BARNABAS
ST CUTHBERT
Millwall
CHRIST CHURCH
Isle of Dogs
ST KATHERINE
ST LUKE

CHAPTER 1

FROM LONDON TO LYTTELTON

To qualify as a true Cockney, you must begin your life within the sound of the church bells of St Mary le Bow in London's Cheapside. Thomas John Edmonds, born in Poplar on 13 October 1858, fulfilled the criterion, as did his father James, who was born in the same East End docklands area in 1814. Although family legend has it that James came from Wales, census information makes this improbable. His wife, Jane Elizabeth Darley, was born in Hull, Yorkshire, probably in the same year as her husband. James had at least two siblings, Charles and Henry.

The industrial revolution from the mid-1700s to the mid-1800s meant that traditional occupations were increasingly made obsolete by new technology and ever-larger factories. Those in search of work often had to travel long distances to previously alien parts of Britain, and many made their way to London. Between 1714 and 1840, the city's population swelled from around 630,000 to nearly two million, and by the end of the Victorian period it was six million.[1] As the east became the manufacturing and commercial heart of the city, it was seen, by the mid-1800s, as a place of refuge for displaced people from other countries, such as impoverished Irish escaping the potato famine. But this huge population explosion brought unprecedented problems: poverty and starvation became all too common.

It was probably the challenge of finding and keeping employment that prompted the Edmonds' many changes of address in east and southeast London. Census records and details from birth certificates show James Edmonds' occupation variously as grocer, shopman to a provision dealer and cheesemaker. Since he was city-born, it is more likely that he was in fact a cheesemonger – someone who sold cheeses but did not make them. James was working as a grocer when the couple's first child, James Darley, was born in Lewisham (then part of Kent) in January 1840. They then moved to the dockland area of Limehouse, north of the Thames, just next to Poplar, where their next two children were born: Alfred John in December 1840 and Anne Elizabeth in November 1842. After a brief period back in Lewisham, where Henry Alfred was born in 1843, they moved a couple of miles north to Deptford. This is where the next four children were born: Charles in about 1848, William in 1850, Edwin Timothy in 1851 and Arthur in about 1857. The next, and probably final move was back over the river to Poplar, some time before the birth of Thomas John in 1858.

This 1898–99 map shows the east London area where Thomas and Jane were born and the loop of the South West India Dock (also known as South Dock) from which the newly-weds departed for New Zealand in June 1879.

James Edmonds was not an unusual name, and there were plenty of cheesemongers and grocers, so the surviving records should be approached with caution. In 1843 the London Post Office Directory listed a cheesemonger of this name living at 6 Brewer Street, Somers Town (a slum area in northwest London also referred to as St Pancras), and a grocer living in Salmon Lane, Limehouse. In July 1845 James Edmonds, grocer and cheesemonger, 'late of Salmon's Lane, Limehouse in the county of Middlesex', was declared bankrupt.[2] As the long lists in the *London Gazette* show, bankruptcy was not uncommon in these tough times, and it was a situation that could be remedied. On 29 February 1848, James Edmonds, late of 6 Brewer Street, shopman to a cheesemonger, appeared in the Court for Relief of Insolvent Debtors and was taken to the Whitecross Debtors' Prison for London and Middlesex. He was still there four years later, on 3 April 1852.[3] It is tempting to believe that the two were the same man, whose fortune declined from bankruptcy to insolvency and incarceration, but the different addresses seem to make this problematical. And unless his family was living with him in the prison, which seems unlikely since Whitecross had wards and not individual rooms like the Marshalsea immortalised by Charles Dickens in *Little Dorrit*, how did James father children born in 1850 and 1851?

Poplar, an area just north of the Isle of Dogs in London's East End, took its name from the black poplar trees that thrived on the moist alluvial soil beside the marshes. At that time the single largest employer in this part of the city was the East and West India Dock Company. In his biography of London, English writer Peter Ackroyd describes the docks, which opened at the beginning of the nineteenth century, as 'the largest single, privately funded enterprise in the history of London', involving 'great fortress-like structures with gates and high walls'.[4] Other docks, such as Millwall in 1868, would follow. Many of the inhabitants of Poplar were either involved with the docks or had occupations that supported the shipping trade: shipwrights, carpenters, dock labourers, lightermen and rope makers.

Although no members of the Edmonds family appear to have been directly involved, they are likely to have provisioned dock workers as well as the local population. In those pre-refrigeration days food had to be bought daily from butchers, fishmongers, bakers, grocers and cheesemongers, who obtained much of their produce from the surrounding fertile fields of the Isle of Dogs. Arthur, the seventh Edmonds son, became a journeyman pork butcher sometime before the 1871 census. He may have worked in a market or perhaps closer to home in a local butcher's shop.

Life in this smoky, malodorous part of London was difficult if you were of modest means. Houses were badly constructed, damp and poorly ventilated. Most had lean-to privies that drained into a common cesspool. Because of the lack of running water, people almost invariably shared communal tanks with many other houses. Wastewater flowed into sewers that were little more than open ditches. Inadequate sewerage and hygiene led to a succession of devastating cholera epidemics; in the worst, in 1866, more than 3000 people died in the East End. Small children were particularly vulnerable to the disease, and it is possible that James and Jane's sixth child, William, born in Deptford in 1850, was a cholera victim, since he does not appear in the 1861 census. Edwin's first child, Eliza Jane, born on Christmas Day 1873, died of bronchitis in November 1878. In 1859, work began on a system of sewers for the whole city, and deaths from disease fell drastically after these were completed in 1875.

• • •

In the 1871 census 13-year-old Thomas is listed as a scholar, but this does not necessarily mean that he was still at school. The term was only vaguely defined in the census taker's instructions and came to be used as a blanket description for the children of a household, whether they were in a classroom or working.[5] Even if the boy had been at school until the age of 12, as required by the Elementary Education Act of 1870, it is very likely that by the following year he was contributing to the family income. He was clearly, however, reasonably well educated by the time he was running his own business. His adult correspondence was articulate and he had a good vocabulary at his disposal, and in a 1915 testimonial addressed to his advertising company he plays with a quotation from Shakespeare's *Henry V*.[6]

Thomas Edmonds' first job is reputed to have been mixing powders, such as the popular sherbet, at the East End factory of Frederick Allen & Sons in Canal Road, Mile End.[7] The company was most famous for its chocolate and cocoa products, promoted for their health-giving properties – the company exhibited at the 1884 International Health Exhibition – but it also produced brightly coloured boiled sweets, lozenges, candied fruit and toffee, and the recently invented sherbet – a powdered mixture of bicarbonate of soda, tartaric acid and sugar that fizzed when added to water. By the time of his marriage in 1879, however, Thomas was working as a furniture salesman.

He may have met his future wife, Jane Elizabeth Middleton Irvine (also known as Jennie/Jenny), in 1873 when his older brother Edwin, a woodturner by trade, married her sister Sarah at St Peter's in Stepney, just a couple of miles from Poplar. The girls' father, David Irvine, had died in 1862. Family tradition says he was a sea captain, but census records show him as a waterman in 1841, ferrying passengers across and along rivers, and a customs officer a decade later. Their mother Eliza was David's second wife; his first wife, Susannah, had died, leaving behind two young children, Henry and Eliza. By 1862, when Eliza was about 40, Henry appeared to have left home, Eliza was 11, Sarah nine and Jane two.

In the absence of any form of social security payments, Eliza Irvine would have needed to work. According to the 1871 census she was a laundress, which involved hard manual work that was poorly paid. The younger Eliza was listed as an unemployed domestic servant and Sarah as a machinist, but it is unclear whether she worked in a factory, in a sweatshop or at home. When she married Thomas Edmonds, Jane was employed as a maid in the Home for Working

Thomas's first job is thought to have been at London confectionery company Frederick Allen & Sons, where he would have gained useful experience for his future work.

and Destitute Boys established on Stepney Causeway in 1870 by Irish philanthropist Thomas Barnardo, who devoted his life to helping deprived children.

By this time Britain was the world's richest and most advanced industrialised economy. Its railway system had grown rapidly and most of the population was living in towns and cities. There had, though, been a number of recessions. The most severe was the worldwide so-called Long Depression, which lasted from 1873 to the early 1890s. In the sluggish market, commodity prices fell and wages dropped, resulting in high levels of unemployment and much financial hardship for the working classes. And although the construction of docks, railway stations and goods yards had replaced the pockets of substandard and slum housing that characterised parts of East London, the resulting displacement of local residents added to the social problems.

• • •

On the other side of the world, at the end of the 1860s, the New Zealand economy was 'not in a good state'.[8] The great goldrush in the south was over, as were the wars in the North Island, and wool was not yet earning money, and these factors led to economic depression in Otago and Auckland, respectively. In 1870 the dynamic colonial treasurer Julius Vogel proposed that over the next decade the country should spend millions of pounds – a sizeable chunk of it borrowed from Britain – to fund the building of railways, roads, bridges, port facilities and telegraph networks and to power increased immigration. The extended title of the 1870 Immigration and Public Works Act summed it up: 'to provide for Immigration and the Construction of Railways and other Public Works and also to promote Settlement'.[9]

The government developed a campaign in England, Scotland and Ireland, run by immigration agents, who used posters, lectures and the testimonies of those who had made good in the New World to attract others keen to escape hard times and build a new life. The target market was married agricultural labourers and single female domestic servants, though

Like many emigrants, Thomas and Jane had their photographs taken just before their departure for New Zealand. These small images, known as *cartes de visite*, were affordable for working-class people.

In the eighteenth and nineteenth centuries, London was the busiest port in the world. Ships lined the Thames until construction of the enclosed docks in East London, beginning in the early 1800s.

the net widened as time went on. There was some financial assistance for migrants between 1871 and 1873, but the long and costly journey remained 'out of the reach of the class that most needed to migrate'.[10] The situation changed dramatically in 1873 when Vogel, now premier, introduced free passage for selected migrants and for those who had been nominated by family already living in New Zealand. In 1870 there were about 250,000 Pākehā in the country; by 1891 that figure was well over 600,000. After a peak of over 30,000 in 1874, the number of arrivals dwindled – to under 12,000 in 1875.[11] By the late 1870s the New Zealand economy was facing another downturn, and in July 1879 the intensive recruiting campaign came to an end. Migrants who had been nominated by others already in New Zealand were still given government assistance in the form of a £5 payment, but this ceased in 1890.

As an experienced woodturner and carpenter, 28-year-old Edwin Edmonds was exactly the kind of immigrant New Zealand was after, and Thomas, though not similarly skilled, was bright, hard-working and intent on bettering himself. They had little to lose. The Irvines were equally convinced. For the younger Eliza, now 28, there was the promise of work – and perhaps of marriage, given the reported overabundance of single men in the colony. The Edmonds and Irvines travelled in steerage, but were not assisted migrants. As the *Lyttelton Times* reported when their ship, the *Waitangi*, arrived in New Zealand, the 186 third cabin or steerage passengers had 'all paid their own passages, and from what was seen of them they appear to be a class that will do well in the land of their adoption. They appear to be a thoroughly respectable and intelligent body of people.'[12]

Edwin and Thomas's father James lived long enough to farewell his sons; he died in 1880. Their mother Jane remained in London, living with her son Charles, his wife Rebecca and their rapidly expanding family. Arthur was presumably settled in his trade as butcher. By 1881 the eldest Edmonds son, cheesemonger James, who had been declared bankrupt in 1872, had 'no occupation' written beside his name on the census. However, in an example of what was known as chain migration, and probably sponsored by his brothers, he did eventually emigrate to New Zealand sometime after he married Dorcas, who was some 20 years his junior, in 1888 – and probably before nomination of relatives ceased in 1890.

Little is known of the couple's life in Christchurch except that James worked as a coal merchant and later a draper, and had a lucky escape in October 1921 when the cart he was

The Edmonds travelled to New Zealand on the *Waitangi*, seen here in a painting by Richard Ball Spencer. The montage opposite shows scenes typical of shipboard life.

driving was hit by a train;[13] he died in 1926. After the third brother, Henry, died in March 1882, his widow Fanny and their three children, Julia, Lydia and Alfred, sailed to New Zealand in 1884, probably sponsored by their family, to settle close to Fanny's sister in Dunedin. Julia's diary entry for 26 May noted that during a stop-off in Lyttelton on their way down to Port Chalmers they 'saw Uncle Tom, Aunt Jenny [Jane] and cousin Willie'.[14]

As for so many other families, the prospect of better employment opportunities and advancement was alluring for the Edmonds family, but the decision to spend some 100 days at sea sailing to an unknown destination on the other side of the world was not one to be taken lightly. Just three weeks before Thomas and Jane, aged 20 and 19 respectively, departed for New Zealand, they were married at St Thomas's church on Bethnal Green on 8 June 1879.

• • •

On the morning of 26 June, the *Waitangi* left the South West India Dock – perhaps only a couple of miles from Thomas's last reported address in Mile End Old Town – and was taken downstream to Greenhithe, where its compasses were adjusted. It then proceeded further downriver to Gravesend, on the south bank of the Thames Estuary, where the 235 passengers embarked that same evening. Before that, Edwin, Sarah, Thomas and Jane Edmonds and the two Eliza Irvines, and their fellow migrants travelling in steerage, would have spent some 10 days in the emigration depot at Blackwall while they waited for their ship.

The *Waitangi*, operated by the New Zealand Shipping Company, was one of the many sailing vessels that dominated the world's shipping lanes in the 1870s. Constructed in Sunderland in northeast England in 1874, it was described as a 'high-class iron clipper ship',[15] a 1145-ton three-master, 210 feet long and with a breadth of 35 feet; sailing 'before the wind' it was capable of 14½ knots. The Edmonds family would not have set foot there, but those travelling in style could enjoy an impressive saloon with a gilt cornice, furnished with marble-topped sideboards and a 20-foot teak table flanked by six long, double-backed velvet settees.[16] Between 1874 and 1897 the *Waitangi* made 25 trips bringing immigrants to New Zealand; nine of them ended in Lyttelton.

On the evening of 26 June, Captain C. Hodder greeted the 25 first-class (or saloon-class) passengers, while senior officers made the 24 second-class passengers welcome. Other, more junior crew directed the 186 steerage passengers to their quarters under the main deck. Once embarkation was complete, passengers had to undergo a final medical examination by a doctor from the British Board of Trade. Also present were the ship's surgeon, in this case Mackintosh Collie, and the emigration officer. With no cure for infectious diseases such as measles, scarlet fever, whooping cough or smallpox, it was imperative to prevent anyone showing symptoms from sailing. The migrants, who were made to wait on the poop deck sometimes for many hours, feared not being passed fit. But as historian David Hastings notes, few people were sent ashore and the examination was often 'quick and cursory'; the Board of Trade doctors 'tended to err on the side of negligence and displayed equal contempt for the migrants, the ships' surgeons and the risk of disease'.[17]

The steerage passengers were accommodated in a cramped, low-ceilinged cargo space beneath the main deck. Its position below the waterline meant that there were no portholes and little natural light. The area would have been sparsely furnished with rows of tiered bunks and a long table down the middle. There were three distinct compartments, each reached by a separate hatchway. The forward area, next to the crew's quarters, was for single men. As married couples, Edwin and Sarah and Thomas and Jane would have been allotted bunks in the middle compartment. The single women in their party, including the two Elizas, were accommodated at the rear of the steerage space.

Privacy within each compartment was limited – at best there would have been a curtain between bunks. Mattresses were provided, but passengers brought their own bedding. During the three-month voyage they had to make do with the few changes of clothing and washing accessories that would fit into a cloth bag hung by their bunks. The rest of their belongings stayed in their trunks, which were stored in the hold throughout the voyage.

On the following day, after passing the government inspection, the ship was towed around the southeast corner of Kent, into the English Channel and then, in the face of fresh westerlies, past Dover, Folkestone, Hastings and Brighton as far as the Isle of Wight. Finally, at 10 o'clock on the morning of the 29th, the *Waitangi* was on its way. But it soon had a taste of conditions to come, gales and 'torrents of rain, thunder and lightning',[18] before passing the Lizard Peninsula in Cornwall, the most southerly point of the British mainland, and heading out into the North Atlantic.

There is no known surviving account of the Edmonds' experience of the next stage of their voyage, across the Bay of Biscay, which lies along the western coast of France and the northern coast of Spain and is regularly beset by some of the Atlantic's worst weather. However, a diary written on the 1879 voyage of the *Stad Haarlem* from Plymouth to Lyttelton indicates just how ferocious conditions could be:

> *During Sunday we entered the Bay of Biscay amidst a roaring hurricane, hatches battened down, and not a soul allowed on deck. The captain's steward ventured, but was dashed against the deck-house, and dropt bleeding and senseless. He was hauled in, and put to bed very much injured. The waves are tearing us along, rolling pell-mell over us. Here comes a smasher, raising his foaming head high above us, and surging and howling like mad, at length swoops down upon the ship with a hideous roar, sweeping our decks from stem to stern, then careering off for another victim, and leaving us to the tender mercies of hundreds of his boiling and merciless successors.*[19]

Routine governed shipboard life, which was busy for those in steerage. Each day there were set times for getting up and going to bed, for cooking, eating and washing and for chores – and for the children to attend school.[20] When Thomas and Edwin's sister-in-law Fanny and her three children travelled to New Zealand on the steamer *Victory* in 1884, 14-year-old Julia wrote in her diary: 'up at 6 with beds up and swept underneath. After breakfast we did our knives and forks and tins, then scrubbed our tables and holy-stoned our floors.'[21] Each week there were days designated for washing clothes and for collecting supplies, though drinking water and items such as meat and eggs were dispensed every morning. All the cooking was done in a central galley, but each mess's food was kept separate. The main course, served in the middle of the day, 'was usually tinned or salted meat, either boiled or baked, with fresh or preserved potatoes and dried vegetables'.[22]

A coal-fuelled condenser distilled fresh drinking water from the sea. Washing facilities were basic and it was difficult to get soap that worked effectively in saltwater. 'It is funny,' Julia Edmonds wrote, 'to see the clothes hanging out. We have not washed any of ours yet but some have and they are so yellow with the sea water.'[23] In the heat of the tropics the men could strip down to their trousers and swim, or stand under a hose on deck. The women sometimes reduced the layers of clothes they wore and some even went barefoot.

The ship's doctor, or surgeon-superintendent, was responsible for both the health of everyone on the ship and for discipline. Seasickness was a problem, naturally, but there were births and deaths, other illnesses – and accidents, especially during storms. A few deaths were not unusual on an emigrant ship but there could be many more if a passenger had brought an infectious disease on board. In 1874, 26 people on the *Scimitar* died of measles and scarlet fever; more than 40 perished on the *Brothers' Pride* in 1863. To keep order on board, there were constables to watch over the male steerage passengers. A matron was in charge of the single women, who were kept separate from any men in an area some called 'the virgins' cage'.[24]

After crossing the equator on 20 July and rounding the southern tip of Africa on 20 August, the *Waitangi* made the run across the Southern Ocean in variable winds. Sometimes there was

contact with other ships. On 17 July, for example, the passengers and crew hailed their counterparts aboard the *Helen Pembroke*, on its way to Calcutta, and on 23 August it was the *Gateside*, heading to Adelaide. The *Waitangi* was off the most southwesterly point of the Australian mainland, south of Perth, on 10 September. Six days later it passed Tasmania, where it experienced the worst weather of the voyage – so bad that no observations were taken for six days. On 21 September the ship passed The Snares, about 125 miles south of the South Island of New Zealand, and from there sailed north.[25] That day, too, the *Waitangi* communicated with the *Mataura*, which sailed into Port Chalmers the next day and could report that all was well on the Lyttelton-bound vessel.[26]

There had, however, been some drama during the voyage. A seaman had fallen from the rigging to the deck but, though badly shaken, he recovered after a couple of days' rest. And steerage passenger Thomas Swain had 'while on the high seas, used profane and insulting language to the surgeon'.[27] On a more serious note, one night Captain Hodder disturbed a steward and the cook's mate helping themselves to the contents of the storeroom, and doing so by the light of a naked candle placed on top of the powder magazine. As the *Evening Post* later suggested, 'The slightest accident might have resulted in blowing the ship to atoms, and hurrying into eternity at a moment's notice the 300 souls on board.'[28]

The bustle and excitement of arriving in Lyttelton is captured in the 1878 etching above. By 1886, as shown in the painting on the following pages by John Gibb, the port had developed considerably.

The journey took 91 days – the other *Waitangi* passages to New Zealand varied from between 77 and 117 days – and 'this favourite representative of the New Zealand Shipping Company's fleet' reportedly arrived in Lyttelton Harbour on 25 September 1879 'in excellent time, and in beautiful order'.[29] The local health officer, Dr J.T. Rouse, made his official visit to check that the ship was free of disease and did not need to be placed in quarantine. A steam tug then towed the *Waitangi* up the harbour so it could berth at Gladstone Pier. 'Neither increase nor decrease in their numbers occurred during the passage, no sickness other than the mal-de-mer, and no accident of a serious character happened from departure to arrival.' When the new immigrants landed on the pier at Lyttelton they were 'apparently in as good health as they could wish to be'.[30]

J. GIBB
1886

CONFECTIONER

CHAPTER 2

COMING TO CHRISTCHURCH

Like all immigrants in those years, the Edmonds family did not spend much time in the busy port of Lyttelton. The *Waitangi* berthed late in the afternoon of the 25th; they disembarked the following morning and boarded a train that took them through the tunnel under the Port Hills into the Heathcote Valley and on to Christchurch. Half a century later, Thomas recalled how they 'emerged from the Lyttelton Tunnel and gazed upon the Southern Alps clad in their mantle of snow'.[1] The steep hills of the port were replaced by the tussocky flatness of the Canterbury Plains, stretching towards those distant mountains. After passing through the railway station in Moorhouse Avenue (then known as the South Belt), an impressive neo-Gothic structure opened less than two years before, they got off the train at Addington Station and made their way to the nearby immigration barracks in Poulson Street.

Back in August 1872, in the early days of assisted immigration, both the *Lyttelton Times* and the *Star* had printed a long account of the barracks. It was undoubtedly intended for those back home: the reporter was at pains to point out the glories of a system under which people were 'housed and fed gratuitously until they obtain suitable and remunerative employment'. There was no charge, either, for the train journey and the transport to the barracks. These, which could house between 300 and 400, were divided into three areas, for single women, single men and families. On the 'third clear day' after arrival, it was time for prospective employers to visit. The afternoon before, printed forms were put up in each barracks compartment, with the current wages for all kinds of labour, skilled and unskilled, 'so that the immigrants know exactly what to ask and what to accept'. The engagements, as they were known, took place under supervision and were governed by several rules.[2]

A far cry from London: Christchurch's Colombo Street seen from the cathedral tower in 1881, and right, Addington Station, painted by George Turner, around the time the Edmonds family stepped off the train in September 1879.

Seven years later, when the Edmonds reached Christchurch, things were different. The *Crusader*, which had arrived the day before the *Waitangi*, was carrying 'an unusually large number of self paid passengers' – 214 of them. Of those, 163 were steerage passengers, many 'doubtless with but very little means at command'.

Immigration officer J.E. March was able to offer these passengers 'the same accommodation at the depot [i.e. barracks] and chances for employment as the Government extends to immigrants, also temporary quarters at the depot until they had an opportunity to secure others of their own ... There was no intention to treat any of the passengers as paupers, the purpose being purely one of assistance to strangers arriving in a new country without homes to go to, and without friends and acquaintances ... to render them assistance or advice.' The same offer, the *Press* reported, would apply to the steerage passengers on the *Waitangi*. The aim was to encourage 'a self-paid stream of immigration from the country whence these new arrivals came, and thus help to lighten the burdens of the colony in respect to assisted and free immigration'.[3] Just a few days earlier, in a report to the under-secretary of immigration, March had noted that there was 'at present little or no demand for labour. On Wednesday last there was a large meeting of the unemployed, and there cannot be a doubt that at the present time a very great deal of distress exists. I am quite sure that fully 600 men are now out of work. I understand, however, that directions have been given to find immediate employment for them on railway works.'[4] This may tie in with the family legend that Thomas initially worked briefly on the railways.

• • •

So what was it like, this city of Christchurch? At the suggestion of Canterbury Association surveyor Captain Joseph Thomas, sent out in 1848 to determine a suitable location for a settlement, it was originally to have been on the other side of the Port Hills, at what is now Teddington, but the amount of reclamation required scuppered that idea. The city would instead be built on the edge of the Canterbury Plains on land that was flat but would prove to be swampy. The port of Lyttelton had its origins in 1849 when Captain Thomas had a jetty and a customs

house built there. The organised European settlement of Canterbury began in December 1850 with the arrival of what are always called the first four ships – the *Charlotte Jane*, *Randolph*, *Sir George Seymour* and *Cressy* – bringing the 773 settlers known as the Canterbury Pilgrims. It was John Robert Godley, leader of the colonists, who named Christchurch, after Christ Church, his old Oxford college. Christchurch became New Zealand's first city by royal charter on 31 July 1856.

But the area where the city would stand – edged by Te Iringa o Kahukura (the Port Hills) to the south, by the sea to the east and by Kā Tiritiri o te Moana (known, far more prosaically, to Europeans as the Southern Alps) to the west – already had a name, Ōtautahi. The colonising drive to recreate a little England on the other side of the world depended on the displacement and deprivation of Ngāi Tahu, the tangata whenua, who had long lived and thrived there. There were two pā near the future town centre, on the banks of Ōtākaro (the Avon River), another at Ōpāwaho (Ōpawa) and a fourth in what would become South New Brighton. From the 1840s the Crown began to 'buy' Ngāi Tahu lands in Te Wai Pounamu, the South Island, for European settlers to occupy. The largest was the Canterbury purchase by Commissioner Henry Kemp in 1848: for just £2000, the Crown acquired a breathtaking 20 million acres of land. Those living there were 'compensated' with meagre and poor reserves that enormously reduced their access to food sources and circumscribed their lives and futures. From 1849 until it was finally settled in 1997, Ngāi Tahu would pursue justice through Te Kerēme, the claim.

Depicted in the image below left, organised settlement of Christchurch began with the arrival of the first four ships in December 1850. The 1887 watercolour below shows the Avon River and the developing city with the cathedral spire in the distance.

A challenge for early settlers arriving in Lyttelton was the difficulty of access across, or around, the Port Hills to Christchurch. Until a road via Evans Pass and Sumner was completed in 1857, the usual route was the steep Bridle Path, made for packhorses and pedestrian traffic. The alternative was by sea. Heavy goods had to be unloaded at Lyttelton and put aboard small craft that were sent around Godley Head and across the perilous Sumner Bar to Ferrymead,

near the mouth of the Heathcote River. Here the cargo would be transferred into wagons, which from late 1863 were pulled to Christchurch by New Zealand's first steam locomotive.

A day or two after the Edmonds family arrived, the *Lyttelton Times* noted that, as of April that year, the population of Christchurch was 14,186. That made it the third largest town in New Zealand – but only just: it was slightly ahead of Auckland (14,163), but well behind both Dunedin (23,261) and Wellington (19,467).[5] It was not London, though: as Thomas would recall, 'Christchurch seemed to us a very small village.'[6] The cathedral at the heart of the city was struggling towards completion. There were many wooden structures, and some impressive Gothic Revival stone buildings, such as Canterbury Museum, which opened in 1870 largely thanks to the determination and enthusiasm of its first director, Julius von Haast; Canterbury College (of the University of New Zealand, later the University of Canterbury); the Normal School in Cranmer Square, which became the country's first teachers' training college in 1877; and the post office in Cathedral Square, which had opened in July 1879.

However, as historian Geoffrey Rice points out, 'the façade of Victorian success and respectability sometimes barely concealed an economic reality of uncertainty, unemployment and hardship for many ordinary people'.[7] By 1879 a land boom in Canterbury was over and wheat and wool prices, so vital to the province, fell. The Long Depression followed. For Thomas, 'the prospects did not appear to be at all bright. There was a soup kitchen in Victoria square. The Barracks were full, and there was also a great deal of unemployment.'[8] The soup kitchen, along with a food and clothing depot, was opened in June 1880 by the Christchurch Benevolent Association in the old post office; on the first day, 273 people turned up for a midday meal. The association, which lasted until 1885, became 'a haven of hope for hundreds of poor Christchurch citizens'.[9]

In the decade before the Edmonds came to live there, Christchurch had been an unhealthy and malodorous place, with high death rates from diphtheria, typhoid and scarlet fever, a polluted Avon River, human and household waste in the gutters, cesspits, and poor or non-existent drainage. But in 1879 work began on what would be the first real metropolitan underground sewerage system in the country, achieved in the early 1880s.[10]

When the Edmonds arrived in 1879, the cathedral (left) was under construction. As the photos opposite show, Christchurch's built environment was extensive by the mid-1880s, including a number of impressive stone buildings. One of those was the Bank of New Zealand, seen bottom right in the lower photo (taken from the cathedral tower facing south).

Its population would soon be surpassed by that of Auckland, but Christchurch beat the northern city to the honour of having New Zealand's first telephone exchange, on 24 September 1881. At that stage there were about 30 subscribers, all 'telephonically in connection with each other'. And allowing for a few mistakes – put down to inexperience – the system gave all the promised results 'with certainty and accuracy'.[11] Similar telephone exchanges soon opened in Auckland and Dunedin.

In the 1880s and 1890s Christchurch was a national leader in two important and closely associated social areas: temperance and women's suffrage. Starting with the Christchurch Total Abstinence Society, established in 1860, the number of local temperance societies grew to over 20 by 1884. In 1887 prominent feminist Kate Sheppard became head of the suffrage campaign being run by the recently formed Women's Christian Temperance Union. That year the first of five suffrage petitions, with ever-increasing numbers of signatures, was submitted to Parliament; New Zealand women won the vote on 19 September 1893. Jane Edmonds, her sister, half-sister and mother would all sign the 1892 petition: their names can be found on sheet 240, page 427.[12] Christchurch was, also, 'the cradle of trade unions and artisan radicalism' in New Zealand during the 1880s. Unionism flourished in this period of unemployment.[13] So did imported sectarian differences: on Boxing Day 1879 there was a serious clash between Catholics and Protestants in Manchester Street as a procession of Orangemen en route to a picnic was set upon by some 30 Catholics hiding behind Barrett's Borough Hotel.

Although life remained hard for many working people throughout the Long Depression, Canterbury survived better than most provinces, thanks to its ability to grow and export wheat, wool and meat. The introduction of refrigerated shipping in 1882 was particularly transforming: the province's first shipment of frozen mutton left Lyttelton for Britain the following year.

But as one newspaper correspondent pointed out in October 1879, New Zealand was 'by no means an exclusively pastoral and agricultural country'. It had 'very considerable' mineral resources and its climate, geographical position and the extent of its coastline and natural harbours made it 'peculiarly suited for an extensive commerce'. If New Zealand were to become 'the Britain of the Southern hemisphere', it needed to follow the example of both 'the Mother Country and our American Cousins in the matter of industrial progress'.[14]

There was certainly a growing amount of industry in late nineteenth-century Christchurch, both within the town belts (later the four avenues) and immediately south of the city, in what was then the borough of Sydenham. This included several foundries such as Anderson's and Scott's, and agricultural implement manufacturers, reflecting Canterbury's pre-eminence as a farming province. Among other notable industries was Aulsebrook's steam biscuit factory and flour mills, which began production in 1863 and moved in 1879 to a large brick factory on the corner of Montreal and St Asaph streets. Another important industrial area of Christchurch was to the southeast, around Ferry Road, which was a major route between the city and Lyttelton. It was here that Thomas Edmonds decided to set up his business.

• • •

Thomas and his family had been struck by the unfamiliar and empty landscape, but they soon discovered that there were other local phenomena to get used to. One was the infamous Canterbury nor'wester, a typical föhn wind that has been described as 'the most notorious gale' in a generally windy country. 'Born in the heart of the mountains, it accelerates down the great valleys east of the Main Divide and roars out across the plains', becoming hot, dry and dust-laden by the time it reaches Christchurch.[15] This wind, especially common in spring when the Edmonds family arrived, could cause minor damage, such as that done to two prized tree ferns in the courtyard of a Cathedral Square business in September 1880,[16] but was also responsible for destructive fires.

Even less familiar, and much more alarming to newcomers, were earthquakes. New Zealand had already had its fair share of these before 1879, especially the huge 1855 quake in the Wellington region. But seismic activity was not confined to the North Island. On 5 December 1881, Christchurch and the surrounding region were hit with a magnitude 6 earthquake, which dislodged a piece of decorative moulding from the spire of the partially completed cathedral. A much more damaging earthquake early on the morning of 1 September 1888 would bring down the whole top portion of the spire. For over 30 minutes, frightened residents endured five distinct shocks that caused crockery to shatter, pictures to fall from walls, windows to break and chimneys to tumble.[17]

The city's development around the turn of the century was proudly showcased on the covers of special editions of local newspapers. Aulsebrook was one of the many Christchurch manufacturers already going strong by 1879, when it moved into the impressive factory shown on this poster.

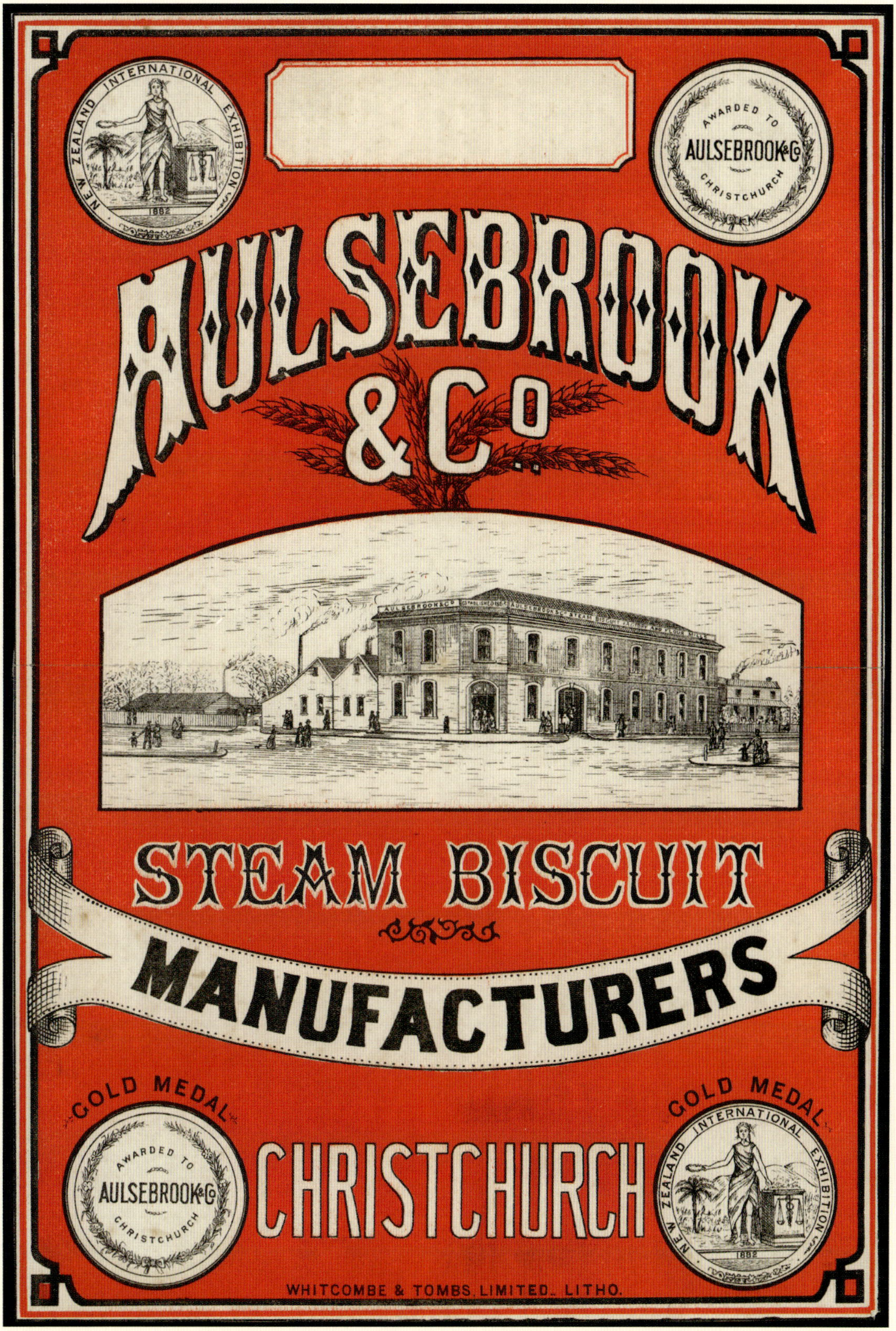

NEW ZEALAND INTERNATIONAL EXHIBITION
1882
AWARDED TO
AULSEBROOK & Co
CHRISTCHURCH
AULSEBROOK
& Co
STEAM BISCUIT
MANUFACTURERS
GOLD MEDAL
AWARDED TO
AULSEBROOK & Co
CHRISTCHURCH
CHRISTCHURCH
GOLD MEDAL
NEW ZEALAND INTERNATIONAL EXHIBITION
1882
WHITCOMBE & TOMBS LIMITED. LITHO.

THE ACORN AND THE OAK

CHAPTER 3

A BUSINESS IS BORN

Family tradition suggests that, as he stepped off the *Waitangi* at Lyttelton in 1879, Thomas found a coin in his pocket, tossed it overboard and firmly stated that he would 'arrive with no money and start from scratch with everything now coming from my own hands'. It seems that he was certainly ready to build a life in New Zealand. Also on the ship was saddler and bootmaker George E. Rowland. According to his great-grandson, John Campbell, Rowland 'had a bit of money, and T.J. Edmonds wanted him to go into business with him', though this did not eventuate.[1]

There is some mystery surrounding Thomas's earliest employment and his role in the burgeoning economy of Canterbury. As mentioned earlier, his first job may have been on the railways, where family legend says he suffered an injury to his hand. He may, too, have sold kerosene door to door, transporting it in a tank mounted on a hand barrow. And he is said to have taken orders for scones and cakes made by Jane, who was an excellent cook.

Edmonds' transformation from small store to large factory was used in advertising in early 1930. The photo of Jane and her son Will dates from 1880.

As Thomas himself wrote in November 1915, 'I ... started my business career in a small grocer's shop, with a turnover of about £20 a week.'[2] That store, which was also the family's first Christchurch home, was two blocks northeast of Ferry Road, in an area then known as Ashbourne. The business was certainly underway soon after the Edmonds family arrived in New Zealand: when Thomas registered their first child William's birth on 12 April 1880, he gave his profession as grocer. The name Ashbourne came from Charles Robert Blakiston, who was involved in both national and provincial politics and was for many years the Christchurch manager of the Trust and Agency Company. He bought Rural Section 110 on Ferry Road and farmed there on the property he christened Ashbourne, after a place in Derbyshire. When the land was subdivided in the 1880s, it was called the 'town of Ashbourne' and Blakiston's Christian names were used for two streets (no longer in existence) that cut across it. In 1893 the area became a borough and the name was changed to Woolston.

The grocery was on the southwest corner of Randolph Street[3] and what was, by February 1886, known as Edmonds Street. The street, sometimes erroneously referred to as 'Edmunds' or 'Edmond's' Street,[4] was clearly named after the family – many city streets took their names

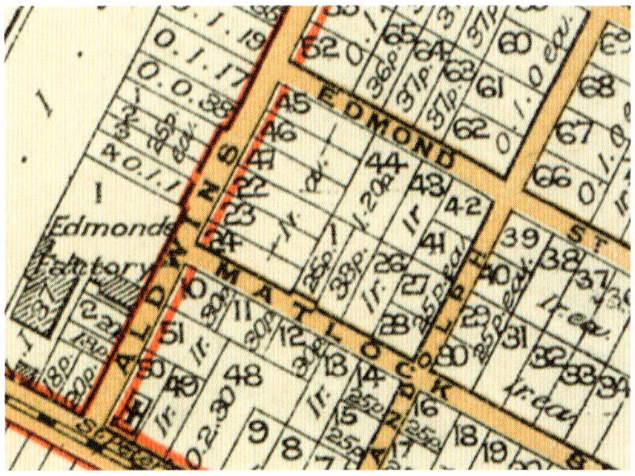

Thomas and Jane's grocery store, in Ashbourne, featured in a 1929 booklet celebrating the business's first 50 years; the *Waitangi* is a link to 1879. The swastika was originally a religious icon that symbolised good fortune. The shop was on the corner of what would become known as Edmond Street, as seen in the 1926 map above. The plan of Ashbourne was a developer's proposal for a town of that name in 1883.

from well-known residents and landowners – but for some unknown reason in 1893 it lost its terminal 's' and became just Edmond. It took 124 years, but in 2017 the error was corrected and, much to the delight of Thomas Edmonds' descendants, the original name was restored.[5] The shop sign had an unnecessary and misplaced apostrophe – 'Edmond's Store'; this would not be the last time this happened to the name.

Another five of Thomas and Jane's eight children were born while they lived at the grocery: Ernest in August 1881, Lilian in October 1883, George in August 1886, Jim in August 1888 and Gertrude in February 1891. Edwin and Sarah lived nearby: their children, Arthur, Rose and Edwin, were all born at Ferry Road, Ashbourne, in the early 1880s. (Ferry Road was used both specifically for the thoroughfare and to refer to the locality.) By 1886 they had moved into 'the seventh house', a four-roomed cottage in Olliviers Road (initially Lane). This was where Herbert and David were born. Their last child, Henry, died aged just 13 weeks in January 1891. Although the main cause of death was given as 'diarrhoea', the death certificate also recorded 'tabes mesenterica', a wasting illness caused by drinking milk from cows infected with tuberculosis. This was not the only family tragedy. Jane and Sarah's half-sister Eliza had married printer Joseph Turner in 1880, and they made their home in Ashbourne. Their daughter Ruby was just nine months old when she died of pertussis, or whooping cough, in May 1888.

Edwin set up a woodturning and cabinetmaking business, Edmonds & Page, in 1886. He became a member, and later secretary and then president, of the Blue Ribbon Gospel Temperance Mission.[6] Originating in the United States, this organisation spread to Britain and to its distant colonies. The name came from a Bible admonition to the Israelites to border the fringes of their garments with a ribbon of blue as a reminder to heed the Lord's commandments. Members wore a blue ribbon to show that they had signed the pledge to abstain from alcohol. Thomas and Jane's seven-year-old daughter Gertrude would do so in 1898 at a pledge station set up at nearby St Peter's Presbyterian Church (though later in life she enjoyed the occasional drink). Sarah, too, took her religion seriously: an 1886 newspaper advertisement wanted it known that Mrs Edmonds of Olliviers Lane was holding a 'Cottage Prayer Meeting every Wednesday, at 2.30'.[7] Such gatherings were not uncommon in those years. In 1889 Eliza Irvine, who had been living with Edwin and Sarah, married widower Henry Allchin: he was one of the city's early Baptists, and services were often held at his home.

• • •

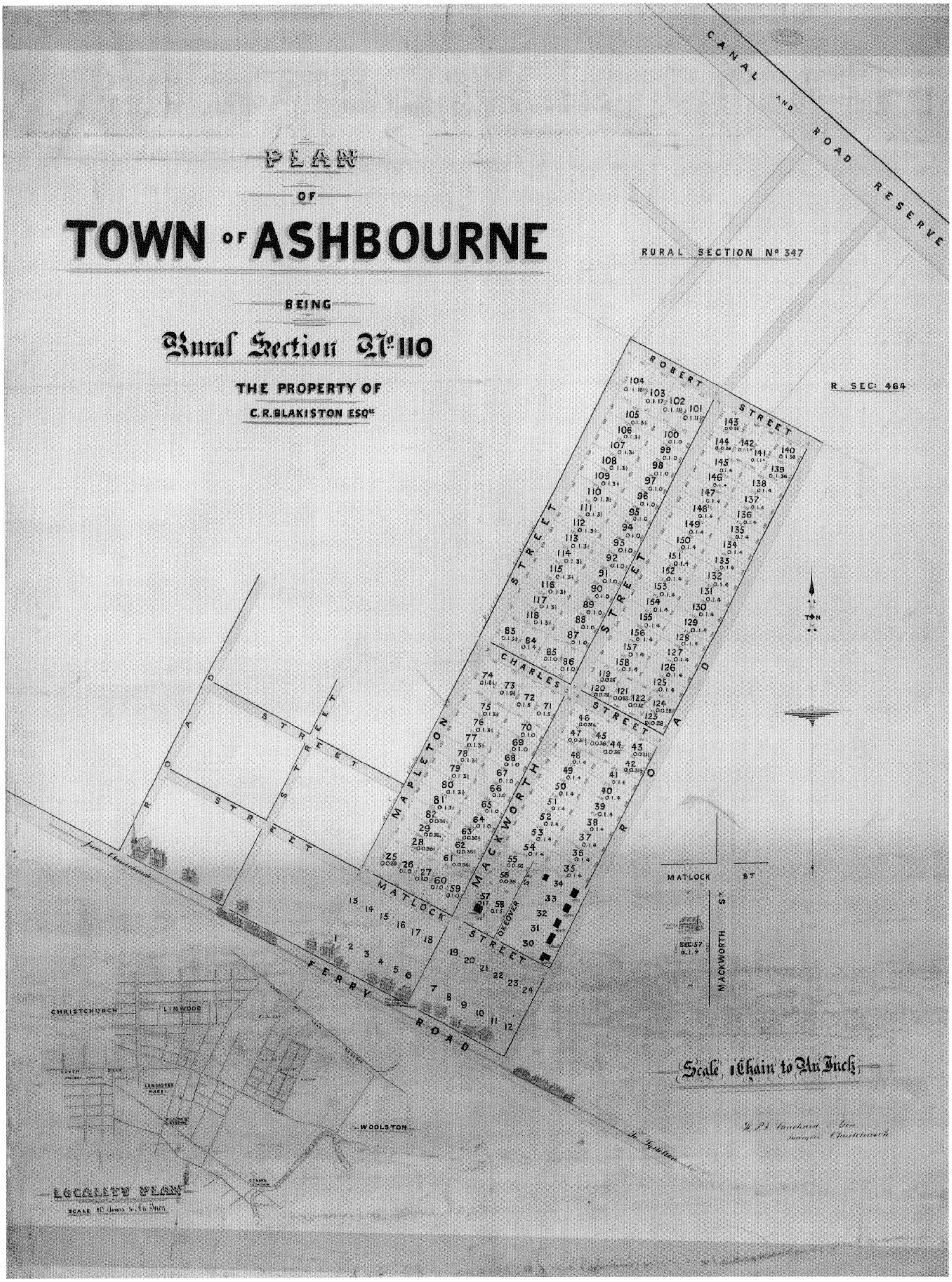
PLAN
OF
TOWN OF ASHBOURNE
BEING
Rural Section No 110
THE PROPERTY OF
C.R.BLAKISTON ESQRE
CANAL AND ROAD RESERVE
RURAL SECTION No 347
R. SEC: 464
ROBERT STREET
STREET
CHARLES STREET
MAPLETON STREET
MACKWORTH STREET
OKEOVER ST.
MATLOCK STREET
ROAD
ROAD STREET
STREET
STREET
FERRY ROAD
MATLOCK ST
MACKWORTH ST.
SEC 57
0.1.7
Scale 1 Chain to An Inch
CHRISTCHURCH
LINWOOD
LANCASTER PARK
WOOLSTON
LOCALITY PLAN
SCALE 10 Chains to An Inch

From June to August 1881 Thomas Edmonds was one of 21 listed agents for Nelson, Moate & Co., wholesale and retail tea merchants, blenders and importers; his location was given as Ashbourne.[8] He was soon an active member of the local community, along with other family members who lived nearby. When a bazaar was held in the Oddfellows Hall just before Christmas 1881 to raise money for the Sydenham Baptist Church building fund, Thomas, Jane and Sarah were among those running stalls. 'A novelty,' said the *Star* report, 'was present in the shape of a grocery stall.'[9] It would be reasonable to assume that this was Thomas's domain.

Electoral rolls for 1882 and subsequent years listed Thomas as a grocer but, as he wrote, 'Some time after entering the grocery line the idea came to me that if I could manufacture a satisfactory baking powder there should be a fair sale.' At the time, imported baking powder arrived in wooden crates and after three months at sea, moisture in the air had often spoiled the powder's active ingredients. Thomas had valuable experience gleaned during his time at Frederick Allen & Sons. (The firm's listing in the official catalogue for the 1884 International Health Exhibition in London mentioned 'Granulated Effervescing Citrate of Magnesia'.) 'Previous to leaving London, I had become acquainted with the use and mixing of powders relative to sherbet making, so I decided to tackle the baking powder business and at once started operations.'[10] In 1915 he recalled that his 'first mixing of baking powder consisted of about 200 tins',[11] but it seems that his product was in fact originally packaged in small paper bags, which Thomas transported in some kind of barrow and is known to have sold in Lyttelton, where there was money to be made by provisioning ships. He later used an adult tricycle, carrying his baking powder in a box on the back. Thomas also used a horse and cart for deliveries. Years later, he recounted how he had mixed a large quantity of baking powder, which Jane had worked late to bag up. He loaded the batch onto his delivery cart, but the horse bolted, upsetting the cart and spilling the precious stock onto the road.[12]

The baking powder was proving popular with the customers of the Edmonds grocery: 'as time went on the women would take two or three tins each for friends'. Based on this encouraging response, Thomas decided to concentrate on 'the scientific blending of the ingredients' that made up his product. 'I was for three years or more studying the problem, during which time other brands began to creep in. This gave an impetus to my investigations and enabled me to produce the powder which has since become a Dominion favourite, and also resulted in my

working out the formulae for egg powder, custard powder, and self-raising flour.'[13] In April 1887 he applied for a patent for 'self-raising egg-flour' and by 1888 he was manufacturing custard powder – 'sold everywhere'.[14]

The source of the Edmonds baking powder recipe became the subject of a legend that James William Morton, a well-known chef and hotelkeeper who taught culinary arts at Christchurch Girls' High School, had given it to Thomas when he came in search of work. Morton's 1887 endorsement of Edmonds baking powder did appear on an early label[15] – 'the best that has come under my notice' – but he also heartily supported an imported American brand called Sea Foam. Although Morton's granddaughter, Margaret Parkes, has suggested that he possibly created the famous Edmonds mixture, there seems to be no evidence of this.[16]

The *carte de visite* of Thomas, Jane and their first three children, Ernest, Will and baby Lilian, was taken in 1883. Thomas reportedly made his early product deliveries by wheelbarrow, later graduating to horse and cart.

Thomas convinced several merchants to take his baking powder. 'By this step I considered good fortune had turned my way, and that all I would have to do would be to supply the demand.' But after three months with no orders, he went back to the retailers, who told him that they had never been asked for his brand. 'Realising that it was not known to the public I set about to create a demand by making a personal canvass. It was my custom, if people whom I saw would not buy, to leave the powder with them without payment on the understanding that if they did not like it I would take it back next visit.' He was proud to remember 'that never one tin was returned, but instead they asked for more'.[17]

While his baking powder business was getting underway, Thomas was manufacturing and marketing other items. Through March and April 1887 he was advertising his Magic Drops toothache cure, which gave 'instant relief' and cost a shilling.[18] For the exhibition of the Canterbury Industrial Association in July 1887, samples of 'baking powder, "Turkish Delight" (a temperance fruit drink), camphorated borax for sanitary purposes, also samples of bread made with the baking powder [surely by Jane] ... were sent by the manufacturer, Mr T. J. Edmonds, Ashbourne, Christchurch'.[19] His 'Turkish Delight' was on display again at Christchurch's Metropolitan Show at the new Agricultural and Pastoral Showgrounds in Addington in November: 'The man who can invent a palatable drink which is not Intoxicant, deserves well of his fellows. Hitherto the way of temperance has been made doubly hard by the exceedingly uninviting nature of the drinks which one who has donned the cerulean ribbon is condemned to ... Mr Edmonds has brought out a new drink, entitled "Turkish Delight," which is effervescent and pleasant.'[20]

Thomas was apparently making use of other retailers too. Magic Drops and what by then was called Edmonds Prize Baking Powder were advertised from March to May 1887 at 'Next Barrett's Hotel in High Street' and in April at 'Oxford Terrace near Cashel Street'. In March 1887 the baking powder was available from well-known agents Trent Bros, who by the beginning of May were also selling Edmonds Self-Raising Flour.[21] Jane contributed to that success: Gertrude recalled her mother spending evenings sewing calico bags for the flour on a treadle sewing machine.[22]

By May, with his patent granted,[23] Thomas was pulling out the advertising stops in a trio of small ads: 'NO More Eggs Required – Use Edmonds Patent Self-raising Egg Flour. Equal to four eggs each pound of flour. Sold everywhere. Trent Bros, agents.'; 'USE Edmonds' Prize Baking Powder. Oxford terrace, near Cashel street 1s tin.'; 'YES. Edmonds' Baking Powders have been analysed, with 7 other makes, and proved superior to all. Sold everywhere.' From June to early September came a new approach, in which 'Mother' was told she could get Edmonds' Prize Egg Custard and Prize Baking Powders at a range of emporiums: 'If your Grocer don't keep it, ask them to get it from any merchant in Christchurch. Sold in 1lb tins. 1s each.'[24]

Through the latter part of 1887, Thomas was telling would-be buyers: '4000LBS Sold in Three Months. Highly recommended by all who use it. Get a 1s 1lb tin, try it and judge for yourself, and you will say Edmonds' Prize Baking Powder is the best. May be had of all grocers and merchants everywhere.'[25] Amounts sold appeared in the newspaper report on Thomas's baking powder contribution to the November 1887 Metropolitan Show: 'Mr Edmonds, who holds the next stall, exhibits baking powder, the results of which in the shape of bread, scones, and cakes made with it certainly stand the test of tasting well ... As a proof of the popularity of the baking powder, it may be noted that three tons has been prepared for the market since March last.'[26]

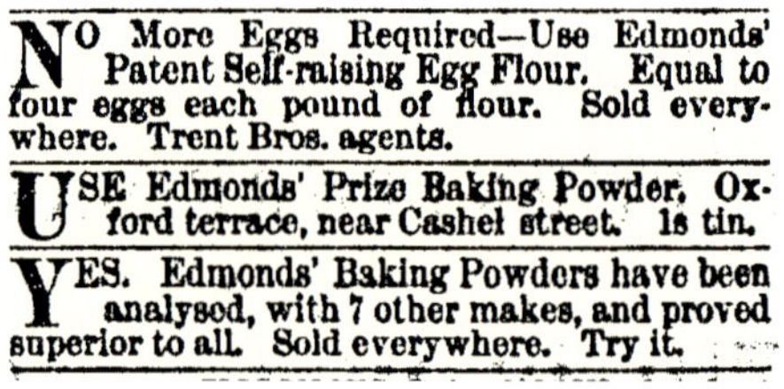
NO More Eggs Required—Use Edmonds' Patent Self-raising Egg Flour. Equal to four eggs each pound of flour. Sold everywhere. Trent Bros. agents.

USE Edmonds' Prize Baking Powder, Oxford terrace, near Cashel street. 1s tin.

YES. Edmonds' Baking Powders have been analysed, with 7 other makes, and proved superior to all. Sold everywhere. Try it.

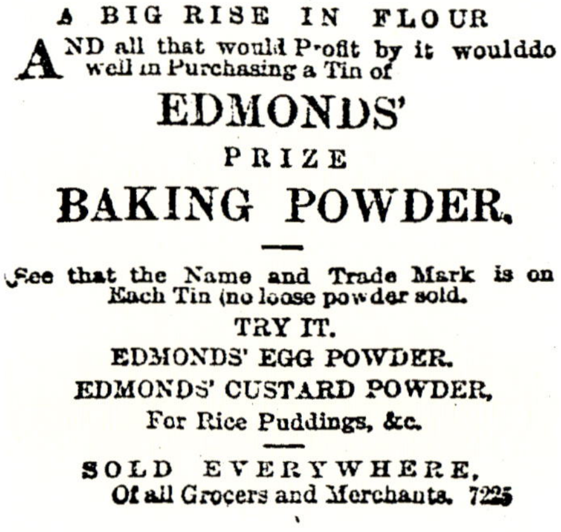
A BIG RISE IN FLOUR

AND all that would Profit by it woulddo well in Purchasing a Tin of

EDMONDS'

PRIZE

BAKING POWDER.

See that the Name and Trade Mark is on Each Tin (no loose powder sold.

TRY IT.

EDMONDS' EGG POWDER.

EDMONDS' CUSTARD POWDER,

For Rice Puddings, &c.

SOLD EVERYWHERE,

Of all Grocers and Merchants. 7225

Inexpensive newspaper classifieds and small advertisements were part of Thomas's early publicity strategy. In the photo above right, by about 1906 delivery by horse-drawn cart had been superseded by a smart four-wheeled carriage. It was driven by Jim Knight, the family's 'General'; Beatrice is seen on the left. On the following pages, Cathedral Square in the early 1900s.

The pre-Christmas advertisements echoed this: 'GOOD Tidings and Great Joy, for Christmas It has come, and Edmonds' Prize Baking Powder is being used all over the Colony. Testimonials are being received from all parts. Over three tons sent out into the Market in six months. Makes everything light and white. Try it next time you bake.'[27] Thomas became a regular at shows and exhibitions. At the Christchurch Industrial Conversazione of March 1888, for instance, 'he demonstrated the efficacy of his egg powder and baking powder, by exhibiting pastry of which the powder formed an ingredient, and which certainly appeared all that pastry should be'.[28]

Thomas, always commercially astute, was keen to protect his territory in the face of growing competition. Although a widely known trademark for the classic Edmonds label was registered in 1913 (see Chapter 6), a trademark that was likely for either the Edmonds name, 'Sure to Rise' or the 'E' logo was prominently mentioned on labels well before that date. Some labels also featured the word 'Registered', suggesting that the correct legal process had been followed. Newspaper advertisements from early 1888 stated: 'SPECIAL Notice to all who use Edmonds' Prize Baking Powder, see that the name and trade mark is on each tin. No loose Powder sold.'[29] A report on Thomas's exhibit at the 1889 New Zealand and South Seas Exhibition in Dunedin referred to 'Mr Edmonds' baking powder, which, according to the trade mark, is "sure to rise" (and trade marks and advertisements are the embodiment of truth and accuracy)'.[30] Before the Trade Marks Act 1953, it was not illegal to imply that a trademark was registered even if it was not,[31] but it seems most unlikely that the highly ethical Thomas would have purposely misled the public. And the 1887 flour patent showed that he was well aware of the importance of protecting intellectual property in an intensely competitive market.

EBROOK'S
BISCUITS
AND COCOA

THE
PREMIER
BAKING POWDER
OF
NEW ZEALAND.

CHAPTER 4

BATTLE OF THE BRANDS

On 23 September 1769, a century or so before Thomas Edmonds arrived in New Zealand, when James Cook's *Endeavour* was a fortnight away from sighting land, botanist Joseph Banks confided in his journal that the bread on board ship was 'but indifferent, occasioned by the quantity of Vermin that are in it, I have often seen hundreds nay thousands shaken out of a single [ship's] bisket'. Ever the naturalist, Banks identified infestation by no fewer than five different kinds of beetles and spiders. 'We in the Cabbin have however an easy remedy for this by baking it in an oven, not too hot, which makes them all walk off ...'[1] There was a small oven on the port side of the vessel, where one-handed cook John Thompson sometimes baked fresh bread and pies for the officers and gentlemen on board, as well as for the sick.[2]

The leavening process then used for making bread usually depended on the fermentation of yeast. In 1754 Scottish chemist Joseph Black had discovered carbon dioxide, the gas that was so vital to bread baking. Mixing and kneading the dough traps and then disperses millions of air bubbles throughout bread dough. The yeast 'metabolizes the starches and sugars in the flour, turning them into alcohol and carbon dioxide gas [which] inflates the network of air bubbles, causing the bread to rise. During rising, the yeast divides and multiplies, producing more carbon dioxide.'[3] Bakers found that carbon dioxide could also be produced by adding sodium bicarbonate (baking soda) and sour milk (which contains lactic acid) to their dough. Although the chemical reaction was still unreliable, the problem would later be solved, when the sour milk was replaced by cream of tartar – a weakened form of tartaric acid and a by-product of the wine industry, especially in France and Italy. As the managing director of Edmonds noted many years later, 'It would be interesting to know what would happen if the world "went dry" ... if there were no wine there would be no cream of tartar, and, therefore, no baking powder.'[4] The mixing of these two uniform components – sodium bicarbonate and cream of tartar – greatly improved the control bakers had over the leavening process, and marked the beginnings of what would become known as baking powder.

Premier Baking Powder was just one of Edmonds' many early competitors. Dressing up to promote local products was a favourite form of advertising in these years – Miss Grimstone splendidly represents Hudson's, which remained a strong competitor for Edmonds until after the First World War.

European settlers in New Zealand in the early 1800s made their own bread. If yeast was available – likely shipped from Australia – one of the challenges was keeping it alive between baking sessions. Bread could be made, too, using leaven – a quantity of dough or a starter saved from a previous batch; or using barm – the foam or froth formed on the top of a fermenting liquid such as beer or wine.[5] In 1842 Aucklanders could buy yeast 'suited for Bakers and private Families' from the Norfolk Brewery in Lower Queen Street for 3s a gallon; and in 1846 a Nelson newspaper provided settlers with a recipe for making their own.[6] For those without access to ovens and rising agents, the most likely form of bread was the simplest: unleavened flour and water damper, probably of Australian origin and also known as bush bread or camp-oven bread. Along with tea and mutton, this was typical fare in early colonial New Zealand.

As greater numbers of Pākehā arrived, bringing with them wheat and flour, Māori 'embraced the art of breadmaking'. They made a flat, round unleavened bread called takakau, as well as two types of leavened bread. For rēwena ('leaven') they used boiled and mashed potato, with flour and sugar added to create a starter or 'bug'. To make parāoa parai or Māori fry bread they used a plain yeast-raised dough that was kneaded, cut into pieces and deep fried. All three kinds of bread are still baked today.[7]

The first modern version of baking powder was produced by British chemist Alfred Bird in 1843. Although this product combined cream of tartar and baking soda, at this stage the two ingredients were kept apart until they were used to prevent them from reacting too early. Four years earlier, in August 1839, while promoting organised settlement, the London-based New Zealand Company published this country's first newspaper, the *New Zealand Gazette and Wellington Spectator*. Of interest to prospective emigrant bakers was an advertisement for carbonate of soda and tartaric acid, which were available in London for 1s and 3s 6d per pound respectively.[8] Regular shipments of these and other basic essentials, including flour, would arrive in New Zealand from London and Sydney, and on 16 April 1840 the entrepreneurial Andrew Duncan began soliciting orders from settlers in Wellington for 'a regular supply of Bread and Biscuit. Dishes covered and baked on the same principle as in London, and on moderate terms.'[9]

Grocers of the period typically had immaculate – and at times precarious-looking – displays of tins, as this 1903 photo (above) shows. Opposite, before Edmonds made its mark, Borwick's and Hudson's were the two dominant brands.

The country's first baking powder may have been the one case that arrived from Sydney on the *Moa* in May 1850, along with other supplies, including 300 bags of flour, 180 cheeses, six kegs of nails, 20 barrels of herrings, 3 tons of sugar and a billiard table.[10] Soon there were advertisements for what was possibly the first identified commercial brand of baking powder to appear here – Hudson's, manufactured by English chemist Robert Spear Hudson.[11] However, this product does not appear to have been on the New Zealand market for long, because the owner handed over his formula to his brother-in-law, George Borwick.[12] Rebranded as Borwick's, and first advertised early in 1859, it went on to dominate the local market until the rise of Thomas Edmonds' product. Promoted under the

heading 'Bread for the Bush', it claimed to be the only effective substitute for yeast; no settler should be without 'a good supply'.[13]

But Borwick's did not have the New Zealand baking powder market entirely to itself: by the 1860s competitors were arriving on the scene. These included the memorably named Harper Twelvetrees from East London, and another import, Corbyn's, whose British Baking Powder claimed to be 'an effectual preventive of Indigestion'.[14] By now there were some locally produced alternatives. An early one came from Nelson chemist and druggist George Elson, whose Egg and Baking Powder was available by 1864, sold in packets and tins, alongside his other proprietary lines such as homoeopathic medicines and corn and wart solvent.[15] But if frequency of advertising was anything to go by, Borwick's had the lead; on just one day, 12 March 1864, it was advertised in no fewer than seven newspapers throughout the colony.[16]

By 1865 Harper Twelvetrees was promising customers that its 'Yeasterine' was 'sure to act' – many years before Thomas Edmonds made a similar claim for his own product.[17] Claims now focused increasingly on the alleged purity of the products, and their freedom from harmful additives and cheap 'fillers' substituted for the real – and more expensive – thing. In 1867 Borwick's warned customers via four testimonials, including one from the private baker at Buckingham Palace, to avoid 'spurious imitations', some of which were 'unwholesome and injurious', and claimed their product was entirely free from the allegedly harmful alum, or sodium aluminium sulphate.[18] Aluminium-based powders were cheaper to produce and therefore provided serious competition for those based on cream of tartar which, as a natural product, was said to be healthful.

Chemists and pharmacists who stocked the vital ingredients were well placed to mix their own powders. H.H. Coggins of Oamaru sold his Superior brand, which was 'in every respect equal to Borwick's', and other competitors included Aickin's Aerated brand from Auckland, Cox's 'second to none' from Shortland (later Thames), and Hill's Colonial Baking Powder manufactured by Auckland chemists Hill and Hudson.[19] For New Zealanders who still preferred to mix their own, the 1874 Christmas edition of the *Daily Southern Cross* provided a recipe for baking powder: its action was 'so rapid' that it needed to be kept in a well-corked bottle. The *Otago Witness* also offered a simpler recipe.[20]

HUDSONS
HUDSON'S
Baking Powder.
HUDSON'S
BALLOON BRAND
BAKING POWDER

With the growing number of baking powders now on the market, there were increasingly outrageous claims regarding their purity and efficacy. In 1878 an analysis of 12 samples of Christchurch bread found two of them had been adulterated with alum, one 'to a considerable extent'.[21] The analysis was carried out by Hampshire-born Professor Alexander William Bickerton, who had arrived in Christchurch in 1874 to take up the post of foundation professor of chemistry at the newly established Canterbury College (see Chapter 11).

The most unfortunate chapter in the history of baking powder concerns the injuries sustained when it was confused with other substances. There were several instances of poisoning when arsenic was mistaken for baking powder, usually because the arsenic had been stored in an empty baking powder tin. In 1889 a Masterton woman died in 'great agony' after eating pancakes containing the arsenic her taxidermist husband used for preparing bird skins.[22] Two years later, some 20 wedding guests at Pahiatua were poisoned, and two died, after eating cakes made with either arsenic or oxalic acid. In 1892 a number of people at a Wairoa hotel survived after eating arsenic-filled Yorkshire pudding; and in 1895 four men at a sheep station in Buller lay 'retching and vomiting for upwards of thirty hours' before recovering, slowly, after eating scones made with arsenic.[23]

As this impressive 1913 display shows, Hudson's 'Bound to Rise' product was a major combatant in the baking powder war, along with many other brands, like those below and on the following pages.

When Edmonds' baking powder first appeared, it faced a growing number of local competitors. Perhaps the most serious of these was Sharland's Moa brand, which had depots 'all through the country';[24] it won first prize at the 1881 Auckland Show and was touted as 'famous throughout New Zealand for its 'absolute purity and strength'.[25] The influx of new baking powder brands – both imported and New Zealand-made – continued unabated. Among the more colourfully named alternatives in the early 1880s were Goodwin's Elephant brand, John Buchanan's South British and Spread Eagle brands, Hercules, Rainbow Star and Royal ('Once Tried, Always Used'). Alfred Bird of England was another newcomer on the market here, with baking powder as well as custard and blancmange powders.[26] In the mid-1880s about a dozen different brands of baking powder were being advertised regularly throughout the country, and by 1887 Thomas Edmonds' product had joined them.

The confident claims for high sales and superior quality of commercial brands would continue. In 1890 Jumbo, 'the best in the market', alleged it had sold over 10,000 tins of baking powder in the previous 12 months, and within a year had 'driven all others out of the market'. At the same time the Kiwi brand apparently had 'an awkward knack of sending pastry flying; won't be kept down'.[27] At least 60 new brands entered the already crowded New Zealand market in the 1890s; consumers were spoilt for choice.[28]

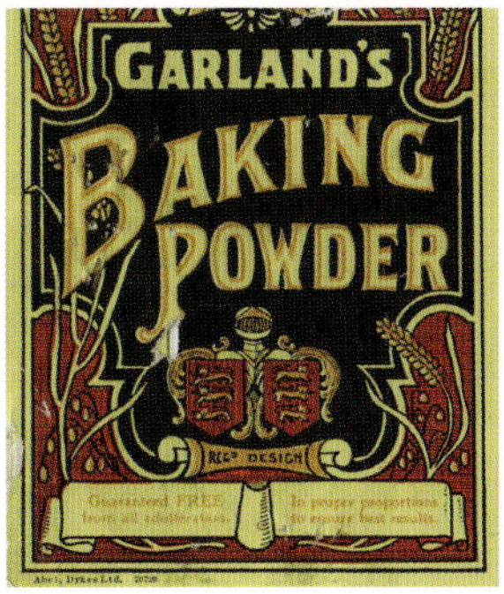

Fairy
BAKING POWDER
PREPARED WITH ACID PHOSPHATE
CONTAINS 14 OZS. NET.
EXCELS IN ITS RISING PROPERTIES
FINE QUALITY
BIG SURPRISE
Just Watch it Rise
VERONICA CHEMICAL PRODUCTS
K
BRAND
BALLOON BRAND
BOUND TO RISE
TRADE MARK.
BAKING POWDER
Q-P
QUALITY PACK
WINSON'S
BAKING POWDER
NOTED FOR PURITY AND EXCELLENCY OF QUALITY
TIN WHEN NOT IN USE.
SHARLAND'S
THE MOA BRAND
ESTD 1865
BAKING POWDER.
GUARANTEED TO COMPLY WITH THE
DRUGS ACT 1908, N.Z., BY SHARLAND
SHARLANDS
MOA
BRAND regd.
CONCENTRATED
EGG
PRESERVATIVE
SUFFICIENT TO PRESERVE
200 EGGS
G.U.S
UNA
BAKING POWDER
W
FOR BETTER COOKING
Winson's
NOTED FOR PURITY & EXCELLENCY OF QUALITY
BAKING POWDER
PACKED BY G. E. WINSON LTD, AUCKLAND
BAKING POWDER
CONTAINS AS AN ACID BASIS
CREAM OF TARTAR
S. KIRKPATRICK & Co. Ltd
NELSON N.Z.
EGG
MOA
SHARLAND & Co. Ltd

'K'
BAKING POWDER
CREAM OF TARTAR
99-100%
CONTAINS AS AN ACID BASIS
99-100%
CREAM OF TARTAR
S. KIRKPATRICK & CO LTD. NELSON
G. E. WINSON'S
BAKING POWDER
NOTED FOR PURITY AND EXCELLENCY OF QUALITY
SELF-HELP
CREAM OF TARTAR
99-100%
BAKING POWDER
ALL BRITISH INGREDIENTS
14 OZS. NETT WEIGHT
TUCKER'S
Sunshine
BAKING POWDER
WINSON'S
Guaranteed
BAKING POWDER
CREAM OF TART
99-100%
BAKING POWD
BOUND TO RISE
BRITISH INGREDI
3 OZS NET WEIGHT
SILO
SILO BAKING POWDER
AUCKLAND
WELLINGTON
CHRISTCHURCH
DUNEDIN
NORTON'S
WATER GLASS
EGG
PRESERVATIV
T. NORTON LTD.
KIRKPATRICK'S
'K'
CREAM OF TARTAR
BAKING POWDER
Self-Hel
CREAM OF TARTAR
BAKING POWDER
PAMS
BAKING POWDER
PUTS PEP INTO YOUR BAKING
CREAM OF TARTAR
BAKING POWDER
BOUND TO RISE
OZS. NETT WEIGHT

tice has developed both Cradd
Mason's crews, with the result t
being well nigh friendless at f
now has a good following. The
Foster's crew—which, physically
the strongest the Club has ever t
—is not at all attractive, and thi
for the falling off in support that
place. But they are the best-co
crew of the lot, and I rather fanc
at them as they have finished,
course between the old Woolv
Cowlishaw's, if it could speal
tell a tale of hard work
man in the boat. I like
Craddock's crew shape, but I do
they will stand the pace set
the first mile. Mason's crew ha
lot of work, and should make thir
for the first portion of the journ
rate. Atkinson has a nice,
balanced crew. In the hands of
like, say A. L. Smith, for inst
crew would have shown a
advance in the five weeks they
before them. As it is they have
the improvement that was to be
after being so long together, and
says they will be last. If they
any rate, hope it will be a goo
some of the crew have worked
tiously. I certainly cannot see
in it but Foster's crew, and if th
finish first it will be very strange

As these remarks have spun ou
a length, I must deal with the rem
the events very briefly.

The Avon R.C. Trial Pairs will
in two preliminary heats and a
Hobbs and Godfrey should take t
in the first heat, and the brother
those in the second. I stand
for the final.

Like the A.R.C., the C.R.C. Tr
will be rowed in three heats.
Styche and Nicoll for the first
Humphreys and Wright for the se
also for the final.

For the U.R.C. Trial Pairs
prefer the favourites, Mills and
with Dyer and Dawe as a likel
despite the fact that they have fe
and row in shocking style. T
event is expected to lie between
Inwood, and Rosewarne, the la
being the favourite. My sel
Craddock.

MARKET REPORTS

The NEW ZEALAND LOAN A
CANTILE AGENCY COMPANY, Lim

CHAPTER 5

SURE TO RISE

'One day a lady customer when persuaded by me to purchase a tin, complained that when using other brands the scones were very flat. I assured her that if she used my brand, her scones would be sure to rise. The name "Sure to Rise" struck me very forcibly ...'[1] Thomas Edmonds knew a winner when he heard it. He was using the now famous phrase by the time he was exhibiting at the New Zealand and South Seas Exhibition in Dunedin late in 1889, where he received two first place awards – for his self-raising flour and, of course, his baking powder.[2]

In the middle of page two of the *Lyttelton Times* on 28 August 1890 sat a distinctive advertisement, tipped sideways. It showed a complex, stylised semi-circular and radiant rising sun, with the phrase 'Sure to Rise' and the words 'Edmonds' Prize Baking Powder And Self-Rising Flour. Sold Everywhere'. The advertisement was repeated in December and January, but by the beginning of February the sun motif had disappeared from the papers and the wording had changed. (The advertisement was, however, used in the fifth edition of the *New Zealand Domestic Cookery Book*, published in 1905.) By early 1891 the advertisements stated that Edmonds had been established in 1879, a proud boast that would remain. A 1923 advertisement showing 'The growth of a Big N.Z. Industry' included a little sketch with the caption: 'This 10 x 12' shed formed our humble and unpretentious factory of 1879.'[3] That date is more likely, however, to mark the beginnings of Thomas Edmonds' grocery business – in the same year he arrived in Christchurch – than the launch of his best-known product.

The first Edmonds logo is thought to be the sunburst shown opposite, a design that first appeared in the *Lyttelton Times* in August 1890. As the cordial label shows, a rising sun was a popular image for many products, particularly in the nineteenth century.

The sun symbol had long been revered by ancient cultures such as the Egyptians and Incas. In 1710 the world's oldest insurance office took the name Sun, and in 1884 the first ever packaged and branded laundry soap was called Sunlight. The sun had a particular resonance in nineteenth-century Britain, which claimed to have built an empire 'on which the sun never sets'. The first graphic representation of the rising sun in New Zealand was perhaps on the masthead of the *Victoria Times*, which was published in Wellington only once, on 15 September 1841.

'Sure to rise' was a common expression in New Zealand, applied variously to property prices, river levels after rain and the prospects of those with social aspirations, but Edmonds appears to have been the first company to make commercial use of the term with respect to groceries and food. This did not stop others from trying to do the same. Graham's baking powder was advertised in a Wairarapa newspaper in 1892 as 'sure to rise'; and another product made equally cheeky use of the phrase in 1902 with the rhetorical question: 'Why is the Sun like the Skylark Baking Powder? They are both sure to rise.'[4] The phrase 'Bound to Rise', which may also have been inspired by the Edmonds label, was employed from 1891 by Hudson's Balloon brand, which was on the market until at least 1921. Sharland's, in 1896–97, also claimed its Moa brand was 'Bound to Rise' – despite that bird already being extinct.[5] Another early feature of the classic 'Sure to Rise' baking powder label was the vertical panel that stated: 'Public/Opinion/Once Used/Always/Used/Try It'. Both Royal and Tucker's Family brands used 'Once Tried, Always Used', and East's claimed: 'Those who have used it once will have no other, try it.'[6]

• • •

As usual, Thomas exhibited at the Canterbury Metropolitan Show in November 1889 – 'Of interest to farmers' wives should be ... a well got-up collection of baking powder and self-raising flour, the efficacy of which was testified to by sundry loaves of bread and cakes made therewith'[7] – and at the big New Zealand and South Seas Exhibition held in Dunedin that same year. But there were no further newspaper advertisements for Edmonds products until those new ones in the *Lyttelton Times* in August 1890. Thomas was instead focusing on the physical expansion of his flourishing business.

The land on which the shop stood, Lot 39, had been part of the original 50-acre Rural Section 99 on the 'North side of Ferry Road'. On 24 September 1889 Thomas bought adjoining Lots 37 and 38, about half an acre of land altogether.[8] On this he operated his first factory, a simple single-gabled wooden building that he either built or converted and

As the business grew, Thomas built a simple wooden factory (left) close to the grocery store, and later opened a new, bigger factory around 1896–97 (right). Above right, Jane's mother, Eliza, with Beatrice, Irene and Gertrude, c.1899. On the following pages, Thomas (centre) poses proudly with his staff. By 1902 his four sons were working for him: Ernest is seated at the back, with James and Will seated below him, and George is standing far right. Jim Knight is on the far left.

subsequently added to over the next few years. This was almost certainly the building with a large 'Tin Store' sign on the side that appeared in Edmonds' (1929) Jubilee Publication (see p. 34). In December 1890, when Jane Edmonds was advertising for a 'useful Girl, about 15', applicants were asked to contact her at 'Baking Powder Factory, Ashbourne'. In a May 1892 advertisement a widow was offering a 'Comfortable Home for One or Two Young Ladies'; those interested were to apply to 'R.F., Edmonds' Factory, Edmonds Street'.[9] But more space was required as sales grew. In July 1893 Thomas purchased '1½ acre land, together with dwelling of 6 rooms ... on Ferry road'.[10] On part of this new site he built his second factory, a two-storey barn-like wooden structure that opened onto Aldwins Road.

In old age, Gertrude described the family moving, around 1895, to a single-storey house built by her father on the corner of Ferry and Aldwins roads, next to the new factory and across the road from St Peter's Church. Their neighbour was John Souter, whose Melrose Nursery occupied land on Ferry Road for many years.[11] The date may have been 1896, since in October that year Thomas was seeking tenders for 'Glazing and Painting House and Factory at Ferry Road'; the specifications could be seen at his office.[12] Since Gertrude was the last child born in the grocery shop, in 1891, and Beatrice was born in 1895, it's possible that the family lived in the old house that had come with the land while they waited for the building work to be finished. The Edmonds' youngest child Irene (Rene) was born in the new home in 1898.

The house was a considerable improvement on the first Edmonds dwelling. A photograph taken in 1898 shows members of the family sitting in a room that boasts a plaster ceiling with decorative moulding and floral wallpaper, and a substantial and ornate fireplace with a large

EDM
ESTD

NONDS'
G POWDER
1879
SURE TO RISE

mirror above it. There was running water, but still no inside toilet. Sissy Ashley, the live-in housekeeper, did most of the domestic work, helped by a general servant. Jim Knight was the handyman: he cut wood, tended the vegetable garden and drove goods from the factory into town in a horse-drawn van;[13] this was very possibly the 'James Knight of Woolston gardener' to whom Thomas sold Lots 37 and 38 in October 1902.[14] In September 1897 Jane Edmonds was looking for an 'experienced General Servant, must be good cook' and in November 1899 she advertised for a 'Good Respectable General [servant]. Apply Mrs Edmonds, Ferry Road, near St. Peter's.'[15] In later years she made use of Mrs R.H. Mitchell's registry office, one of several recruitment agencies in the city for domestic staff.[16]

Although neither Jane nor Thomas played an instrument, both loved music and it was an important part of family life: the photograph shows a piano and a canterbury for the sheet music. Thomas also bought an Aeolian self-playing organ, or organola – a version of a pianola, with music rolls – which stood at the far end of the dining room.[17] In 1905 he donated this to the Baptist church in Colombo Street, and he bought another one for the next family home in Gloucester Street.

Thomas put his sons to work in the burgeoning business. Ernest started in 1896, aged 14 or 15, and by 1900, 20-year-old Will had been at the factory for at least five years. That year, though, there was a reward: he and his cousin Arthur, Edwin and Sarah's son, travelled to Europe. In August, according to the 'Anglo-Colonial Notes' in the *Lyttelton Times*, the pair were 'among the Christchurch "boys" at present enjoying life in the Old Country'. After sailing to England on the *Gothic* and spending a few weeks in London, Will had gone to Paris for three weeks, where

Thomas, Will, Jane and Ernest in the living room of the new Ferry Road house in 1898. Patty Pan baking powder (opposite) had a unique added attraction – lids that could be used for baking. In the 1908 factory photo on the following pages, Thomas and Will are in the office, with tins of baking, custard and egg powder ready for dispatch.

Arthur later joined him, and together they visited the Exposition Universelle, a spectacular celebration of the new century. The cousins were next bound for Scotland. So far Will had, said the reporter, 'enjoyed himself greatly'.[18]

• • •

By the last decade of the nineteenth century, baking powder was in high demand. The 1891 census revealed that, since 1886, the number of factories built to produce baking powder in New Zealand had quadrupled, from two to eight, and the number of employees had risen from nine to 27.[19] But while such brands as Borwick's, Balloon, Moa, Jumbo and Dragon were advertised regularly nationwide, Thomas kept a relatively low profile, with only occasional small classified advertisements in Canterbury newspapers. There were, however, regular reports of his success in various exhibitions. At the 1893 Metropolitan Show he received a 'very high commendation' for his baking powder and self-raising flour, and at the Industrial Exhibition in 1894 he was praised for the 'well-arranged trophy [formal arrangement] of calico and paper bags of self-raising flour, and of prettily-adorned cannisters containing his custard, egg and baking powders'.[20] In September 1895 both Thomas and his brother Edwin had displays at the Industrial Exhibition: in the Workers' Department, Edwin 'with his wood-turning lathe' had 'an excellent collection of products – ranging from Indian clubs to napkin rings – all in native woods'.[21] Thomas was 'as usual ... to the fore' with his baking powder display at Christchurch's Metropolitan Show in 1896. The next year, there was reference to his Sure to Rise baking powder, with 'quite a stock of tins on view ... The hearts of the thrifty housewives who make their own bread will no doubt be rejoiced at the bags of self-raising flour exhibited.'[22]

By this time Thomas had some local competition. Near the Edmonds display at the 1896 exhibition was that of Hayward Bros, with their 'justly celebrated' Flag Brand 'pickles, bottled fruits, sauces, olive oil, vinegar and baking powder, all most appetising, and "put up" in very attractive style'.[23] Hayward's had started making baking powder in 1892 and, according to the advertising, it promised to supersede all imported kinds. It was 'supplied in neat tins, which enable it to be carried without detriment to the contents, and to any distance'.[24] In 1901 the tin was the focus of its next innovation, 'An Ingenious Contrivance': 'a baking powder named the "Patty Pan" ... because the ends of the tin in which it is enclosed are formed of two pattypans ... which can be utilised in baking operations'.[25] After being advertised heavily as 'all the rage' and even 'The Novelty of the Century',[26] this 'very special' baking powder surprisingly disappeared from the pages of the country's newspapers after July 1912.

In 1893 Thomas sought a 'strong young man, about 18 or 20', for his 'baking powder manufactory'.[27] And in 1894 he began to advertise beyond Canterbury, in South Taranaki, Wellington and in Auckland, where he invited 'Ladies who can appreciate a really first-class article' to give his 'Gold Medal' baking powder a trial.[28] Between 1897 and 1899 Thomas advertised for five extra staff, specifically strong, smart, active lads aged between 16 and 18. In the first year of the twentieth century he was after the services of both a 'strong useful boy' and a 'strong cob or cart horse, sound and quiet, with a trial'.[29] The business was clearly expanding.

EDMONDS
PRIZE
KING POWDER
Z LARGE
EDMONDS
PRIZE
AKING POWDER

THE TRADE PRIZE SUPPLIED
BAKING POWD
MANUFACTURE
EDMONDS PRIZE BAKING POWDER
EDMONDS PRIZE BAKING POWDER
EDMONDS BAKING POWDER

EDMONDS'
PRIZE
ESTD 1879
BAKING • POWDER
SURE TO RISE
TRADE MARK
(REGISTERED)

CHAPTER 6

A HOUSEHOLD NAME

Christchurch, as a loyal outpost of the British Empire, marked Queen Victoria's Diamond Jubilee in 1897 with military parades, concerts and dinners, and erected a highly decorative clock tower at the intersection of High and Manchester streets. Then, towards the end of 1900, came Canterbury's fiftieth jubilee, celebrating the arrival of the first four ships in December 1850 and the beginning of organised Pākehā settlement. On 1 November an exhibition opened in the new Agricultural and Industrial Hall, also known as Canterbury Hall, in Manchester Street. Appropriately, the plan of the exhibition honoured those famous vessels, and near the west end of Cressy Avenue was the T.J. Edmonds display. As well as baking powder, it included the company's self-raising flour and egg powder, 'a first-class substitute for real eggs' and usable for all kinds of cakes and puddings.

New Zealand was by now involved in its first foreign war. On 28 September 1899 Prime Minister Richard Seddon, with the enthusiastic support of a parliamentary majority, offered troops to help the Mother Country in a conflict that was clearly about to break out between the British and the Boers of the South African Republic. Of the 6000 New Zealand men who went to fight in this war, 230 would lose their lives, the majority from disease rather than from wounds. Ten contingents went to South Africa; the third, raised in Canterbury, left Christchurch in February 1900. The veldt was a hostile environment, fiercely hot by day and freezing at night, and supplies were basic and sometimes meagre. One of the items missing from the men's diet was baking powder; in letters home, more than one man wrote of having to use the indigestion remedy, Eno's Fruit Salts, as a substitute when making scones and bread.[1] Back in New Zealand, patriotic Diamond brand capitalised on the conflict by claiming their baking powder 'rises just as easy as British Gun Powder', while admitting that the latter 'goes off much louder'.[2]

This striking detail comes from the oldest Edmonds label known to exist, probably dating from 1890 or shortly after.

• • •

Irrespective of its trademark claims, Edmonds did not yet have the rising sun motif or 'Sure to Rise' slogan to itself. Brown, Barrett & Co. joined the fray with the claim that their UNXLD baking powder 'Always Rises at the Proper Time'.[3] Everyone was taking liberties. In January 1905 Hudsons complained that other manufacturers were closely imitating the labels and style of

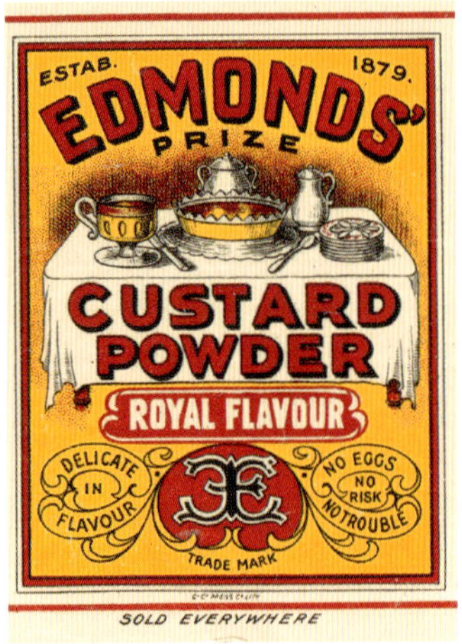

Baking powder was always Edmonds' signature product, but custard and egg powder, both developed in the 1880s, were also popular, beautifully labelled and won awards.

their 'well-known' Balloon brand.[4] Edmonds, too, was the victim of such tactics. The company advised a few months later that loose baking powder was being 'palmed off' as their product; it offered a reward of £5 for 'information that will lead to a conviction', and it reminded customers that 'Edmonds baking powder is sold in tins only'.[5] But at least Thomas's product was now making it to other parts of the country – perhaps largely by sea. According to shipping reports, five cases of baking powder left Lyttelton on the *Wakare* for Napier in March 1902, followed by eight cases to various destinations in April. In October the *Zealandia* carried five cases to Whanganui.[6]

By 1904 Thomas was placing large, eye-catching display advertisements in newspapers.[7] In 1906 he claimed that, despite the fact 'he had never tried to push his goods to any extent', orders were 'received daily' from all parts of the country. The output of his baking powder in 1894 had been 100,000 tins; this rose to 350,000 in 1904 and 370,032 in 1905. It was expected to reach 400,000 in 1906, but the actual number of tins sold was 429,780.[8] Thomas pulled out all the stops for his display at the 1906–07 New Zealand International Exhibition in Hagley Park in Christchurch: it incorporated a miniature working railway, complete with station and tunnels, as well as a model of the countryside, with a picnic party and cars on the road. But the main focus was that 'well-known article', tins of Sure to Rise baking powder in 'well-arranged pyramids'.[9] Although Mrs Pugh, winner of a cooking contest at the exhibition, chose to use Chef rather than Edmonds baking powder, each of Edmonds' four products – baking powder, custard powder, egg powder and self-raising flour – was awarded a Special Gold Medal.[10] The Edmonds baking powder label already included medals awarded at the 1889–90 New Zealand and South Seas Exhibition in Dunedin and the 1900–01 Canterbury Jubilee Industrial Exhibition. The latest success could now be added to the line-up.

Towards the end of 1906 there were also important business developments. Edmonds' factory was employing nine hands; more than this was 'unnecessary' because everything was done by 'up-to-date machinery'. And, addressing another concern of the day, 'hygienic' conditions in the workplace rendered Edmonds' mixtures 'immune from impurities.'[11] By the beginning of February 1907 the firm had embarked on another initiative: placing 'GOOD RECIPES For Cakes, Scones, Pastry, Pikelets, Bread, Pancakes, and Puddings' in each tin of baking powder.[12] These were developed and tested by Thomas and Jane's daughter Lilian and by their son Will's wife Alice. By March the advertisements were shouting, 'New Recipes! NEW RECIPES! New Recipes!', and by August the copy was more specific: 'cocoanut cakes, exhibition buns, rock cakes, brown scones, pikelets etc.' A 1908 advertisement described them as 'simple recipes for healthful and tempting dishes'.[13]

The recipes were printed on discs of a parchment-like and slightly transparent paper, about 3 inches in diameter, that sat on top of the contents of the tins, fitting snugly under the overlapping lids. These inserts later carried advertisements for Edmonds' egg powder, self-raising flour, cake powder and cornflour, as well as baking powder and the Edmonds cookery book – which suggests they may have been included with the company's other products. The

RECIPES
FOR
COCOANUT CAKES,
EXHIBITION BUNS,
ROCK CAKES,
BROWN SCONES,
PIKELETS, etc.,
In each Tin of
EDMONDS'
PRIZE
Baking Powder.
Ask your Grocer for it.

The medal won by Edmonds at the 1906–07 exhibition quickly found its way onto the baking powder label. As the newspaper advertisement notes, around the same time Edmonds began to include recipes printed on a paper disc inside each tin. As the following pages show, over the years discs were used for a range of promotional purposes.

discs also sometimes promoted other things, such as children's stories in the early 1920s, *The Edmonds Custard Fairy Book* in 1931, and the National Savings Movement during the Second World War. Surely these recipes – and the public response to them – were the genesis of the Edmonds cookery book (see Chapter 7). At least one other competing brand used the same idea: by 1910 tins of Daisy baking powder were including recipes for 'several tasty tea cakes, scones etc', and back in 1903 and 1904 each 1s tin of Sharland's Moa brand included a coupon, 10 of which entitled the consumer to a copy of the 428-page *Presidential Cook Book*.[14]

Sales of Edmonds baking powder continued to grow steadily. In 1908 they reached 655,668 tins, prompting an advertisement that observed that 'Quantity speaks for quality'. Sales in 1909 were an even more impressive 743,976 tins and the product could by now justifiably claim to be 'the Dominion favourite'.[15] The popularity of baking powder, regardless of brand, meant more empty tins. In 1905 it was suggested that these made 'excellent molds in which to pack ice cream for serving'. With holes punched in the lid, they could also be converted into suitable sprinklers for a cleaning mixture made of one part pumice powder and three parts soap powder. Another, more novel form of recycling was a caricature of the mayor of Christchurch in a university students' capping procession: his mayoral robe was a 'dirty window curtain', and his chain consisted of the lids of baking powder tins.[16]

And many of those tins were being made at the Edmonds factory. In early April 1903 the Arbitration Court sat at the Provincial Council Chambers to hear the application that several companies, including Aulsebrook and Edmonds, 'should be brought under the conditions of the industrial agreement between the Tinsmiths' and Sheet Metal Workers' Union and the employers'. Thomas asked to be exempted from the proposed agreement 'as the firm made tins only for its own use'.[17] Two meat companies, plus Aulsebrook and Edmonds, were granted exemptions.

• • •

There has been speculation, based on family memories, that the design of the baking powder label, or a variant of it, involved the input of English-born artist Philip R. Presants, who came to New Zealand from his hometown of Norwich in 1897.[18] He began his career in this country with the Christchurch Press Company, and later designed material for exhibitions, including the award Thomas won at the 1900–01 Canterbury Jubilee Industrial Exhibition. Presants was also a friend of the Edmonds family: his daughters Lilian and Myrtle often played with Thomas and Jane's youngest daughter, Rene. It does not, however, seem likely that he had a part in designing the original label, given that the design – and those for egg powder and custard powder – had been around for some time. It is possible, though, that he reproduced or printed a label around 1905, since a photograph shows a precut sheet of labels on a promotional wall in the design area of the *Press* offices, where he worked (see pp. 236–237).[19] He may also have had a hand in one or more of the cookery book covers (see Chapter 7).

By 1910 Edmonds was placing advertisements more regularly, employing images with text and exploring a range of different approaches. An early

WHEN
EGGS ARE SCARCE
OR EXPENSIVE
USE
EDMONDS
CAKE BAKING
POWDER
NEW EDITION
Free!
EDMONDS
'Sure to Rise'
COOKERY
BOOK 6th edition
PLEASE TURN OVER
Have you got your
7th Edition
FREE Cookery Book?
If not send your name and address to
Dept. B.P.
T. J. EDMONDS Ltd.
P.O. Box 472
Christchurch
N.Z.
COUPON
POST TO EDMONDS
BOX 472
SURE TO RISE
CHRISTCHURCH
Name Mrs A. Brown
Address Okains Bay
Banks Peninsula
I have used your baking
powder for 20 years
AND RECEIVE POST FREE
4TH EDITION
COOKERY BOOK
A GOOD
BOILED CUSTARD
1 breakfastcup milk, 1 egg,
1 heaped teaspoon Edmonds Custard
Powder (Standard flavour),
1 teaspoonful sugar.
METHOD: Put milk into saucepan, bring to the boil. Mix Custard Powder with little of the cold milk, and stir it into the hot milk. Cook a few minutes then pour on to the egg previously beaten with the sugar, stirring briskly. Return to fire and stir till egg is set.
(Note, the custard must not boil.)
MERRY CHRISTMAS
CHRISTMAS CAKE
1 lb. butter
1 lb. currants
1 lb. raisins
lb. sultanas
lb. mixed peel
lb. almonds
4 breakfastcups flour
2 breakfastcups sugar
10 eggs
1 heaped teaspoonful
Edmonds' Baking Powder
Wine glass brandy
BEAT butter to a cream, add sugar, then eggs one by one (unbeaten); mix baking powder with flour, and put in, then fruit dredged with flour. Brandy. Cook 4½ hours moderate oven.
SEND NAME & ADDRESS TO EDMONDS BOX 472 CHRISTCHURCH
EDMONDS
SURE TO RISE
COOKERY
BOOK
FIFTH EDITION
& RECEIVE POST FREE 5TH EDITION COOKERY BOOK
Write Name & Address on Back
THE PRICE
OF
EDMONDS "SURE TO RISE"
BAKING POWDER
IS CONTROLLED
BY
THE BOARD OF TRADE
EDMONDS
"SURE TO SET"
JELLY CRYSTALS
SERVED
Partners in Perfection
WITH
EDMONDS CUSTARD
STOCKED BY ALL
LEADING GROCERS
BATTER
FOR FISH
Ingredients: 4 oz. flour, 1 teaspoon EDMONDS CAKE POWDER, salt to taste, about ½ cup milk; Method: Mix dry ingredients together; add enough milk to make a smooth batter.
ORIENTAL
SUNDAE
2 packets EDMONDS JELLY CRYSTALS (any flavour), 1 sponge cake, a variety of fruit (bananas, oranges, passion fruit, etc.) Method: Cut sponge into squares, put a layer into a dish, then a layer of fruit, and so on until the dish is full. Make the jellies and pour over sponge and fruit. Leave to set and serve with EDMONDS CUSTARD.
When buying
BAKING POWDER
see that the label states
that the
PRINCIPAL
acid ingredient is
CREAM OF TARTAR
Strength 99%
TRIFLE
TAKE some stale sponge sandwich, spread with raspberry jam, cut into small blocks and put into a dish; then make a pint of custard and pour over. Let stand till cold, then spread whipped cream on top. This dish is improved by adding a little sherry or wine to the cut sponge.
WHEN COMPARING PRICES
Remember!
ONE DESSERTSPOON OF
EDMONDS CUSTARD POWDER
WILL MAKE ONE PINT OF CUSTARD
The Best
is the Cheapest
in the end
The one thing needful
to ensure
LIGHT, WHOLESOME
CAKES IS
EDMONDS'
COLOURED
CAKE
BAKING POWDER
FREE
SEND YOUR NAME & ADDRESS TO
EDMONDS
Box 472, CHRISTCHURCH, N.Z.
AND RECEIVE POST FREE A COPY OF THE
SURE TO RISE
COOKERY BOOK
ON RECEIPT OF THE COOKERY BOOK
YOUR POSTAL AUTHORITIES WILL
PROBABLY ASK FOR THE PAYMENT
OF 1½D., WHICH IS A DUTY IMPOSED
BY THE TASMANIAN
GOVERNMENT
4TH EDITION

Spanish Cream
1 packet Edmonds Jelly Crystals, $1\frac{1}{2}$ cups Boiling Water, 1 Egg, 1 teaspoon Sugar, $1\frac{1}{4}$ cups Milk. Method: Dissolve jelly crystals in boiling water, mix egg yolk and sugar with $\frac{1}{2}$ cup of milk, heat remainder of milk, add mixture, and bring to boil, stirring all the time. Mix in the melted jelly and lastly beaten egg white. Pour into a mould to set.
SCOTCH RUM FILLING AND ICING
Ingredients: $\frac{1}{4}$ cup sweetened condensed milk, 1 cup water, about 3 tablespoons EDMONDS' CUSTARD POWDER, 3 oz. butter, 2 oz. light brown sugar, few drops rum flavouring. Method: Mix the custard powder to a thin cream with a little water. Bring the rest of the water and condensed milk to boiling point, pour this on to the moistened custard powder and stir vigorously. Return all to pan and boil for few minutes. Place lid on pan, stand till custard is cold. Beat the butter and sugar to a very creamy consistency. Add the custard mixture gradually, beating the mixture well till very light and fluffy, using a dover beater. Add flavouring to taste. Put between cakes and use as an icing on top of cakes.
EDMONDS' PRIZE BAKING POWDER
SOLD IN THREE SIZES, VIZ.:
SMALL $6\frac{1}{2}$ OZS. MEDIUM 12 OZS. LARGE $14\frac{3}{4}$ OZS.
ONE QUALITY ONLY
THE BEST
RICE CAKES (without Eggs)
1 cup flour
$\frac{1}{2}$ cup ground rice
$\frac{1}{4}$ lb. sugar
$\frac{1}{4}$ lb. butter
$\frac{1}{2}$ cup milk (good measure)
1 heaped teaspoonful Edmonds' Cake Powder
Pinch salt
METHOD: Cream butter and sugar, sift and mix dry ingredients into same, mix all thoroughly with the milk, add flavouring, and bake in patty pans in moderate oven from 10 to 12 minutes.
WARNING
We desire to warn all users of EDMONDS' POWDERS that same are sold in TWO SIZED TINS ONLY, viz.:—large and small. The LARGE tins of EDMONDS' BAKING, EGG, and CUSTARD POWDERS are the most economical on the market.
SOLD EVERYWHERE
SAMPLE.
EDMONDS' CUSTARD POWDER
TO MAKE A CUSTARD.
From a pint of new milk take sufficient to mix smooth the contents of this sample; sweeten the remainder of the milk with a dessertspoonful of sugar and when the milk is boiling pour the mixed custard into the saucepan, stir, and when it boils again pour into a jug, grate a little nutmeg on top if desired.
Delicious, hot or cold.
EDMONDS
New!
DELICIOUSLY DIFFERENT
"SURE TO SET" JELLY CRYSTALS
EDMONDS CUSTARD POWDER
Try VANILLA flavour with Gooseberries, Figs or Plums. Try LEMON flavour with Stewed Apples, Pears, Pineapple or Bananas. Try ALMOND flavour with Apricots, Cherries or Peaches. Try STANDARD flavour with Milk Puddings, Cereals, etc. Try RASPBERRY flavour with EDMONDS RASPBERRY JELLY CRYSTALS. Try BANANA flavour with EDMONDS LEMON JELLY CRYSTALS. Wholesome and Nutritious.
TEA CAKES WITHOUT EGGS
1 lb flour
4ozs. sugar, 4ozs. butter, 2 teaspoonsful
EDMONDS' EGG POWDER,
half lb dates (or sultanas) chopped, milk to mix, salt a pinch.
Rub butter into flour, add all dry ingredients, mix all together to a paste with milk, turn out on board, form into a roll and cut in equal parts, put on a cold greased and floured tray, and bake in quick oven.
SANDWICH CAKE
1 cup flour
1 heaped teaspoon Edmonds' Baking Powder
3 eggs
Pinch of Salt
$\frac{3}{4}$ cup sugar
$1\frac{1}{2}$ ozs. butter
2 tablespoons hot milk
TENNIS BISCUITS
6 oz. butter, $2\frac{1}{2}$ oz. icing sugar, 6 oz. flour, 2 oz. EDMONDS VANILLA CUSTARD POWDER, about 1 oz. each of cherries, peel, almonds (chopped finely and mixed together). Method: Cream butter and sugar, then add remainder of ingredients; roll into small balls, flatten, decorate each with a small piece of cherry, and bake 15 to 20 minutes at 350° F.
JOIN THE NATIONAL SAVINGS MOVEMENT
LEND to Defend the Right to be FREE!
JOIN THE NATIONAL SAVINGS MOVEMENT
TO MAKE ICE CREAM
From a pint of milk take sufficient to mix smooth a large dessertspoonful of Edmonds' Custard Powder (vanilla flavour preferred), to which add a beaten egg. To the remainder of the milk add four heaped dessertspoonfuls of sugar, and when the milk is boiling, pour the mixed custard into it, stir, and pour into a jug. When cold, mix half a pint of cream in with the custard, and pour into receptacle in churn, then break ice into small pieces, and pack round receptacle, putting a good sprinkling of salt between each layer of ice. Churn until frozen, replacing ice and salt as it melts. Excellent ices can still be made if the cream is left out.
SERVE EDMONDS' CUSTARD WITH STEWED BOTTLED OR CANNED FRUITS—IT MAKES ALL THE Difference
VELVET PUDDING
2 cups milk, 2 dessertspoons EDMONDS CUSTARD POWDER, 2 eggs, 1 dessertspoon butter, 4 tablespoons sugar. Method: Mix custard powder with a little of the milk and stir in the egg yolks. Heat remainder of the milk, pour in the mixture, add butter, cook 5 minutes then pour into a pie dish. Beat egg whites stiff, add sugar and pile on top. Brown in a cool oven.

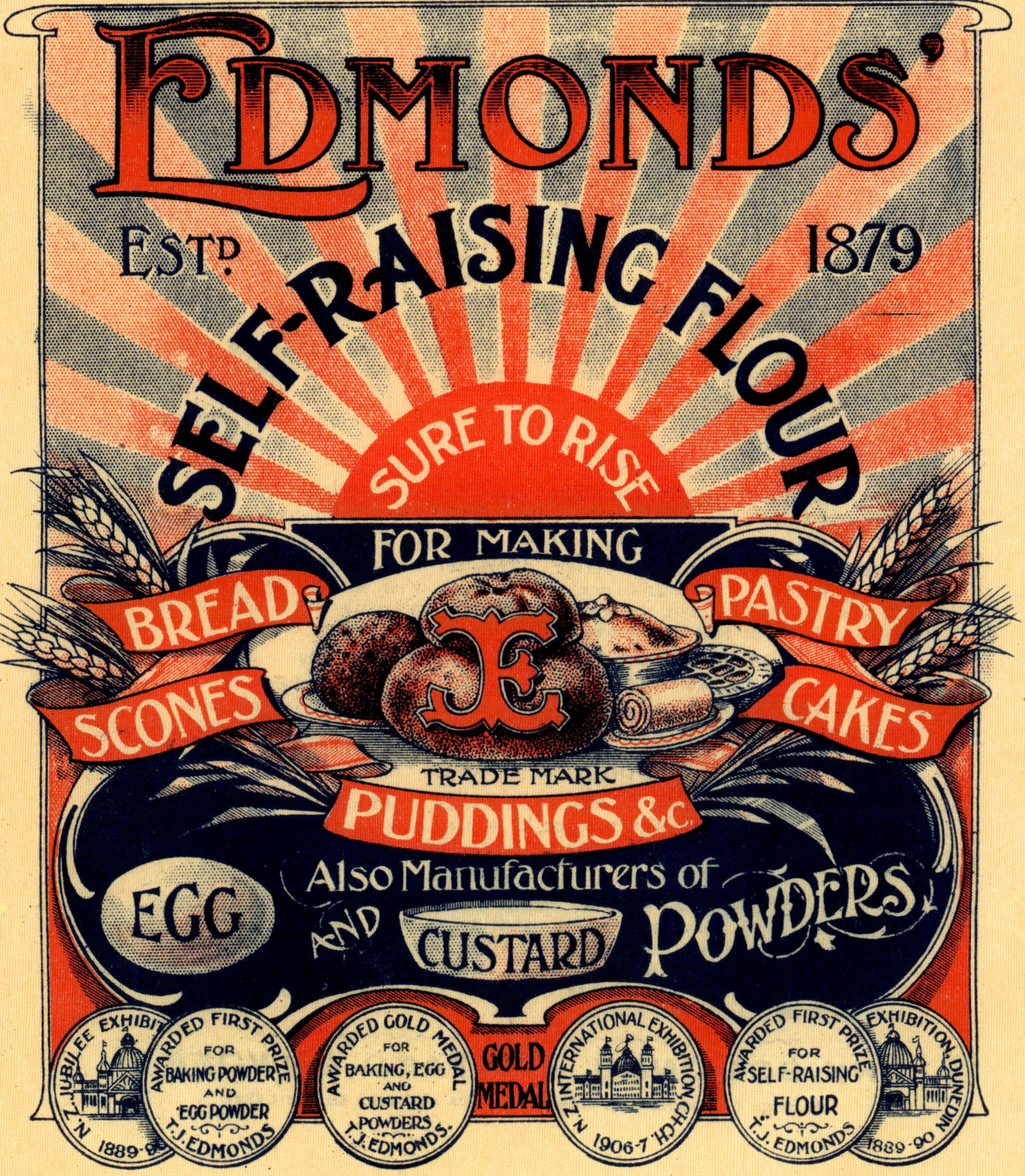
EDMONDS'
ESTD 1879
SELF-RAISING FLOUR
SURE TO RISE
FOR MAKING
BREAD
SCONES
PASTRY
CAKES
TRADE MARK
PUDDINGS &c.
Also Manufacturers of
EGG
AND
CUSTARD
POWDERS
N.Z. JUBILEE EXHIBIT
1889-9
AWARDED FIRST PRIZE FOR BAKING POWDER AND EGG POWDER T.J. EDMONDS
AWARDED GOLD MEDAL FOR BAKING, EGG AND CUSTARD POWDERS T.J. EDMONDS.
GOLD MEDAL
N.Z. INTERNATIONAL EXHIBITION CH-CH. 1906-7
AWARDED FIRST PRIZE FOR SELF-RAISING FLOUR T.J. EDMONDS
EXHIBITION, DUNEDIN 1889-90

example, which appeared around November that year, showed a flotilla of yachts with their sails spelling out the message 'Try It Next Time You Bake' against the backdrop of a rising sun emblazoned with 'Sure to Rise'.[20] These advertisements were presumably commissioned and therefore original, but another from around the same time, showing a happy housewife holding aloft a plate of successful baking, was likely to have been an existing standard 'cut'.[21] Then, around April 1911, an image appeared of an arrow piercing a baking powder tin and aimed at the rising sun. This was part of an intensive nationwide campaign, and over two years it appeared in at least 17 different newspapers, from the *Northern Advocate* to the *Mataura Ensign*.[22] In that month, too, one of the most unusual of all Edmonds advertisements first appeared. It was dominated by the image of a large right hand and the message 'The Hand That Does the Cooking Has a Finger in the Pie' and the reminder to 'Ladies' that Edmonds baking powder 'Will Aid You to Keep Your Supremacy'. In the background was the now ubiquitous rising sun. But perhaps the public found the image unsettling: it appeared only occasionally over a 10-month period.[23]

Edmonds was not the only manufacturer looking for a new promotional angle. In 1911 Aunt Janet's offered a £3 3s prize for the best limerick about their baking powder,[24] which may have prompted an Edmonds advertisement that incorporated the following rhyme:

> Anyman of Anytown
> Likes his Cooking Light and Brown;
> And, in Choice of Wife, advises
> One who's Cooking Always Rises.
> EDMOND'S BAKING POWDER, then
> Makes Good Cooks and Happy Men!

A number of these men were depicted beaming at a plate of baked delights. The initials on the illustration, FHC, were those of Rangiora-born and First World War artist, Frederick Herbert Cumberworth.[25]

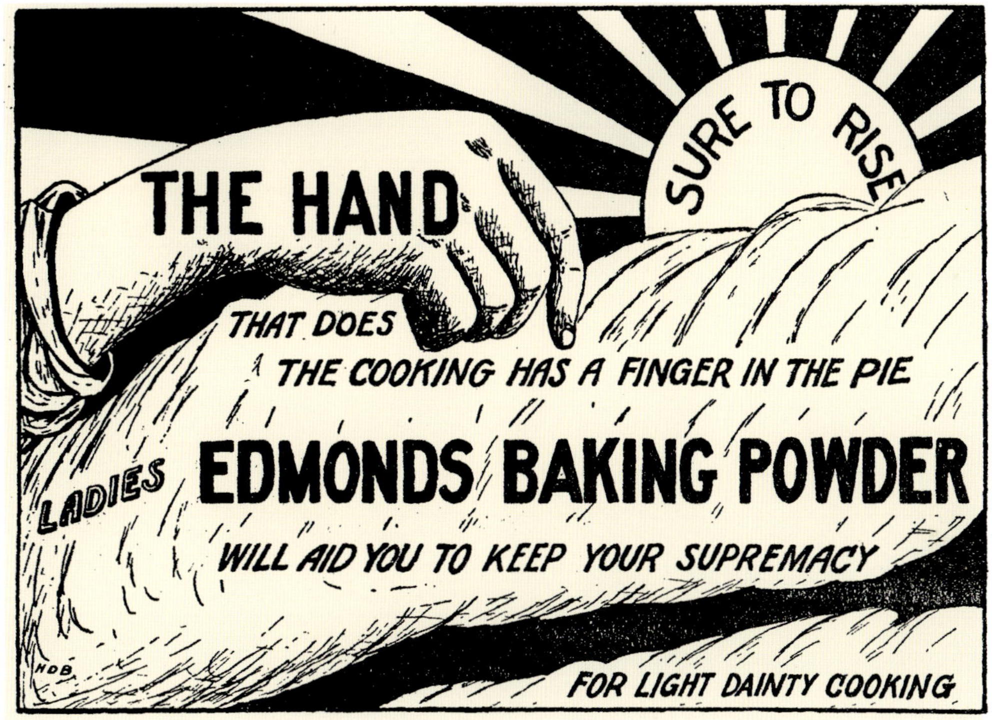

• • •

'For years,' Thomas Edmonds wrote later, 'I had indulged in a mild sort of advertising, but had never looked at it in a very serious light.' By mid-1911, when the annual sales of baking powder stood at 878,268 tins, and after 'giving the matter very serious thought', he 'somewhat dubiously' decided to employ Ilott Advertising Ltd for 12 months.[26] The agency was founded in Wellington in 1892 by Irish-born John Ilott. His first business was placing advertisements on behalf of South Island, and later North Island newspapers, and this later led to designing advertisements as well. Early major clients were Wood's Great Peppermint Cure in 1894 and Glaxo in 1903; and others who joined the growing company between 1909 and 1912 included, along with Edmonds, Shell, Bank of New Zealand, Fleming's Creamoata and Cadbury. In the advertisements Ilott designed for Edmonds, a 'house style' soon became apparent.[27]

On the previous pages, a wordy 1907 leaflet extolling the virtues of baking powder, and an immaculate design from the same period, possibly by Philip Presants, decorating a paper bag. On these pages, in 1910 jaunty little yachts carried Edmonds' message, while the next year 'The Hand' was one of their most unusual – and unsettling – advertisements.

Perhaps the earliest advertisement that can be positively attributed to Ilott dates from September 1911, promoting the company's baking powder ('For the heaviest pudding or the daintiest pastry') and the cookery book (which now contained 'hundreds of fine recipes').[28] But although Ilott's were soon producing a large number of advertisements for Edmonds, they were not responsible for the company's Christmas 1911 promotion, depicting a jovial Santa with a large Edmonds tin on his back filled with baking. This advertisement, which included recipes for Christmas cake and plum pudding, and appeared every Christmas until 1919, was the work of Fred Cumberworth.[29]

The benefits of employing professionals were impressive. Thanks largely to Ilott's 1911 campaign, Edmonds' sales grew during that year by 200,000 tins –

"SURE TO RISE"
The fruits of the earth are produced and developed for the benefit of mankind.
In course of that development the nation has hailed with delight the advent of
EDMONDS BAKING POWDER
"SURE TO RISE"
ILOTT STUDIO
7997

more than double any previous increase. 'It was this factor that so strongly illustrated to me the benefits of advertising executed by capable hands. The remarkable success achieved by this first campaign turned me into an ardent believer in advertising.'[30] Just before Christmas 1915 Thomas wrote a testimonial to John Ilott and his team: 'Your handling of our campaign, though handicapped by unfortunate shortages as regards our stocks' – it was wartime – 'has been highly successful, and left us more firmly convinced than ever, in your undoubted capabilities as Advertising Agents. To sum up the position as seen through our own glasses, and to ask your pardon for pirating Shakespeare, we think the following phrase fits the bill. "If conscientiousness and thoroughness constitute a sin, you are the most offending souls alive."'[31]

In 1911, Edmonds began a long-running partnership with Ilott Advertising, a Wellington firm that specialised in 'art & business' for best results. 'As Light as a Fairy' was one of hundreds of Ilott designs. The 1923 advertisement, left, links baking to the origins of cream of tartar: the planting of grapevines.

During the course of that first campaign Thomas adopted what he termed a 'tabulated system', which covered the whole of New Zealand and enabled him to follow and compare each year's results.[32] Sales were still booming, and sailed past the magic one million mark for the first time in 1912. An advertisement celebrating this achievement first appeared in February 1913 and was used frequently for the next four and a half years.[33] By 1915 sales had reached 1,250,000 tins, and to keep up with demand the company was using more than 20 tons of cream of tartar every month.[34]

The regular display advertisements Ilott's produced for Edmonds were distinguished by three main elements: an attention-grabbing headline, an accompanying section of text and a hand-drawn illustration. An early example was 'As Light as a Fairy', which first appeared in late 1911 and depicted a winged female in a diaphanous gown bearing a 'beautifully light' large cake made thanks to Edmonds.[35] And in a 1912 advertisement headed 'The Height of his Ambition', a young boy has used a stepladder to

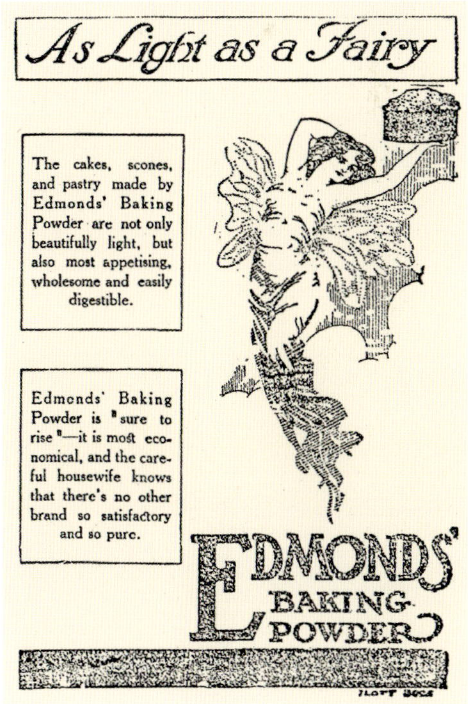

gain access to the baking in the cupboard. Poetry was obviously not Ilott's strong point, however, as this mid-1912 refrain demonstrates:[36]

Pastry as light as a snowflake,
Cakes as tasty as can be,
Scones that are highly nutritious:
With all doth such cooking agree.[37]

A year after the first officially recognised controlled powered flight by a heavier-than-air machine in New Zealand, at Papakura on 5 February 1911, a monoplane featured in an Edmonds baking powder advertisement, with the caption: 'It raises itself.' Promoting the product's 'snowflake lightness', the plane made numerous appearances until 1915. That year several newspapers reported the story of a shopkeeper's confusion over a request for 'a tin of aeroplane', until he realised that his customer wanted Edmonds baking powder.[38] The company's advertising was usually designed with the housewife in mind, but two new advertisements that ran from 1913 to 1915 appealed to the rural market: they featured men in the shearing shed and out in the paddocks, 'sons of toil' who needed their 'tucker' in the form of puddings, scones and buns made using Edmonds.[39] The invalid market was also targeted: from 1916 through to 1921 Edmonds advertised in *Kai Tiaki: The Nurses' Journal of New Zealand*, stressing the purity, wholesomeness and safety of its product.[40]

By the time the First World War broke out, the 'Sure to Rise' slogan was firmly attached to Edmonds. When 16-year-old Reginald Palmer was taken before the magistrate in September 1914 for riding his bicycle on the footpath in Wainoni, he was asked where he worked and how much he earned a week. When he replied that he was an employee of the Edmonds Baking Powder Factory and was paid 15s a week, the magistrate said, 'It's sure to rise.' He then imposed a fine of 3s without costs.[41]

• • •

As Edmonds grew and advertised widely, it was subject to regulatory scrutiny in the pre-war years. Its best-known product was mentioned in a voluminous 1912 report from a specially appointed Cost of Living Commission, which noted that monopolies were profiting by maintaining high commodity prices, and that reductions in duty on some articles had not been handed on to consumers: 'They have obtained control, and fixed higher prices.' Among the commodities in the firing line were sugar, matches, cocoa, soap and candles, and other such well-known food products as Colman's mustard, Robinson's groats and barley, Highlander condensed milk – and Edmonds baking powder.[42] Nothing concrete resulted from the commission's report, which was not even discussed in Parliament until April 1914.

In April 1913 another Edmonds product, egg powder, was affected by a rule change. A major promotion, starting in 1911, described it as a 'perfect substitute for eggs' and 'much more economical'. It was, apparently, 'impossible' to distinguish between cakes made with the egg powder and those made with the real thing.[43] A more imaginative advertisement pointed out that a 1s tin of Edmonds egg powder equalled 30 eggs, and asked, 'How many eggs will a 6d tin save a housewife?' The *'Sure to Rise' Cookery Book* would be dispatched free to all those who sent in their answers.[44] There was, as well, a successful gift scheme: a 6d tin of

Advertisements targeted many different types of customer: this one dating from just before the First World War was designed to appeal to rural women feeding a hungry male workforce.

Mathieson, Lieutenant R., Irish Guards, killed near Ypres, on Nov (Marton).

McNab, Surgeon Captai London Scottish Regime in action (Southland).

Rawlins, Corporal G. County of London Regi tists' Rifles), killed on 11th while cutting enem wire entanglements, a which he volunteered (T

Russell, Captain W. amptonshire Regiment action October 23rd (Haw

Steele, Captain Oliv Berkshire Regiment, kil tion, October 25th (Auck.

Tait William, King's tish Borderers, killed in Europe.

Taylor, Second Lieu H., 1st Battalion York caster Regiment, died brouck Hospital of February 9th (Auckland).

Tomson, Lieutenant K. Cavalry, killed in action (Wanganui).

Todd, J. S., killed in Europe on January 19th Gisborne).

Watts, Captain C. H Battalion Northamptons ment, killed in action in (Nelson.)

THE NAVAL FOR

The following were ki serving with the naval fo

Custance, Dr. G. W. M. in loss of H.M.S. Hawke.

Knowles, William Edwa Philomel, killed in February 8th, with a lan

Moreton, John Thoma H.M.S. Philomel, killed on February 8th with party.

Powell, William Oli petty officer, killed in loss Bulwark (Wellington.)

Reardon, seaman, lost Australian submarine AE

Stanbury, William, H. mel, wounded in action ary 8th with a landing died shortly afterwards.

Woodlands, seaman, HM.. Australian submari

NEW ZEALAND FO

The following membe New Zealand expedition have met their deaths outside the Dominion:—

Bell, Surgeon Captai Terras, Mounted Field died in Abassia Hospital ber 29th (Christchurch.)

Burlinson, Private G. Corps, Wellington Moun died on January 8th at C injuries caused by falli horse (Levin.)

Campbell, Private Malc Mounted Regiment, died January 10th, from pneum borne.)

Cooper, Private A. Hawke's Bay, Company, Infantry Battalion, d

Edmonds' egg powder for every tin of Edmonds baking powder bought, with a disc tucked into the lid required as proof of purchase. Eggs were given a bad press: 'You can't possibly tell whether the egg is good until you've broken it – but you've got to pay for it just the same.'[45] But eggs – and poultry farmers – got the last word. From March 1913, new 'Pure Food' regulations required the proper labelling of food products and high standards of 'cleanliness and freedom from contamination'.[46] Every label attached to egg powder had to carry the following message: 'This powder is artificially coloured to resemble eggs, but possesses none of their nutritive qualities.'[47]

A few months later, the Dominion Laboratory in Wellington published a report revealing that of 10 samples of baking powder tested, two (unidentified) did not comply with the regulations. (This was a minimal improvement on the 1878 analysis.) One newspaper's view of this potentially alarming news was that 'capitalism ... had not destroyed incentive' – in this case 'the incentive to adulterate'.[48]

• • •

In her book, *Baking Powder Wars: The Cutthroat Food Fight that Revolutionized Cooking,* Linda Civitello outlines the battles and the struggles that surrounded this crucial product in nineteenth- and twentieth-century America. In New Zealand, too, by the early 1900s baking powder was a hotly contested market, made even more so by the intrusion of rules and regulations and changing customer expectations. As Thomas had found, advertising was crucial to business success, which depended on the authenticity, uniqueness and customer appeal of a company's product claims. Edmonds had long recognised this: the company had relied on its trademark since 1887, but this was no longer enough. It is possible, too, that Thomas was spurred on by the legal changes resulting from the recent Patents, Designs and Trade-marks Act of 1911, designed to 'make Better Provision for the Grant of Patents and for the Registrations of Designs and Trade-marks'.[49] The relatively new relationship with Ilott's may have also been a catalyst. On 1 November 1912, when he was employing 16 people and the business was continuing to grow, Thomas took the major step of applying for a trademark for the 'Sure to Rise' baking powder label. The image itself was on the application, No. 10823, published in the *Patent Office Journal* on 28 November 1912, and when registration was granted by the Patent Office on 1 May 1913, it was recorded as a 'label trademark'.[50] The registration has been renewed many times since, and the design – one of the most famous trademarks in the history of intellectual property in New Zealand – has remained fundamentally the same for some 120 years.[51]

The advertisement opposite highlighted the benefits of egg powder. The 'Sure to Rise' label registration in 1912, though not Edmonds' first intellectual property protection, remains one of New Zealand's best-known trade marks. The manipulated factory photo on the following pages appeared as an advertisement in 1912. Thomas and Will stand together in front of the factory next to the car.

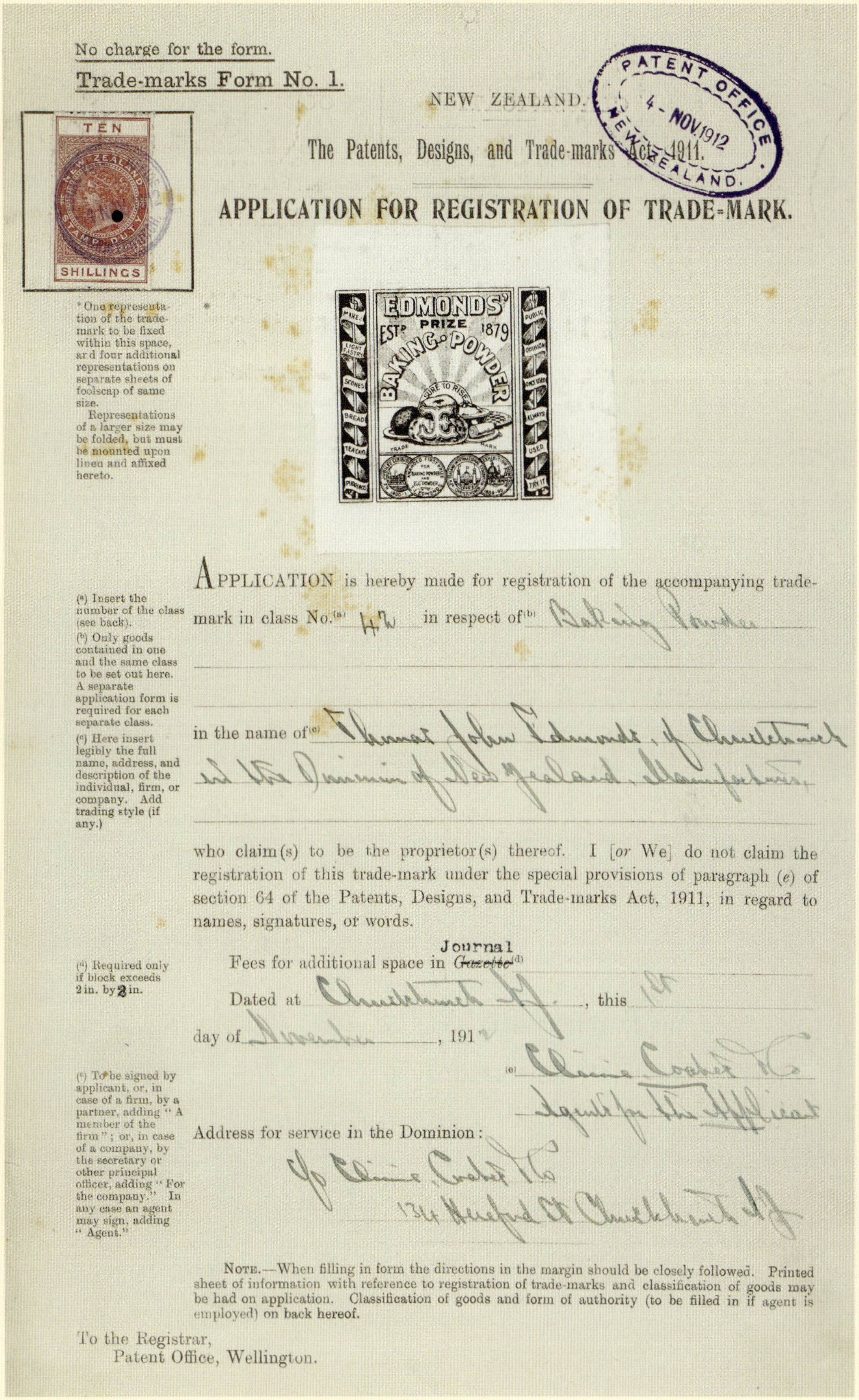

No charge for the form.

Trade-marks Form No. 1.

PATENT OFFICE 4-NOV 1912 NEW ZEALAND.

NEW ZEALAND.

The Patents, Designs, and Trade-marks Act, 1911.

APPLICATION FOR REGISTRATION OF TRADE-MARK.

TEN SHILLINGS

* One representation of the trade-mark to be fixed within this space, and four additional representations on separate sheets of foolscap of same size. Representations of a larger size may be folded, but must be mounted upon linen and affixed hereto.

APPLICATION is hereby made for registration of the accompanying trade-mark in class No.(a) 42 in respect of(b) Baking Powder

in the name of(c) Thomas John Edmonds, of Christchurch in the Dominion of New Zealand, Manufacturer,

who claim(s) to be the proprietor(s) thereof. I [or We] do not claim the registration of this trade-mark under the special provisions of paragraph (e) of section 64 of the Patents, Designs, and Trade-marks Act, 1911, in regard to names, signatures, or words.

Fees for additional space in ~~Gazette~~ Journal(d)

Dated at Christchurch NZ, this 1st day of November, 1912

(e) [illegible]
Agents for the Applicant

Address for service in the Dominion:
[illegible]
134 Hereford St Christchurch NZ

(a) Insert the number of the class (see back).

(b) Only goods contained in one and the same class to be set out here. A separate application form is required for each separate class.

(c) Here insert legibly the full name, address, and description of the individual, firm, or company. Add trading style (if any.)

(d) Required only if block exceeds 2 in. by 2 in.

(e) To be signed by applicant, or, in case of a firm, by a partner, adding "A member of the firm"; or, in case of a company, by the secretary or other principal officer, adding "For the company." In any case an agent may sign, adding "Agent."

NOTE.—When filling in form the directions in the margin should be closely followed. Printed sheet of information with reference to registration of trade-marks and classification of goods may be had on application. Classification of goods and form of authority (to be filled in if agent is employed) on back hereof.

To the Registrar,
Patent Office, Wellington.

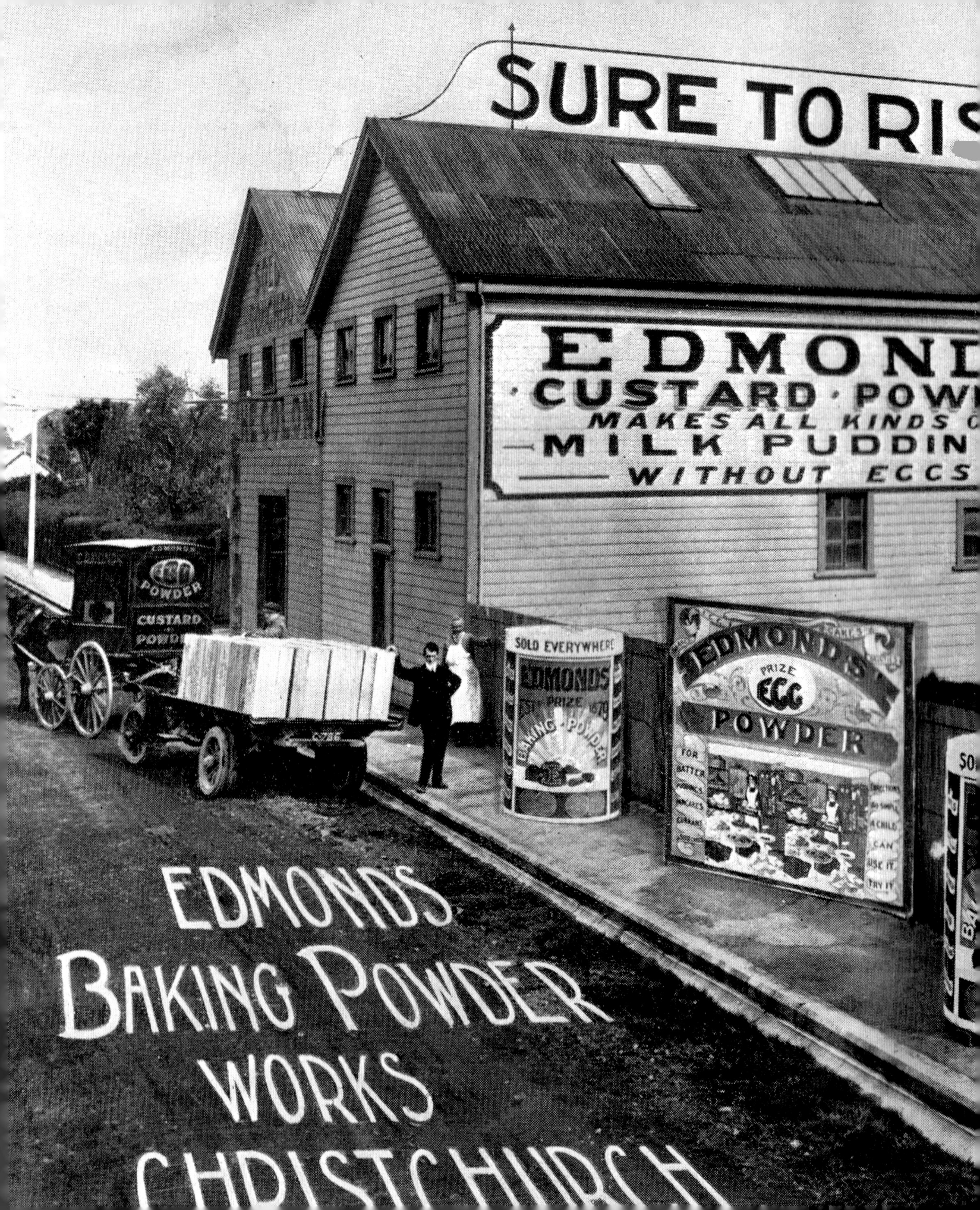
SURE TO
CUSTARD
MAKES ALL KINDS
MILK
WITHOUT
POWDER
CUSTARD
SOLD EVERYWHERE
EDMONDS
PRIZE
BAKING POWDER
EDMONDS'
PRIZE
EGG
POWDER
EDMONDS
BAKING POWDER
WORKS
CHRISTCHURCH

SOLD OVER
30
YEARS
EDMONDS'
BAKING POWDER

LIGHT BAKING
SURE TO RISE
LIGHT BAKING
3RD EDITION
4th Edition
4th Edition

CHAPTER 7

RECIPES FOR SUCCESS

There were many other cookery books out there – Mrs Beeton's famous *Book of Household Management*, and books by Hannah Glasse and Eliza Acton, but also the *New Zealand International Exhibition Cookery Book* compiled by Mrs Patrick Gill after the great 1906–07 event in Christchurch, a very popular Australian offering from Mrs Maclurcan, Mrs E.B. Miller's *Economic Technical Cookery Book*, a one-shilling *Everyday Cookery Book* from Whitcombe & Tombs, and even a *Middle Class Cookery Book*. There was a vegetarian offering and one specifically for cooking on gas stoves. Some were published to raise money for schools, Plunket or the church,[1] like the *Hinemoa Cookery Book*, on sale for a shilling and 'published in the interest of the Webb Street and Newtown Primitive Methodist Church Debt Reduction Funds'. Some households may still have had copies of *Brett's Colonists' Guide and Cyclopedia of Useful Knowledge*, published in 1883, which included more than 100 pages of recipes, 12 of them for biscuits and cakes.[2]

A colourful array of the 'Sure To Rise' cookery book's first four covers. The advertisement for the first edition appeared in 1908.

Cookery books were sometimes given away: the well-known British Liebig Extract of Meat Company, for instance, had been offering its *Practical Cookery Book* in New Zealand since November 1889, and in April 1894 Christchurch grocer F.A. Cook was giving all his customers a free copy of his book, which was usually worth a shilling.[3] In 1903 one of Edmonds' competitors, Sharlands, also joined in, offering a free copy of the 428-page American *Presidential Cook Book* in exchange for 10 coupons as proof of purchase of their Moa baking powder.[4]

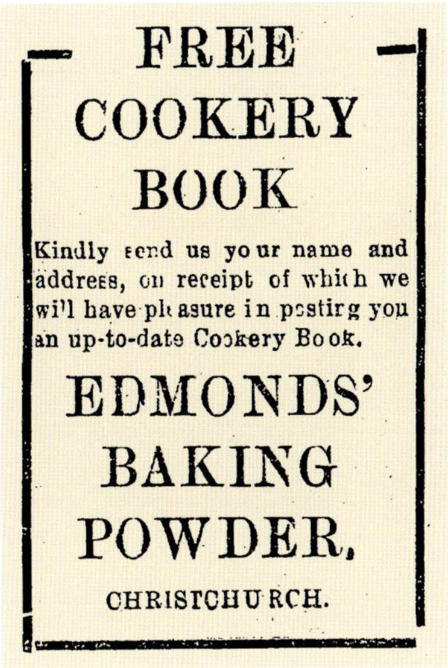

But when it published a free 'up-to-date Cookery Book' in 1908, Edmonds became the first local baking powder manufacturer to use a kind of promotion already popular and well tested overseas. In the United States and Britain, where a multitude of new brands had sprung up, manufacturers had been producing recipe books, which 'served as both marketing and instruction manuals' by featuring their own products.[5] The Edmonds version would become a New Zealand phenomenon.

In its own words, the first edition of the 'Sure to Rise' Cookery Book was 'especially compiled', and contained useful everyday recipes as well as cooking hints. It would be 'posted free to any address, on receipt of

LIGHT BAKING
SURE TO RISE
SURE TO RISE
COOKERY
BOOK

one penny stamp'.[6] The publication was printed by Smith & Anthony Limited in Christchurch, suggesting that the company quite possibly also designed the cover. Despite extensive efforts, however, the artist remains unknown. The cover was particularly striking - a strongly coloured hand-drawn illustration in a much looser and more informal style than most design of the era. In the foreground was an early morning rower looking out to sea (possibly at Cave Rock in the seaside suburb of Sumner) and admiring a dramatic sunrise emblazoned with the words 'Sure to Rise'. On the horizon in the image was a steamer, perhaps carrying that essential baking powder ingredient, cream of tartar. Surrounding it all was a border with leafy flourishes reflecting the then fashionable Art Nouveau style, with the words 'Light Baking' at the top. The upper two corners of the border enclosed images of a loaf of bread and a decorative letter 'E' (in fact a combination of Thomas's initials, TJE), which appeared on the label of the Edmonds tin. In the two lower corners were plum duff puddings garnished with holly leaves, suggesting that in addition to everyday recipes there were ideas for Christmas dinner. Curiously, the name Edmonds was nowhere to be seen, though the back cover (see p. 83) sported a large graphic illustration of the baking powder tin, and 'T. J. Edmonds, Baking Powder Manufacturer, Christchurch' appeared in large print on the title page.

There have been suggestions that the first edition appeared in 1907, but no evidence has been found to support these claims.[7] The first indication of the cookery book's existence seems to be a letter to T.J. Edmonds dated 1 July 1908,[8] in which the correspondent notes that a friend 'has a copy and the recipes seem very good' and requests 'two copies of your "Sure to Rise" Cookery book', one each for Captain Knipe and Miss Knipe of Balclutha and Invercargill respectively. Two penny stamps were enclosed. The letter is responding to an offer included in the cookery book itself, but quite how it reached the public's attention this early in the year is uncertain. The earliest newspaper advertisement so far found, a modest typographical arrangement (see p. 79), appeared in the *Manawatu Standard* on 29 October 1908. From then on, the cookery book was increasingly and more frequently advertised in a range of papers nationwide.

From September 1909, the copy was much more confident: 'HINTS ABOUT COOKING. And useful everyday recipes will be forwarded by return post to any address. FREE If you send a postcard to Edmonds' Baking Powder works, Christchurch, for this useful work. The recipes are simple, economical, and up-to-date. You will never be at a loss for appetising dishes if you have EDMONDS' COOKERY BOOK.'[9]

With its striking cover, the first edition of the cookery book proved so popular that it was reprinted the following year. In releasing recipe books featuring its own products, Edmonds was following the example of overseas manufacturers. There were also many cookery books by other food manufacturers available in New Zealand.

As food historian Helen Leach notes, however, the first few editions 'in no way served housewives as an all-purpose recipe book. It took seven editions and thirty years before there were sections that covered the range of dishes cooked in New Zealand kitchens on a daily basis.'[10] According to family lore, the first edition was put together by Lilian Edmonds and her sister-in-law Alice, who was a trained typist. It contained almost 100 popular and familiar recipes – just over half of them, understandably, for baked goods: scones, bread, buns, pikelets, cakes and pastry.[11] Rita's Apple Pudding was named for Will and Alice's eldest child, and Rene's Kisses for Thomas and Jane's youngest, then aged nine.[12] The instructions for the kisses were minimal – it was assumed that the cook knew what to do, and this was in the days before ovens had a temperature dial: 'Mix until quite light; drop in teaspoon lots on hot tray, and bake in quick oven. When cold fasten together with jam.'

There is, of course, no copyright on recipes, and as has always happened with cookery books of whatever type, Edmonds 'borrowed' recipes from local and overseas sources, both for these early editions and later on. Helen Leach found that many 'Edmonds' recipes had been in print

Opposite, Thomas's daughter-in-law Alice and daughter Lilian, pictured with a young David Cropp, compiled the first edition of New Zealand's most famous cookery book. Two recipes, Rene's Kisses and Rita's Apple Pudding, were named after Thomas's youngest daughter and eldest granddaughter (photos right). The back cover of the first edition is seen below.

years, if not decades, before. These, and dishes already popular in New Zealand homes, 'found their way into Edmonds' cookery books, not always very rapidly, and sometimes not at all if they didn't use as an ingredient a product that Edmonds made'.[13] The publications produced by Royal, one of the largest American baking powder producers, are thought to have been used in the Edmonds factory, judging by company stamps and pencil-marked text changes on the pages.[14] Early Edmonds editions also echoed features, styles and details common in overseas examples.

By July 1910 the second edition had been printed and was being advertised and sent all over New Zealand. (The 1908 edition was also reprinted in 1909; as Helen Leach has acknowledged, there is still much work to be done on 'unravelling the many editions, variants, and reprints'.)[15] Based on comparisons with his other illustration work, Cathy Tuato`o Ross has suggested that Philip Presants may have designed the cover, which was also used for the third edition.[16] This is certainly possible, since it shares Presants' immaculate production style and features elements present in his other designs. He would, though, have needed to complete the cover before he left on a trip to Britain in February 1910.[17]

The 1910 book, with a print run of 150,000, included such no-nonsense recipes as Good Plain Cake, and Ham or Tongue Omelet,[18] and proved immensely popular. The third, equally successful, edition was produced in 1914. Inside the front cover was a firm reminder: 'As all Baking Powders are not made alike, we cannot vouch for good

LIGHT BAKING
DAINTY COOKING
SURE TO RISE
SURE TO RISE
COOKERY BOOK
2ND EDITION
CH CH PRESS CO LTD

The cover of the 1910 second edition used an accomplished illustration that may have been the work of Philip Presants. It was also used as the third edition cover in 1913 although, as shown right, the back covers were different. Under the fold-out, the fourth edition had two different cover designs, both presenting idyllic rural scenes.

cooking if other brands are used ... Your Grocer Sells EDMONDS' ORDER A TIN and TRY the RECIPES.' Among the cooking hints were several stern admonitions: 'Cakes should be baked as soon as they are mixed', 'Raisins should always be stoned', 'Test the oven before baking – don't guess', 'Never slam the oven door when cooking, it spoils cakes, pastry, and puddings'. And for the first time, this edition had a page of written testimonials.

By July 1919 the cookery book had gone to 'practically every corner of the globe .... Some 250,000 copies had also been distributed throughout New Zealand.'[19] Was it the third edition that Jean Gant of Auckland lost when her brown leather suitcase went missing on a tramcar between Customs Street and the Remuera Post Office in January 1923? The *Police Gazette* scrupulously listed the contents, which included her clothes (among them 'a mauve-crepe dress-piece with a spray of daisies on left breast') along with such personal items as a silver trinket box with pink lining, a Swan fountain pen, a celluloid pig – and an *Edmonds Cookery Book*.[20]

The cookery book was available to those who wrote in, and it was often sent to engaged couples; Edmonds family members are said to have scoured the engagement columns in the local newspapers and pinpointed addresses. The thousands of requests were often accompanied by a note praising Edmonds baking powder and professing years of loyalty to the company's products;[21] and one writer touched on the ethics of requesting the free book while using another brand of baking powder. A correspondent who claimed, in 1909, that she had been using Edmonds' for over 30 years must have qualified as one of Thomas's very first customers. Another from Morningside, Auckland, wrote in 1925 to say that her grandmother was one of the first to use the powder in Christchurch, and that the family, 'without exception', had done so ever since, and other early converts in Rakaia and Greytown boasted that same year that they had been using Edmonds baking powder for 40 years. Letters arrived from all over New Zealand; there were several from Tasmania, and one from a woman who had used Edmonds baking powder in England before coming to New Zealand. Several customers described themselves as 'constant users' – a tin a week for nine years, for example, or five tins a month. A Blenheim cook managed to get through three to four tins per week: they were responsible for feeding 15 men who were 'very ravenous' for cakes baked with Edmonds.

Correspondents were unstinting in their praise for Edmonds baking powder. It was

LIGHT BAKING
DAINTY COOKING
SURE TO RISE
SURE TO RISE
EDMONDS
COOKERY BOOK
4th Edition
Whitcombe & Tombs Ltd.

LIGHT BAKING
DAINTY COOKING
SURE TO RISE
SURE TO RISE
HOME
COOKERY BOOK
4th Edition

'excellent in every way', 'a first class powder', 'most splendid', 'indispensable' and, perhaps most originally, 'Kapai te Edmonds'. Several writers claimed they had 'never had a failure', and one who hailed it 'absolutely the best on the market' noted it was 'a little dearer than other powders', but more economical. Another, describing Edmonds products as the best she had used, added that she had been a cook in England so 'ought to know a wee bit about it'. Typical comments were 'I do not care for any other brand', 'I can use no other' and 'I will have no other', but perhaps the most positive was this emphatic endorsement from New Lynn, Auckland, in 1925: 'I have *always* used Edmonds Baking Powder and *always* will.'

Much of the correspondence was personally addressed to Mr T.J. Edmonds, and grateful cooks sent follow-up letters acknowledging delivery of the cookery book, which was often needed to replace previous editions that had been lost, borrowed, had torn and missing pages or, in one instance, had been 'accidentally burnt'. In early December 1923 one eager cook from Maungatapere, near Whangārei, asked if her new book could be sent as soon as possible because she needed to get on with her Christmas baking. Predictably, the vast majority of the letters came from housekeepers and housewives. One wrote that, thanks to Edmonds, her husband's digestion did not suffer, while a new bride believed her 'matrimonial bliss' would be 'assured' thanks to the cookery book. Ten-year-old Winnie Castle of Ōtāhuhu, Auckland, requested a copy for 'mother', and a husband from the Bay of Islands wrote, rather patronisingly: 'The wife has used your Baking Powder for years & will look at nothing else in that line.'

In response to advertisements and other forms of publicity, including word of mouth, Edmonds received thousands of customer letters requesting a copy of the cookery book and often praising the company's products.

The introduction of 12 'Sick Room Dishes' (later 'Invalid Dishes') in the fourth edition in 1923 was likely a response to the 1918 influenza pandemic,[22] but also, perhaps, intended for the many returned soldiers still struggling with ill health. It gave instructions for making gruel, described as nutritious and causing perspiration, with oatmeal, water, salt, butter and nutmeg, or perhaps Tripe Fricassee, linseed tea or Fruit Salts – Good Aperient, which had a slightly alarming ingredient list: bicarbonate of soda, tartaric acid, Epsom salts, magnesia, cream of tartar and lemon essence.[23] Two versions of the cover were produced. One, featuring sheaves of wheat, showed a comfortable rural house with a gently smoking chimney and the word 'Home' inscribed on the roof. On the second, an Edmonds delivery truck wound through a utopian countryside, complete with grazing sheep; no destination, clearly, was too remote. The wheat had been replaced by bunches of grapes, perhaps a reminder of the cream of tartar essential to the making of baking powder. Both scenes, like the seaside illustrations on the earlier editions, were bathed in a radiant, sure-to-rise glow. Although these covers have some stylistic similarities to Presants' design style, given that he was no longer living in

May 28th 1910

North Bank

To Mr Edmonds
Baking powder Manufacturer
Christchurch

Thank you verry much for your Cookery Book. now Mr Edmonds as a cook of 35 years standing about Blenheim i can positively state that of all the Compounds of Baking powder i have used, in my cooking experiences i have never came across any thing in the shape of Baking powder to hold a Candle to your celebrated and champion Baking powder, i have used home made Colonial made powder but none have come within a mile of your famous powder, the beautiful things i have had from you baking powder have discarded all Soda & acid from every station i have cooked on and i can lick any town Baker at making a loaf of Bread with your powder thanking you for your Book and wishing you every prosperety i Remain Respectfully
James Galbraith North Bank Wairau Valley
Blenheim. N.Z.

MERRY XMAS

Christchurch they are more likely to have been executed by another artist. There were eight pages of colour illustrations in the fourth edition; and it, like its successors until 1988, was printed by Whitcombe & Tombs (later Whitcoulls).[24]

The fifth edition, now expanded to 61 pages, featured photos of the factory, and the cover, which abandoned the graphic illustrations of its predecessors, was a clear nod to Art Deco, with long rays stretching out from the rising sun.[25] The publication year has been extensively recorded as 1930, though 1933 seems much more likely based on newspaper archives. One advertisement showed two elegant, coiffured housewives in aprons asking admiringly, 'Isn't the New 5th Edition Delightful?' This edition was described as 'Edmonds New Cookery Book, printed in colours, contains scores of delightful recipes' - and it was once again available on receipt of a postcard.[26] A little over 60 per cent of the recipes in this edition were new, compared with 42 per cent in the previous version.[27]

Art Deco flair replaced colour illustration on the fifth edition of the cookery book. The festive table opposite appeared in the 1955 De Luxe edition; from then on the cookery book was no longer free.

For the next edition, published in 1936 and expanded to 71 pages, the advertising was even more enthusiastic: 'This sixth edition of Edmonds famous Cookery Book is a better edition than ever! New ideas! New recipes! New illustrations! This splendid little book costs you nothing! It's entirely free! Send for your copy at once to avoid delay!'[28] In another innovation, there was a section that featured recipes using the range of Edmonds' jellies now available. Curiously, too, for such a popular cookery book, this was the first edition to include a recipe for pavlova as we know it today - though it was called a meringue cake - a confection that had been around since the mid-1920s.[29]

Each new edition of the cookery book was a reflection of the times in which it was published. In 1939 it was Edmonds' diamond jubilee, but it was also the first year of the war and there appears to have been no newspaper advertising. A small section with recipes for poultry and game was added: three of the eight recipes were for rabbit, which was inexpensive and easy to come by.[30] By this time there were homegrown cookery book competitors: Brown & Polson's Cornflour gave away a free book, famous radio personality Aunt Daisy's publication was wildly popular, and the Self Help grocery chain brought out its own publication.

In 1955, a year after Edmonds' seventy-fifth anniversary, the first De Luxe edition of the cookery book was published, with a print run of 120,000 copies. And, in another break with tradition, the cookery book was no longer free: the price was a shilling. There was also an economy edition: an 84-page stapled book that contained 500 recipes and cooking hints, an extensive index and a number of colour pages. Another innovation was the cover: for the first time it featured a photo of the Edmonds factory and garden. This has continued until the present day, although from 1982 the photo was replaced by a hand-drawn illustration.

A Perfect CARNIVAL CAKE
Edmonds
SOLD EVERYWHERE
EDMONDS
EST 1879
PRIZE
BAKING POWDER
2 good breakfast cups flour
2 level ,, ,, sugar
2 level teaspoons
Edmonds Baking Powder
6 eggs 6 oz. butter
2 tablespoons boiling water
Vanilla Essence
Beat eggs and sugar for 15 min.; sift in dry ingredients; add butter (melted) then boiling water last of all. Divide mixture in three and when cold put together with raspberry jam, ice with plain icing. Decorate with angelica, cherries and nuts.
EDMONDS 'Sure to Rise' BAKING POWDER

The cookery book had always been a vehicle for promoting Edmonds' products. By the early 1930s it included attractive colour advertisements and illustrated recipes, providing visual relief from pages of dense text: these pages appeared in the cookery book in 1936. Carnival Cake was a popular recipe; it was beautifully presented in the illustration opposite, although the method omitted any instruction to actually bake the raw mixture.

The 1955 book was much larger, and over 290 recipes – more than half the content – were new. As Helen Leach discovered, only a few recipes, about 2.5 per cent of the whole book, were 'still recognisable from the first and second editions'.[31] At last, too, there was a section on preserving fruits and vegetables, and some distinctively Kiwi recipes, such as Toheroa Soup, Aotea Biscuits, Whitebait Fritters and Tree Tomato Jam.[32] In the words of Helen Leach, *Edmonds' Sure to Rise Cookery Book* 'was finally a product in its own right and one that New Zealanders came to rely on for the next fifty years' – and more.[33] This was the recipe book everyone had on their shelf, the one that was given by grandmothers to mothers, and mothers to daughters (and later sons).

The 1955 edition had exhorted housewives to send in any problems to Elizabeth Edmonds, who from the mid-1950s recommended such 'Recipes of the Moment' as Caramel Souffle and Jelly Cream – tasty treats that, naturally, required Edmonds' products.[34] Elizabeth, like her predecessor Mrs Active Acto (see Chapter 13), was entirely fictitious. These imaginary women giving manufacturers a human face followed in the footsteps of the more famous American Betty Crocker, created in the United States in 1921. The most durable New Zealand equivalent has been Pam, who has lent her name to Foodstuffs' grocery lines since the 1930s.

Edmonds, of course, recognised their cookery book as an ideal vehicle for both advertising and increasing sales of their own products: baking powder, followed by custard powder, egg powder (which was renamed 'cake baking powder' by 1923, and was advertised intensively in the mid-1930s) and jelly crystals. The percentage of recipes that specified an Edmonds product was 69% in the first edition, and 79% by the third edition. It decreased after that, to 44% in the 1955 De Luxe edition. In the space of half a century, the publication made the transition from 'advertising brochure to cookbook in its own right'.[35]

As the years went by, although old favourites and essential basics remained, the recipes changed with the times. To modern eyes, some older recipe names have a slightly quaint charm: Elsie's Fingers, Auntie Cakes, Mysterious Pudding, Express Cake, Tennis Cake, Picnic Dainties … . Recipes in the revised edition of 1967 reflected the company's broadening range of products, including pasta and additional cake mixes and puddings. On the other hand, there were now some notable exclusions, such as the recipe for tripe. Occasionally, deletions caused disapproval, as Edmonds food technologist Ron Hooker recalled. 'We discontinued a rabbit recipe and later had to restore it in response to public demand. Sometimes it is assumed that some old recipe cannot possibly still be of interest. Housewives quickly correct that. Even as apparently innocuous an item as a trifle recipe had to be put back.'[36]

From around 1955, the fictitious Elizabeth Edmonds was introduced to promote products and share recipes. Colour photographs replaced graphic artwork in the cookery book from 1977; the display of coffee and cakes opposite has a distinctly 1970s flavour.

Edmonds also produced a series of numbered recipe leaflets – single sheets printed on both sides and folded – covering a variety of subjects. No. 17, for instance, featured 'More Meal Suggestions Mainly for Men', and No. 25 offered 'Further Simple Recipe Suggestions for Beginners'. These, Hooker recalled, were 'included in any letters mailed out by Edmonds and given away to visitors, at demonstrations and at fairs and shows'.[37] Elizabeth Edmonds, whose image sometimes appeared despite her non-existence, compiled and tested some of the leaflets and even wrote messages to the readers. No. 13, 'Children's Parties', gave the recipes for Mystery Jelly, Nougat Dessert, Party Marshmallow, St Clement Slices, Alphabet Blocks (squares of jelly with whipped-cream letters) and Bunnies in the Field (with pear halves for the rabbit bodies). 'I trust,' wrote Elizabeth, 'they will give much joy to the Little Folk.'

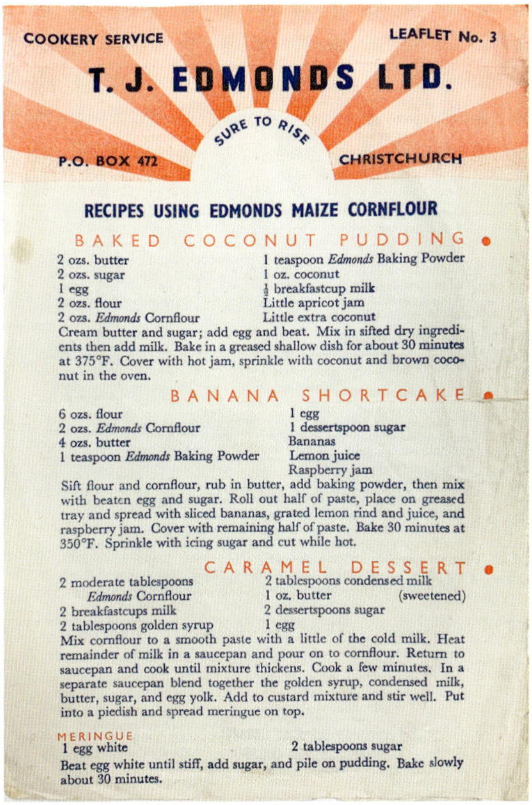

COOKERY SERVICE LEAFLET No. 3

T. J. EDMONDS LTD.

SURE TO RISE

P.O. BOX 472 CHRISTCHURCH

RECIPES USING EDMONDS MAIZE CORNFLOUR

BAKED COCONUT PUDDING

2 ozs. butter
2 ozs. sugar
1 egg
2 ozs. flour
2 ozs. *Edmonds* Cornflour
1 teaspoon *Edmonds* Baking Powder
1 oz. coconut
½ breakfastcup milk
Little apricot jam
Little extra coconut

Cream butter and sugar; add egg and beat. Mix in sifted dry ingredients then add milk. Bake in a greased shallow dish for about 30 minutes at 375°F. Cover with hot jam, sprinkle with coconut and brown coconut in the oven.

BANANA SHORTCAKE

6 ozs. flour
2 ozs. *Edmonds* Cornflour
4 ozs. butter
1 teaspoon *Edmonds* Baking Powder
1 egg
1 dessertspoon sugar
Bananas
Lemon juice
Raspberry jam

Sift flour and cornflour, rub in butter, add baking powder, then mix with beaten egg and sugar. Roll out half of paste, place on greased tray and spread with sliced bananas, grated lemon rind and juice, and raspberry jam. Cover with remaining half of paste. Bake 30 minutes at 350°F. Sprinkle with icing sugar and cut while hot.

CARAMEL DESSERT

2 moderate tablespoons *Edmonds* Cornflour
2 breakfastcups milk
2 tablespoons golden syrup
2 tablespoons condensed milk (sweetened)
1 oz. butter
2 dessertspoons sugar
1 egg

Mix cornflour to a smooth paste with a little of the cold milk. Heat remainder of milk in a saucepan and pour on to cornflour. Return to saucepan and cook until mixture thickens. Cook a few minutes. In a separate saucepan blend together the golden syrup, condensed milk, butter, sugar, and egg yolk. Add to custard mixture and stir well. Put into a piedish and spread meringue on top.

MERINGUE

1 egg white
2 tablespoons sugar

Beat egg white until stiff, add sugar, and pile on pudding. Bake slowly about 30 minutes.

Free recipe leaflets were a popular innovation to attract customers and encourage the use of Edmonds products. The cookery book's photographs have a nostalgic appeal for many New Zealanders: the example opposite shows lamingtons and custard cups.

The eleventh edition, published in 1971, responded to recent trends with a special gas cooking version. Five years later the cookery book was spiral-bound for ease of use while cooking. It contained a convenience foods section; and for the first time, measurements were given in both imperial and metric. To keep abreast of changing tastes and dining habits, the 1980 cookery book had a cake mix section, and more poultry recipes, now that chicken and turkey 'no longer need be reserved only for special occasions'. And, in a sign of the times, the 1988 edition included an expanded microwave baking section – but the section on food for invalids was dropped.[38]

Naturally, there were changes in the people who tested and selected the cookery book recipes. Lilian and Alice made way for Connie Stevens who, in 1940, test-baked scones in the factory kitchen. In 1944 she was succeeded by Mrs Law, cookery demonstrator at the Christchurch Gas Company, who was invited by factory manager Tiny Cox to test bake and to work on the cookery book. From 1963 Judy Aldridge, appointed home economist for quality control and product development, helped Mrs Law, who gradually pulled back, leaving the laboratory, run by Dr Rosa Stern along with Tiny Cox, to carry on with the cookery book and the leaflets. Laboratory managers and marketing personnel were involved, and there was also input from Ilott's.[39] In 2016 art historian and food authority Alexa Johnston had the task of giving the famous book its biggest revision and update since the 1990s. In went contemporary items such as homemade pasta, gluten-free recipes, bliss balls and Portuguese tarts, and some old favourites were reintroduced, including a 1976 marshmallow shortcake.[40]

By the time of the centennial edition in 1978, 'suitable for gas and all other cooking appliances', Edmonds was claiming staggering total cookery book sales of around 3 million. (It should be remembered, however, that the first four editions were free.) According to the company, building on the 150,000 print run of the second edition, it distributed 130,000 copies of the third edition and 150,000 of the fourth, in what Leach suggests must have been 'one of the most successful advertising campaigns of the twentieth century'.[41] It has been said – including by Edmonds themselves – that it is the 'best-selling book ever published in this country'. Cookery books can go through many editions but, as Helen Leach points out, 'they can undergo dramatic revisions, losing old recipes and gaining new ones'. It is, she suggests, 'more accurate to say [*Edmonds Cookery Book*] has been the most successful cookbook series in New Zealand history'.[42] Nonetheless, the numbers were impressive. A 'little ripple' ran through the New Zealand publishing world in December 1989 when the *Edmonds Microwave Cookbook* sold 103,000 copies in less than three months – 'an all-time record for a New Zealand title. Prominent publishers, usually pleased if they sell 3000 copies of a book with "literary merit", were observed to get misty-eyed at the news ...'[43] The latest fully revised edition took the number six spot in the top 10 best-selling cookbooks for 2020, just behind one by internationally popular chef Yotam Ottolenghi.[44]

In whatever edition, however stained and dog-eared from years of use, the *Edmonds Cookery Book* remains, in the words of Ron Palenski, 'as much a part of New Zealand kitchens as a stove and knife', relied on and cherished as a beloved and essential part of this country's cultural history.[45]

Edmonds custard powder, cornflour and jelly crystals were all key ingredients in these recipes for cold sweets in the 1955 De Luxe edition, which was typeset in the classic pink-red and blue. Opposite, now into its sixty-ninth edition, the cookery book has had a range of cover styles over the decades.

COLD SWEETS

● ICE CREAM (2)

1 pint Milk
1 breakfastcup Sugar
2 teaspoons *Edmonds* Custard Powder
2 teaspoons Flour
1 tin Unsweetened Condensed Milk

Place tin of milk in boiling water. Boil 5 minutes, chill. Heat milk in a saucepan, leaving out sufficient to mix flour, custard powder and sugar to a smooth paste. Pour hot milk on to this and cook in a double boiler until it thickens. Cool. Beat condensed milk till fluffy and add to the custard mixture. Beat well. When half frozen remove from tray, place in a bowl and beat well. Return to refrigerator to freeze.

● ICE CREAM (Easy) (3)

Make a blancmange (see page 40). Cool, then add 1 tin of Sweetened Condensed Milk. Beat well. Pour into trays and freeze.

● ICE CREAM PUDDING

2 ozs. Butter
2 ozs. Sugar
1 oz. Flour
1 Egg
1 pint Milk
Vanilla Essence

Cream butter and sugar, add flour then gradually add beaten egg. Pour on the hot milk and return to the saucepan. Bring to the boil and cook 5 minutes, stirring all the time. Add vanilla. Serve cold.

● LEMON FLUFF

1 oz. Gelatine
2 breakfastcups Cold Water
2 Lemons
½ breakfastcup Sugar
2 Eggs

Soften gelatine in cold water, add grated lemon rind and sugar. Boil 2 minutes. Add lemon juice and leave to cool. Fold in stiffly-beaten egg whites. Pile spoonfuls into glass dishes or set in a wet mould. Serve with custard made from egg yolks.

● LEMON SOUFFLÉ

2 cups Cold Water
1 cup Sugar
2 heaped tablespoons *Edmonds* Cornflour
Juice of 1 Lemon
Whites of 2 Eggs

Bring water and sugar to the boil, mix the cornflour to a thin, smooth cream with a little cold water and add to the first mixture when boiling. Set aside to cool, add lemon juice. Beat egg whites to a very stiff froth, add by degrees to mixture, beat well then set aside in a wet mould. Make a custard (boiled) with the yolks if liked or serve with cream.

● MELROSE CREAM

Equal quantities of custard made with *Edmonds* Custard Powder and liquid jelly made with *Edmonds* Jelly Crystals. Mix together when cool and set in a wet mould. An attractive dish can be made by surrounding the mould with different coloured jellies from small moulds. (Egg cups will do.)

42

STEAMED RAINBOW PUDDING ●

3 ozs. Butter
3 ozs. Sugar
1 teaspoon Vanilla Essence
2 Eggs
¼ breakfastcup Milk
6 ozs. Flour
1 moderate teaspoon *Edmonds* Baking Powder
Pinch of Salt
1 teaspoon (heaped) Cocoa
Few drops of Cochineal

Cream butter, sugar and vanilla essence together. Beat the eggs and add alternately with the sifted flour and baking powder. Add milk with last of the eggs. Divide the mixture into 3 equal portions. Leave one white, add the cocoa to the second, and the cochineal to the third. Grease a basin and drop in spoonfuls of different coloured mixtures so the pudding will have a marbled effect when cut. Cover with buttered paper and steam 2 hours.
Serve with *Edmonds* Custard.

EDMONDS SURE TO RISE COOKERY BOOK
SIXTH EDITION
Edmonds SURE TO RISE Cookery Book
7th EDITION (Reprint)
Price: SIXPENCE
Edmonds SURE TO RISE Cookery Book
ECONOMY EDITION
Price: ONE SHILLING and SIXPENCE
EDMONDS SURE TO RISE COOKERY BOOK
EDMONDS SURE TO RISE CookeryBook SURE TO RISE
30 NEW RECIPES
EDMONDS CookeryBook SURE TO RISE
16 New pages 80 New recipes All measurements now in Metric and Imperial.
EDMONDS Cookery Book SURE TO RISE
The Trusted Name in Food
25th ANNIVERSARY EDITION
NEW EDMONDS MICROWAVE COOKERY BOOK SURE TO RISE
Your Microwave Recipes for Success
Edmonds cookery book
standard edition 20c
sure to rise
EDMONDS PRIMA COOK BOOK
new american recipes!!!
SELECTED AND ADAPTED FOR USE IN THE N.Z. KITCHEN BY T. J. EDMONDS LTD.
EDMONDS Illustrated COOKBOOK II
EDMONDS
ESTD 1879 EDMONDS SURE TO RISE
COOKERY BOOK
INSPIRING NEW ZEALANDERS' LOVE OF BAKING AND COOKING
The New Edmonds Junior Cookbook
Over 70 yummy recipes illustrated with simple, step-by-step instructions
EDMONDS
EDMONDS
food for flatters
over 200 recipes
for small budgets,
small spaces
and big ideas
ESTD 1879 EDMONDS SURE TO RISE
EVERYDAY
OVER 300 of your FAVOURITE RECIPES

RENE'S KISSES.

½ lb. cornflour
½ lb. butter
½ lb. sugar
½ lb. flour
4 eggs

2 teaspoonfuls Edmonds' Baking Powder

Mix until quite light; drop in teaspoon lots on hot tray, and bake in quick oven. When cold fasten together with jam.

RITA'S APPLE PUDDING.

Mix thoroughly a teaspoon of Edmonds' Baking Powder with a breakfastcup of flour. Beat 2 eggs well, add 1 gill of milk and a tablespoon of butter, beat all together 15 minutes. Place 2 inches of stewed apples in a pie dish. Pour in batter and bake in quick oven. Serve hot.

In the first edition, Rene's Kisses and Rita's Apple Pudding were named for family. Rene (Irene) was the youngest daughter of Thomas and Jane. Rita was the eldest daughter of their son William and his wife Alice, who helped to compile the first cookery book. Rita's Apple Pudding eventually became simply Apple Pudding, but Rene's Kisses could still be found in the 125-year celebration edition of 2004.

BUFFALO CAKE.

1¼ breakfastcups flour
¼ lb. butter
2 eggs
¾ breakfastcup sugar
2 teaspoonfuls Edmonds' Baking Powder

Cream butter and sugar, add eggs beaten, mix flour and baking powder, and add to mixture, then enough milk to make thin. Cook in sponge sandwich tins. Put together with lemon honey or raspberry jam. Icing on top.

Four American recipes made their way into the first edition: besides Buffalo Cake, there were American Pudding, Pop Overs and a recipe for Doughnuts. According to Helen Leach, the last two recipes came almost directly from *Dr. Chase's Third, Last and Complete Receipt Book and Household Physician*, only substituting Edmonds Baking Powder for cream of tartar and baking soda. Thomas and Jane may have encountered or even bought the popular book while in the United States.

YORKSHIRE TEA SCONES.

¾ lb. flour (or 1½ large cups)
1 oz. butter (or a tablespoonful)
1 desertspoonful sugar
½ cup milk
2 teaspoonfuls Edmonds' Baking Powder
1 egg

Put butter into a saucepan, when dissolved put in the milk and make warm; place sugar in a basin and pour on the warm milk. Then place flour in mixing bowl and mix in Edmonds' baking powder, make a well in centre and drop in the egg, then pour on milk and mix well. The paste should be thin, roll and cut into shapes, place on hot floured oven shelf, and bake in hot oven 10 minutes.

Yorkshire Tea Scones was the first recipe of the 100 or so in the first, 1908, edition of the cookery book. Although these are called scones, rolling the paste thinly according to the instructions results in something more like a modern biscuit. Yorkshire Tea Scones was one of eight scone recipes given, along with Scotch, Girdle, Up-to-date Brown, Sultana, Currant, Brown and Plain. The family of Jane Edmonds' mother, Eliza, is thought to have come from Yorkshire.

VEGETARIAN ROAST.

Bread	Milk,
Peanuts	1 onion
Seasoning	

METHOD: Brown some crusts of bread in the oven, shell peanuts and put them through the mincer, putting the bread through the mincer afterwards.

Take a cup of the bread crumbs, pour on them a little milk, just enough to moisten, but not to make them too soft.

Mix with them half a cup of the ground peanuts, salt, and a little powdered herb, either sage or thyme, and one minced onion, put all into a buttered pie-dish, and bake slowly till nicely browned. If it appears to be getting too dry, a very little water may be put on top as it is cooking, or a few pieces of butter on top makes a fine improvement.

Among the many new recipes in the 1923 cookery book were six in an inaugural Salads section, plus one for Brown Bread (below) and another for a Vegetarian Roast. The Radiant Living philosophy, with its emphasis on healthy eating, was central to the lives of Thomas and Jane and their family.

BROWN HEALTH LOAF.

1 large breakfastcup flour
1 large breakfastcup wheatmeal
½ teaspoonful salt
2 good teaspoonfuls Edmonds' Prize Baking Powder
1 dessertspoonful golden syrup
½ cup milk
½ cup water

Mix well all the dry ingredients in a basin, dissolve the treacle in the hot water, and when cold add the milk; mix all together into a light dough, put into a caketin covered with a lid, and bake in a moderate oven for one and a quarter hours.

LEMON HONEY (For Sponges or Tarts.)

½ lb. sugar
Rind and juice of 2 lemons
2 ozs. butter
2 eggs

Grate only the yellow part of the lemon rinds (avoid white part, as it is bitter), strain the juice, beat eggs a little, put all ingredients into enamelled pot; cook slowly until thick and smooth. Do not let it boil. Put in jar, and cover when cold.

Lemon Honey and Pikelets seem to be the only two recipes that have been constant cookery book inclusions from the first edition of 1908 until the latest edition of 2016 which was updated by food writer Alexa Johnston.

PICKLED ONIONS

Pour hot water over pickling onions to loosen the skin, then peel (a stainless knife is best). Put in a basin and cover with hot brine. Let stand for 24 hours, then drain. Wipe the onions, put into jars, cover with spiced vinegar and cork well. If onions are desired white, after taking out of brine, put into cold milk and bring to the boil. Remove from fire, let stand till cold, wipe, and bottle, using white vinegar. Leave for 2 or 3 weeks before using.

In alphabetical order for the first time, the fourth edition boasted new sections dedicated to fish, meat, stuffings, vegetables, eggs and savouries, plus jams, jellies (fruit set) and pickles. One of the nine recipes in this last section was for Pickled Onions, a well-known favourite of Thomas Edmonds.

CAPTAIN AND SHIP

For the boys' party! Set **Edmonds Greengage Jelly** in flat glass dishes, one for each person. Cut the ship from a quarter orange or grapefruit rind, well stripped inside. Place in the greengage jelly before quite set. Fill ship with a cargo of chopped nuts, banana cut small, bits of sponge cake, raspberry jam, and cover well with **Edmonds Vanilla Custard** poured over when cool, and top with dabs of whipped cream. Use a cocktail stick for the mast, with a sail and flag cut from cellophane. Make the Captain by spiking two cherries together with a piece of cocktail stick, using them also for legs and arms, and put a green angelica telescope under his arm and a piece of almond stuck on for a peak cap.

A new section of 22 recipes was added to the cookery book in 1936 under the simple heading of 'Jelly', but as far back as the first edition there had been a Pineapple Jelly recipe that called for a tin of pineapple and 2 packets of jelly 'chrystalls'. The typically bright colours of the jellies were inspired by flowers from the Edmonds factory garden, particularly begonias.

AOTEA BISCUITS

7 ozs. Butter
3 ozs. Brown Sugar
5 ozs. Flour
2 *heaped* tablespoons *Edmonds* Cornflour
1 teaspoon *Edmonds* Cake Baking Powder
Pinch of Salt
1 breakfastcup Kornies

Cream butter and sugar, add sifted flour, cornflour, Cake Baking Powder and salt together. Lastly, add crushed Kornies.
Form into small balls, place on cold, greased trays, flatten with a fork and bake 20-30 minutes at 350°F.

The earlier Edmonds cookery books were peppered with recipes that harked back to 'Mother England'. The 1955 first De Luxe edition included these Aotea Biscuits. Until then, the only use of te reo Māori had been in several recipes using kumara and one for toheroa soup. Aotea means white cloud but the biscuit is round, brown and flat.

SPONGE ROLL OR SANDWICH.

1 cup flour
1 teacup sugar
3 eggs
1 teaspoonful Edmonds' Baking Powder
2 tablespoonfuls cold water

Beat the eggs and sugar till stiff and frothy, sift flour and Baking Powder, add water to eggs and sugar, then stir in the sifted flour and baking powder lightly and quickly, pour into greased tin, and bake in hot oven from 8 to 10 minutes. This recipe will also serve for a Jam Sandwich.

In the view of Alexa Johnston, 'a tender and lofty sponge cake, generously filled with jam and whipped cream [is] the crowning glory of any afternoon tea table'. Although a sponge roll had featured on the Edmonds label since their first use of labels, there was no recipe in the cookery book for a sponge roll (or cake) until 1923. By 1957, however, 'sponges were struggling and no longer illustrated' and so in her rewriting and reshaping for the 2016 edition, Johnston brought back the classic 1950s recipe.

CHAPTER 8

A FAMILY FLOURISHES

The big changes in the company after the turn of the century were mirrored by changes on the family front. In November 1902 Ernie, who seems to have worked for his father for some years before turning to farming, married Ethel Maud McCausland, from the tiny settlement of Doyleston, near Leeston on the Canterbury Plains. Lilian, who was a talented singer, had already travelled to Sydney to take singing lessons from Norman Alston, a young English baritone who had come to Australia in 1898, and Tom Riccardi, a bass baritone who had had a successful operatic career on both sides of the Tasman. In 1903 Thomas decided to take Lilian to Italy, to study in Milan. They set sail for Europe on New Year's Eve, presumably leaving Will in charge of the factory. The *Lyttelton Times* reported that after 'disembarking at Naples and seeing something of Rome, Florence and Genoa' they had 'a lengthy stay at Milan, where Miss Edmonds underwent a course of training which has greatly improved her vocal powers'. While Lilian was studying, Thomas took business trips to Marseilles and Montpellier – most likely to arrange for supplies of cream of tartar from the winemaking industry there. When Lilian's lessons were over, they visited Venice, the Italian lake district, Paris and Dieppe before crossing the Channel. After 'an enjoyable two months' business-cum-pleasure tour in the Old Country' they came home. The report concluded that Thomas was 'well content to return to New Zealand, for in his travels he has seen no fairer country nor one that suits his fancy half so well'.[1]

Early in 1905 Lilian set up as a 'teacher of voice production and singing' in Victoria Street, Auckland. Her first advertisement, under the heading 'Voice Culture', noted that she had been studying 'for some time under the Best Masters in Milan' and had been a pupil of Riccardi and Alston.[2] At the beginning of May she made her debut at the first concert of the season by the Auckland Liedertafel (later the Royal Auckland Choir), conducted by well-known composer Alfred Hill, and she went on to be a popular performer.

Beatrice and Rene, the youngest of the Edmonds children, pose for a studio photo in their best velvet dresses, c.1908.

On 16 June 1904, while Thomas and Lilian were overseas, Will, aged 24, married 25-year-old Alice Victorine Hart, one of ten children of Jane and George Hart. A reporter on the *Press* for many years, George Hart rose to be chief of staff and drama critic for the newspaper. Will and Alice lived in one of the two houses adjacent to the factory, and it was here that three of their four children were born: Rita (1905), Nelma (1908) and Keith (1909). They later bought a house at 23 George Street

(now Oram Avenue) in popular New Brighton, where their daughter Brenda was born in 1914.

There were real estate changes for Thomas and Jane too, although there is some uncertainty about these, owing to lack of records. According to Gertrude, Thomas 'built three houses, two in Gloucester Street and one in Worcester Street. The family lived in one of the Gloucester Street homes, "Minion", and let the other two houses.'[3] This cannot be entirely correct, however. The move from Ferry Road to 67 Gloucester Street, opposite today's CoCA Centre of Contemporary Art Toi Moroki, was probably made about 1904, after Thomas and Lilian returned from Europe; but Thomas did not build this house. By 1903 'Mignon' (not Minion) was being advertised as a boarding house offering 'superior accommodation' in large single and double rooms.[4] Were houses being built while the Edmonds lived at Mignon and while they were in Australia in 1905? In the spring of that year, Thomas, Jane, Lilian, Beatrice, Rene and Gertrude rented a house in the beachside Sydney suburb of Coogee, where they spent the next 18 months.

The next two addresses at which the Edmonds family lived were 240 Gloucester Street and 203 Worcester Street, which back onto each other in the block just east of Latimer Square. It is thought that Thomas built two two-storey houses on these sites: the houses no longer exist, but there are photos. However, there was already a house at 240 Gloucester Street, which had been there since the 1880s, offering 'superior private board and residence'. In January 1910, one W.J. Gregory was selling 'his Valuable Properties, situated 238 and 240 Gloucester Street'. One of the two houses had 'every possible modern convenience', the other was 'not quite so up-to-date. Both let to good tenants ... This offers a great chance to a speculator.'[5] Was that speculator Thomas? He had been granted a building permit for Gloucester Street on 17 July 1908.[6] Did he know the house was coming up for sale, and plan to rebuild on the site? The Edmonds were certainly living at 240 Gloucester Street by at least March 1912, when Jim advertised a flute for sale at this address.

The house had five bedrooms (the younger children had to share) as well as a dining room, living room and sitting room. Each room had a bell pull to summon the staff from the kitchen. There was electric lighting and a telephone that Gertrude was allowed to use to talk to her friends. Advances in plumbing technology meant that the family had the luxury of two inside toilets (one upstairs and one downstairs) and a shower. The washhouse, which was attached to the house, had a gas-fired copper.

Perhaps 203 Worcester Street merely underwent a transformation. This address, too, was a boarding house from 1905 until after the First World War. Although family lore says that Jane and Thomas gave 240 Gloucester Street to Lilian and her husband Bert Cropp as a wedding present, they do not appear to have left that house until the early 1920s; they and the Cropps possibly shared it until then. When Jane sold 203 Worcester Street in 1933, to a Miss O'Leary, it was described as a 'large two-storey residence of nine rooms, together with thirty-two perches of land'.[7]

• • •

Gertrude recalled that medical advice was the reason for the lengthy 1905–06 break in Australia: Thomas needed to take a rest. Beatrice and Rene attended a local school, while Gertrude focused on piano lessons. The family went to concerts and enjoyed the open-air sea baths, where Gertrude learnt to swim.[8] Jane and the girls sailed home to Lyttelton on the *Moeraki* via Wellington, on 19 October 1906; Thomas had probably returned earlier to prepare for the big exhibition that opened in Hagley Park on 1 November.

Lilian did not return to Auckland; she made her Christchurch debut as a soloist, singing a Rossini aria, at the 25 July concert of the Banjo, Mandolin and Guitar Orchestra in the Choral Hall. The *Lyttelton Times* admired her 'pleasant, well-trained and expressive soprano voice, its only noticeable fault being a roughness in the lower register'.[9] By the following year she was sharing the stage with Albert Leonidas (Bert) Cropp, a young bass who was already making a name for himself throughout New Zealand: he sang with the Fuller's and Musgrove opera companies and later with Williamson's Grand Opera Company. By April 1909 Lilian

Lilian and Bert Cropp enjoy a game, c.1917, and, opposite, Will Edmonds is pictured with his wife Alice and their first two children, Nelma and Rita, c.1908.

and Bert were appearing on the same bill. When they sang at a concert held to raise money for the Akaroa Regatta in July that year, the local reporter noted that their voices 'blended most harmoniously'.[10] In September 1909 Bert headed for Sydney to try his luck there, but he was back in Christchurch by mid-1910 and performed frequently from then on, occasionally with Lilian. The couple were married on 20 August 1913. Just before the wedding, the Dresden Piano Company, where Bert worked, presented him with a silver salver. (Because of anti-German sentiment during the war, Dresden changed its name to the Bristol Piano Company.)

Gertrude, too, was a talented musician. On 1 May 1908 she appeared at the Theatre Royal in Christchurch as part of a performance by Tom Pollard's Lilliputian Opera Company, a hugely popular series of children's troupes that he had established in Tasmania in 1880. Children would join one of the Pollard troupes as they toured Australia and New Zealand. As music historian Peter Downes noted, they 'became a national institution ... Towns turned out to welcome them wherever they went, and at times their popularity exceeded theatre capacity. Windows were flung open so eager audiences could watch the shows from outside, even perched in the branches of trees.'[11] Gertrude recalled her appearance in the popular Christmas show *Bluebell in Fairyland*, in which she had one line: 'Here Bluebell, have some of mine.' She preferred, however, to be in the chorus rather than taking a leading part.[12] She continued having piano and singing lessons, and often accompanied the family to musical and orchestral society performances; and she and her parents invited friends to enjoy musical soirées at their Gloucester Street home.

As a successful businessman Thomas was able to indulge his expensive passion for cars, including a 1905 10hp Cadillac and the progressive electric vehicle seen here, c.1921, a Milburn Light Electric, Model 27L, which went on the market from around 1920.

Ernest was the only Edmonds sibling who did not learn a musical instrument. In January 1909 nine-year-old Rene was placed third for her rendering of 'Husheen' in the Irish Song section of the Christchurch Competitions. She sang 'prettily and with confidence, and showed excellent appreciation for her years', and the judge, Charles Baeyertz, a well-known critic and editor of the arts magazine *Triad*, remarked that she was 'a little artist in embryo [who] sang with much better feeling than many of the older competitors'.[13] In December 1910 Rene was performing with Mrs Mills' Midget Merrymakers. The following April she won prizes for singing and violin playing, and she took home 10s 6d in May 1914 when, aged 15, she won another violin solo: 'Miss Edmonds had alone been up to the requirements of the class.'[14] Rene was also proficient on the piano and had a good ear for music: 'She'd hear a bit of music on the radio and then go and sit down and play it.'[15] Beatrice had musical talent, too. In 1919, she and Lilian were part of a concert party that provided entertainment at a dance held at the New Brighton Ladies' Miniature Rifle Club.[16]

Jim, like his brothers, worked in the family business. He was a racing pigeon enthusiast and enjoyed showing poultry. In December 1904 his pigeon Provincial came second in the Canterbury Flying Club race from Invercargill to Christchurch, a distance of 292 miles.[17] He kept hens, beautiful white Wyandottes, which he entered in competitions. A family friend, Phil Presants, who was also probably involved in Edmonds' design work, shared Jim's interest: in April 1906 *Star* columnist 'Crow-Black' noted that 'Mr P. R. Presants has disposed of his team of Silver Wyandottes competing at the Lincoln College competition to Mr Edmonds of Woolston.'[18] Jim was something of an athlete: he competed in the 220 yards and the half-mile handicap foot races held at Lancaster Park by the Christchurch Cycle and Motor Club in March 1910, and over the next few years his name often appeared in reports of athletics competitions. Motorcycles were a passion for Jim, though sometimes things could go wrong.

On 18 September 1913 he appeared before the magistrate for 'having driven a motor-cycle on the beach road between Allandale and Governor's Bay, contrary to a by-law of the Mount Herbert County Council'. He pleaded guilty and was fined 10s and costs.[19]

Thomas was interested in animals, too – though in his case it was dogs. In August 1902, with Ferry Jigs, he won the Toy Terrier Puppy class at the annual Kennel and Collie Club Show, although the *Lyttelton Times* felt that the 'Toy and other Terriers call for little notice'.[20] Like so many people in flat-as-a-pancake Christchurch, Thomas took to cycling; in December 1902 he competed in the Christchurch Cycling Club meeting at Lancaster Park.[21] But his real obsession, when it came to transport, was the internal combustion engine. At the 1906–07 New Zealand International Exhibition he was so impressed by the exhibit of American cars that he bought a 1905 10hp Cadillac. The next step was to join the recently established Canterbury Automobile Association. Fellow members included John Deans, son of one of the first European settlers to arrive in Canterbury; Arthur Rhodes, a former MP and mayor of Christchurch; and Percy Hallenstein, of the prominent retail family. When Thomas was elected to the management committee of the Canterbury AA in March 1907, he officially joined Christchurch's moneyed motoring elite. Later he bought a Milburn Light Electric, Model 27L car, an expensive status symbol in its day – President Woodrow Wilson drove one in the White House grounds – and an unusual and extremely progressive vehicle among petrol-fuelled cars that required cranking. As his grandson Murray – George's youngest son – recalled, the car was 'steered with a tiller ... and made a whirring noise ... it was like being asked to go for a ride in a spaceship'.[22]

The family enjoyed frequent car trips to Hanmer Springs: Beatrice, Gertude, Thomas and Irene are seen at the resort in 1908. There was overseas travel too: Thomas and Jane are pictured opposite with Bert and David Cropp at Sydney's Taronga Zoo, c.1916.

Thomas soon saw the advantages of horsepower over horses for his business as well, and motor vans were introduced. But new ways brought new problems. In November 1913, Edmonds employee C. Webster, who had been driving a motor lorry for four years, appeared at a sitting of the Arbitration Court. The Canterbury Motor-car, Horsedrivers' and Livery-stable Employees' Industrial Union of Workers was asking for a wage increase and a 45-hour week. 'This,' noted the *Star*, 'was the first dispute of its kind in New Zealand as the use of motor delivery vans had only come into vogue during the last few years. There were more vehicles of that kind in Christchurch than in any other city in New Zealand'; there were 26 drivers in Christchurch, 'all of whom were Drivers' Union members'. Their lawyer considered that the drivers 'were called upon to perform more work and responsibility than the ordinary carter, who used a horse vehicle'. The men were asking for a weekly wage of £3 'with overtime rates on a proportional increase'. Webster, who was receiving only £2 14s for his 45 hours, had driven a horse and cart for three years and 'could easily see the difference ... With the motor-van it was necessary for him to always keep his attention on his vehicle as well as on the traffic of the road, whereas with a horse and cart the worry was considerably less.'[23] The old-fashioned methods had not gone entirely, though: as late as 1918 the company was wanting to buy a 'Quiet, Staunch Van Horse, young and sound'.[24]

• • •

Thomas and his family were becoming important figures in the city's life, reported in the social pages of the newspapers. They took the waters at the fashionable Hanmer Springs in North Canterbury: there were visits in March 1907 and 1908, and again in 1909, when Will and Alice were there, possibly chaperoning Lilian and Bert.

In January 1911 Thomas sailed for Britain on a business trip, accompanied by 15-year-old Beatrice, who required surgery after an accident. They stayed in London with Alexander Bickerton, who had left New Zealand in 1910, and his daughter Alice. When the British census was taken on 2 April Thomas, a 'manufac. of baking powder', and Beatrice, a 'scholar', were listed as boarders at 1 Leinster Gardens in West Paddington. Like all visitors to London, Thomas made himself known to the New Zealand Government Office in Victoria Street, Westminster.[25]

But for all his enjoyment of an increasingly good and comfortable life, and the provision of the best education for his daughters, Thomas never forgot his modest and straitened beginnings. When his children asked their father why he always gave money to the constant stream of beggars who came to their door, pointing out that he was only encouraging them, he replied that he had known hardship in his own life and that he would always help someone if they asked.[26] He was unfailingly generous to good and deserving causes, both public and private. He and Jane supported many organisations, including the Red Cross and Plunket societies, St Saviour's Orphanage, the Salvation Army, Rotary Club and the YMCA. In November 1901, after the earthquake at Cheviot, north of Christchurch, he donated £25 to the relief fund. That same year he gave land for an extension of the footpath in Ferry Road, on the condition that 'a near fence be erected'.[27] He donated money to the Children's Ward of the hospital in 1909, and the following year contributed 105s to the National Shilling Fund 'for the purpose of defraying the cost of Professor Bickerton's proposed trip to Great Britain in the interests of his theory of Partial Impact'; the fund raised a total of 1427 shillings.[28]

As his grandson David Cropp recalled, Thomas was 'a quietly spoken man. He had a very clear complexion and he didn't smoke and he didn't drink, and he didn't talk much. He was quiet and very private. He was a soft touch. If anyone wanted money, they would ask him. He didn't care. But on the other hand, he lived very frugally. I can see him opening a [wooden] case and he took the nails and straightened them out and put them into a glass jar. I remember thinking as a boy, "My goodness, why?" But it was a way of life with him.'[29]

The photo on the following pages shows the extended family in 1901. Top row: Will and Arthur Edmonds; second row: Henry Turner, Rose Edmonds, Thomas Edmonds, Ernest Edmonds, Lilian Edmonds, Joseph Turner; seated: Walter Turner, Eliza Turner, Joseph Turner, Jane Edmonds holding Irene, Dorcas Edmonds, Granny Eliza Allchin (previously Irvine), James Edmonds, Sarah Edmonds, Edwin Edmonds, Edwin Edmonds Jr; front row: William Turner, George Edmonds, Gertrude Edmonds, Beatrice Edmonds, (David) Walter Edmonds, Herbert Edmonds, James Edmonds.

James Edmonds with Ginger

Thomas and Jane with Irene, c.1912

Irene and Alice Edmonds (née Hart), c.1913

Ernest Edmonds, middle row, 2nd from left, Woolston Primary School, c.1887

Julia Blackwood, née Edmonds, 1892, author of a shipboard diary (1884)

Edwin and Sarah Edmonds (née Irvine), and family, c.1901

Edwin Edmonds (Thomas's brother) in later life

Ernest Edmonds with family, c.1920

Thomas and Jane, c.1915

Crab hunting at Castle Rock, Sydney, Australia.
Gertrude centre front, c.1918

Will Edmonds in his 1912 Mitchell (Touring)

Outside the wooden factory, c.1918

'On the beach at Waikiki': Irene, Thomas and Jane, with Gertrude and Beatrice (seated), c.1916

'Bathing at Waikiki' with Diamond Head in the distance: Jane, Beatrice, Gertrude, Thomas and Irene, c.1916

Irene in Waikiki, Hawaii, c.1916

'Our guide, and Rene expecting to lose her life any minute,' Glacier Point, Yosemite National Park, USA, c.1916

Beatrice, Irene and Gertrude with friend

Beatrice, on the voyage to Hobart to perform with the Cheer-Ohs, c.1917

Gertrude with her camera, c.1917

Beatrice, Irene and Gertrude with the ship's captain and Mrs Bennett White, Cheer-Ohs director, c.1917

'The fashion of 1916': in costume, Gertrude in the centre and Beatrice on the right, with a fellow Cheer-Oh Girl on the left

Beatrice and ukulele, Hawaii, c.1917

Gertrude and ukulele, Hawaii, c.1917

Beatrice and her Cheer-Oh Kewpie doll, c.1917

Beatrice, Gertrude and Irene, c.1917

Cheer-Oh Girls, c.1918

Keith Edmonds and David Cropp, overlooking Auckland Zoo, c.1924

Eileen and Edna Edmonds, c.1920

George and Clara Edmonds' children, Nola, Thelma, Jack and Ray, c.1920

James and Edith Edmonds' daughter, Marijean, c.1923

Eileen Edmonds with sister Edna and cousin David in the barrow, c.1916

Thomas and Jane at their daughter Beatrice's wedding, Sydney 1920

Thomas and Jane Edmonds with granddaughter Pamela, c.1922

Lilian with son David, c.1917

The four Edmonds sisters with David Cropp. Left to right, Gertrude, Beatrice, Irene and Lilian, c.1917

Thomas in the centre with Will's widow Alice (née Hart) on his left and their two youngest children, Keith and Brenda, and some of the Hart clan, c.1918

Lilian and Jane Edmonds, c.1920

Ernest and family, c.1914

Brenda and Keith Edmonds and David Cropp, c.1918

Family group, Jane Edmonds centre, holding baby Pamela, Gertrude to her left, c.1922

CHAPTER 9

TRAGEDY & TRAVEL

On Saturday 1 August 1914, at about 11 p.m., Will Edmonds died at his New Brighton home, aged only 34. Will had belonged to the New Brighton Surf Club and the Christchurch Beautifying Association, and had enjoyed motoring and cycling – but his great love was golf. He and Alice were among the first members of the nine-hole New Brighton Golf Club and often played together in mixed foursomes. Gertrude, Beatrice and Rene were also keen players, as was Bert Cropp. In fact Gertrude met her future husband, Harry Williams, on the golf course in 1913.

On the afternoon of 1 August Will, Alice and the children were strolling on the golf links when Will suddenly collapsed on the eighth green. He remained conscious briefly, and was able to say a few words to his family, before a hastily summoned doctor administered an anaesthetic and Will was driven home. There was a moment of hope when he regained consciousness sufficiently to speak with Alice but he then failed to rally, and died late that evening. The cause of death was given as heart failure. Will's daughter Brenda always believed that her father had strained his heart at work, holding up some machinery that had toppled over, but it seems more likely that he had some pre-existing medical condition, such as untreated rheumatic fever in childhood.[1]

Will Edmonds, c.1904, destined to lead his father's company, was only 34 when he died suddenly of heart failure in 1914.

When Will's estate was assessed for death duties in September 1915, it was valued at £3835.[2] According to his will, all the household effects, furniture, books, chattels and so on went to Alice, along with any money from his life insurance. The estate and the rest of the property was to be overseen by the public trustee, who was to convert it into money and invest it. One third of the proceeds would go to Alice, plus another third as long as she remained a widow. The remaining third was for the upbringing and education of the children. It is difficult, therefore, to know how much money Alice had.[3] The Widows' Pensions Act had been passed in 1911, and Alice, with four children, would have qualified for £30 a year, but this amount would have been reduced by a pound for every pound over £30 she received from other sources.[4] Brenda recalled her grandmother Jane slipping money to Alice when Thomas was not watching – although this seems counter to his usual generosity. Alice was certainly resourceful: when the soles of her shoes wore out, she would put cardboard in them to cover the holes; she grew plenty of vegetables and fruit in her extensive garden, and a tame duck laid an egg a day at the back of the section. Rita left school at 15 to work and help support the family. In later years, Alice enjoyed a lively musical and social life. According to Brenda, her mother 'never spoke one word about Daddy' after his death. Alice and the family appear to have remained in their George Street house until March 1925, when it was sold 'on account of the District Public Trustee, executor of the will of T.W. Edmonds, deceased',[5] and Alice and Brenda moved to Wellington.

A grieving Thomas had to face the task of replacing Will as general manager. It is likely that he had offered Bert Cropp a role in the company when he married Lilian, and after Will's death Thomas asked Bert to take over the top job. Bert later became managing director, and he served the firm until 1942. As his son David recalled, Bert 'didn't know anything about business. He was making money in shows, singing, and he was also working in the Bristol Piano Company ... I remember him telling me what a thrill he got when he learnt double entry bookkeeping.'[6]

On 1 April 1915 T.J. Edmonds Ltd was incorporated as a private company under the 1908 Companies Act. In practical terms, this was really a reincorporation in a new form, and seemingly influenced by Edmonds' relatively new advertising relationship with Ilott's. John Ilott later described himself as a 'close friend' of Thomas and 'mainly responsible for [his] deciding to form his business into a Limited Liability Company'.[7] The capital was £25,000 and the subscribers were all family members. Thomas held 17,999 shares; Ernest, George and Jim, each described as 'works manager', held 1000 each; Lilian, Gertrude, Beatrice and Irene had 1000 shares; and Bert Cropp, 'accountant', held the remaining single share.[8]

• • •

On the steps of Parliament House in Wellington, at 3 p.m. on Wednesday 5 August 1914, the governor, Lord Liverpool, announced that New Zealand had declared war on Germany. Britain had done so the day before. There was wild patriotic enthusiasm throughout the country at the prospect of war and fundraising events were organised for the men who were to serve overseas. Among these, in Christchurch, was a 'monster procession' with decorated cars, bands, groups and associations of all kinds and displays from many local retailers and companies, including Edmonds.[9]

In the commercial world, manufacturers were about to face challenges as restricted shipping caused disruptions to supply. For Edmonds, this meant difficulties in importing the vital ingredient, cream of tartar – and an inevitable price rise that was described as 'phenomenal'. By mid-September 1914 the price of baking powder had reportedly shot up by 74 per cent, and Prime Minister William Massey was asked in Parliament if the government was aware of the situation.[10] In November a disgruntled letter-writer noted that Edmonds baking powder, 'appropriately labelled "Sure to Rise", was retailed before the war at 11d per tin, and is now 1s 6d for the same quantity'.[11]

Alternative recipes for baking powder were published, and Edmonds' competitors leapt into action: Sharland's, for example, was 'still sold at BEFORE-WAR Prices'.[12] The situation was hardly helped in May 1915 when the cost of cream of tartar 'bounded up', increasing by £35 a ton: 'Owing to the difficulty of securing the raw material', Edmonds would 'be able to supply only small quantities in the meantime.'[13]

Not long after this, an Edmonds advertisement rather startlingly announced 'Peace

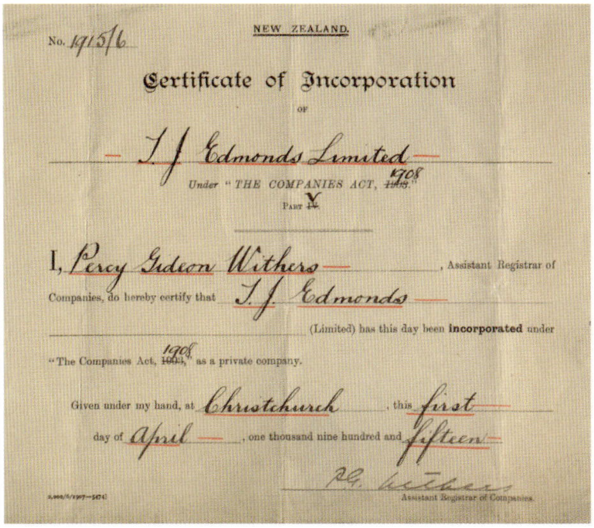

NEW ZEALAND.

No. 1915/6

Certificate of Incorporation

OF

T. J. Edmonds Limited

Under "THE COMPANIES ACT, ~~1903~~ 1908."

PART ~~IV~~ V

I, Percy Gideon Withers, Assistant Registrar of Companies, do hereby certify that T. J. Edmonds (Limited) has this day been **incorporated** under "The Companies Act, ~~1903~~ 1908," as a private company.

Given under my hand, at Christchurch, this first day of April, one thousand nine hundred and fifteen.

P.G. Withers
Assistant Registrar of Companies.

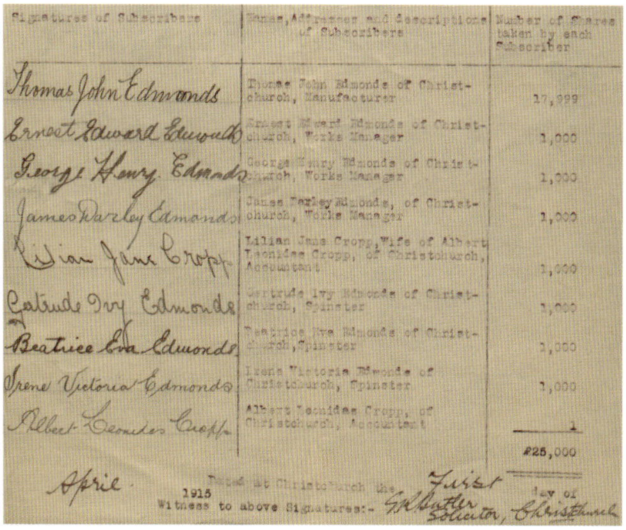

Signatures of Subscribers	Names, Addresses and descriptions of Subscribers	Number of Shares taken by each Subscriber
Thomas John Edmonds	Thomas John Edmonds of Christchurch, Manufacturer	17,999
Ernest Edward Edmonds	Ernest Edward Edmonds of Christchurch, Works Manager	1,000
George Henry Edmonds	George Henry Edmonds of Christchurch, Works Manager	1,000
James Darley Edmonds	James Darley Edmonds, of Christchurch, Works Manager	1,000
Lilian Jane Cropp	Lilian Jane Cropp, Wife of Albert Leonidas Cropp, of Christchurch, Accountant	1,000
Gertrude Ivy Edmonds	Gertrude Ivy Edmonds of Christchurch, Spinster	1,000
Beatrice Eva Edmonds	Beatrice Eva Edmonds of Christchurch, Spinster	1,000
Irene Victoria Edmonds	Irene Victoria Edmonds of Christchurch, Spinster	1,000
Albert Leonidas Cropp	Albert Leonidas Cropp, of Christchurch, Accountant	1
		£25,000

Dated at Christchurch the First day of April 1915

Witness to above Signatures:- G.K. Butler Solicitor, Christchurch

Declared!', though the next line read 'Cross out the eggs', which were 'the most serious element of uncertainty on baking day'. But if you used Edmonds egg powder, you would 'introduce a powerful ally into your baking operations'.[14] The company also reminded customers that: 'Owing to the non-arrival of shipments it has not been possible to fill all orders for Edmonds Baking Powder. The tens of thousands of housewives who have tried and proved that there is nothing to equal Edmonds, should know that nevertheless there has been no increase in price in the last six months, and should therefore refuse to pay any advance if asked to do so.'[15]

Perhaps inevitably, by late August 1915 Edmonds was 'reluctantly' forced to raise the price of both its baking powder and egg powder by a penny per tin, though the formula had not been altered and the baking powder was still made with 'real grape' cream of tartar that was 'pure and wholesome'.[16] The company soon felt compelled to respond to the not unreasonable 'rumour' that its product was more expensive, and to 'invidious comparisons between it and other brands'. A widespread, year-long advertising campaign, 'The Case For and Against Edmonds Baking Powder', was designed to clarify the situation by pointing out the 'true facts' – principally that each large Edmonds tin contained more 'pure' powder than in other brands; it was 'false economy' to buy "cheap" baking powder'.[17] Before the war, grape cream of tartar had cost between £75 and £85 a ton, but by April 1918 it had skyrocketed to almost £400.[18]

Bert Cropp, Lilian's husband, took over the management of the company after Will's death and later became managing director. The 1915 certificate of incorporation and shareholder register are important company artefacts.

In August, Edmonds was running an advertisement headed 'Cream of Tartar Has Risen £315 a Ton', and making 'a special appeal to every housewife'. Only the 'highest grade genuine cream of tartar', it declared, would be used in 'Sure to Rise' baking powder; the company 'steadfastly' refused to use any substitutes. 'Stand by us in this matter,' it implored, and help conserve dwindling supplies. 'It is better to *use less* of the best, than be compelled to come down to cheap inferior brands.'[19]

Not until some months after the war ended did Bert Cropp admit that frequent shortages of raw materials had forced the Edmonds factory to close down on three or four occasions.[20] By early 1919 the company could report that changes to shipping and the possibility of receiving raw materials at more regular intervals would allow them to resume full production.[21]

But if baking powder was in short supply at home, the situation at the front was far worse.

The troops were issued flour as part of their rations, but not baking powder. According to Major Eugene O'Neill, a surgeon with the New Zealand Medical Corps, writing from the Dardanelles, 'The ideal thing would be to send a Santa Claus ship of provisions to the Gallipoli Peninsula – frozen lamb, flour, etc., and do not forget the baking powder.'[22] Late in 1915 Sister Jean Ingram, serving with the New Zealand Army Nursing Service and writing home from Cairo, said that the nurses 'bought men leaving for the front packets of baking powder, which were greatly appreciated'.[23] Among the necessities that a returned soldier advised a young private to take with him, along with extra socks, bootlaces, spare underpants and a wristwatch with luminous dial, were '6 packets of baking powder'.[24] However, as they had in the war in South Africa, enterprising New Zealand soldiers at Gallipoli compensated for the absence of baking powder by resorting to Eno's.[25]

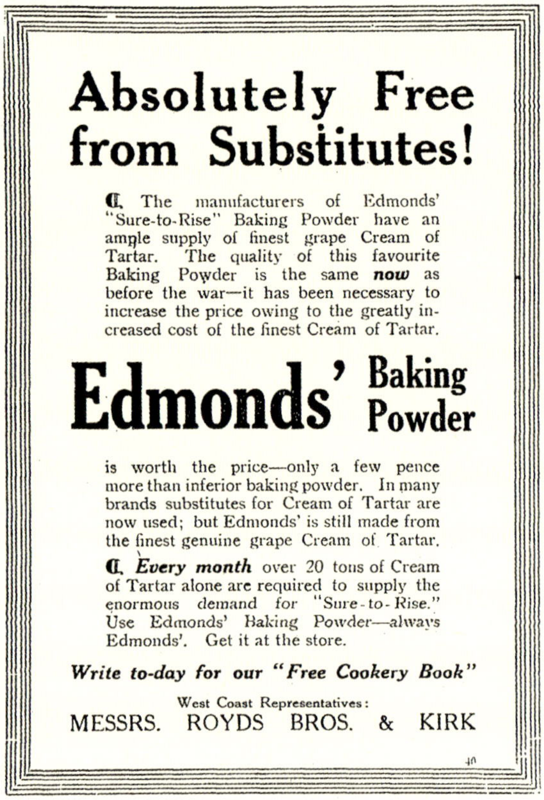

• • •

Soon after war was declared, Thomas gave £50 to help support the troops. Later that month he and two others contributed 'a large number of patriotic song sheets' to be sold and, it was hoped, raise more than £30. He bid enthusiastically for the fat lamb that was auctioned at a patriotic concert in mid-1915.[26] There were donations, too, to the Blankets for Britain fund, £500 for a Soldiers' Girl Queen Contest, and £200 to a nationwide Red Triangle Day held to support YMCA war work.[27] Edmonds also did its bit by donating packing cases for the food, bedding, clothes and 'comforts' that the Christchurch Red Cross sent overseas. In October 1916 the *Press* reported that over 6000 parcels – Christmas presents for the men in the trenches – had been sent to England. 'There were 157 cases in all, the boxes being presented by the Edmonds Baking Powder Company.'[28] Early in March 1918 the Red Cross thanked Edmonds and the Christchurch Gas Company for generous gifts of packing cases that had been used in February to send much-appreciated goods to France, Britain, Egypt and Salonika, Greece. Baking powder tins were in demand, too, for sending foods such as honey, sugar and baked treats to the troops.[29]

Other family members worked for the war effort at home. Rene took part in a Grand Concert by the Christchurch Orchestral Society in November 1914 to raise money for the Belgians. (Germany's attack on Belgium on 4 August and its subsequent shocking treatment of the civilian population raised ire and sympathy throughout the world.) 'Three million Belgians Starving! They're helping us. Help Them! Be at the Colosseum tomorrow night.' Jane and her daughters knitted socks for the troops; and in October 1915 the New Brighton War Relief Committee gratefully acknowledged monthly donations from Alice.[30]

Although conscription had begun in 1916, operating on a ballot system, men could still volunteer. Jim, who was a few weeks away from turning 25, registered at the Christchurch recruiting office on 19 June 1917, giving his profession as 'manufacturer'.[31] For some reason – possibly medical, or that he was required at the factory – he did not serve; he was still at home in Gloucester Street in September that year, advertising a cycle-car for sale. Many young men who were itching to enlist were held back by family expectation and duty. Meanwhile Jim had been doing his bit at home: in October 1914 he joined the Christchurch Citizens' Defence Rifle Club, a group of men who were 'going to give up a great deal of their leisure in order to learn how to defend their country should occasion arise'.[32] As the war ground on, married men with one child, and then with two children, were called up in April and June 1918. 'Edmonds, Ernest Edward, manufacturer, 229, Linwood Avenue, Christchurch' was listed in the local paper on 19 June;[33] he was attested and went into the military training camp at Trentham, outside Wellington, on 5 November that year, but the war ended before he could go any further, and he was demobbed by the end of that month. There is no military record for George, but by 1914 he had three children and would not have been called up.

Bert Cropp, who had been passed fit in June 1918, entered training camp early in October and was made a corporal before he was discharged on 18 November.[34] Harry Williams, who later married Gertrude, went overseas in August 1917 and was wounded three times in France: the first time was accidental; he then suffered a bullet wound to his neck in March 1918, and in August he received a gunshot wound to his right knee. He was promoted to sergeant, and he came home on the *Ajana* in April 1919.[35] Members of the Edmonds staff, such as assistant foreman Colin Hart, also served overseas.

Above, Jim, the youngest Edmonds son, did not serve in the First World War but joined a local citizens' defence group. The war placed pressure on the supply of cream of tartar. In its advertising, Edmonds confidently asserted its superiority, and was keen to assure customers that their baking powder still contained the critical ingredient.

A year after Will's sudden death, the Edmonds family was facing more trouble. In June 1915 a Christchurch newspaper reported Ethel Edmonds' application for separation maintenance and guardianship for two children against Ernest, her husband of 13 years. For the last 18 months, she said, her life 'had been a misery'. Ernest was a drinker (in a teetotal family); racing occupied much of his time – he had four trotters; and there was another woman.[36] The unsavoury details, which included much discussion of the company, were reported at length in the *Star* and featured in a large article in the sensationalist weekly, *N.Z. Truth*.[37] The magistrate awarded custody of the older daughter Lily to Ernest, and the younger daughter Edna to Ethel, who was awarded a separation order and £2 a week. Ernest would be allowed to see Edna every Saturday afternoon.[38]

After the trauma and shame of the court case, an extended overseas holiday seemed an excellent idea. On 4 September the 'For Women Folk' section of the *Star* reported that 'Mr and Mrs T.J. Edmonds, of Gloucester Street, accompanied by the Misses Edmonds' – Gertrude, Beatrice and Irene – were leaving Christchurch in a few days en route for San Francisco. 'After two months in that centre, during which time they will thoroughly do the Panama Exposition, they intend to visit Southern California, making Los Angeles their headquarters. Miss I. [Rene] Edmonds is developing brilliantly as a violinist and composer, and will make the most of the musical opportunities of her tour. Visiting artists who have heard her predict a great future.' Thomas told his talented daughter that he wanted her to have chances with music that had not been possible for him.[39]

On 15 September the travellers boarded the SS *Ulimaroa* for the night sailing from Lyttelton to Wellington, where they transferred to the Union Steam Ship Company's handsome and superbly furnished *Marama*. This would be its last voyage before it was converted into New Zealand's second wartime hospital ship. Gertrude recalled that at night they had to travel in total darkness for fear of being torpedoed by a German raider, but the voyage was uneventful.[40] The extravagant Panama Pacific International Exhibition, which ran from February to December 1915 – the United States was not yet at war – was staged primarily to celebrate the completion of the Panama Canal but also to showcase San Francisco's recovery from the huge and destructive 1906 earthquake.

After two months the family went on to Los Angeles, where they stayed for a few weeks before returning to San Francisco and renting a house in Berkeley, very close to the university: Gertrude walked through the campus on her way to weekly French and singing lessons.[41] Beatrice and Rene, too, learnt French, and Rene studied violin with an Italian teacher, Antonio de Grassi. The family enjoyed concerts and cultural performances at the Greek

Theatre in the university grounds and saw world-famous Russian ballerina Anna Pavlova. The time in San Francisco may also have borne business fruit for Thomas. It is likely that he met John Stauffer of the Cream of Tartar Company, from whom he would purchase cream of tartar during the war, and Stauffer later became a business partner in the 1926 Australian Cream Tartar Company (see Chapter 10).

On 27 November 1916, almost exactly a year after they arrived in California, they sailed for home via Hawaii, where for three weeks they rented a cottage at Waikiki, and Suva, Fiji, where they stayed at the sumptuous Grand Pacific Hotel, designed to give guests the illusion of still being on an ocean liner. After reaching Auckland on 8 January 1917, Thomas and Beatrice travelled down to Christchurch, while Jane, Gertrude and Rene went on to Sydney, where Rene was to continue her music studies at the Sydney Conservatorium; Thomas and Beatrice joined them there several months later.

An unusual opportunity to help the war effort came when Gertrude and Beatrice were invited to join the Cheer-Oh Girls, a dancing and singing company that had been founded in November 1916 by Meta Hayter – who was always referred to as Mrs Bennett White and was, apparently, a male impersonator – to raise money for patriotic funds. The versatile and popular troupe of between seven and 10 young women, which began in Mosman, performed around New South Wales and toured Tasmania in May 1918. Throughout the war and for four years afterwards, the Cheer-Ohs raised an impressive £55,000 for a range of patriotic and repatriation funds.[42] Each concert had its own cause, such as the Red Cross, the Flying Corps, the Trench Mortar Battery, the War Chest Fund, the Railway Comforts Fund, or coffee stalls for the troops in France.

Opposite, Ernest and Ethel Edmonds are seen with their daughters Lily and Edna, c.1915. Irene, a talented musician and composer, poses with her violin, c.1915. Above, Jane and Thomas enjoy playing tourist in Portland during the family's American sojourn, c.1916.

Gertrude and Beatrice were members from 1917 to 1919; and Rene was involved in 1918 and 1919. During the highly successful Tasmanian tour, which raised £500, the Hobart *Mercury* noted that 'Misses Gertrude and Beatrice Edmonds were excellent in their Hawaiian songs and playing on very tuneful Hawaiian guitars' and that the programme ended with Beatrice 'and the girls in Maori costumes singing the "Waita [sic] Maori" chorus, followed by a vigorous performance of the "Haka"'; the chorus was probably Alfred Hill's most famous song, 'Waiata Poi'.[43] The Cheer-Oh Girls were giving a show at the Liverpool military camp in southwest Sydney when they heard that the war was over. The Armistice came into effect at 11 a.m. on 11 November 1918. As Gertrude recalled, 'The show finished early and everyone went into town to celebrate!'[44]

The Cheer-Oh Girls, below, photographed during their busy wartime touring in Australia, 1918. Beatrice is standing second from right, next to Mrs Bennett White; Gertrude is at the front on the left. Opposite, Gertrude and Harry Williams on their wedding day in 1921. This was the third post-war family wedding: Lilian had married Bert Cropp in 1919 and Beatrice had married Peter Fripp in 1920.

The relief of the war's end was clouded by the influenza pandemic, known then as the Spanish Flu, which killed close to 9000 New Zealanders from mid-October to mid-November 1918. Christchurch, with the 'twin advantages of early warning and excellent organisation',[45] suffered fewer losses than Auckland and Wellington, but hundreds died. The city mobilised an impressive relief effort to fight the disease, centred on Cathedral Square; the remainder of the city was organised into blocks, where volunteers identified the sick and arranged for doctors and nurses to visit. Vast quantities of soups and other invalid foods were made in soup kitchens and widely distributed to the sick and needy. Among the many gifts of food to the city's soup kitchens acknowledged in the *Star* at the end of November were 'corn

flour and jellies from Edmonds and Co.', and the *Press* reported a couple of weeks later George Edmonds' 'very generous supply of jellies and cornflour also fomentation cloths' to the North Linwood and Dallington relief committee. The company donated £25 to the Leyden Street Influenza Depot, which was not far from the Edmonds factory.[46] By mid-December the city was returning to normal, and so too were much-needed supplies. 'Edmonds' baking powder,' reported the *Press* commercial editor, 'has been scarce for some time, but the stocks now held are ample for Christmas requirements.'[47]

The peace celebrations were postponed until 1919. When they finally took place, members of the Edmonds family were on hand. In September Bert and Lilian, 'wearing a lovely gown of white net over satin, with embroideries of gold and emerald', attended a grand Anzac Ball. In November Bert and Gertrude, who had returned to Christchurch before the rest of the family to spend some time with Lilian and her new baby, contributed musical numbers at a banquet for returned soldiers held in the Pier Hall in New Brighton.[48] The company was also still donating goods: prizes of tins of baking and custard powder for the married women's race at the annual New Brighton Gala, with all proceeds going to the Naval Heroes' Fund and the Returned Soldiers' Memorial.[49]

• • •

Harry Williams returned in April 1919, and he and Gertrude had just three months together before he sailed to London in July to take up a job as manager of warehousemen and manufacturers Butterworth Brothers, for whom he had been working in Christchurch before the war. The couple announced their engagement in the *Star* on 26 April 1920. On 18 November Beatrice married Captain Samuel Trude (Peter) Fripp of the Royal Flying Corps at St Chad's Church in Cremorne. Beatrice wore 'a simple gown of pale pink georgette'; Rene, who was her bridesmaid, was dressed in pale blue; and Jane wore 'a smart gown of black silk'.[50] Gertrude arrived in Sydney shortly after the wedding and, on 4 December, sailed for London with Beatrice and Peter. While they were en route, Harry was told that he could return to Christchurch and serve as Butterworth's manager there. When he explained that his fiancée was 'on the water', however, his position in London was extended for another two months; and on 25 January 1921, 29-year-old Gertrude and 40-year-old Harry were married in Christ's Church, Russell Square.

SURE TO RISE

CHAPTER 10

A LANDMARK FACTORY

New Zealand's economy suffered in the decade after 1918: a post-war boom was followed by a sharp recession in 1921–22, and another downturn around 1926. One effect was a steady rise in the cost of essentials such as tea, cocoa, sugar – and baking powder. 'The burden of the housewife,' said the *Otago Witness* in February 1920, 'grows heavier and heavier, and one wonders will these increases on household commodities ever cease.'[1] An indignant editorial three months later revealed that it now cost more than twice as much to maintain a pre-1914 standard of living, and that wages had not gone up in proportion. A damning list of percentage increases was topped by clothes pegs (300 per cent), and both cream of tartar (243 per cent) and baking powder (150 per cent) featured prominently.[2] Edmonds pointed out that, while other baking powders were a penny or two cheaper, a large tin of 'Sure to Rise' contained between 2 and 4 ounces more than other brands, and that a tin of Edmonds 'goes further because you don't have to use so much'.[3]

By 1919, T.J. Edmonds Ltd was using 25 tons of cream of tartar a month and producing between 1.25 and 1.5 million tins of baking powder a year: 'It would not be exaggerating to say that in the pantries of 90 out of every 100 good New Zealand housewives one could find a "Sure to Rise" tin.'[4] The wooden factory buildings, and even the three-storey brick building behind them, which had been added by 1912, could no longer cope with the increasing demand. (Thomas had been granted building permits for Aldwins Road in November 1907 and July 1908, and on 4 February 1910 and 1 May 1913.)[5] At the beginning of July 1920 architects J.S. & M.J. Guthrie were inviting tenders for 'NEW FACTORY AND OFFICE BUILDINGS (in Brick), Ferry Road, for T. J. Edmonds, Ltd'. Brothers John Steel Guthrie and Maurice James Guthrie had a thriving architectural practice in Christchurch in the first half of the twentieth century; their projects included Christchurch Boys' High School and St George's Hospital.[6] In late October the builder, William Williamson, was granted a building permit for 'Edmonds & Co. Ferry Road'.[7] Williamson was responsible for a number of well-known city

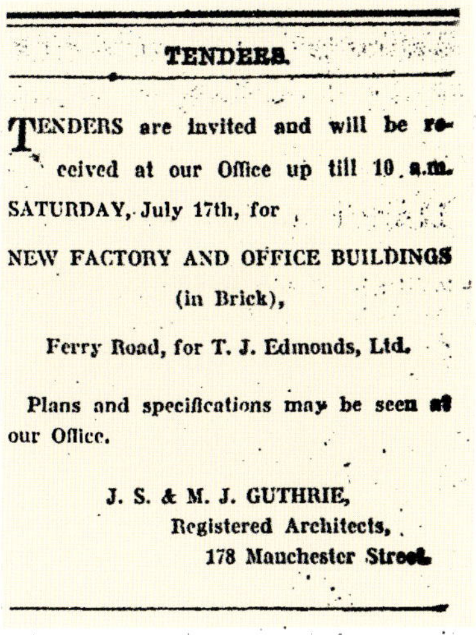
TENDERS.

TENDERS are invited and will be received at our Office up till 10 a.m. SATURDAY, July 17th, for

NEW FACTORY AND OFFICE BUILDINGS (in Brick),

Ferry Road, for T. J. Edmonds, Ltd.

Plans and specifications may be seen at our Office.

J. S. & M. J. GUTHRIE,
Registered Architects,
178 Manchester Street.

With its striking façade and gardens, the new Edmonds factory, commissioned in 1920 and completed in 1922, became a nationally famous landmark.

buildings, among them the Nurses' Memorial Chapel at Christchurch Public Hospital. (A year later, on 21 July, Thomas bought land with frontages on both Aldwins and Ferry roads,[8] but it must have been extra acreage for the future; work would surely already have started before then for the factory to be completed by early 1922.)

The new factory was a three-storey brick structure with a cement plaster façade, and a sawtooth roof with inset glass panels to allow the maximum amount of air and light into what the company later described as a 'scientifically constructed building', which housed the 'most modern machinery' that was 'electrically controlled, so that dust and smoke are eliminated'.[9] The imposing structure, surmounted by the familiar sun symbol with the 'Sure to Rise' slogan, quickly became one of Christchurch's best-known industrial buildings and a prominent landmark that was synonymous with the company. It was a major feature of many advertisements, and of the cookery book. (Thomas was not alone in his creation of an up-to-the-minute factory that helped to proclaim and market his company; go-ahead businesses overseas were doing the same. In 1911–12, for example, the Canadian firm E.W. Gillett Co. Ltd., which produced Magic Baking Powder, had built an impressive castellated factory in Toronto that trumpeted its products on the top and on the walls.)[10]

In late February 1922, shortly after the opening of what was 'probably the most modern baking powder factory in the world', the *Press* 'special representative' was invited to make an inspection, and the subsequent lengthy puff piece was published in a number of the nation's newspapers. In his 'long chat', managing director Bert Cropp announced that he expected sales for 1922 to exceed 2 million tins, and that the factory had an annual 'output capacity' of over 6 million tins. This was because 'one of the biggest English firms selling to grocers and storekeepers had been making careful tests of Edmonds' Baking Powder for a very considerable period, and had come to the conclusion that there was nothing on the English market which could even compare with it'. The company was therefore 'confident that huge sales could be expected in the Motherland'. Bert had returned from a recent world trip with samples of baking powder brands from various countries, including Canada, the United States and England, and these had been tested by 'expert chemists'. Edmonds' product had been deemed superior to all others and was, in Cropp's opinion, 'the finest baking powder in the world'. Edmonds was also enjoying increasing sales for its custard powder, which was now

Robert Percy Moore photographed the Edmonds factory on Ferry Road soon after its completion. The new factory quickly became a central feature of the company's advertising. The photo on the following pages by George Edmonds shows the proximity and integration of the old and new factories and houses occupied by staff.

FACTORY

The Largest Baking Powder Factory South of the Line

The whole of the premises are surrounded by beautifully laid out lawns and gardens

OFFICES

SINCE 1879 Edmonds "Sure-to-Rise" Baking Powder has steadily grown in public favour. The first year's output was barely 1,000 tins; in 1911 sales had increased to 878,000; last year the output exceeded one and three-quarter million tins. This year it is confidently expected that sales in this Dominion will reach over two million tins. This enormous consumption averages over seven and a-half tins per annum for every family in New Zealand.

The secret of Edmonds wonderful success lies in the fact that the greatest care has always been taken to maintain quality Only the finest grape cream of tartar is used, and even during the war, when the utmost difficulty was experienced in maintaining regular supplies of this necessary ingredient, the Directors of the firm actually closed the factory down for periods totalling six months, sooner than lower the quality standard.

EDMONDS
"SURE-TO-RISE" BAKING POWDER

The new factory has an output capacity of over six million tins per year. Every modern appliance for labour saving has been introduced, and the utmost care has been taken by the architects to see that the greatest amount of light is secured. Modern machinery for filling and weighing has been installed, and the powder throughout the entire process of manufacture is untouched by hand. Robbins & Myers' Motors have been installed throughout the factory.

To-day the Dominion housewives will take none other than Edmonds "Sure-to-Rise" brand. They know that the unvarying high quality is always maintained, and that successful cooking is always assured when Edmonds is used in the mixing.

Edmonds Baking Powder is sold by every storekeeper in the Dominion.

FILLING ROOM

SURE TO RISE

URE TO RISE
G.H.EDMONDS
CH-CH. N.Z.

The new factory and brick office, probably with Bert Cropp and Thomas in the doorway, were illustrated in the 1923 edition of the cookery book. The photo opposite shows the head office staff in 1929: R.J. Murly, Bert Cropp, Veda Coton, Thomas Edmonds, his sons Jim and George, and F.S. Taylor.

being produced in the old factory: its growing popularity was attributed both to its high quality and the fact that it was cheaper than imported brands.[11]

Bert ushered the visiting journalist through the new complex, which consisted of the factory and a separate office block right on Ferry Road. (On 23 February 1922 he had advised the appropriate officials that the registered address of the company was now no longer 13 Aldwins Road, but 375 Ferry Road.)[12] His own office was fitted out with some 'exceptionally fine pieces of New Zealand-made furniture'. A feature of the factory was the installation of labour-saving measures such as the latest devices for weighing and handling materials. There was a laboratory, to test and analyse raw ingredients. A vital part of manufacturing the company's various powders was the production of both the tins and cases needed to package and transport them. From timber supplied to specified sizes, 24,300 cases per annum were assembled on the premises. Bert offered other impressive statistics:

> Over 680 tons of baking powder are sold every year, which means that 14,000 tons of carting and handling has to be done by shipping companies and railways from one end of the Dominion to the other. To give an idea of what this means ... if one-ton motor trucks were loaded up with raw material brought into the factory, and also with the manufactured baking powder, they would form a procession five miles long, and would require approximately 1360 motor-lorries; while the tin used would cover an area approximately one million square yards.

The *Press* reporter met Thomas, who was now chairman of directors: 'It is [due] to Mr Edmonds's ingenuity and acumen that the foundations were laid which made the rise of this splendid business possible.'[13] The company's fame soon spread to London: it was awarded a certificate of honour and a medal for its participation in the British Empire Exhibition in Wembley, which ran for several months in both 1924 and 1925.[14]

FURTHER EXTENSIONS *to*

EDMONDS Model Factory made necessary by the ever increasing demand for EDMONDS QUALITY PRODUCTS

The present model factory of T. J. Edmonds Ltd.

Extensive additions made necessary by increased sales

Sold by every grocer in NEW ZEALAND

All EDMONDS' PRODUCTS are sold only in containers bearing the well-known EDMONDS labels.
ACCEPT NO SUBSTITUTE

IT is many years since the founder of Edmonds ran his business in a tiny factory. But, even then, he saw the Edmonds of the future, a mighty model factory, in a setting of glorious flowers and cool green lawns—a model factory wherein people worked well because they were happy and contented.

All this has come to pass. Edmonds progressed. And with them, their employees progressed. Long before it was on the Statute Book, the 40 hour week was in force in Edmonds Model Factory—the healthy, sunny, model factory which has the unique distinction of being the largest Baking Powder Factory in the Southern Hemisphere.

To-day, the discerning public insist on Edmonds Products. In tiny townships, in cities, in towns, people *must have—Edmonds*. And so great is the demand that extensions are being made to Edmonds Model Factory. With tradition behind them, Edmonds Products to-day are unchallenged for quality—unchallenged for value.

There is no Substitute for Quality
INSIST ON
EDMONDS

'*Sure-to-Rise*' BAKING POWDER
'*Sure-to-Please*' CUSTARD *and* '*Sure-to-Set*' JELLIES

EDMONDS 'Sure-to-Please' CUSTARD, in six delicious flavours, in 4-oz. (6d.), 10-oz. (1/-), 4-lb. (5/-) and 28-lb. tins.
EDMONDS 'Sure-to-Rise' BAKING POWDER, in 4-oz. (6d.), 14-oz. (1/4), 5-lb. (6/9) and 28-lb. tins.

EDMONDS 'Sure-to-Set' JELLIES, in 12 delicious flavours, in 4-oz. (6d. each and 2/9 half doz.) and 1-lb. (1/8) packets. Packed in cellophane to retain the flavour.

By 1937 extensions to the factory were needed: a new store was constructed of steel frame and concrete, and timber and 400 sheets of roofing iron were sold off.[15] Even before the work was finished, a company advertisement was proclaiming this latest structure as the realisation of Thomas's dream to create a 'mighty model factory … wherein people worked well because they were happy and contented'[16] – set in a garden that would become famous in Christchurch and beyond.

• • •

The 1920s brought a spate of price-cutting wars. One such outbreak in Christchurch in 1923 reflected the keen competition between rival grocery firms, and a number of lines, among them dried fruits, soap, bacon – and Edmonds baking powder – were sold at much lower prices than usual.[17] Edmonds appealed to the housewife by including a message in its tins:

> Dear Madam, Because of a Price Cutting War, retailers from Auckland to Bluff are selling 'Sure to Rise' at practically cost. The law forbids our taking any action to regulate retail selling prices. When the grocer ceases to get a profit on any line, he does not want to sell any more of it, and we have been threatened with boycott. This can only be done by the housewife taking what the grocer wants to sell her. You will probably be asked to try some other brand 'just as good' (?). Insist on 'Sure to Rise', it will not fail you.

In late 1927 the price of baking powder went up again, once more because of the high cost of cream of tartar. But before long an unspecified manufacturer, described as 'one of the largest … in the local trade' – most probably Edmonds – advised merchants of a reduction in the cost of their product.[18] By then, however, Thomas had developed a contingency plan. In 1926 his firm was a co-founder of the Parramatta-based Australian Cream Tartar Company, established to produce this essential ingredient much closer to home. The other partners in what the *Press* described as 'a real business romance'[19] were the Stauffer Chemical Company (Australia) Ltd and British firm Kemball-Bishop Ltd. These three companies each held 25 per cent of the shares; the rest were held in Australia.[20]

As the *Press* noted, 'The idea began with Mr T.J. Edmonds, the well-known baking powder manufacturer', who had 'bought largely' from Stauffer's San

Continued growth required expansion of the factory complex in 1937. The diorama was made by George Edmonds after the alterations were completed. He made several such dioramas over the years, one of which survives, having been rescued by locals when the factory was being demolished.

Francisco company when British cream of tartar was unavailable during the war. Thomas suggested that 'a factory in New Zealand would be a profitable concern, but the company preferred Australia'. This led to the multinational partnership and the construction of a factory, 'ideally situated' on the Parramatta River, with a planned monthly capacity of 100 tons each of cream of tartar and tartaric acid. Both products are from argol, the acid incrustation that forms inside vats used for aging wine. The new company planned to use local argols, previously discarded by Australian winemakers. Dissolved and boiled, the argols were then crystallised before being subjected to more boiling, followed by filtering and drying, and then ground.[21]

By 1949 Edmonds was importing raw materials from all corners of the Commonwealth, including Britain, Canada, South Africa and Australia. The photograph opposite, showing the storage of such vital ingredients, is from the 1955 film *Cookery Nook*. The illustration on the following pages is from the 1952 edition of the cookery book.

• • •

In the wake of the December 1919 general election, which returned the Reform Party with William Massey as prime minister, Ilott's came up with a topical advertisement for Edmonds: 'One candidate secures enormous majority. By an overwhelming majority the people of the Dominion have decided that Edmonds' baking powder is by far the best'; this 'great victory' resulted from its 'marked superiority ... over any other candidate'.[22] Ilott's adopted a novel approach with a campaign based on five 'Leaves from the Diary of a Successful Cook'. These were handwritten entries, from Monday to Friday, documenting the progress from buying the

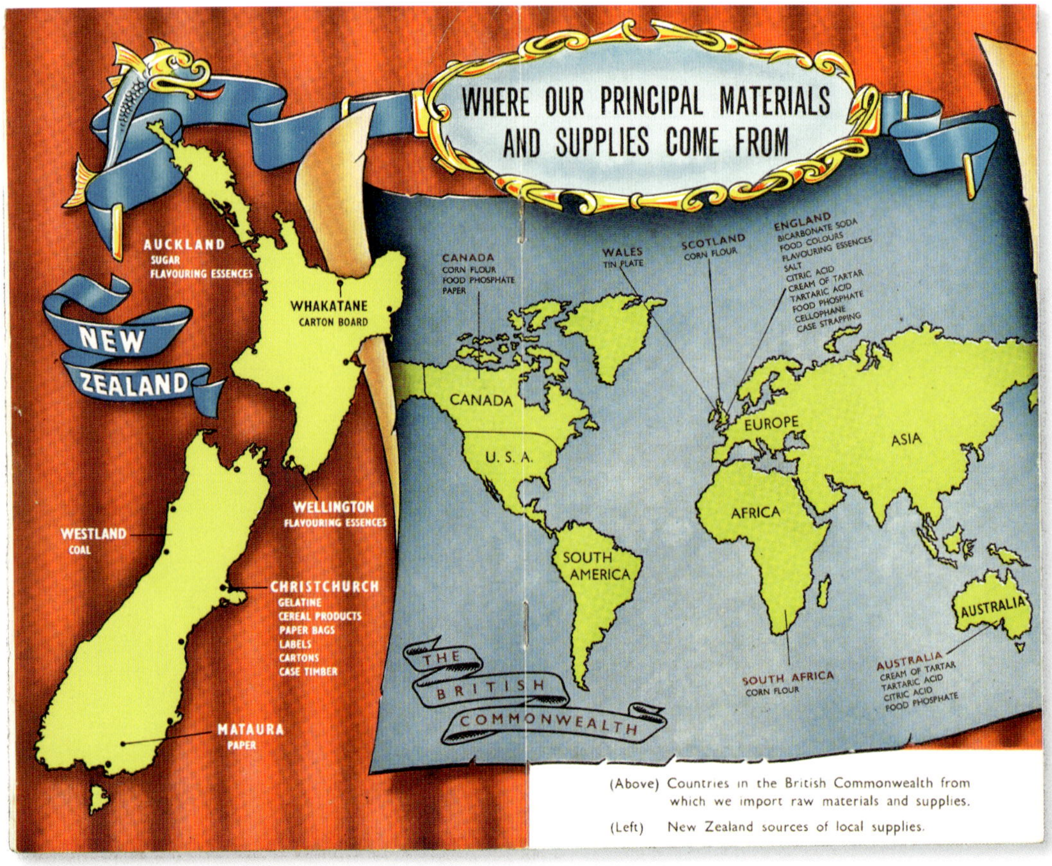

URE TO RISE

essential baking powder to cooking, the arrival of guests and the inevitable outcome: 'Party a huge success ... everyone congratulated me on my cooking.'[23] Another imaginative promotion was a children's competition to guess the number of tins of Edmonds displayed in the window of H. Allen's Strand Cash Grocery store in Tauranga. The correct number was 319 and the closest guess was 320, submitted by Dorothy Miller, who won 7s 6d.[24]

Edmonds baking powder had become a household name – to such an extent that it often made an appearance at fancy dress occasions. A Sure to Rise headdress stood out at a Christchurch roller skating party in 1911, and costumes at a Ladies' Ball at Mangatoki, southern Taranaki, in July 1920, included a Miss L. Wright as 'Edmonds' Baking Powder'.[25] At poster balls, people wore ingenious costumes that represented well-known household products. Attending one such event, in aid of the Queenstown Brass Band, also in 1920, were Mrs Melville as Indian Root Pills, Mr Jack Summers as Strang's Gold Medal Maori Coffee, and Miss Philp as Edmonds Baking Powder.[26] Held regularly, these occasions no doubt provided a welcome diversion during the grim days of the Depression and the Second World War. And Edmonds baking powder was the inspiration for the best decorated bicycle at the 1935 Ponatahi Sports, in South Wairarapa.[27]

By the late 1920s Edmonds was being promoted as 'the lightest possible' baking powder, a quality endorsed by the inclusion of butterflies in a series of advertisements. Edmonds asked customers to put the matter to the test by half-filling several tumblers with water, adding a teaspoon of different brands of baking powder to each and stirring: the product that generated the most bubbles had the greatest leavening power and, unsurprisingly, Edmonds performed 'with flying colours'.[28] The bubbles were, of course, carbon dioxide, and baking powder was required by law to produce not less than 10 per cent by weight of the gas.[29]

Edmonds' increasingly impressive sales inspired someone at Ilott's to go vertical. Having explained that Aorangi, the Māori name for Mt Cook, meant cloud piercer, the copy took off: 'Now imagine (if you can) a column of Edmonds Baking Powder Tins, rising from the ground, piercing the clouds and towering upwards into space 58½ times higher than our great mountain. Such comparison gives a vivid idea of the quantity of Edmonds Baking Powder sold in one year.' As a helpful illustration showed, the 733,333 feet of 'tin upon tin' left the 12,349-foot mountain far below.[30] In 1924 Ilott's came up with an even more imaginative concept: a single cake baked from a year's worth of Edmonds baking powder would be no less than 4000 miles high, equivalent to 1710 mountains the height of Mt Cook stacked one on top of the other.

Left, until at least the mid 1950s, labels were affixed to tins by hand. Right, with Edmonds' sales booming in the early 1920s, Ilott's advertising campaigns used local landmarks such as Mt Cook to illustrate the phenomenal sales and popularity of their baking powder.

This admittedly read like 'a page from Jules Verne', but it was 'absolutely true'; and next year the cake would be 5000 miles high.[31] Mt Cook featured in another campaign over 1928 and 1929, called 'The Big Things of N.Z.', which were numbered one to six: the Franz Josef Glacier, the Forest Giant Kauri, the Remarkables, the Mighty Swordfish, Mt Cook, and the Otira Tunnel, completed in 1923. All were extraordinary in their own way, as the persuasive copy explained, but Sure to Rise baking powder also qualified as 'a big one', with sales reaching 2½ million tins in 1928.[32]

Cooking properly – with Edmonds – was regarded as an essential skill and, according to the advertisements, the housewife who did not use Sure to Rise risked failed baking and family disappointment. Ilott's understood its market. For the first issue of *The Ladies' Mirror*, founded in 1922, the agency created a full-page advertisement that told, in three 'chapters', the story of 'a young wife who thought she couldn't cook'. When Miss Office becomes Mrs Cook, she manages the roast dinner but produces only leaden cakes, pastry and scones. Despite her husband Jack's comment that he had 'seen worse when he was boarding', she realises that the lack of Edmonds Baking Powder is the problem. After she has purchased a tin, Jack is delighted to find that her cooking is 'just as good as Mother's – and better'.[33] Edmonds continued to advertise in *The Ladies' Mirror* and its successor, the *Mirror*, for 35 years. Newspaper advertisements followed the same line. One showed a young woman being admired by a trio of men; the caption read, 'Charming but I wonder if she can cook?' Apparently it would not matter yet: youth could have 'its joyous fling' and then she would be saved from domestic disaster by using Edmonds.[34]

Campaigns also targeted younger consumers, such as one in 1920 and 1921 called 'A Series for the Children', that used well-known children's stories: the genie produced a tin of Edmonds for Aladdin from his magic lamp; and the wicked wolf followed Little Red Riding Hood because her basket contained 'lovely cakes and other dainties' made with Edmonds.[35] In 1931, *The Edmonds Custard Fairy Book*, designed and illustrated by Valentine Studios in Christchurch, offered children 'fine pictures which you can paint'.[36]

Edmonds' steadily increasing sales suggested the effectiveness of these and other advertising campaigns. When a *Press* reader wondered whether certain products, including Edmonds baking powder, Adams Bruce cake, Sunlight soap and Bournville cocoa, were more expensive thanks to the cost of advertising, it was pointed out that advertising actually made such commodities cheaper because, without it, they would not be sold in anything like the same quantities.[37]

In its efforts to appeal to consumers, Edmonds did not overlook children. A special children's edition of the cookery book was also published. The advertisement opposite is from 1914. There were colouring competitions and, in 1931, the release of *The Edmonds Custard Fairy Book*.

SOLD EVERYWHERE
EDMONDS'
PRIZE
ESTD 1879
BAKING·POWDER
MAMA'S FAVOURITE

Tin production, c.1950, 200 completed tins per minute

Tin making, c.1950

Packing sponge mix, c.1950

Factory floor, 1922

Filling room floor, 1923

Engineers' workshop (left) and case-making department, c.1950

75th anniversary celebrations, 1954

Staff receiving awards for 25+ years of service, 1951

Colin Hart in the laboratory

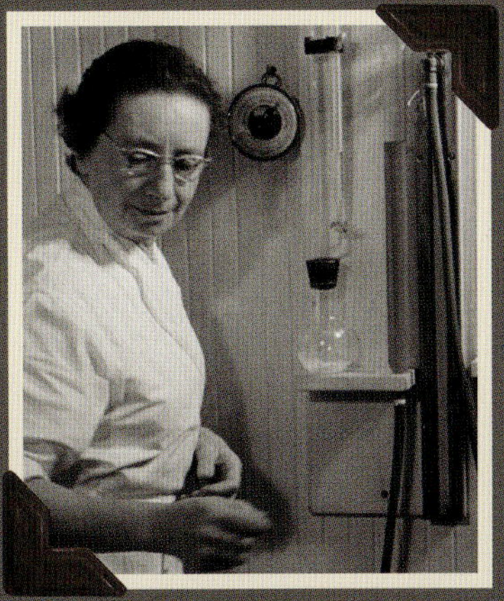

Dr Rosa Stern, scientist, 1955

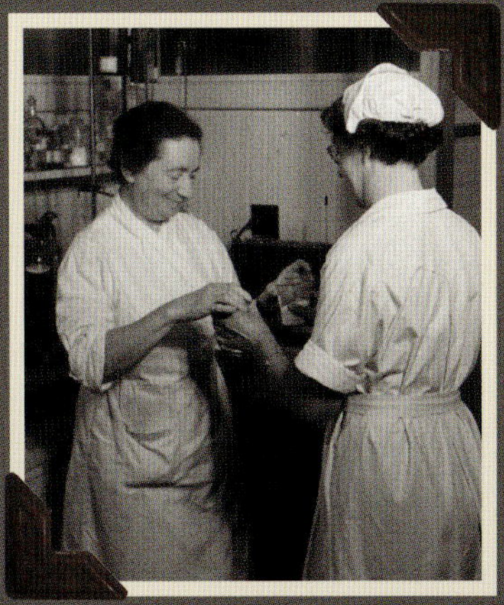

Dr Stern & colleague

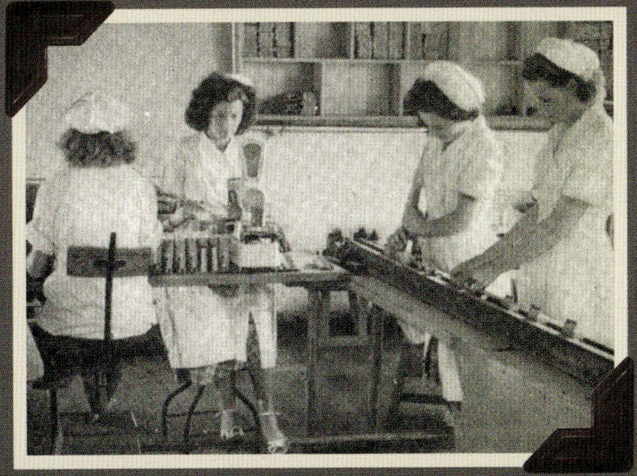

Packing jelly crystals, c.1950

Staff, 1950s

Staff of T.J. Edmonds Ltd, March 1937

CHAPTER 11

BENEFACTORS & BELIEVERS

'This being the 50th anniversary of our arrival in Christchurch ... it is my duty to perform the very pleasant task of unveiling the foundation stone of this clock tower, telephone cabinet, and letter box, which Mrs Edmonds and myself desire to present to the citizens of Christchurch, as a memento of the many years of happiness we have spent in your City ...'[1] Thomas Edmonds was speaking to a group of dignitaries and citizens gathered on the corner of Chester and Madras streets on a Thursday in the spring of 1929. The date, 26 September, was significant: it was 50 years to the day since he and Jane had disembarked from the *Waitangi* to begin a new life. As always – and perhaps unusually for the times – Thomas gave full credit to the role his wife had played. The clock tower, neo-Gothic in style, stood 32 feet high and, the *Press* noted, was made of stone brought from a number of South Island quarries, as well as from Connemara in Ireland and from Italy. Its two dials faced east and west; on the north and south sides were figures of Father Time carved by William Trethewey, who would find his greatest fame as the sculptor of Christchurch's magnificent war memorial in Cathedral Square. Gargoyles looked out from the corners and, below them, carved trusses added to the ornamentation.

The photo opposite shows the band rotunda in 1932. Below, Thomas and Jane at the official unveiling of the inscription tablet marking their gifting to Christchurch of the clock tower, telephone and letter box.

After the unveiling, the speeches and the cheers, everyone walked along Cambridge Terrace to the future site of another Edmonds gift to the city: a band rotunda, which was to stand on the bank of the Avon between the Manchester and Colombo street bridges. Thomas was very fond of brass-band music. A 'considerably larger crowd' was on hand as he unveiled the tablet for the rotunda that would, boasted Mayor John Archer, be 'the largest of its kind in the Dominion and probably south of the Line. It was a beautiful building, and when lighted would provide a source of delight to the thousands who would come to hear the concerts which would be given on summer evenings by City bands.' At the ensuing afternoon tea in the Caledonian Hall, Thomas proudly announced that the cake was made from self-raising flour.

An interesting superstitious note appeared in the proceedings. Deputy mayor Henry Thacker mentioned that Thomas was the thirteenth member of his family, 'and that it might be observed that the date of the ceremony was the 26th – just double the number 13'. In making a toast to Thomas and Jane at the Caledonian Hall, the mayor also mentioned that both were born on 13 October, though 'he was not going to say who was the older'. He added that when Jane 'had had her fortune told by a gipsy on one of the public commons in England ... she had been told that she would have a husband who would travel to a distant place and his name would become a household word' – and, he said, 'the prophecy has come true.'

It was a busy day. Everyone then adjourned to the Radiant Hall in Kilmore Street, where Thomas unveiled a marble tablet bearing the inscription: 'Dedicated to God for the promotion of health and the arts in the service of humanity.' The money for the building had been raised by the Radiant Health Club as a home for its members, and to meet 'a long-felt want in supplying accommodation for numerous societies'. As the club's president explained, Thomas and Jane were the patron and vice-president respectively. The hall had been built by Radiant Hall Ltd, of which Thomas was chairman of directors, and the largest shareholder: he had met a good portion of the £7000 cost. The mayor was 'very much impressed with the suggestive name of this hall ... I hope that the club will not confine its radiance to its own members, but will cast a radiance all over the city.'[2]

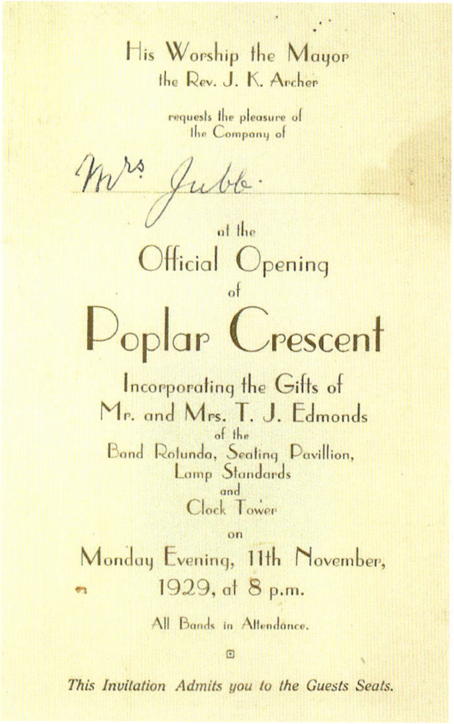
His Worship the Mayor
the Rev. J. K. Archer
requests the pleasure of
the Company of
Mrs Jubb.
at the
Official Opening
of
Poplar Crescent
Incorporating the Gifts of
Mr. and Mrs. T. J. Edmonds
of the
Band Rotunda, Seating Pavillion,
Lamp Standards
and
Clock Tower
on
Monday Evening, 11th November,
1929, at 8 p.m.
All Bands in Attendance.
This Invitation Admits you to the Guests Seats.

Construction delays meant that the clock tower, the circular stone telephone cabinet and a drinking fountain mounted on a stylised acanthus leaf were about a fortnight away from completion, and the Radiant Hall was expected to open its doors in about six weeks. The hope that the rotunda would be completed early in November was not quite realised, but the opening was held on the evening of Armistice Day, 11 November, and it was a memorable occasion, even reported in the Brisbane *Telegraph*, which described a crowd of 'well over ten thousand people' and 'a grand concert by the massed bands of Christchurch'. When the rotunda lights were switched on at 8 p.m., to 'magnificent effect', a great cheer arose from the banks of the river and the Manchester Street bridge. Jane Edmonds then cut the striking orange ribbon.[3] The national anthem was followed by the inevitable sincere speeches, and the reminder that, in accordance with Thomas's wish, the stretch of river where the new rotunda stood would be known as Poplar Crescent after the trees planted there, and after his London birthplace, 'a very populous part of London which would now be immortalised in Christchurch'.[4] In his words of thanks, the deputy mayor said that 'for a long time in Ferry Road there had been a big sign, "Sure to Rise", and Mr and Mrs Edmonds had risen that night'.[5] The occasion was rounded out, of course, with a band concert, led by the Canterbury Caledonian Society's Highland Pipe Band. Thomas and Jane had also given six streetlamps – a gift that was matched by another six from the Christchurch Beautifying Association. The clock tower soon became a point of reference in the city and often featured in advertisements: '298 Oxford Terrace, Furnished and Unfurnished Rooms to let, conveniences; near Edmonds' Clock.'[6]

• • •

Throughout their lives Thomas and Jane were drawn to what would now be called alternative philosophies and spiritual beliefs. The family regularly attended St Peter's Presbyterian Church, on the corner of Ferry and Aldwins roads, and Thomas and Jane supported the Baptist church, but their interests and inclinations also took them into spiritualism, theosophy and the Radiant Living movement.

Spiritualism, which is based on the belief that the spirits of the dead are able to communicate with the living, to their moral and ethical benefit, was extremely popular worldwide, especially after so many men were killed in the First World War. Jane Edmonds, in particular, seems to have been drawn to what was termed Christian spiritualism, which had a strong social element. As a newspaper article explained, it 'concerns itself no longer with phenomena merely, but undertakes to explain the mysteries of the Christian religion, of which [its followers] consider themselves the faithful exponents'.[7] Jane was inspired by

As seen in the invitation to the opening of Poplar Crescent, Thomas and Jane made significant gifts to Christchurch; these were also celebrated in *Through the Changing Years*, Edmonds' 1929 jubilee publication.

the visits to Christchurch of Jane Elizabeth Harris, who had made a name for herself as a writer under the pen name 'Jenny Wren' but 'was eventually won over by the prospect of a purposeful life after death' and became a successful medium, renowned for her 'trance lectures'.[8]

In early March 1898 Harris gave her first Christchurch lecture, at the Choral Hall in Latimer Square, which was followed by others on subjects that included 'Women's Work and Influence: Past, Present and Future', 'God, Who is He? Where is He? What has He done for Man?' and 'The Cry of the Children'. By the time she returned to the city at the end of 1899, a local group had been established, to which Jane belonged. The *Press* advertisement for Harris's 'Inspirational Lecture' on 'Footfalls of Humanity' noted, as well, the 'Wednesday Meeting, Theosophical Hall, Lichfield street, 8 p.m. Friday. Public Circle, 8 p.m. Daily Clairvoyante Readings, 2 to 5, at Mrs Edmonds', Ferry road, near St. Peter's'.[9]

Rather more troublingly, Thomas and his sister-in-law Sarah became involved with Oakley Crawford, an American bigamist and swindler who called himself Arthur Bently Worthington when he arrived in Christchurch in 1890. After making his presence known via a series of well-attended lectures, he and his supposed wife Mary Plunkett, later known as Sister Magdala, proceeded with a plan to establish a new sect known as the Students of Truth. His gift of the gab and easy charm ensured a large number of enthusiastic disciples. On the corner of Madras and Gloucester streets, opposite Latimer Square, arose an impressive classical Temple of Truth, which was opened in 1892. But Worthington's dodgy dealings soon became clear. In July 1894 one Elizabeth Mary Ingram sued the Students of Truth Society Trust Board to recover the interest on debentures issued by this group: one of the eight trustees, who had bought the land for the temple and later leased the building to Worthington, was T.J. Edmonds. He had acted

Below, Thomas's interest in alternative philosophies led to his involvement with the Temple of Truth. Opposite, the Edmonds clock tower became a favourite meeting spot and remains a beloved feature of the city.

in good faith and from genuine belief, as had Sarah, who had already expressed her anger in a feisty letter to the *Press* on 18 May. When she called on Worthington, 'as he chooses to call himself', to ask when he intended to pay the long-awaited promised interest on a £50 loan advanced for the Temple of Truth:

> Instead of receiving a courteous answer from a gentleman, he used towards me most abusive language, put his hands upon me, notwithstanding my protest, and then took me by the shoulders, and by brute force pushed me out of his front door.
>
> Now, Sir, how long is this man to be allowed to fool and victimise the people as he is doing? I hear he has another victim on hand, whom he condescends to allow on his platform, and that simply because of his money. Should he succeed in getting that he will simply cast him off, as he has already done the woman and her children he brought here with him, and who but for others would now be helpless and destitute.[10]

Worthington, his past laid bare, fled to Tasmania. When he returned to Christchurch early in September 1897, he was met by friends, but after his first public lecture was 'immediately assailed with hooting, groaning and personal remarks'; he and his companions, 'escorted by several policemen', were followed by between 200 and 300 angry and vocal men and women. For the only time in the city's history, the Riot Act was read.[11]

The Edmonds family – particularly Thomas, Jane and Beatrice – had a keen interest in Theosophy, a religious movement founded in New York in the late nineteenth century by Russian émigrée Madame Helena Blavatsky. The Theosophical Society lists its three main beliefs or objectives as: '1. To form a nucleus of the universal brotherhood of humanity, without distinction of race, creed, sex, caste, or color. 2. To encourage the comparative study of religion, philosophy, and science. 3. To investigate unexplained laws of nature and the powers latent in humanity.'[12] As early as 1893 the society was at pains to point out that 'Mr Worthington had not, and never had, any connection with the Theosophical Society, nor did the majority of the local Theosophists attach any value to his teaching, the substance of which had long since been condemned by Madame Blavatsky.'[13]

From June 1894, when a Christchurch branch was established, the Theosophical Society held frequent public meetings and lectures. Thomas, Jane and Beatrice were definitely involved by late

November 1919, when an advertisement for a lecture of 'Ideal Education' promised that Miss Beatrice Edmonds would be the soloist,[14] and she performed again in October the following year. In the 1933 edition of *Who's Who*, Thomas Edmonds' religion was given as Theosophy.[15]

With no official home of its own, the Christchurch Theosophical Society met in various places – in the Opera House in Tuam Street and at addresses in Lichfield, Armagh and Manchester streets. In 1925, when the society planned to build a permanent hall at 267 Cambridge Terrace, it employed leading Christchurch architect Cecil Wood to design the building. The estimated cost of £5000 was to be raised partly by public appeal and thereafter a loan. After checking out the plan and the cost, Thomas generously donated the £500 needed to buy the land, and loaned the balance at 5 per cent interest. He also advanced, from 1 August 1926, the sum of £2500, 1.5 per cent of which would be a yearly donation to the building fund until the money was paid back.[16] Wood designed a handsome two-storey neo-Georgian building made of brick and stone that featured 'a columned portico, quoins, multi-pane windows and a hipped roof of slate'. The foundation stone was unveiled at a very precise time in 1926: 4.43 p.m. on the afternoon of Sunday 25 July – said to be the date and time at which the Buddha had preached his first sermon in India.[17]

Thomas and Jane generously supported the development of the Theosophical Society Building, above, and the Radiant Hall, later known as the Repertory Theatre.

In July 1929, Thomas and Jane judged the best costumes at a 'Theosophical Dance' held in the Cambridge Terrace hall: the 'most original lady' was a Miss F. Maclay, who came as 'Radiant Health'.[18] The Radiant Living movement grew out of the late-nineteenth-century American philosophy of New Thought, and the movement and its Radiant Health Clubs were propounded

in New Zealand and elsewhere by Phoebe Holmes. Her disciple, the colourful Herbert Sutcliffe, established his first School of Radiant Living in Providence, Rhode Island, in 1931. Another 36 schools were established over the following 20 years, 12 of them in New Zealand.[19] The precepts of Radiant Living were fairly complicated and hard to pin down, but they involved holistic psychological, physical and spiritual health; diet was also important.

Sutcliffe did not visit New Zealand until 1938, but Phoebe Holmes lectured here well before that and gathered many enthusiastic followers. After she left Christchurch in January 1929, a local reporter noted that she would 'long be remembered by all who came in touch with her'. The Christchurch Radiant Health Club was formed in Christchurch to carry on the 'benevolent work' she had begun;[20] Jane and Thomas were two of the 14 foundation members. The club held weekly meetings, and included 'in its province of activities the study of Christian psychology, health, diet, and solar plexus breathing'; by late February its membership had reached almost 300.[21]

In early April the *Press* reported that the club had bought a section 'for the erection of a hall to be utilised for the club's activities and for the spiritual teaching of Christian psychology and healthful exercises',[22] and tenders for the building, designed by H.F. Willis, were called for. Well-known local builder Charles Luney won the contract: his company built many of the city's most famous buildings, including the Christchurch Town Hall. The Radiant Hall was a notable piece of architecture – a combined theatre and hall, with seating for 800 and a stage designed by Professor James Shelley, founding professor of education at Canterbury College and a leading figure in the city's arts scene. The hall later became the home of the Repertory

Theatre, which Shelley had founded in 1928. The stage, 'one of the largest in the Dominion', was 57 feet wide and 48 feet deep, with a proscenium arch 28 feet across, and was fitted with 'a complete modern cyclorama'. The theatre was decorated in ivory and bronze, and the exterior was 'in Spanish mission style'.[23]

When the hall was opened on 13 November 1929, 500 excited members of the Christchurch Radiant Health Club were on hand to celebrate 'the accomplishment of many months of scheming, planning, and anticipation'. Jane named the hall 'Radiant', turned a special golden key to open it, 'and the eagerness of the waiting people made the wide doors seem too small'.[24] Unfortunately, like the Theosophical Hall, this building fell victim to the 2010 and 2011 Canterbury earthquakes.

• • •

Thomas had yet another gift to bestow on his beloved city, this time to mark the province's eightieth birthday in December 1930. As he wrote in a letter to Mayor Archer, he had much pleasure in giving 'a parcel of land of seven building sections at the corner of River and Wainoni roads, this land to be held in trust by City for the purpose of a public reserve for the free use and enjoyment of the people of Greater Christchurch'. Thomas had bought the land two years before 'for the purpose of safeguarding the riverside boulevard, which work, I trust, will be carried to completion at an early date'. He added a special request: 'It is my desire that permission be granted for the placing of a suitable memorial to the late Professor Bickerton on the north-east corner of the above reserve.'[25]

Late nineteenth-century Christchurch was, in Geoffrey Rice's words, 'an exciting place, buzzing with new ideas' and 'full of radicals, reformers and eccentrics',[26] and the most famous – some would say notorious – among them was Alexander William Bickerton. He had arrived in Christchurch a few years before Thomas and his family, to become the first professor of chemistry at Canterbury College. But he ended up going well beyond his original remit: he also taught physics, gave public science lectures, and served as a government analyst – it was probably in this capacity that he first met Thomas Edmonds, while testing his baking powder. He clashed with the university over teaching duties and administration, and on larger issues concerning its general approach to education.[27] Bickerton began pursuing what became, for him, a lifelong passion – his theory that 'the partial impact of heavenly bodies was the origin of new stars and the cause of other unexplained astronomical phenomena'. His theory of 'a self-sustaining universe with no transcendent God' won scant support.[28] However, his bohemian way of life and outspoken socialist and anti-war ideas did not help.

Thomas Edmonds donated land for a reserve to honour his old friend Alexander Bickerton (left), an eccentric professor of chemistry who also created a popular pleasure park in Wainoni. In the hand-coloured photo on the following pages, taken around 1930, the rotunda, clock tower and telephone cabinet donated by Thomas and Jane can all be seen.

The Federative Home Bickerton founded at his Wainoni house in 1896 worked on cooperative principles. A few members ran small industries on site, among them a fireworks factory. After Bickerton was eventually fired by the university in March 1902, he established the Wainoni Remedy Manufacturing Company, producing patent medicines, and he turned his property into a public pleasure park that included popular attractions such as a zoo and a Punch and Judy show; it also became famous for its spectacular firework displays. Bickerton left for England in July 1910, and never returned.

Thomas, with his own interest in chemistry and astronomy, was drawn to Bickerton and the pair became good friends. Gertrude and Beatrice remembered him as 'the sort of man who when he came into a room left an impression' and as 'a great character'. Both sisters recalled 'the short, black-coated, bearded figure coming up the path to their home'; Beatrice spoke, too, of his 'strange high laugh'. He would bring with him a flax bag that Jane always filled with food.[29] In England, Bickerton continued to fight for acceptance of his partial impact theory, with financial assistance from fellow New Zealander Ernest Rutherford. Not long before his death in London on 22 January 1929, the college with which he'd had such a vexed relationship made him professor emeritus and the New Zealand government granted him an annuity. Bickerton's eldest son, Alexander, also served as an analyst in Canterbury and reported on a diverse range of commercial products, including hair tonic, beer, cocoa and Edmonds baking powder.

CHAPTER 12

FAREWELL TO THE FOUNDER

By the time of Edmonds' fiftieth anniversary in 1929, annual sales figures of its 'Pure Grape Cream of Tartar Baking Powder' stood at nearly 3 million tins. One advertisement celebrating that glorious jubilee year focused on the long-standing importance to the New Zealand housewife of this core product. Others likened the growth of the company from its origins in a 'tiny store' in Christchurch to the story of the acorn and the mighty oak.[1] The beginnings of the Edmonds empire were related to landmark historical events, such as the laying of the first submarine trans-Tasman telegraph cable in 1876, and the 'great Tarawera Eruption' of 1886.[2]

The company's jubilee was marked with the publication of a handsome commemorative booklet, *Through the Changing Years*, in which Thomas expressed his 'appreciation of the long-continued patronage accorded … by the housewives of New Zealand': over 50 years it had been his 'constant aim' to serve them.[3] Thomas himself was not forgotten. His loyal and appreciative staff presented him with a signed, illuminated testimonial as a 'token of their high estimation' for a man who had 'gained golden opinions'. At the bottom were two Latin tags: 'Suaviter in modo fortiter' (Pleasantly in manner, powerfully in deed) and 'Venit, Vidit, Vicit' ('He came, he saw, he conquered' – after the phrase attributed to Julius Caesar).

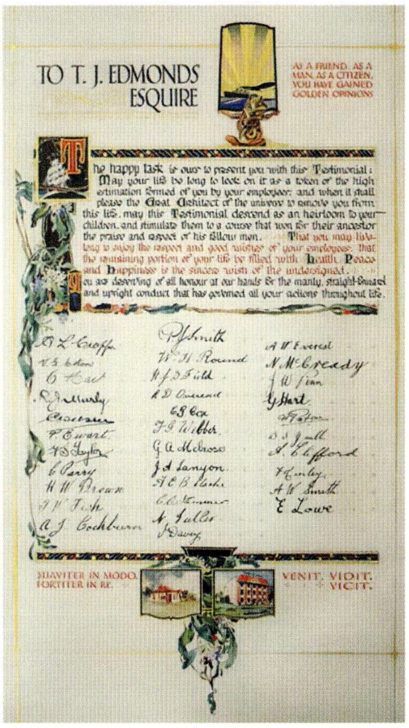
TO T. J. EDMONDS
ESQUIRE

AS A FRIEND, AS A MAN, AS A CITIZEN, YOU HAVE GAINED GOLDEN OPINIONS

The happy task is ours to present you with this Testimonial: May your life be long to look on it as a token of the high estimation formed of you by your employees; and when it shall please the Great Architect of the universe to remove you from this life, may this Testimonial descend as an heirloom to your children, and stimulate them to a course that won for their ancestor the praise and respect of his fellow men. That you may live long to enjoy the respect and good wishes of your employees; that the remaining portion of your life be filled with health, Peace and happiness is the sincere wish of the undersigned. You are deserving of all honour at our hands for the manly, straightforward and upright conduct that has governed all your actions throughout life.

SUAVITER IN MODO. FORTITER IN RE.

VENIT. VIDIT. VICIT.

The photograph of Thomas in 1908 was inscribed 'My Jubilee', a reference to his fiftieth birthday. The decorative testimonial was given to Thomas by Edmonds staff as part of the company's 1929 jubilee celebrations.

There were changes on the product front, too. Custard powder, including some flavours, had long been an Edmonds staple but, come 1932, consumers 'in main towns' could purchase additional flavours in handy little tins that cost 6d.[4] Sure to Set jelly crystals were also launched in 1935, a range of 'table jellies' available in 12 flavours: lemon, cherry, raspberry, pineapple, mandarin, red currant, strawberry, lime fruit, nectarine, greengage, orange and peach. Easy to make, they were guaranteed to produce 'quivering, sparkling shapes of radiant colours',[5] a visual strength that would quickly underpin some bold and attractive advertisements.

In another development in 1929, the company launched baking powder in a 5-pound tin – a move expected to find favour with 'large establishments' such as boarding houses and hotels.[6] This innovation was touted as an ideal Christmas present for those at 'Home' (back in Britain): 'Give a Gift that is Made in New Zealand ... Show the folks overseas what New Zealand can do!'[7] The 'Sure to Rise' baking powder range was further extended a year or two later with the launch of a 4-ounce tin – 'the useful little size in Edmonds that has been needed'[8] – and a huge 28-pound container in 1935. A suggestion that the latter would allow grocers to sell the powder 'loose' drew a rapid and sharp response from the company, which advised that the tins were intended as a 'special pack ... for large users only ... and not for any other purpose'.[9]

The celebration of Edmonds' achievements coincided, of course, with the Great Depression, which was sparked in October 1929 by the Wall Street crash and went on to cause widespread unemployment and hardship, and riots in New Zealand's main centres in the autumn of 1932. As the effects of the slump deepened, there were growing requests for donations of essential foodstuffs to assist the unemployed. Loose baking powder was one of the staples, along with butter, that were sought by voluntary relief workers at the mayor's St Andrew Street depot in Dunedin.[10] A culture of 'making-do' was especially prevalent during the Depression, and empty baking powder and kerosene tins contributed to this Kiwi ingenuity. Members of the Women's Institute made footstools from clusters of baking powder tins; one, from Manawatū, was padded and covered with cretonne.[11] The Otago Home Economics Association made toys for distribution to children in needy families – including two watering cans made from 5-pound baking powder tins, with nozzles fashioned out of perforated tobacco tins. A popular toy was a telephone set made from a pair of baking powder tins, their open ends covered with brown paper and connected by a length of stout string.[12]

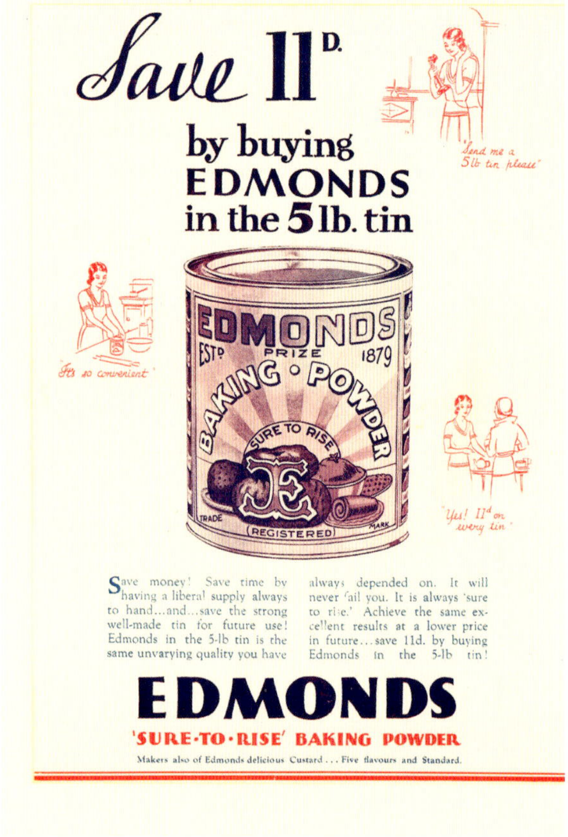

A collection of handy hints for farmers that appeared in the 1930s included what was surely one of the most creative uses of an empty baking powder tin: by smearing it with butter and setting it on a shaft at the top of an empty kerosene tin, it became a mousetrap. The hapless mouse, attracted by the butter, would jump onto the slippery tin, only to lose its grip and end up trapped at the bottom.[13] Such cunning ideas may have accounted for a number of empty tins, but the majority likely ended up in rubbish tips. Christchurch, a city where so many baking powder tins were produced, had its own solution to the problem: the discarded containers were rolled flat to make a firm and solid foundation for the construction of roads.[14]

• • •

Unlike many other businesses, Edmonds prospered in the hard years, thanks, as David Cropp put it, 'to the habits of the New Zealand housewife'. Baking was always considered a necessity, and although the family was 'conscious that there was a Depression on … it never hurt us'.[15] But there were challenges. Back in 1921, the rising cost of consumer goods had led to the establishment in Wellington of a Self Help Co-operative grocery store, and by early 1930 there were 20 such stores in the Auckland region alone. By March 1931, however, Self Help claimed it was 'on the black list for a leading brand of baking powder' because it refused to make a 36.7 per cent profit on cost.[16] Edmonds was not alone in this; at one point Self Help refused to stock several other well-known domestic products, including Lane's Emulsion, Aspros, Bell Tea and Marmite, for the same reason. Edmonds responded by lowering the price of its 5-pound tins in the main centres, first to 7s (in 1931) and later to 6s.[17] Self Help had its own brand: the 'large household size' sold for 1s, compared with 1s 1d for Edmonds, and so it could claim to be 'again to the fore in reducing the cost of living'.[18]

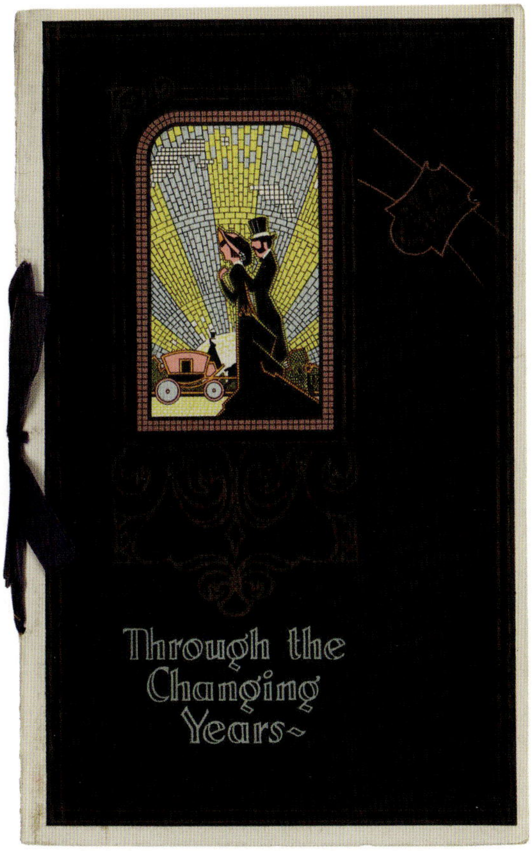

The launch of the 5-pound tin in 1929 provided an opportunity for a new advertising angle. In the same year, the cover of Edmonds' jubilee publication made striking use of Art Deco styling.

But that was not the end of the matter: the disagreement between Edmonds and Self Help reached the Supreme Court in Christchurch in November 1931 – and possibly set a precedent for exhibiting tins of baking powder in a courtroom. Edmonds sought an injunction to restrain Self Help from using the words 'Bound to Rise' printed over a sample of baking, in this case a cake; and it made a related claim that the products looked too similar and could deceive customers. The defence pointed out that Self Help's 'Bound to Rise' trademark was in existence 25 years before Edmonds registered its 'Sure to Rise' label trademark in 1913. After a great deal of often entertaining legal tit for tat, Mr Justice Adams eventually concluded that 'the striking differences as to colour and appearance generally are so obvious that no reasonable person could be deceived' and reserved judgement in favour of Self Help. It is hard not to think that the judge rather enjoyed the case: at one point he told the Edmonds lawyer, 'Your client says that the proof of the pudding is in the baking powder.'[19]

Self Help was soon able to report that sales of its baking powder were increasing, appropriately, 'by leaps and bounds',[20] a growth helped no doubt by the fact that the cooperative now had 125 stores throughout New Zealand – and by the recent publicity of the court case. Perhaps taking another leaf out of Edmonds' book, in late 1932 Self Help produced a 242-page publication of recipes and household hints. The book cost 2s 6d, but was offered free to customers who purchased goods to the value of £1 in one order.[21]

• • •

This enchanting 1933 advertisement, with its levitating tin, conveyed a sense of progress (although the suggestion of neon lighting was for effect only) and needed no advertising copy. As seen in the illustration of Christchurch's Cathedral Square opposite, bright lights and cinemas offered a welcome diversion during the dark days of the Depression.

STAR
TIMES

Grocer Manufacturer Philanthropist

Death of Mr. T. J. Edmonds,

Founder of

T. J. Edmonds Ltd.

Christchurch

THE death of Mr. T. J. Edmonds, Chairman of Directors of T. J. Edmonds Ltd., Christchurch, removes from our midst an outstanding personality. A native of London, Mr. Edmonds was born 74 years ago. He, together with Mrs. Edmonds, arrived in Lyttelton on the ship "Waitangi" in 1879, starting in a very small way in business as a grocer in premises in Ferry Road, near to the present site of the well-known factory of T. J. Edmonds Ltd. The grocery trade fifty years ago was vastly different from what it is to-day, and it would then occasion no surprise in that Mr. Edmonds drifted into making his own baking powder, from which small beginning grew the large and flourishing business of to-day, a business which may be regarded as unique among the manufacturing industries of New Zealand. The business was, a few years ago, formed into a private company, and though Mr. Edmonds ceased to participate actively in the business, he ocupied the position of chairman of Directors until his death. He was also very closely associated with the Australian branch of the business, the Australian Cream of Tartar Company from which the raw material for "Edmonds" Baking Powder is obtained. From one point of view Mr. Edmonds would not be regarded as a public man, yet he always manifested a keen interest in public affairs. Many of our readers will remember how but a few years ago we had pleasure in publishing an account of the celebration of the golden jubilee of the arrival of Mr. and Mrs. Edmonds in New Zealand. It was on that occasion he presented the city of Christchurch the very fine band rotunda on the North bank of the Avon between the Colombo and Manchester Street bridges, whilst on the South bank further east he provided a clock tower with telephone and letter boxes. The presentation was a fitting acknowledgement of what Mr. Edmonds regarded he and his wife owed to the city, whose citizens had, he considered, contributed in no small measure to whatever success had been theirs. With considerable foresight Mr. Edmonds had chosen the eastern portion of the city, hoping that others might be imbued with a desire to make Christchurch the City Beautiful, as its pioneers had originally planned. Amongst other benefactors was the gift of a section at Wainooni for the erection of a memorial to Professor Bickerton. Another gift was the provision of an organ in the new Colombo Street Baptist Church. Whilst prominence is given to the forementioned gifts, they probably fall into insignificance having regard to the private benefactions, for it is recorded of Mr. Edmonds that he never turned a deaf ear when approached for assistance for any deserving cause.

It may be said of Mr. Edmonds that in business he was straight-forward and honourable in all his dealings, and having once fixed his course he turned not neither to the right hand nor the left. From the path of business integrity he never swerved.

He is survived by his widow, by a brother Mr. Edward Edmonds, New Brighton, by three sons, Messrs Ernest, T. H., and J. D. Edmonds, of Christchurch (his eldest son, Mr. T. W. Edmonds, died in 1914), and by four daughters, Mesdames A. L. Cropp, H. S. Williams, K. Ballantyne, of Christchurch, and Mrs. S. T. Fripp, of London.

To the above we tender our very deep sympathy. The funeral of the deceased gentleman took place at the Linwood Cemetery amidst a great assembly of the public, making an imposing tribute to his public benefactions, and showed the high regard in which he had been held by all sections of the community. Among those present at the grave-side was the Mayor (Mr. D. G. Sullivan, M.P.), who delivered a eulogy on the life and character of Mr. Edmonds. The Mayor paid a very fine tribute, making special reference to the high ideals that had always characterised Mr. Edmond's business relations, at the same time stating that those who knew him best know that he not only possessed high ideals, and an unblemished character, but added to these an exceedingly warm and kind heart.

A few months after the Self Help squabble ended, T.J. Edmonds Ltd lost its founder. Late on the evening of 2 June 1932, a few weeks after returning from a trip to Australia to see the opening of the Sydney Harbour Bridge, Thomas died at Lewisham Hospital in Christchurch, aged 74. He had been in a prime position to observe the official ceremony, in a seat next to the vice-regal stand, and had seemed in good spirits when he got home, giving interviews to both local papers and advancing his thoughts on the international situation – 'The world is in trouble, which has been brought about mostly by the past great World War' – and about the state of affairs across the Tasman. He told the *Star* reporter that, in his opinion, 'Matters were not at all promising in New South Wales.' Not only was the daily interest bill on the new bridge £15,000, but businesses, including buses and charabancs, were 'very heavily taxed and the general responsible opinion was that there would be no improvement until a new Government had taken office'.[22] 'Business people and private individuals alike are sick of conditions as they exist at present in Sydney,' Thomas informed the *Press*, and a drop in imported goods meant 'many wholesale warehouses were feeling the pinch and were in danger of going into liquidation'. The city's business people were 'far from being optimistic'.[23]

Thomas 'appeared to be in his usual good health' and many friends 'remarked how well he was looking'. It was a shock, therefore, when 'he complained of not feeling very well, and on the advice of his medical man he took to his bed, heart trouble having been diagnosed'.[24] His death was widely reported and the obituaries were full of praise for 'one of the most generous of public benefactors Christchurch has ever known ... A man who took a pride in his city and in its growth and improvement, Mr Edmonds has left behind him many monuments of his sincerity of purpose and extreme generosity.' His love of beauty was lauded: he 'not only strove to improve the appearance of the city by giving freely, but he surrounded his business premises in Ferry Road with a garden which is the delight of residents of the district and visitors'. And, of course, he had watched his company 'grow from small beginnings to a flourishing business'.[25] John Archer, the former mayor and a Baptist minister, described Thomas as 'a fine man and a valued citizen, who loved his city and did a lot of kindness in more ways than one'; he added that the one word he would always associate with Thomas was 'Radiance'.[26]

Thomas's death in 1932 led to an outpouring of condolences and tributes, among them this obituary from *The N.Z. Bakers' & Grocers' Review.*

Thomas's funeral, held at Linwood Cemetery on 5 June, was attended by a 'great assembly of people', and the graveside service 'made an imposing tribute to his public benefactions and showed in what high regard he has been held by all sections of the community'. Many cars followed the cortège from Worcester Street to Linwood, where the Woolston Brass Band, playing that favourite of the period, the 'Dead March' from Handel's *Saul*, led the funeral procession into the cemetery. The bandsmen then stood around the grave for Thomas's favourite hymn, 'Lead, Kindly Light'. Everyone sang 'Abide With Me', before Mayor Dan Sullivan began his eulogy. Thomas's business dealings had always been scrupulously honest, Sullivan said, 'but those who knew him best knew that he had not only high ideals and an unblemished character but an exceedingly warm and kind heart. Many citizens would be sorrowing at his death, for he was never known to send away empty-handed any who approached him in their hour of distress.' It was clear to the city that someone of stature had died: for two days the flags on the Christchurch Municipal Chambers and the Municipal Electricity Department were flown at half-mast.[27] Thomas was buried alongside his eldest son, Will.

The newspapers were quick to report that Thomas's generosity had continued after his death: he left £1000 each to Plunket and to St Saviour's Orphanage. His family, of course, were the main beneficiaries of the will. Ernest was to have the income from an invested £4000, paid six-monthly, 'for the remainder of his lifetime'. Thomas explained this arrangement was made 'because of his mode of living and that I have already made advances to him in lifetime which … are hereby forgiven him'. He left £500 each to Ernest's wife Ethel and their two daughters. Beyond that, the estate was to be equally divided between Jane, Lilian, Gertrude, Beatrice, Irene, George, James and Will's widow, Alice. Thomas left his 'rolled gold watch (chiming)' to George, his 'gold albert' (watch chain) to James and his 'wearing apparel' to Ernest.[28]

• • •

As New Zealand struggled to find its way out of the Depression, there were changes in the world Thomas had known. It was around this time, August 1932, that Edmonds began producing a second baking powder, Acto. (The name may have implied 'active', or followed the style established with Jell-O; it may also have been an acronym for the Australian Cream Tartar Company.) Acto was advertised frequently throughout the 1930s, its main selling point being that it was cheaper than Sure to Rise. In March 1933, for example, one retailer was advertising a tin of Acto for 11d, compared with 1s 3d for Edmonds Sure to Rise.[29] Like Sure to Rise, Acto was at this point made with cream of tartar, and the reasons for its lower price are unclear; perhaps it indicated a different grade of that vital ingredient, or possibly it was the same product, branded differently and sold at a lower price to attract other customers and make it harder for competitors to find space on grocers' shelves. Although it was manufactured by Edmonds, the label appears to have kept this a secret (something that piqued the interest of the health regulator), as did all but a handful of newspaper advertisements.[30]

This portrait of Thomas Edmonds was by well-known Christchurch artist Archibald Nicoll. Opposite, Edmonds released Acto in 1932 as a second cream of tartar powder and a cheaper option (possibly the same powder), but kept their name off the label. Grocers' advertisements often promoted both powders together and sometimes let the secret slip.

A good deal happened in 1935. In a sign of the times, and of the profile of the company, in March managing director Bert Cropp accepted a nomination from the Radio 3ZM Club as South Island listeners' representative on the newly established Broadcasting Board.[31] He made sure, too, that the spirit of generosity lived on at the company. From late May to the beginning of November, T.J. Edmonds Ltd supplied the 500 children of Woolston School with half a pint of milk a day. A number of other firms throughout the country did the same in other schools, in a response to concerns about the 'seriousness of the deficiency in the diet of many children [in] the economic conditions of to-day'.[32]

Then, on 5 August, the Edmonds directors, having unanimously agreed that it was 'desirable to reconstruct the company', passed a special resolution to liquidate it and reregister under the same name. The reasons for this technical change are unclear, though it may have been related to the provisions of the Companies Act 1933 or perhaps a desire to tidy up administratively following Thomas's death. The company's share value had grown enormously, from £25,000 to £200,000. Ten family members, including Will's widow, Alice, and Jane, held all but £4000 of the shares, which went to long-serving factory manager Philip Smith, who had been a shareholder for some time.[33]

In November 1935, the company instituted a 40-hour week for its staff. This initiative was enshrined in a growing number of industrial awards throughout the 1930s, and the long-fought-for shorter working week was made law in 1936 by the Industrial and Conciliation Amendment Act and the Factories Amendment Act.[34] The move made sense in a period of high unemployment. As the *Thames Star* reported, 'The principle of the shorter working week has been accepted by the firm of T.J. Edmonds, Ltd … to allow the continued employment of a number of extra hands engaged for work in the factory some time ago. Though the firm is not interested in being credited with pioneering the 40-hour week in Christchurch, it is understood that it is the first considerable firm to make the change.' The factory usually employed about 50 hands but had recently taken on 'a number of extra men … to make up arrears of work'. Although that crisis was over, 'it was realised that by closing the factory altogether on Saturdays it would be possible to keep the additional men in employment'. As manager F.S. Taylor explained, 'The step has actually involved a certain small sacrifice, but we find that no efficiency at all is lost. We decided that it was the only feasible way of dealing with unemployment.' And there had been no rashness involved: the change had 'been under consideration for the last three or four months'.[35]

According to David Cropp, there was a practical reason for the innovation. 'We used to fill the tins in the morning and label them in the afternoon', but on a Saturday, when the staff worked only in the morning from 8 a.m. to noon, this caused 'a bit of

Baking Powder, Acto, per tin 0 11
We guarantee this to be equal if not superior to any 1/- baking powder on the market.
Edmond's Baking Powder, the best in the world, 8d and 1 3

ACTO BAKING POWDER, 1/- tin.
Made by Edmond's. Have you tried this?

a muddle'. Bert Cropp 'decided they wouldn't come back Saturday morning'. Prime Minister Michael Savage praised the move as 'very enlightened; but it was only convenience'.[36] Fred Kinley worked at Edmonds for many years. He recalls that one Friday he came home and said, 'Guess what, family … I don't have to go to work tomorrow morning!' There had been a staff meeting and an announcement about quarter to five: 'Nobody has to come to work tomorrow … As from now I'm reducing your time to 40 hours a week … and the wages will stay the same.' This initiative was a continuation of Thomas's attitude towards the staff, as Fred's son Ian noted: 'Mr Edmonds [George] was a man who everyone wanted to work for. He had a waiting list of staff who wanted to work at the factory. He never put an advertisement in the paper. He looked after the staff very well. He was very supportive. If anyone was ill they [still] got paid.'[37]

By February 1936, Edmonds was still upbeat about the new working week, although not everyone was entirely convinced. The company, however, described the experiment as 'a great success … The staff was contented because they worked fewer hours with no loss of wages, and the management was satisfied because its production had decreased not at all.' It was true

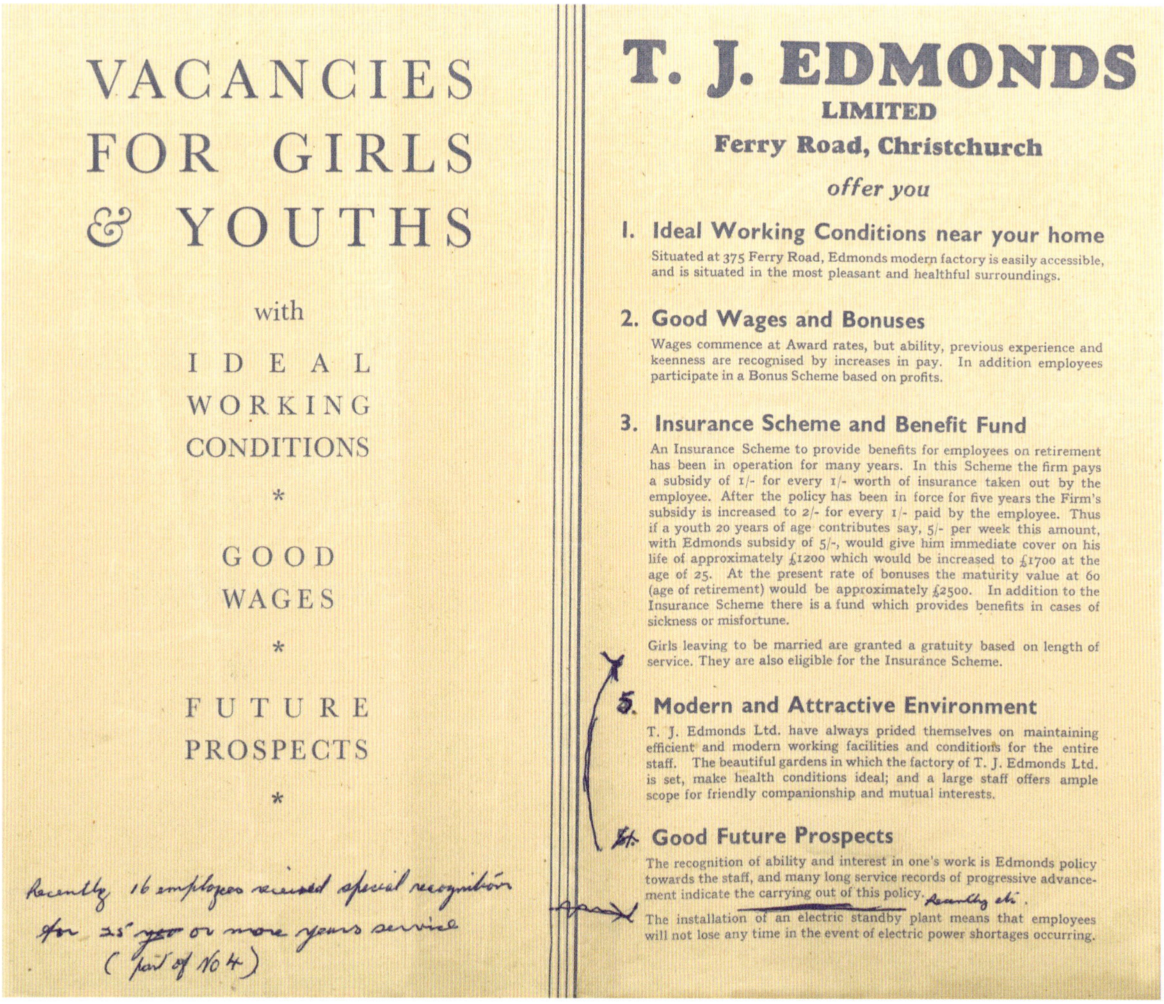

This recruitment leaflet targeted 'girls & youths' with the offer of progressive working conditions. The official staff jubilee photo was taken in September 1929 (see image credits for names).

that Edmonds could shut its plant down in minutes and that its labour charges were not as high as those in many other industries, but closing completely on Saturdays had not been a problem. 'Several hands who were previously listed as temporary employees, although they worked almost full time, have now been absorbed into the permanent staff.'[38]

The press coverage of the 40-hour week mentioned only male employees at Edmonds, but there were a few women working at the factory by then. A 1929 jubilee photo of the staff includes one young woman wearing a dustcoat, whose name is given as Miss V. G. Coton – she was Veda Gladys, aged 17. By 1932 a dozen women were employed.[39] One woman who worked at Edmonds during the Second World War until she was old enough to join the Women's Auxiliary Air Force, and later returned to the company, had a job in the jelly department. 'We used to start in the morning making greaseproof inners which we folded around a wooden mallet and then some girls made up the cardboard packets and we inserted the greaseproof inside. Jelly was measured in by hand and then passed to the weigher and put on a belt where the tops were turned in ready for the girl at the end to glue them down again manually.'[40] It was a long way from Jane sewing flour bags in a little shop on a Woolston street corner. By the time of the seventy-fifth anniversary in 1954, there were 19 women on the payroll.

• • •

The loss of her husband after more than 50 years of marriage was a dreadful blow for Jane, who was left lonely and restless. In the months after Thomas's death she visited Wellington for a few days in June and again in August; in late October Beatrice came home from London to visit her mother, and stayed until Boxing Day. In mid-October the following year, 1933, the furniture at 203 Worcester Street was sold and it was reported that Jane had 'given up her house' and was living at Warner's Hotel in the Square.[41] There was, said the *Press*, 'spirited bidding throughout the sale and excellent prices were obtained'. 'This is one of the best sales of Furniture held in recent years, the lovely Furniture and Carpets being practically new and purchased regardless of cost.' Everything went under the hammer: paintings – two of them by noted British-born New Zealand artist Charles Nathaniel Worsley, Axminster carpets, a suite in rosewood and tapestry and one in moquette, two handsome bedroom suites, a leather easy chair, rugs, mirrors, tables of all shapes and sizes, bronze figures, stair runners – and much more, including even the lawnmower, the 'deposit safe', the radiators, the Hoover carpet sweeper and the linoleum. This had been the comfortable home of a successful self-made couple, who began their lives in impoverished East London. The occasion was both remarkable and sad.[42]

Jane saw much change in her 78 years, from life as a maid in East London, to an important public role as the wife of a successful and prominent businessman.

Jane continued to travel. She went to Sydney in March 1934, and made frequent trips to Wellington, where she stayed at the grand Spanish Mission-style Midland Hotel on the corner of Johnston Street and Lambton Quay. In late April 1935 she returned to New Zealand from a sojourn in Britain. She was in Wellington again in February 1938, living at the Midland, when she was knocked down in the street by a taxi. In a semi-conscious state 78-year-old Jane was taken home to her family in Christchurch where, like her beloved Thomas, she died in Lewisham Hospital on 12 April: a post mortem gave the cause of death as heart failure. In complete contrast to her husband's grand farewell, Jane's interment was private and there were no flowers.[43] Her will was generous to a number of causes, such as the District Nursing Association, the Salvation Army, Plunket, the YWCA and the Woolston Brass Band.

David Cropp knew his grandmother 'much better' than his grandfather. 'She had a restricted education, as most people had in those days. She was inclined to embrace religion, not that she was unpleasant with it – she wouldn't try to proselytise – but she got a lot of comfort from it. She would get hold of mediums. I remember there was one in particular who said she could get grandma in touch with T.J. [after he died], and she was very pleased with that one.'[44] It was Jane's hope of reaching Thomas 'on the other side' that had taken her to her favoured clairvoyant in Wellington who, sadly, deprived her of a good deal of money.[45]

SOLD EVERYWHERE
EDMONDS
ESTD
PRIZE
1879
BAKING • POWDER
SURE TO RISE

CHAPTER 13

WAR & PEACE

Thomas had been right about the world being in trouble. On 3 September 1939 New Zealand, alongside Britain and Australia, formally declared war on Germany after it invaded Poland two days earlier. Before long, this dramatic turn of events would once again affect this country's imported grocery lines, and there was concern that certain essentials, such as baking powder, along with almonds, currants, dates and ginger, would not be available for that year's Christmas cake.[1] By early October such shortages had become a reality, and other staples were affected. Storekeepers began rationing, and shortly nearly 300 lines of goods were placed on a list of prohibited imports.[2] As in the Great War, cream of tartar was 'exceedingly scarce' and soared in price: 'Merchants are at their wits' end to maintain some semblance of stocks.'[3] In some cases baking powder was sold only when purchasers included it in a general order for groceries; loyal customers of Ashburton grocers Fletcher Bros were allowed, with their usual weekly order of perhaps 15 or 20 shillings, a packet of cornflour, a packet of matches or a tin of Edmonds Sure to Rise.[4]

The baking powder situation was not helped when the Union Steam Ship Company vessel *Waikouaiti*, returning from Sydney, ran aground at Dog Island in Foveaux Strait on 28 November 1939. All the crew were rescued, but the ship broke up and among the lost cargo destined for southern ports were some 70,000 pounds of tea, 'a big proportion of the new season's figs' and, even more important than the 'considerable quantity of rum' on board, a load of cream of tartar, 'local stocks of which are practically exhausted'. Because import licences were necessary for such goods, there was little chance of replacing them in the immediate future.[5] Suggestions of panic buying did not help either.

This 1939 advertisement reflects a new, industrial look. The dynamic image of the tin suggests positivity and progress, much needed qualities during the war-time years. Such was the power of the Edmonds tin that it could be used without any explanatory advertising copy.

Maybe the solution to the problem lay elsewhere. 'Grandmother', in a letter to the *Press*, asked, 'Why all the fuss … over the shortage of baking powder? If eggs are used in the making of cakes and the eggs and the cake mixture are well beaten, there is no need to add baking powder. In my day we were not afraid to use time and strength to ensure good results.' To help ease the situation, members of the Women's Division of the Farmers' Union compiled and proposed to circulate recipes that needed neither baking powder nor cream of tartar.[6] In an attempt to stabilise grocery prices, from the beginning of

September 1941 the New Zealand government fixed the prices of 38 essential commodities, including baking powder.[7]

As had happened in the First World War and the Depression, baking powder tins were put to good use. During a power cut in late 1939 the Pleasant Point Town Board in Canterbury was forced to conduct one of its meetings 'by the light of a solitary candle reposing in a baking powder tin'. 'Do not throw away ... baking powder or cocoa tins,' implored the *Patea Mail* in May 1940, 'as these are excellent for packing goods to send overseas. If you have no use for them, hand them to the nearest Women's Institute, and they will distribute them.'[8] By 1941, with the national situation worsening and concern that the country was vulnerable to enemy attack, empty baking powder tins were called up for a more active role. In Cambridge the members of the Home Guard were collecting tins to make homemade bombs. 'While they are called "jam-tin" bombs, actually jam tins are not very suitable, as the tops have to be cut. Tins with close fitting lids, such as have contained baking powder or treacle are the best.' The Home Guard in Whangārei went even further, beseeching housewives to save cocoa and baking powder tins 'so that small bombs can be made to defend your home and property'.[9]

The outbreak of war had threatened to disrupt a national celebration, the New Zealand Centennial Exhibition, marking 100 years since the signing of the Treaty of Waitangi and the beginning of organised European settlement. It was decided, however, that the show must go on as a much-needed national morale booster. The exhibition opened in Wellington on 8 November 1939, and by the time it closed on 4 May 1940 there had been 2,641,043 visitors, an astonishing figure given that the population was then about 1,600,000. Edmonds was on display in the New Zealand Manufacturers' Court, in a complex of structures reflecting the progressive modernism promoted by the event. A tall circular structure, surely inspired by an Edmonds tin, housed a scale model of the company's factory and garden complex at Ferry Road, made especially for the event

Shown below, the Edmonds display at the 1940 Centennial Exhibition. Photographs of the factory, like those opposite, appeared in various editions of the cookery book. The 'jelly ladies' in the lower photograph were among the first women employed as factory workers in the early to mid-1930s.

by George Edmonds. Behind, set into a sweeping curvilinear wall, were displays of company products, and potted palms added a touch of elegance.[10] Visitors to the Edmonds display were also invited to discuss their cookery problems with a trained specialist, a home science graduate, who demonstrated how to make 'delicious cakes, jellies, custards and other dishes'.[11]

Edmonds was also represented at the exhibition in a model of Christchurch, later displayed at the city's Industries Fair. In mid-1941, though, it was discovered that some 20 of the more imposing model buildings were missing from where they were being stored by the Christchurch City Council. Among those presumed to have been 'souvenired' were the cathedral, the Regent Theatre and the Edmonds clock tower.[12]

The Edmonds factory, at full size, had been nominated as perhaps the country's best-known public building 'pictorially' in a late 1939 article urging citizens to help the war effort by buying New Zealand-made goods. It was a 'model edifice': 'The rooms are large, well-lit, lofty and airy, and the general impression of alabaster immaculateness is increased by the white coats, aprons and caps worn by the workers.' Perhaps unaware of the looming crisis, the writer pointed out that the vineyards of France made possible 'the delectable cream-cakes at a Taumarunui afternoon tea'. The Edmonds building was special because it was 'the expression in stone, cement and glass, of a unique personality'. And the staff were loyal: 'On the wall in the manager's office was a group photograph of the whole personnel taken in 1929, and, with three exceptions, the picture would do for to-day's assembly.'[13]

In October 1940 the price of baking powder came before the Price Tribunal, which explained that without the government measures the cost would have 'increased substantially long before this'. The problem was cream of tartar, which had risen in price by up to 100 per cent in the space of a year. By December it looked as though, come February, there would be 'practically no baking powder made with cream of tartar'. Manufacturers would need to make 'phosphate baking powder', a replacement that would be 'in every way satisfactory'.[14] The shortage of cream of tartar sometimes meant that the Edmonds staff could not work a full week, though employees were always well looked after during the war.[15]

Wellington-based W.T. Rawleigh Co. Ltd had been peddling its Good Health Phosphate baking powder door to door since the early 1930s. In response to the current crisis, in 1940 the GUS (Grocers United Stores) chain, which had more than 100 stores throughout the South Island, introduced its own Una baking powder, 'a highly purified phosphate aerator'.[16] Edmonds unblushingly followed suit in March 1941 – after reassuring the public the previous month, under the headline, 'No Cause for Alarm', that a halt to cream of tartar supplies would not mean the disappearance of its famous baking powder. The company's scientific staff had been on the job. 'Rather than alter the formula of their famous "Sure-to-Rise" Baking Powder, and so as to avoid the disappointment and concern that a complete withdrawal from the market would cause, Edmonds have therefore decided to introduce ACTO Baking Powder.' They had 'formulated' a phosphate-based alternative and repurposed the Acto brand name – but this time proudly owned by the company.[17] Given that Acto as a brand had been around for almost 10 years, Edmonds was slightly stretching the truth in implying that it had 'introduced' a new product in order to 'keep faith with the women of New Zealand'. But needs must in 'meeting a war-time emergency'.[18] It was also a major reversal: in 1932 Edmonds had proudly reminded its customers that, during the last war, it had 'temporarily *stopped manufacturing*, losing thousands of pounds of trade, rather than use an inferior ingredient'.[19]

Edmonds had long criticised phosphate-based powders as inferior. However, with cream of tartar in short supply during the war, Edmonds switched its Acto brand to a phosphate powder and now included the company name on the label. Sure to Rise was still unavailable in 1945 when the spectacular advertisement opposite – a veritable apotheosis of Edmonds products – promoted the superiority of Acto.

By the mid-1940s, with no cream of tartar baking powder left on the market, manufacturers had little choice but to promote the phosphate-based alternative. Conveniently, the pre-war powders were now said to have offered only aeration, whereas the new phosphate type was not only a 'miraculous rising agent' but a 'priceless health ingredient' – at least according to its importer, who also claimed that phosphate, an element that was lacking in New Zealand soils and foods, was essential for nerves, teeth and bones and 'general bodily tone'.[20] The product was promoted so aggressively on the radio that one Wellington listener complained about music programmes being interrupted by advertisements asking, 'for the millionth time', whether they had tried 'the new phosphate baking powder'.[21]

On 7 May 1945 Germany surrendered, bringing an end to hostilities in Europe. Three months later, Japan followed suit. The war was over. Cream of tartar was still in extremely short local supply, and Edmonds anticipated it might be at least six months before it could start making Sure to Rise powder again. But Edmonds Acto was in 'plentiful supply' and, perhaps to accommodate those who had grown accustomed to this alternative, Edmonds promised to continue producing it when Sure to Rise was back on the market: the company looked forward to the day when it could supply 'the best cream of tartar baking powder ... and the best phosphate baking powder'.[22]

EDMONDS "SURE-TO-RISE" BAKING POWDER.

Now that the war is over, we are receiving numerous inquiries as to when Edmonds "Sure-to-Rise" Baking Powder will again be available. The position, however, is that cream of tartar is still in extremely short supply, and we anticipate that it will be at least six months before we shall be able to recommence manufacture of "Sure-to-Rise" Baking Powder, and even then supplies will be limited for a few months. Meanwhile, Edmonds "Acto" Baking Powder is in plentiful supply, and this will continue to be manufactured even when "Sure-to-Rise" is again available. We look forward to the day when we can supply both "Sure-to-Rise," the best cream of tartar Baking Powder, and Edmonds "Acto," the best phosphate Baking Powder. T. J. Edmonds, Ltd., Christchurch, manufacturers of Edmonds "Sure-to-Rise" Baking Powder and Edmonds "Acto" Baking Powder, and also Edmonds Custard Powder and Jellies.—Advt.

Factory and Gardens of
T. J. EDMONDS LTD., CHRISTCHURCH, N.Z.

FOR SUCCESSFUL COOKING
EDMONDS
ESTD PRIZE 1879
BAKING · POWDER
SURE TO RISE
(REGISTERED)
EDMONDS
SURE TO PLEASE
CUSTARD POWDER
6 FLAVOURS
Edmonds
sure to set
RASPBERRY
JELLY CRYSTALS
Edmonds
RASPBERRY
JELLY CRYSTALS
Edmonds
QUALITY PRODUCTS

Finally, in July 1946, Edmonds announced that Sure to Rise was back, but supplies were limited and customers were advised to buy only for their immediate requirements.[23] There was no such problem with Edmonds Acto, now promoted by a new persona, Mrs Active Acto, a busy housewife who, thanks to the reliability of her eponymous baking powder, could be 'out for the afternoon' – 'baking never keeps her in'.[24] And although Sure to Rise and Acto were different products, both were advertised as 'the Peak of Perfection', sitting together on a snowy summit.[25] The reality could, however, be rather different. Ian Kinley recalled that, after the war, his father Fred was required to visit stores around Christchurch, uplift their stocks of Acto and replace them with Sure to Rise. Back at the factory, 11-year-old Ian helped his father to open the Acto tins and tip the contents into barrels, which were then emptied at the Burwood rubbish dump – several truckloads of them. The emptied Acto tins were then relabelled and refilled, presumably with Sure to Rise.[26] As New Zealand home bakers knew, phosphate baking powder could have a bitterness that had to be masked by using plenty of sugar. And, unlike the cream of tartar version, Acto and its like did not begin aerating a mixture until it was heated.[27]

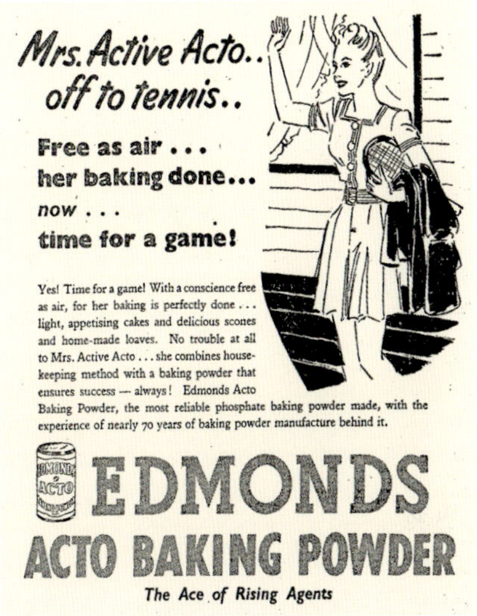

After the war, phosphate Acto and Sure to Rise were advertised side by side, 'Both the Peak of Perfection'. The phosphate powder even had its own voice through Mrs Active Acto.

• • •

'We welcome you to Edmonds Garden Factory. It's a pleasure for us to make your visit one of interest and instruction. We hope you will enjoy your glimpse of a New Zealand industry. Seeing how Edmonds Quality Products are made will convince you that New Zealand is right up-to-date in manufacturing methods which combine efficiency and hygiene with pleasant and comfortable working conditions.' It was about 1949, and as New Zealand began to enjoy a period of post-war prosperity and calm, Edmonds, now a popular visitor attraction, had produced a 15-page, highly illustrated (in colour and black and white) souvenir booklet entitled *Your Visit to Edmonds*, which was given to those who toured the factory and garden.

The visitor would see 'Baking Powder, Custard Powder and Jelly Crystals in various stages of manufacture and packing'. The first stop was the tin-making room on the ground floor, where automatic presses converted tinplate into tins at the rate of 110 per minute, and two engineers were permanently engaged on repair and maintenance work. Each day 12,000 tins were filled with baking powder, and a gummed label was applied that covered the bottom of the overlapping lid and shrank when dry to ensure a perfect seal. The process of placing jelly crystals in packets that were then sealed by a gluing machine designed and built by Edmonds engineers was a 'most entertaining sight'. At no point in the whole manufacturing process were Edmonds products touched by hand; they were safeguarded 'with all the care that modern science can give them'. Even the boxes in which the products were dispatched were nailed together by machine.[28]

By 1952 New Zealand's population had reached 2 million, boosted mainly by the 'baby boom' but also by a large influx of migrants, most of them from Britain. The great majority of export earnings came from agriculture. More than half of New Zealand's sheep and dairy products went to Britain, and Britain was the source of nearly half of the country's imports. When it came to the evening meal, New Zealanders settled for the traditional 'meat and three veg'; dining out and a taste for exotic or ethnic recipes lay in the future. And because home baking was still standard practice, Sure to Rise baking powder continued to be in demand.

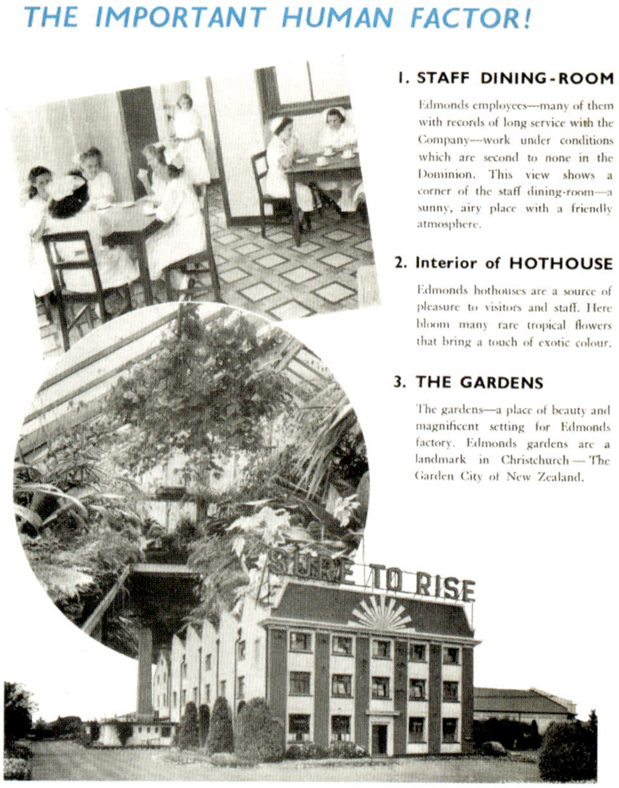

The souvenir booklet, on a page headed 'The Important Human Factor!', had noted that many Edmonds employees, working under 'conditions second to none in the Dominion', had 'records of long service'. In 1951 the company honoured 16 'long-service men' who had each worked at the firm for 25 years or more and whose combined contribution was an impressive 503 years. The list was headed by manager Philip Smith, who had retired after a record 50 years of unbroken service.[29] Those receiving presentations were invited to choose their own gifts: many went for clocks. 'To my knowledge,' Ian Kinley remembered, 'my father didn't work anywhere other than Edmonds. He was there for 25 years anyway. He'd go over on Saturday and Sundays as well. He had to pick up a lot of stuff from the boats at Lyttelton and bring it to the factory, or take it back or to the railways. If it was at the weekend or in the school holidays, I used to go with Dad.'[30]

Ian, who worked at Edmonds himself after the war, recalled the annual staff picnic. 'They held that at different beaches – Waikuku, Woodend, Kairaki. Dad used to drive one of the Bedford trucks and someone else used to drive the other one. They would put seats down the sides and also double sided down the middle. Everyone went to the grounds on Sunday morning and they were then driven to the picnic and driven home again at night. Edmonds supplied food, but not alcohol. We had races for the staff, their children and grandchildren – 100-yard races, 200 yards, things like that. And there were prizes for every race.'[31]

Always keen to use imaginative forms of advertising, in 1955 Edmonds turned to celluloid with a 15-minute film called *Cookery Nook*, produced by well-known New Zealand filmmakers Roger Mirams and John O'Shea. As O'Shea recalled, this 'comedy short ... must have some sort of record as being one of the longest-lived sponsored documentaries ever made for a client'.[32] The film, which never actually mentions Edmonds but features its products and premises lavishly, was a semi-dramatised account of a day of domestic crisis for one suburban household. A woman, when she is told over breakfast that her husband's boss and 'the London representative' are coming for afternoon tea, refuses to change her plans, and 'poor beleaguered Dad' is left to face 'the prospect of a day's baking'. Of course he gets into a hopeless mess, from which he is rescued only by the culinary talents of his daughter Rosina and her friends, trained in cookery lessons at their intermediate school. The 'story' features a cameo of Aunt Daisy reading, naturally, from the *Edmonds Cookery Book*; a cooking demonstration for 'an interested audience of housewives and business girls'; and a visit to the Edmonds factory and garden by members of the Rangiora Housewives Association. There could be no doubt about the gender roles, emphasised by a sonorous BBC-style voiceover: in class, the girls know 'that orderliness and neatness on their cooking tables are habits that later in life will enable them as housewives to organise their time to the best advantage', and the 'London representative' states, 'There is nothing like a man with a wife who knows how to entertain her guests.'[33]

Cookery Nook proudly emphasised the role of testing and checking in the anonymous factory's laboratory. Ron Hooker confirmed this: 'There were endless rounds of quality control ... Every day, the home economists would bake batches of scones, rolling the dough out to a uniform half inch.' Once these were baked, the height of five scones would be measured to check the rise in the baking powder. Home economist Geraldine Evans had similar memories. 'We used to test the baking powder off the line – if it didn't fizz, we knew something was missing. All the testing had to be very precise. The cakes were all in the same size tins; we had electronic scales to check the ingredients.'[34]

Edmonds promoted the superior working conditions in its factory in a souvenir booklet. Driver Fred Kinley, pictured opposite, was one of many who stayed for over 25 years. Above, a still from the innovative short film *Cookery Nook* made by Edmonds to showcase its factory in 1955. On the following pages, the Edmonds legacy was celebrated as part of Christchurch's centennial in 1950.

It was a mark of Edmonds' pre-eminence that it was the only producer of baking products included in a 1959 compilation of 160 New Zealand manufactories. In his preface to this publication, Prime Minister Walter Nash noted that local industries faced 'real problems', such as lack of mineral resources and a small and dispersed national market. He pointed out, however, that the country's population had reached the point where, for the first time, many industries could be economic, which was 'a major advance'. At this stage the food industry group was the national leader, employing nearly 30,000 people and with a value of output far exceeding all others. By now Edmonds had added sponge mix and wheat cornflour to its product range, and was still knocking out 110 tins of baking powder per minute. Nash described the Edmonds story as 'one of the finest advertisements of the manufacturing potential of this vigorous young Dominion', and confidently predicted it would continue to progress.[35]

Milestone

1879

In the back portion of this building, the first Edmonds Baking Powder was made.

1900

At the turn of the century — Edmonds "Sure to Rise" factory about 1900.

Seventy-one years ago, Edmonds factory was porti
To-day, Edmonds Garden Factory — the largest of i
Zealand — produces, every year, millions of packag
"Sure To Rise" Baking Powder, Acto Baking Po
Powder and Jelly Crystals.

EDMONDS 1879-1950

T.J. E

In 1879, the late Mr T. J. Edmonds founded the firm of T. J. Edmonds Ltd. Throughout the changing years, Edmonds have built " firmly and secure."

of a shop.
kind in New
of Edmonds
er, Custard

DMONDS LTD.

CHRISTCHURCH

tang
BREAKFAST

CHAPTER 14

A NEW ERA

The 1960s was a decade of major change for T.J. Edmonds Ltd. In 1963 the company listed on the stock exchange, and Bill Revel, who was appointed general manager, oversaw the transition. It was later suggested that the company was 'in a somewhat somnolent state', and Revell arrived 'with all sorts of bright ideas for pepping up the operation'.[1] In 1963 Ron Hooker was appointed as chemist – or food technologist – with the all-important aim of developing new products, and the chemical analysis laboratory – the test kitchen – which included fume cupboards and titration equipment, was extended. Hooker spent 20 years at Edmonds and oversaw the development of about 200 new products, which sometimes appeared at the rate of one per month. He employed university home science graduates to assist with product development and in the laboratory, where test baking was carried out almost continuously. Every batch was tested, and the resulting cakes, sponges and scones were put to good use by factory staff. Ron's daughters used to go to the factory in the school holidays to try new products and provide feedback. Laboratory staff also gave cooking demonstrations in stores and fairs, spoke to groups, conducted tours of the factory and judged bake-off competitions. New Zealand families were demanding greater convenience and variety, and this was reflected in the growing appetite for more ethnic culinary influences such as curry pastes and sweet and sour sauces.[2] When the company achieved a record gross profit in 1965, the increase in sales was due entirely to new products, about 40 of them, including five cake mixes and five different cooking oils.

Inspired by the need to diversify and keep the business growing, in 1969 the firm's directors made a takeover bid for Henry Berry Ltd, which had been supplying food preparation equipment to the catering industry since the first decade of the twentieth century. Edmonds suggested that Henry Berry Ltd shareholders would have 'a bright future indeed – with Edmonds', but the Berry directors begged to differ and recommended the offer be rejected.[3] By this time, Edmonds was well into expansion mode. There were already subsidiary and associate companies: Instant Foods (manufacturer of freeze-dried foods), bakery firm G.E. Winson Ltd, and Edmonds White

By the 1960s, advertising styles had further changed and Edmonds was producing a wide range of products, including the popular orange drink Tang.

Wings Ltd (established in 1964 in association with Sydney-based White Wings to make packed dry goods products and cake mixes).[4] In 1969 Edmonds acquired the Auckland-based Pakenham Products Ltd, which added pickles, mayonnaise, gherkins and sandwich spreads to the Edmonds range. This was run by Thomas's eldest grandson, Keith Edmonds. The Christchurch bottling company Nabob, which had been making pickles and sauces since at least 1874, was another acquisition. But perhaps the most consequential of these subsidiaries were those associated with the venison industry.

• • •

Edmonds had been exporting modestly since before the Second World War, but it was now important to establish stronger and more diverse overseas markets. Another factor driving this was that New Zealanders were doing less home baking. The company decided to venture into the deer industry. In 1968 it established Edmonds Game Consolidated Ltd, a processing plant for exported venison, as well as crayfish and eels. This enterprise would export mainly to Germany, but also to Sweden, Switzerland, France, the United States, Japan, Australia and the Far East. There were markets, too, for processed deer velvet and tails. In 1969 Edmonds extended its commitment to the deer industry and deer recovery by acquiring Timaru-based Utility Helicopters Ltd. And in 1970, diversifying further, the company opened a new Oxo factory, and it purchased premises in Kaiapoi for Edmonds Food Services Ltd, which supplied ready-cooked food, generally to caterers, hospitals, hotels and cafeterias.

The 1970s was a decade of dramatic economic and social change for the country. In 1973 Britain joined the European Economic Community (the Common Market).

Long-serving Edmonds food technologist Ron Hooker is seen opposite (far right) with laboratory and food technicians, early 1970s. Hooker's contribution to food technology is still recognised by an industry award in his name (administered by the New Zealand Institute of Food Science and Technology). Winning the prestigious Governor-General's Award for Exporting (below) in 1979 reflected Edmonds' successful strategies of product diversification and international growth.

This and the decision by Arab producers to cut oil supplies had severe consequences in New Zealand, causing increased freight costs, wage rates and retail prices, as well as unemployment and inflation. That same year, T. J. Edmonds Ltd won a Trade Promotion Council Export Award in recognition of three years of outstanding export performance. In 1974 the company had to deal with government-imposed price control restrictions, which once again included cream of tartar. By then, however, the company's exports – including Oxo beef cubes and game products – were at a record high. (In 1979 Edmonds exported over 2 million Oxo cubes, which 'if placed end to end, would stretch 50 kilometres'.)[5] And the company set up a joint venture company, Edmonds Fong Lee Ltd in Fiji, which mainly mixed baking powder and sourced most of its dried commodities from New Zealand. Apart from all this, the 1970s was a decade in which the company had to keep up with innovations such as the microwave and the fan-bake oven, and accurately determine the time and temperature settings for making recipes using these appliances.

Despite the 'abnormal difficulties and restrictions', 'the continuing ravages of inflation' and severe price control regulations, in 1975 the Edmonds group trading profit was up. For the rest of the decade there was continuing record group profit, largely thanks to an expanding export market and the introduction of more new products at home. In 1976, taking advantage of government incentives for exporters, the company sent 32 different products to 39 different countries.

The year 1979 was an important one for Edmonds: the company celebrated its centenary, and it won the prestigious Governor-General's Award for Exporting – 'New Zealand industry's most coveted award'.[6] From turnover of $40 a week to export markets worth an annual $6.2 million – how different things were since the modest beginnings of a baking powder business a century before. The company now sent custard powder, labelled in Arabic, to the Persian Gulf, where it was popular during the month-long Ramadan fast – but only after modifying the product, for cultural reasons, to remove alcohol-based flavouring and changing the

Long after his death, Thomas's initials were prominent on the company's plane. Around the same time production was shifted to the Auckland factory pictured below. Opposite, radical changes in packaging design for products destined for Edmonds' overseas markets.

packaging from an unacceptable yellow to blue.[7] By 1979 T.J. Edmonds Ltd comprised six other companies, including Edmonds Deer Farms Ltd, and there were 10 associate companies. Game products – including deer and deer byproducts, chamois, thar, goats and pork – were the company's most important exports that year, but there was a surprising mixture of other exports, too: jelly crystals, cornflour, cake mix, powdered drink, disinfectants and detergents as well as custard powder to the Arabian Gulf, powdered drinks to Jordan, canned kiwifruit to Germany, Tropic powdered drink mix (made and sold in New Zealand as Tang) to the South Pacific and Middle East, and canned tomatoes, potatoes and mushrooms across the Tasman – as well as customwood panels to Australia.[8] This high-flying company even had its own aircraft, a twin-engined Piper Aztec acquired in 1978 and bearing the appropriate registration letters ZK-TJE.[9] And finally, in July of the centennial year, the now 50-year-old Edmonds Band Rotunda underwent an upgrade.

But 1979 may have marked the end of the good times. The company had been moving away from its traditional core baking products and investing heavily in the deer market when it was at its peak. Venison, though, was a 'boom and bust' business, and when deer prices inevitably fell, Edmonds was one of the many businesses that suffered. In 1982 it became the target of a takeover bid from H.W. Smith Ltd, a private Christchurch-based investment company whose directors were closely linked with Brierley Investments Ltd, and it was subsequently subjected to a complex mix of business deals and changes of ownership. All the Edmonds directors recommended acceptance of the offer, which consisted of one fully paid ordinary share in brushware manufacturer Bunting and Co. Ltd, which was associated with

H.W. Smith, and 20 cents in cash for each Edmonds ordinary share. Bunting subsequently purchased Edmonds' food operation from H.W. Smith, which retained ownership of all Edmonds' other activities.[10] Ron Fuller, whose father Bert worked at Edmonds for 45 years and who was an employee himself, was perhaps not far off the mark when he suggested, many years later: 'They made a mistake with all that diversification. They had the baking powder, jelly and custard powder market tied up. They took their eye off the main factory bit and tried to do all these other things, trying to be what they weren't ... They had the deer farm. What the hell – they were a factory, not a primary producer!'[11]

Towards the end of 1982, Bunting sold half the capital of Edmonds Food Industries, which owned the traditional food manufacturing activities of T.J. Edmonds Ltd, to established Auckland-based W.F. Tucker Ltd, known for its Sunshine brand. The head office and the manufacture of Edmonds' baking products were relocated to Auckland. By 1983 Bunting wholly owned some 25 companies, among them Tjmond Properties Ltd – an insulting renaming of T.J. Edmonds Ltd – whose only assets now were shares in Edmonds Food Industries Ltd (one of Bunting's associate companies), and the Auckland and Christchurch factories. There had been considerable discussion about whether Bunting would retain a manufacturing facility at the old Edmonds Ferry Road factory, and whether the gardens would survive, but no commitment was made about their future.[12] The final chapter in the dismantling of T.J. Edmonds Ltd took place in 1984, when Brierley Investments Ltd (BIL) planned a merger with Bunting & Co., offering nine shares in BIL for every 10 Bunting shares. With this acquisition BIL took over what was left of T.J. Edmonds Ltd.

CHAPTER 15

THE NEXT GENERATION

For the children of Thomas and Jane, their lives took different paths. The older children were brought up in a much humbler way, when the business was just getting underway and there was not much money to spare. The last three daughters, by contrast, had the benefit of their parents' steadily increasing wealth. There was a gender difference too: the boys were taken out of school at the age of about 14 and expected to work in the family business, whereas the girls were mostly educated until they were 18, and lived a privileged and pampered existence. And, of course, all the surviving siblings – even Ernest – were able to live very comfortable lives thanks to their inheritance.

As far as the business was concerned, the early death of Will, who was able and dynamic, almost certainly altered Thomas's plans and hopes. Although George remained involved, Bert Cropp became the driving force, particularly after Thomas's death. (John Ballantyne, Irene's son, remembered his mother saying that Bert 'didn't want any of the boys meddling with the firm too much ... George was the only one who knew very much about the machinery because he'd made it. So he was given free access ... The others weren't invited there much at all.')[1] In a report on the company's seventy-fifth anniversary in September 1954, the *Press* noted that 'Four men will be remembered as playing prominent parts in the growth of the business': Thomas, Will, Bert Cropp and Philip Smith. There was continuity: 'Sons of these men have been, and in many cases, still are associated with the company.' The sons mentioned were George; Will and Alice's son Keith; and Lilian and Bert's son David.[2]

Opposite, siblings together: Irene, James, Gertrude, George and Beatrice. Below, Ernest with his daughters Eileen and Edna, c.1905.

After their 1915 separation, Ernest and Ethel's 'splendid residential property' in Dallington, with its 4.5 acres of land, was sold. The couple reunited later that year and bought a house in Linwood, but this property, too, was sold at the end of 1916. Life at a nearby address proved no better. Finally, in 1920, Ethel went to court seeking a maintenance order against Ernest, 'on the grounds of persistent cruelty'. Her maintenance was fixed at £150 a year, with an additional £10 for Edna, who lived with her. Lily was 'to be boarded out at a place to be mutually agreed upon'.[3] By the 1920s Ernest was farming; in 1928, to the acute embarrassment of his family, he began driving a taxi in Christchurch. The couple had been living apart since 1919 when, in late March 1933, Ernest petitioned for divorce, but this was refused because his treatment of Ethel had caused the original separation.[4] Although Ernest received only 1600 shares when T.J. Edmonds was reincorporated in 1935, this allowed him to live well in Christchurch – at one point in a Pages Road house that bore his initials 'EEE' in large letters on the front fence – until his death in 1950 at the age of 69. Ernest had other brushes with the law, but his relationship with his daughters remained warm and loving.

Lilian was 30 when she married Bert Cropp in 1913, and they had two children, David and Elaine. The family was close to Thomas and Jane: there was a gate in the fence between the two adjacent properties. Bert continued to perform frequently as a singer, often with the Liedertafel, after he took on his new role, and Lilian made occasional musical contributions for a good cause. In January 1924, for example, she took part in a 'musical programme of unusual merit' held at Sir George and Lady Clifford's Fendalton home to raise money for the Lewisham General Hospital Fund.[5] There was travel, too: a trip to the United States with Bert in 1922, a holiday in Sydney in 1925, a voyage to Britain in 1931, the United States again in 1933 ... In 1935 Lilian's photo was in the paper when she was 'selected as the queen for the No. 7 group (Manufacturers' and Industrial Group) in the Metropolitan Queen Carnival for the relief of distress in the city'.[6] By August she was in first place, ahead of her sister Irene, who was queen of the retailers' group; she went on to win, and the carnival raised more than £15,000. Bert died in 1948, and Lilian died in 1967 at the age of 84.

George, who worked in the family firm for many years, was a clever man who, if he had had an education, could have been a first-class engineer. He had five children with Clara Thomson, whom he married in 1910; and after they divorced in 1930 he married Dorothy Welsh. When he died in 1973, George was described as a 'retired manufacturer', but he had many other talents and interests. John Ballantyne recalled the 50 rocking horses that George made for the children at the Cholmondeley Home. 'George was fantastic. He was a bit of a dare-devil. He arrived at Coldstream [Irene's home] on a new Velocette motorbike – one of the latest. It was shaft driven ... He used to run it around the rose garden and out the back lawn and all over the place ... He'd be in his best suit, and no helmet!'[7] When Bert and Lilian held a musical evening for charity in 1936, George,

'recently returned from a trip abroad, showed a series of very interesting moving-pictures of places he had visited'.[8] His son Murray recalled that when George received his inheritance after Thomas's death, he spent some of the money on cameras. When he travelled the world after retirement, he 'took huge quantities of 16mm film, carting a large tripod and a very heavy camera'.[9] After George died his personal possessions were not kept, but his impressive film collection, including footage of the 1937 *Hindenburg* disaster, found its way to a junk shop, where it was spotted and later donated to Ngā Taonga Sound & Vision film archive.

Jim also worked for Edmonds. He married Edith (Edie) Daniels, who was Australian, in 1915, and their daughter Marijean was born in 1921. They lived in a large house in Moncks Bay, near Sumner. His granddaughter, Cassandra Philpot, remembered that Jim 'was interested in beautiful things. In the late 1930s he went to Asia ... on buying trips. He shipped an enormous amount of stuff back – and filled the Moncks Bay house. People then came around and bought things such as ivory Buddhas, silk robes, cloisonné boxes, lacquer coasters, jade ornaments and furniture.' Marijean adored her father, who was a 'quiet, intelligent, gentle and thoughtful man'. Edie, who died in 1948, suffered from rheumatoid arthritis and was often bedridden.[10] Jim married Thelma Stone not long after Edie's death; and he died in 1955.

The photo far left features Lilian with her children Elaine and David, c.1927. The other photos show the four sisters in younger years – Irene, Beatrice, Lilian (behind) and Gertrude, and in later life – Beatrice, Lilian, Gertude (behind) and Irene.

Gertrude, who was still able to slide stylishly down a banister when she was 95, lived a happy and busy social life in Christchurch with Harry Williams. The couple had three children – Pamela, Elizabeth and John. They lived in Manchester Street from the early 1920s, then in the mid-1930s they built a large house called Ranui in Clyde Road. In 1942 Gertrude and Irene revived the Cheer-Ohs, this time as producers. Gertrude's daughter Pamela was one of the 14 girls in the company, which performed for such local groups as the Red Cross and the Mayoress's Parcel Fund, and travelled to Wellington to put on a show for the men in the local military camps.[11] Gertrude died in 1987.

On the occasion of Beatrice's hundredth birthday in November 1995, her 'minder and friend' Betty Snell put Beatrice's long life down to the 'fact that she has been a lacto-vegetarian since 1958, she travelled the world until she was 94-years-old and her Radha Soami faith [an Indian spiritual movement]'.[12] Her life was full of incident and intrigue. On a return journey to Britain in February 1933 she met Leslie Jauncey, a trained chiropractor who later gained a PhD in economics at Harvard. The relationship developed rapidly: on 30 March Beatrice's husband Peter Fripp began divorce proceedings, citing Jauncey as co-respondent. As soon as the divorce was final Beatrice and Leslie were married in London in January 1934. From 1940 to 1959 they lived in the United States, where they had an active role with the Camp Fire Girls, a movement similar to the Girl Guides. After Leslie died in 1961, Beatrice lived in Britain and later returned to New Zealand, where she died in 1996.[13] Peter Fripp's niece, Jane Lee, met Beatrice in London in

1977. 'We talked over a silver service lunch, for which she graciously paid, as if we had known each other for decades and as if there was no age gap between us. She was intelligent, glamorous, smart, engaging, bright and delightful. How much greater impact she must have made when she was a young woman!'[14]

Rene, the youngest of the family, continued her musical studies after leaving the Sydney Conservatorium. For two years she lived in St John's Wood, London, while she took violin tuition from leading violinist and teacher Maurice Sons. Back in Christchurch, she lived at home until she married Ken Ballantyne, of the well-known Christchurch department store family, on 9 December 1925. The couple had three children – Day, Jan and John. Music and philanthropy were central to Rene's life, and she performed frequently on radio. In 1935 she and Ken built Coldstream Lodge in Fendalton, designed by the notable Christchurch architectural partnership of Heathcote Helmore and Henry Cotterill. The large music room included in the design had a concert grand piano on a stage at one end and was often used for concerts given by Rene and her trio or quartet, and some by such luminaries as the young Yehudi Menuhin, Noël Coward and Todd Duncan. Rene followed another family tradition, in a modest way: in the mid-1930s she wrote a cookery book for sale at the St Saviour's Orphanage Fair, though only a cyclostyled typed copy has survived.[15]

Like several other members of the Edmonds family, Rene had spiritual leanings that were outside the mainstream. As a younger woman she was involved in Radiant Living, but in her eighties she was baptised and confirmed as an Anglican at St Luke's. Her grandson Philip Richards, who was at the church that day, recalls her speaking of Radiant Living, and he is sure it influenced her

The wedding of Irene and Kenneth Ballantyne, 1925, with, left to right, Thelma Edmonds, Frank Morrison, Ronald Ballantyne and Gertrude Hudson. Opposite, a glamorous studio portrait of Irene, c.1935.

dietary habits. 'As a child, for breakfast, I was fed grated apple with sultanas and wheatgerm whenever I went to stay with my grandparents. She also had a passion for juiced vegetables and fruit ... On one occasion she asked the gardener to deliver some grass clippings so she could juice them. She got him to drink the product, and he fell ill afterwards.' Philip remembered his grandmother saying that when she and Ken retired to their farm in 1950, she sold her Stradivarius 'and no longer felt under pressure to perform, though she kept her practice violin and continued to play at family concerts for the rest of her life. Her first love in later years was the piano, which she played by ear, and she turned to composing, submitting entries for the Australian national anthem, the 1974 Commonwealth Games song and a number of hymns. By playing the violin she was, in some ways, fulfilling her father's dreams, which were definitely beyond his reach growing up in the East End.'[16] Rene died in 1989.

SURE TO RISE

CHAPTER 16

A FAMOUS GARDEN

Thomas's dream of a 'healthy, sunny model factory' always incorporated 'a setting of glorious flowers and cool green lawns'.[1] His love of plants, and his desire for Christchurch to be truly a garden city, led him to establish one of New Zealand's first, and most famous, factory gardens. These special landscapes had their origin in initiatives by late-nineteenth-century British industrialists such as William Lever and George Cadbury to improve the lives and environment of their workers. They each built model villages for their employees, complete with recreational facilities – Lever at Port Sunlight, close to Liverpool, and Cadbury at Bournville, southwest of Birmingham. In his 1898 book, *To-Morrow: A Peaceful Path to Real Reform*, revised in 1902 as *Garden Cities of To-Morrow*, British urban planner Ebenezer Howard had proposed the establishment of 'garden' cities, combining the best of town and country living in self-contained communities. The resulting Garden City movement spread around the world, and New Zealand, in the years after the First World War, was no exception.

The Edmonds Factory Garden was first laid out in 1923 by company employee Rupert (Rube) Overend, who lived in the house next to the wooden factory building. Thomas had asked him if he knew anyone who would be interested in doing the work and Overend, a keen amateur gardener, had put up his hand. The area to be developed ran from the front and one side of the factory to the small office block and low boundary wall on Ferry Road. Overend favoured geometrically shaped flower beds, filled with bright annuals, set into wide swathes of velvet smooth, bright green lawn. Later he created long borders, planted with shrubs and small trees, using annuals to fill the gaps. Its bright floral displays soon made the garden a greatly admired local attraction. When the Beautifying Association inspected the factory gardens in Woolston in March 1924, their first port of call was Edmonds. 'The gardener, Mr Overend, met the visitors at the gates and took them round the lawn in and amongst the splendidly-designed flower beds, all ablaze with colour. Particularly beautiful were the antirrhinums, celosia and

Ray Leech and Norm Griggs at work in the Edmonds' award-winning garden, which attracted large numbers of visitors.

> *The Beautiful Garden Factory*
> *of* **T.J. EDMONDS LTD.**
> CHRISTCHURCH, N.Z.
>
> The magnificent garden surrounding the Edmonds Factory is known all over Australasia. Two full-time gardeners are employed, and each year some twenty thousand plants are necessary to make the flower-beds a mass of glorious colour.

asters. The lawn was in excellent condition, despite the exceptionally large number of fierce nor'westers experienced this summer.'[2] Rube Overend would have been especially delighted about the praise for the lawn, which was his obsession and delight, watched over zealously from his house after hours. He had other triumphs, such as the 'magnificent collection of pot plants and flowers' that won him awards at the Canterbury Horticultural Society show in 1925.[3]

Thomas bought more land in the mid-1920s: a large paddock next to the factory and fronting onto Ferry Road in November 1924 and, in May and July 1925, two neighbouring residential properties. The first of these was a section on the corner of Ferry and Aldwins roads; the second was the adjacent one in Aldwins Road. By 1929 the garden stretched westwards into the paddock, a new fence had been put up, there were three new beds and others were being redesigned, and a glasshouse had been built to house Thomas's prized tropical plant collection.[4] There was more expansion between 1930 and 1935: greater space for the garden meant the loss of three houses on Aldwins Road, one of which had almost certainly been the Edmonds family's former home. Bert Fuller, who was the company caretaker for many years, lived with his family in one of the houses until 1934, when another was built further down the road, at No. 25. As his son, also Bert, recalled, after the head gardener's house came down, he moved around the corner to Ryan Street, which ran off Ferry Road. 'The third [house] was taken to Charlie Williams, the carrier, who was across Ferry Road. They shifted it with the traction engine.'[5]

These stills from the 1955 film *Cookery Nook* show the Rangiora Housewives Association walking through the gardens before a factory tour and (right) the gardens being enjoyed by Edmonds s taff. The colour print on the following pages is a reproduction of a V.C. Browne photo used in company advertising.

When the first Christchurch factory gardens competition was held in 1931, the A1 Challenge Trophy went to T. J. Edmonds and Company, 'whose garden is always worth looking at, probably thanks to the personal interest taken in it by the proprietor and manager of the firm ... they have

set an example and they hope that other factories will follow it, even if they overtake them in doing so.'[6] Bert Cropp accepted the cup, but gave all the credit to Rube Overend. Edmonds won again in 1934, this time under the next head gardener, Malcolm Gilpin, whose son Huia was appointed assistant gardener the following year. (He later became superintendent of the Christchurch Botanic Gardens.) In 1935 Christchurch landscape architect Edgar Taylor designed a garden extension. His formal neo-classical design incorporated Italian cypresses, flanked by hydrangeas, on either side of a pergola. Beneath the pergola were a stone seat and a fountain statue, imported from England, of a young girl holding a bowl of brimming water. In a lily pond edged with local Halswell stone, special containers for the waterlilies were made by the well-known Christchurch potter Luke Adams. When Edmonds triumphed again in 1936, winning the Canterbury Milling Company's Challenge Cup (in Class A, for factory gardens), the pond in the middle of the garden received special mention in the judges' report.[7]

But it was the thousands of brilliantly coloured annual bedding plants, grown from seed and supplemented by countless cuttings raised in the greenhouse and frames, that made the garden such an attraction. Usually it was just for the enjoyment of the employees but, as Murray Edmonds recalled, the factory was 'a much visited place ... my recollection of it was the begonia houses [dating from the late 1930s], which were simply superb and I often moved with large crowds of people through there in the weekends. The scents and the sights, and the skill of the full-time gardener in those gardens and in the begonia houses were quite remarkable.'[8] The gardener was also responsible for attending to the factory's boilers, looked after the large conservatory and separate begonia house, provided fresh flowers and pot plants for the offices and pruned the roses in the company managers' private gardens. (Later, food technologist Ron Hooker would even select a petal from the begonia house to inspire and match the colour of a

URE TO RISE

Marmaduke Matthews drew this beautiful pencil sketch of the factory and gardens for an Edmonds Christmas card. Opposite, the spectacular Edmonds gardens in the 1970s.

new pudding or similar product.) Strong support from management inspired great staff loyalty. Even after the introduction of the 40-hour week, the gardeners still appeared for duty every day and put in long hours if necessary.

In May 1945 T. J. Edmonds Ltd gifted the 4.5-acre unused paddock behind the factory to the city as a park, but on one condition: the council must allow part of the land to be used by the Plunket Society and the Christchurch Free Kindergarten Association for any buildings they might want to erect. With an eye to future expansion, the company wished to retain the front portion of the land as a reserve, but until then it was happy for it to be part of what became known as Edmonds Park.

Since opening early in 1939, the Woolston Kindergarten, which 'supplied a long-felt need in the closely populated [suburb]', had been using the McDonald Hall in Aldwins Road, but hoped it might soon be able to 'erect a modern kindergarten in this district'.[9] That hope was fulfilled in 1950 when the kindergarten moved to a new building in Edmonds Park, and was renamed Edmonds Park Kindergarten 'in recognition of the financial assistance of Messrs T.J. Edmonds Ltd'. This would not be the firm's only kindergarten initiative. In 1970, when the Cotswold Avenue Kindergarten was transported to Smith Street in Linwood and re-erected there, 'the total cost of the move and the development of the site was borne by Messrs T.J. Edmonds Ltd'.[10] The Edmonds Park Kindergarten was taken down in the 1970s but the Smith Street Kindergarten, as it became, survives today as a Kidsfirst centre.

The 1950s brought more changes to the garden: a semicircular 'rainbow border' opposite the fishpond, and what garden historian Thelma Strongman has described as a 'raised and tilted border … bedded out in French marigolds imitating the sun's rays of the company's logo'.[11] Crosby Moran succeeded Malcolm Gilpin as head gardener in 1951, followed by Stan Dwyer in 1954. And, of course, from 1955 the gardens appeared on the cover of every edition of the *Edmonds Cookery Book*. In the 1960s, new glasshouses, cold frames and plant cradles went up on the land to the west of the garden. A rockery area – an 'outdoor room' – was created in 1970 by an apprentice from the Melbourne Botanic Gardens, on the spot where the factory social room had previously been. To make life easier for the gardening staff, lawn was replaced here by gravel.[12]

After becoming head gardener in 1973, Ray Leech made his mark with a special display to mark the city's hosting of the 1974 Commonwealth Games, and with a more natural style of gardening that included a small pond, later extended towards the west to become a winding creek leading to another, larger pond. Over the next few years three small wooden bridges were built and soil excavated from the pond was used to construct mounds planted with rhododendrons, low shrubs and groundcovers.[13] The garden was a popular venue for annual garden parties, Christmas carols and other public events, and for weddings, of which, on some Saturdays, there were up to three.

But changes were coming. In 1982, for the first time, the garden was not entered in the Canterbury Horticultural Society Competition. By 1984 there was 'word that the garden was to be scaled down', and the assistant gardener was made redundant.[14] After the Brierley Investments Ltd (BIL) takeover, the Ferry Road gardens slipped into further decline. By 1986 the glasshouses had been dismantled and sold to a Papanui milkman, and the formal beds replaced with lawn. The original neo-classical symmetry of the garden was destroyed, and Ray Leech, the last of the gardeners, was made redundant in 1987, though for another two years he went in one day a week to keep the grounds tidy. After the glasshouses had gone, he 'grew all the annuals at his own home, until he was asked not to bother with them further'.[15]

The much-loved factory building was also under threat. The people of Christchurch had successfully rallied in the 1960s to prevent roads being cut through Hagley Park and Latimer and Cranmer squares, but they could not stop the Edmonds demolition. (In 1977, in what might have been seen as an ominous sign of things to come, the original corner grocery shop in Woolston was demolished.) Among the groups fighting valiantly to prevent the factory's destruction were the Historic Places Trust (now Heritage New Zealand), which had marked it for protection and given it a B classification in 1985, and the Charleston Neighbourhood Association. In 1987 the landmark 'Sure to Rise' sign was removed from the façade of the factory in the hope that it might be preserved, but its present whereabouts is unknown. (A story that it went to the heritage centre at Ferrymead proved to be untrue.) Locals, too, were concerned. John Hoskin who, with his wife Jenny, would be a prime mover in resurrecting the garden, said later that had he and others 'known there was such a local feeling about that building, we could have saved it ... We were concerned and the Historic Places Trust was concerned, but we had no cohesion. By the time we did rally, it was too late.'[16] In 1990, Linwood High School, which adjoined the old Edmonds site, was keen to turn the building into a theatre and auditorium, but, as *Listener* journalist Bruce Ansley put it, 'The deal was sewn up. The factory was to be demolished. So nothing was to be done about it ... And five days later, the building started to fall.'[17]

The factory's destruction in late 1990 was a major loss to New Zealand's architectural heritage. Jack Hislop and Joe Smart take a tea break during the demolition.

In October 1990 the building and the older formal areas of the garden were levelled, in preparation for replacement by a Mobil service station. All that was left of the original garden was a strip less than 3 metres wide. Christchurch lost, in Thelma Strongman's words, 'not just a notable factory building but also a unique palimpsest of the progression of our twentieth century garden history ... We have exchanged a symbol of local civic values for a symbol of multinational dominance and power.'[18] Thomas Edmonds would surely have agreed.

• • •

Among those who rescued Edmonds memorabilia from a skip after the demolition – a damaged portrait of Thomas; the Tickler file box that for years had housed the baking powder recipe on a shelf in the factory; a scale model of the factory made for the 1940 Centennial Exhibition – were John and Jenny Hoskin. They were instrumental in founding the Friends of Edmonds Factory Garden, which held its inaugural meeting in November 1990. The country's best-known factory building would never rise again, but the garden could.

BIL had already offered the site to the Christchurch City Council but the offer had been turned down. With the

Owners see no merit in Edmonds building

By NAOMI JAMIESON

The Edmonds factory building, under threat of demolition, has no architectural merit, structurally, aesthetically or commercially, according to its owners.

Mr Martin Lekner, chief executive of Brierley Properties Ltd, which owns the building, said the company disagreed with the building's Historic Places Trust B classification, which merits a building with permanent preservation because of "historical significance and architectural quality".

"We have an appreciation of the Historic Places Trust throughout New Zealand and we support them, but we differ with them as to the classification in this case. The cookbook is part of the country's heritage and should be preserved in libraries, but not the building," he said.

The Historic Places Trust's regional officer, Mrs Pam Wilson, said: "It is true that the landmark status of the Edmonds building has diminished with the loss of the 'Sure to Rise' sign but the Edmonds name is still a very marketable asset. I feel that Brierleys might be able to see how highly the public hold the building in their esteem, and capitalise on this."

Brierley Properties had "no specific position or building plan", but Mobil NZ was interested in the site, according to Mr Lekner. Brierley Properties agreed to give Mobil an option while Mobil applied to the Christchurch City Council for permission to build a service station.

"Our biggest worry is that street kids will get into the building, a fire will break out and someone will die," he said. Vandals and burglars have plagued the vacant building in the last six years.

"We don't need another service station in Ferry Road," a counsellor at Linwood High School, Mr Rodger Alexander, said.

"I think the building could be developed as a tertiary performing arts centre, perhaps in conjunction with the Polytechnic," he said.

considerable combined support of the Friends of Edmonds Factory Garden, Linwood High School, the Historic Places Trust, the Civic Trust, the Christchurch Beautifying Society, the New Brighton Lions and the Christchurch Central branch of NewLabour, another representation was made to the council, which bought the site in 1991 for $450,000.[19] Then came the hard work for the Friends, with council backing: drumming up wider support to rebuild the gardens. After Bluebird Foods took over the business in 1989, manager Roy Simmons was keen to help, and so John Hoskin, in his own words, 'looked at the 10-year plan (largely completed in five years) and selected the most expensive item' – the 1935 oval garden – then asked for $27,000 to recreate it. If Bluebird agreed, he suggested they could feature the result on the cover of the *Edmonds Cookery Book*.[20] The first $13,000 cheque was handed to Mayor Vicki Buck in July 1992, and she was there in 1994 to officially open the new Edmonds Factory Garden. Linwood High erected a marquee for the 300 guests and provided music with a quartet; home science students supplied the food, and the school's theatre arts group, dressed in Edwardian costume, served the drinks. There, once more, were Rube Overend's 'velvet' lawn, the pergola, pool and fountain – all the 'formal symmetry and Italianate character' of Edgar Taylor's design, but requiring rather less maintenance.[21] A memorial rose garden was opened on that day too – sponsored by Ken Ballantyne in the name of his wife Irene (Rene), Thomas and Jane's youngest daughter. The cream, gold and rusty red of the blooms echoed the bright sunray colours on the packaging of Edmonds' baking powder.[22]

Rescued when the factory was demolished, the Tickler file box was purportedly used to store the recipe for New Zealand's most famous baking powder. The plaque, installed in 1991, commemorates the factory and gardens and their designers. Opposite are Jenny and John Hoskin, dedicated and hardworking founders of the Friends of Edmonds Factory Garden, which is now once again a haven of beauty on Christchurch's busy Ferry Road.

A bronze plaque, donated by BIL in 1991, was installed in the garden: it acknowledges the designers of the factory and gardens, but doesn't identify who was responsible for their destruction. In 2002 Will Edmonds' youngest daughter Brenda, who was just a baby when Will died in 1914, dedicated a plaque to the memory of her father; she had also paid for the construction of two of the bridges in the garden.

Thanks to the work of the Friends of Edmonds Factory Garden, which has been under the presidency of John Hoskin for its entire existence, the garden has continued to develop, with more natural areas featuring easy-care evergreens and dwarf conifers. The 2010–11 Canterbury earthquakes brought challenges: there was 'liquefaction all over and a big hole opened up in one lawn'. The Friends still care lovingly for the rose garden and scented garden, weeding, pruning, running working bees and fundraising: by 2018 they had raised more than $120,000. The city council looks after the rest of the garden.[23] There is a children's playground and a large parkland area next door, and entry, through a metal gate with the famous 'Sure to Rise' symbol, is free. Those strolling in this beautiful and peaceful place – a favourite wedding venue and home to a popular annual picnic – can pause and relax on one of the artisan-made macrocarpa seats, their backs shaped like the unforgettable Edmonds image of the rising sun.

EDMONDS FACTORY GARDEN
SURE TO RISE

EDMONDS
ESTD PRIZE 1879
BAKING POWDER
SURE TO RISE
TRADE (REGISTERED) MARK
2.27 kg Net
EDMONDS ACTO
115g NET
BAKING POWDER
EDMONDS
ACTO
CAKE
BAKING POWDER
EDMONDS
PRIZE 1879
BAKING POWDER
SURE TO RISE
EDMONDS
ACTO
COLOURED
CAKE
BAKING POWDER
COLOURED
CAKE
BAKING POWDER
EDMONDS
SURE TO PLEASE
CUSTARD POWDER
ARTIFICIAL VANILLA
EDMONDS
CUSTARD POWDER
RASPBERRY
SURE TO RISE
ACTO
2.27 kg NET
EDMONDS
1879
BAKING POWDER
SURE TO RISE
ARTIFICIAL VANILLA
CUSTARD POWDER

EPILOGUE

More than 140 years since young Thomas Edmonds stepped off the *Waitangi* in Lyttelton with his wife Jane, their achievements are seen in tens of thousands of New Zealand kitchens, in some of Christchurch's most distinctive architecture, and in a memorable slogan and an outstanding piece of graphic design. As a new century dawned, the ownership of the Edmonds brands changed hands again, passing from Bluebird Foods to global food manufacturer Goodman Fielder in 2002, but the founder's name and the bright rising sun survive on a wide range of baking-related products, especially that famous baking powder, and on a legendary cookery book.

The landmark Art Deco Ferry Road factory has gone, but the buildings that Thomas and Jane presented to Christchurch in 1929 still stand, though their history has been chequered. In 1987 the Thomas Edmonds Restaurant (later renamed Retour) opened in the band rotunda, but the building, which had a Category 2 Heritage rating, was badly damaged during the 2010–11 Canterbury earthquakes. The 80-tonne copper-sheathed dome was saved and removed in 2012, to sit next to the ruined rotunda. Restoration began in March 2020 and by November the dome was lifted back into place, supported on scaffolding until the rotunda's new columns were made.[1] By April 2021, the rotunda was nearing completion; the most recent achievement was 'the reinstatement of lights on the rotunda's columns, which have once again made the structure a clear beacon at night'. The work was finished by the spring, 92 years after Jane first cut the ribbon.[2] Since 2015 the city council has restored Christchurch's other Edmonds-funded landmarks: the telephone booth (which was previously repaired and had opened for business in 1999), the pavilion (next to the band rotunda) and the clock tower. Another restoration was attended to in 2018 when a petition succeeded in having Edmond Street in Woolston changed to Edmonds Street.

Edmonds tins and packaging are enduring items of Kiwiana. In 2018, after lobbying from John Edmonds (pictured) and other descendants of the Edmonds family, the original name was restored after having been shortened to 'Edmond' in 1893.

There has been recognition, too, for Thomas's achievements as a leading entrepreneur and industrialist. In 2005 he was listed at number 45 – between prime minister Sir Robert Muldoon (44) and painter

Colin McCahon (46) – in a television programme called *New Zealand's Top 100 History Makers*: eight 'well-known New Zealanders' offered their choices over six episodes and the public's picks were revealed in a final live show.[3] Twelve years later, in 2017, Thomas was admitted into the New Zealand Business Hall of Fame, which recognises individuals who have made significant contributions to the nation's economic and social development – in his case in 'food manufacturing and commerce'.[4]

But perhaps the most ubiquitous legacy of this pioneering manufacturer and philanthropist is that essential piece of Kiwiana, the baking powder tin and its instantly recognisable label. In 2008 the decorative 'E', that cunning typographical treatment of Thomas's initials, was included in New Zealand Post's 'A to Z of New Zealand' collectable stamp series, between D for Dog of *Footrot Flats* and F for fantail.[5] Just how embedded the 'Sure to Rise' slogan and those rays of sunshine are in the New Zealand psyche, especially in Christchurch, became clear in a unique way after the devastating Canterbury earthquakes of 2010–11. It was a tin of Edmonds baking powder that inspired designer Rebecca Lovell-Smith when she created an enormously popular

souvenir tea towel. As she later explained, 'There was a group called Rise Up Christchurch – it was a charity – and my husband said, "You'd think they would have called it Sure to Rise" … And I spent the next day doing the design.' There was the familiar tin, showing Christchurch Cathedral and including words of the earthquake moment, such as 'munted' and 'kia kaha'. 'I didn't want to do a negative image. I wanted to do something that was focusing on the positive, because I expected that Christchurch would rise again. So I thought Sure to Rise was a very appropriate slogan.'[6]

So did Thomas Edmonds, all those years before, when he reassured a housewife, worried about her flat scones. The millions of baking powder tins that followed, along with other successful and indispensable products; the continuing editions of that essential and much loved cookery book; the lovely gardens that once surrounded his landmark factory; and, above all, that immediately identifiable symbol and slogan, now so firmly embedded in New Zealand culture – the visionary and determined young man from the East End of London has left an extraordinary legacy in a country on the other side of the world.

Whether on a stamp, in the cover art for a musical or as an emblem of hope after the Canterbury earthquakes, the famous Edmonds name, slogan and rising sun are an intrinsic part of New Zealand's social history.

CHRONOLOGY

1858 Thomas John Edmonds is born in East London.

c.1870 Thomas works for confectionery company Frederick Allen & Sons.

1879 Thomas marries Jane Elizabeth Middleton Irvine. They emigrate to Christchurch on the *Waitangi*.

1880 The Edmonds grocery store opens. Will is born, the first of eight children born between 1880 and 1898.

1880–83 Thomas develops a baking powder recipe.

1886 Edmonds Street is first mentioned in a newspaper.

1887 Edmonds Prize Baking Powder and Egg Powder are first mentioned in advertisements. The first patent, for self-raising egg flour, is also registered.

1888 Edmonds custard powder is first advertised.

1889 The first factory is built on Aldwins Road.

1889–90 Edmonds wins two first prizes at the New Zealand and South Seas Exhibition. The medals become a central feature of the label.

1890 The first sunburst appears in an advertisement.

1891 A logo that looks like the beginning of the baking powder label appears as part of a newspaper advertisement.

1894 100,000 tins of baking powder are sold. Around this time the grocery store is sold and Will leaves school to work for the company. He becomes works manager about five years later.

1896–97 The family moves to the corner of Ferry and Aldwins roads. The second factory is built.

1904 The family moves to the central city.

1905–07 Thomas, Jane and the youngest three girls live in Sydney.

1906 The factory is employing nine people, including Thomas's four sons. More prizes are won at the New Zealand International Exhibition.

1907 Loose recipe discs are included in tins.

1908 The first edition of the cookery book is published, then reprinted in 1909.

1910 The second edition of the cookery book is published.

1911 A long-running relationship with Ilott Advertising begins.

1912 A milestone is reached: one million tins of baking powder and other products are sold during the year. Around this time, a brick building is added behind the factory, which has 16 employees.

1913 A trade mark is registered for the Edmonds Sure to Rise label. Lillian marries Bert Cropp, who will play a central role in the company.

1914 Will dies suddenly, aged 34. Bert Cropp is made manager. The third edition of the cookery book is published.

1914–18 War affects production because of cream of tartar shortages.

1915 The company is incorporated as T.J. Edmonds Ltd.

1916 Thomas, Jane, Gertrude, Beatrice and Irene spend most of the year in the United States.

1917–19 Gertrude and Beatrice join the Cheer-Oh Girls and entertain audiences in Australia. Irene also takes part in some performances.

1920 Tenders are invited for a new factory and office buildings on Ferry Road.

1922 The famous Edmonds factory opens. Two million tins are sold and products are being exported.

1923 The famous factory gardens are created. The fourth edition of the cookery book is published.

1924–25 Edmonds has a stand at the Empire Exhibition in London. About this time, more land is bought next to the factory.

1926 Thomas is a founding shareholder of the Australian Cream Tartar Company in Sydney.

1928 A new black label is introduced for custard powder, probably to better differentiate it from baking powder.

1929 To mark the company's jubilee, Thomas and Jane make significant gifts to the city, including a band rotunda. There are now 28 factory employees. The factory gardens are extended.

1931 Thomas gifts land to protect the riverside boulevard, for what becomes Bickerton Reserve.

1932 Thomas dies, aged 74. The medals that had long characterised the baking powder label are removed. A cheaper baking powder brand, Acto, is introduced.

c.1933 The fifth edition of the cookery book is the first to move away from illustrated covers.

1935 Edmonds is the first Christchurch firm to introduce a 40-hour working week. Sure to Set jelly crystals are introduced, plus 28-pound tins of baking powder for commercial use. The first women are employed in the factory, which now has 50 workers.

1937 With annual sales now over 2.5 million tins, the factory is extended.

1938 Jane dies, aged 79.

1939–40 An impressive Edmonds display features at the Centennial Exhibition.

1941 War again affects cream of tartar supplies and the Acto brand becomes a phosphate-based powder.

1945 A large paddock beside the factory is gifted to the city, now Edmonds Park.

1952 The company wins a national competition for factory gardens.

1954 Edmonds celebrates its seventy-fifth anniversary.

1955 The publicity film *Cookery Nook* is released. With the release of the first 'De Luxe edition', the cookery book is sold for the first time, for 1 shilling.

1963 The company is publicly listed on the stock exchange.

1968 Edmonds Game Consolidated Ltd is established.

1973 With products being exported to 42 countries, the company wins a Trade Promotion Council Export Award.

1977 The original Edmonds grocery store building is demolished after nearly 100 years as a corner store.

1978 The centennial edition of the cookery book is published.

1979 In its centennial year, the company wins the prestigious Governor-General's Award for Exporting. There are now 125 employees.

1982 Edmonds is taken over by H.W. Smith Ltd, who soon sell some of the operations to Bunting & Co. Ltd who, in turn, sell part to W.F. Tucker Ltd. These changes shift the head office and product manufacturing to Auckland.

1984 Bunting sells its residual stake in Edmonds, including the Christchurch factory, to Brierley Investments Ltd.

1989 The Tucker Group becomes part of Bluebird Foods Ltd.

1990 The famous Edmonds factory is demolished. John and Jenny Hoskin establish Friends of Edmonds Factory Garden.

1991 Christchurch City Council purchases what remains of the factory garden from Brierley Investments for $450,000.

2002 The Edmonds brand is sold by Bluebird Foods Ltd to Goodman Fielder.

2008 The sixtieth edition helps to celebrate the 100th anniversary of the cookery book. Edmonds is selected as the 'E' in New Zealand Post's A to Z of New Zealand stamp series.

2011–12 Several of Thomas's gifts to the city, including the band rotunda, are severely damaged in the Canterbury earthquakes.

2016 Significantly updated by Alexa Johnston, the sixty-ninth edition of the cookery book is published.

2017 Thomas is admitted to the New Zealand Business Hall of Fame.

2018 After losing this over time, an 's' is returned to Edmonds Street in Woolston.

2021 The Edmonds Band Rotunda is reopened after restoration and repair.

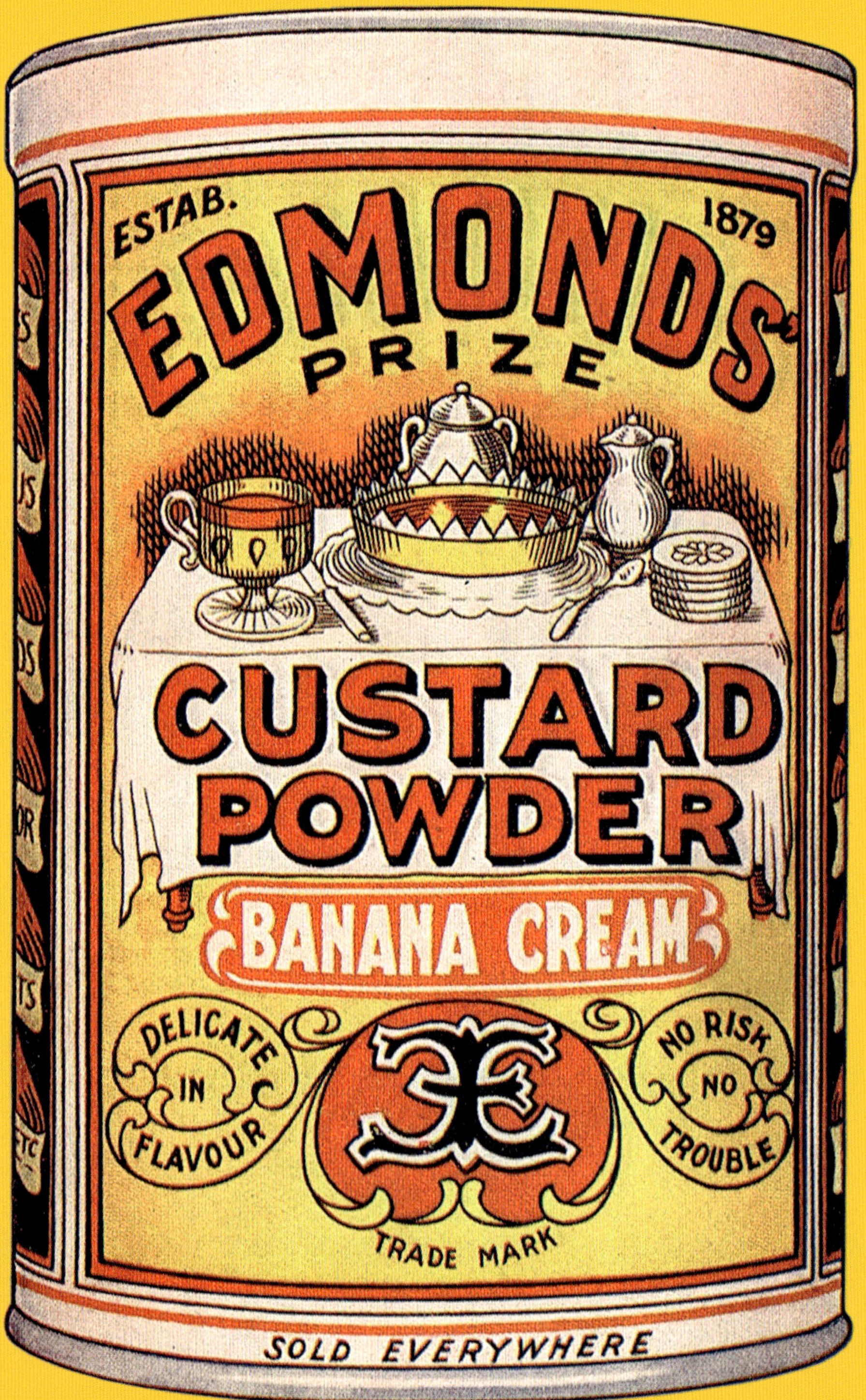
ESTAB. 1879
EDMONDS'
PRIZE
CUSTARD
POWDER
BANANA CREAM
DELICATE IN FLAVOUR
NO RISK NO TROUBLE
TRADE MARK
SOLD EVERYWHERE

GALLERY

THE STORY OF A DESIGN

The Edmonds baking powder label is one of New Zealand's most enduring and recognisable brands. Unusually, the design has remained remarkably stable. The combination of diverse elements, strong, positive colours and the universally appealing themes of sunshine and cooking, has ensured its popularity. It has become a mainstay of both Kiwiana and this country's culinary culture.

Yet, as extensive research has revealed, there have been a number of modest changes to the label over the years. One aspect, however, remains a stubborn secret: the identity of the label's designer.

The biggest changes to the label were perhaps those made at the very beginning. The earliest such designs were published as advertisements in August 1890 and January 1891. Curiously, both designs were rotated 90 degrees and printed on their side. This certainly created significant visual impact, but the reason may have been purely practical: a single column advertisement was cheaper.

The earliest known design was a strongly geometric starburst, prefiguring the label's now familiar sunrise but in a far more abstracted and architectural form. Like its predecessor, the second design did not include a single item of baking; it also discarded the sunrise in favour of a perfunctory typographical arrangement. This introduced the company and its prize product in what looked very much like the top part of the label we know today. 'EDMONDS' appeared in a decorative Victorian font, soon discarded in favour of a more classical font, but the original typographic touch would

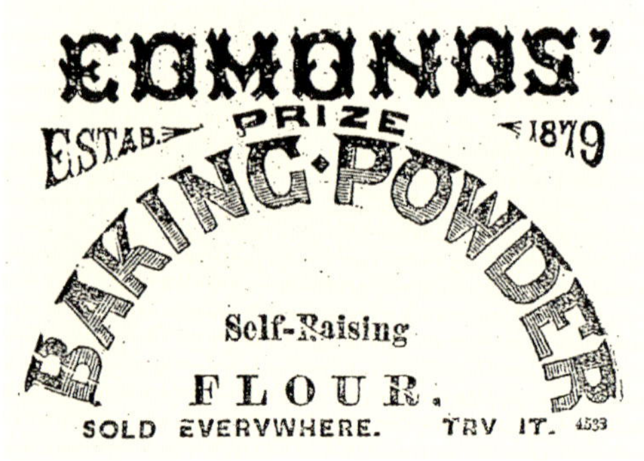

The two earliest Edmonds logos thought to exist are shown left, from August 1890 (top) and January 1891. The earliest label known to exist is shown opposite, likely from the early to mid-1890s. The iconic Edmonds 'E', shown top right, is now thought to be a clever graphic device combining Thomas's initials – TJE – using a Victorian font.

live on in the form of the famous Edmonds 'E'. This apparently stylised capital letter is, in fact, a composite arrangement of the founder's initials, TJE – Thomas John Edmonds. Now over 130 years old, and close to 90 years since Thomas's death, this attractive device must surely qualify as one of the most persistent and pervasive tributes to any New Zealand businessperson.

It is not known how soon after the company's beginnings in 1879 the first Edmonds label was designed. Newspapers offer some clues, though they are not necessarily definitive. Edmonds applied for a patent in April 1887 for 'an invention for self-raising egg flour, for making cakes, puddings, etc', and by February 1888 advertisements were warning customers that there was 'no loose powder sold' – presumably worried about illicit trade – and urging them to 'see that the name and trademark is on each tin'.

Based on an assessment of two details, it seems likely that the earliest label dates from the early to mid-1890s. The first detail is the presence of medals from the 1889–90 New Zealand Jubilee Exhibition in the bottom panel (and not medals from 1901 and 1906–07 exhibitions that were later used). The second detail is a testimonial by James W. Morton on the back panel. Dated 18 November 1887, it was unlikely to have been used for long, given the importance of remaining current and the large volume of other testimonials Edmonds could have used. In fact, the label even encouraged people to 'See Testimonials and Receipts Enclosed'.

Unusually, the early Edmonds label does not carry a printer's mark but discreetly includes a fine print code, 30738. This number matches one used on a very early label for egg powder (see p. 228), in which the identifier, most likely a repeatedly used customer reference, is integrated with the printer's name, 'Weeks Ltd. Lithos ChCh'. This discovery raises the real possibility that

Label details can provide important clues for production dates. For example, Custard Bay, as profiled in the label panel above, was part of Edmonds display at the 1906–07 International Exhibition. The iconic medals, used on the label until around April 1932, also helpfully demarcate labels to before or after events. Shown in the middle of these pages, decorative scrolls were a long-running feature on Edmonds' baking powder tins and some wider packaging. Different designs, like those shown far right, were also pressed into lids to support the overall presentation of tins.

an artist from Weeks Ltd was responsible for Edmonds' original label designs or at least one of the earliest variants.

Although Philip Presants of the Christchurch Press Company almost certainly did not design the original baking powder label, as was once thought, an uncut sheet of labels can be seen in a photograph of Presants at work in late 1904 or early 1905 (see p. 236). The outline of the design components, particularly a plaque on the back panel with the shape of an honours board, links it to a design style used until about 1916.

Under the banner of 'Exhibition Chorus', one such label used the plaque to present a poem titled 'Custard Bay'. This was the name of part of the Edmonds' installation at the 1906–07 New Zealand International Exhibition, which was dedicated to the 'very popular and high-class article' of custard powder. Sans 1906 medals, the label was probably produced especially for the event. The Custard Bay display included a steamer waiting at a wharf to carry the goods to every port, a park in the foreground and the poem, heralding custard powder's merit, in the centre. Coloured lights were included for night-time effects.

Like other ephemera, early labels were inevitably damaged because they were made of paper and were attached to containers used in messy and steamy kitchens. Early tins in immaculate condition are very rare, though Goodman Fielder holds an old scrapbook that includes near pristine labels for several Edmonds products. This archive has been important to better understanding the baking powder label's evolution and history, though the absence of any dates leaves room for many uncertainties.

Dating baking powder labels is not always easy but various clues can help. Generally, reference to the name of the incorporated business, T.J. Edmonds Ltd, dates a label after the company's incorporation on 1 April 1915. This helpfully distinguishes earlier tins from the very large majority of (later) tins and labels that still exist. The presence or absence of medals at

the bottom of a label shows whether it dates from before or after April 1932 – a best estimate of when medals were removed from the design. Specific medals clearly link designs to events such as exhibitions. Early labels between 1906 and 1915 can also be dated because the previous year's tin sales figure is included in the design. The back panel of the 1916 label also provides a sales chronology.

Several other differences are also evident in labels throughout the decades, though actual dates are hard to pinpoint. For example, the baking delights on the earliest known label included three triangular pieces on the right-hand side – probably scones – that were subsequently permanently replaced by a single round pie in that area of the baking line-up. After early outings, the sun shrank in size and retreated to the horizon – perhaps a more earnest attempt to portray it as rising. This change also reduced the size of the words 'SURE TO RISE' (there were also variations in the size and position of the 'TO'). With more room to shine, the rays themselves – stopping at or penetrating the 'BAKING POWDER' arc – varied in expanse and colour intensity as the years went by. Also changeable was whether supplementary white lines were overlaid to exaggerate the sun's glistening effect. The apostrophe on EDMONDS' was a mainstay of early labels and company advertisements until it was largely dropped around 1915, possibly related to the company's incorporation.

Much remains to be discovered about this iconic and beloved design. It has helped to underpin Edmonds' success as one of New Zealand's most enduring and best-known brands – a credit to the original, unknown designer. The marketing experts say that a brand is far more than a logo, but, as the Edmonds story makes clear, a logo is most certainly an essential part of a brand.

EDMONDS
PRIZE
ESTD 1879
BAKING POWDER
SURE TO RISE
TRADE MARK
(REGISTERED)
EDMONDS
ACTO
115g NET
BAKING POWDER
REGD
MONDS
ESTD 1879
COLOURED
CAKE
BAKING POWDER
SURE TO RISE
EDMONDS
ACTO
CAKE
BAKING POWDER
REGD
EDMONDS
PRIZE
CUST
POWD
TRADE MARK
EDMONDS
ESTD PRIZE 1879
BAKING POWDER
SURE TO RISE
REGISTERED
RASPBERRY
EDMONDS
CUSTARD
POWDER
RASPBERRY
EDMONDS
PRIZE
ESTD 1879
BAKING POWDER
SURE TO RISE
TRADE MARK
(REGISTERED)
EDMONDS
PRIZE
ESTD 1879
BAKING POWDER
SURE TO RISE
TRADE MARK
(REGISTERED)
Edmonds
ARTIFICIAL
VANILLA
CUSTARD
POWDER
VANILLA
EDMONDS
SURE TO PLEASE
CUSTARD
POWDER
TRADE MARK
EDMONDS
ACTO
BAKING POWDER
REGD
EDMONDS
ESTD PRIZE 1879
BAKING POWDER
SURE TO RISE
TRADE MARK
(REGISTERED)
28 lbs. NETT WEIGHT
ACTO
BAKING
POWDER
REGD
28 LBS
T. J. EDMONDS LTD.
EDMONDS
PRIZE
ESTD 1879
BAKING POWDER
SURE TO RISE
(REGISTERED)
28 LBS
Prepared with CREAM OF TARTAR
T. J. EDMONDS LTD
EDMONDS
CUSTARD
POWDER

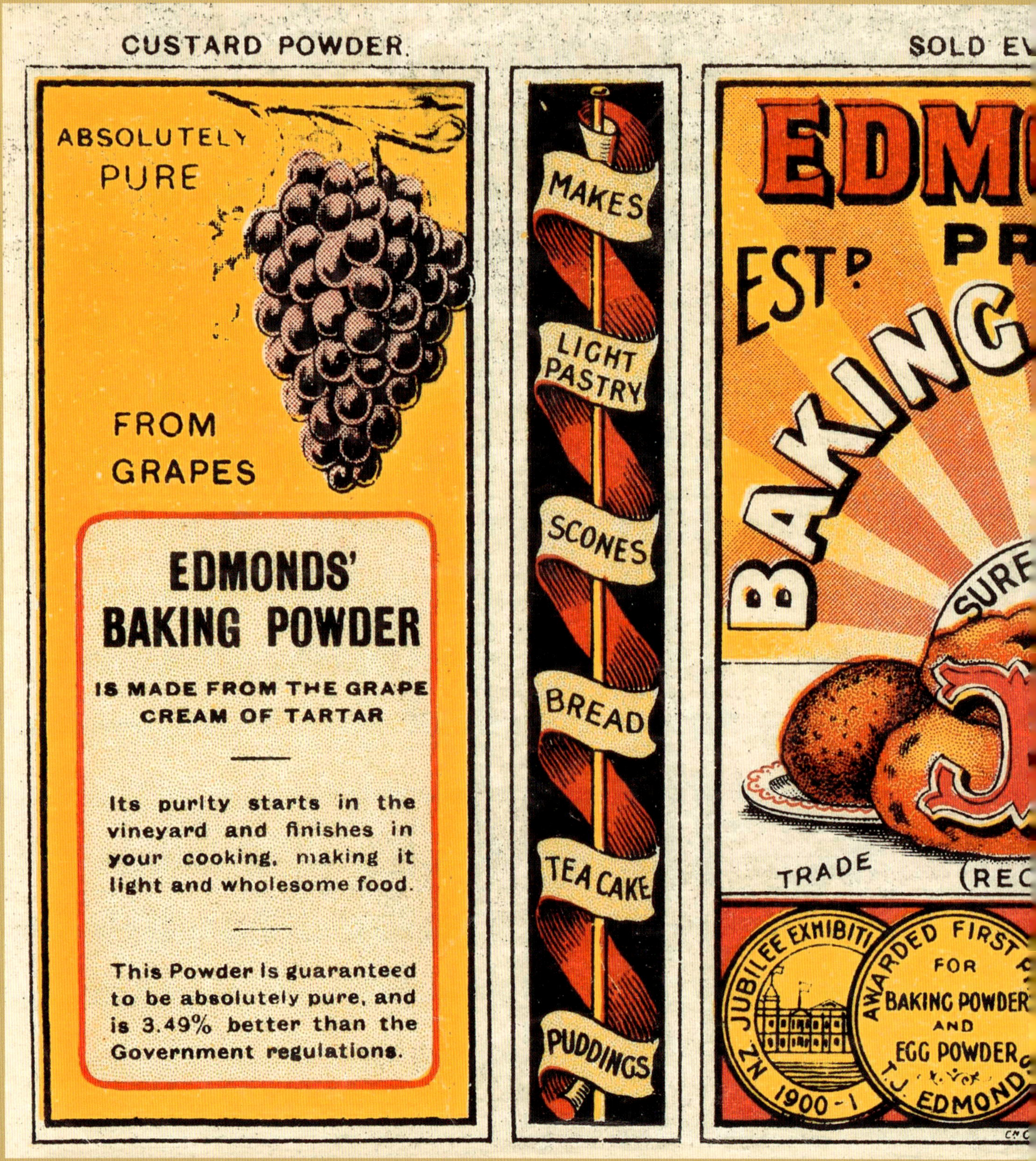
CUSTARD POWDER.
SOLD EV
ABSOLUTELY
PURE
FROM
GRAPES
EDMONDS'
BAKING POWDER
IS MADE FROM THE GRAPE
CREAM OF TARTAR
Its purity starts in the vineyard and finishes in your cooking, making it light and wholesome food.
This Powder is guaranteed to be absolutely pure, and is 3.49% better than the Government regulations.
MAKES
LIGHT PASTRY
SCONES
BREAD
TEA CAKE
PUDDINGS
EDM
ESTD
PR
BAKING
SURE
TRADE
(REC
N.Z. JUBILEE EXHIBITI
1900-1
AWARDED FIRST
FOR
BAKING POWDER
AND
EGG POWDER
T.J. EDMONDS

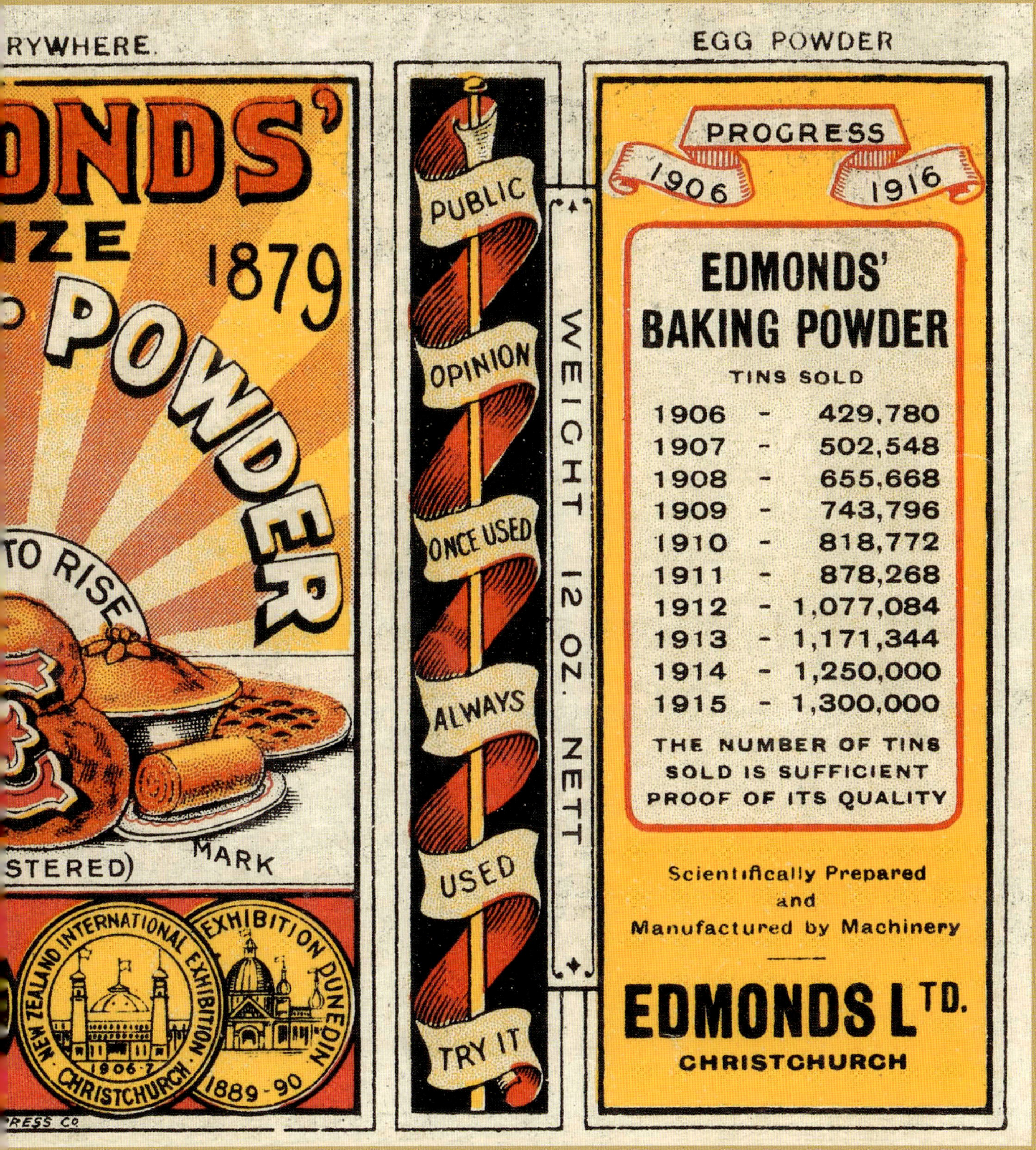
RYWHERE.
ONDS'
IZE
1879
POWDER
TO RISE
STERED)
MARK
NEW ZEALAND INTERNATIONAL EXHIBITION
1906-7
CHRISTCHURCH
EXHIBITION DUNEDIN
1889-90
RESS CO
PUBLIC
OPINION
ONCE USED
ALWAYS
USED
TRY IT
WEIGHT 12 OZ. NETT
EGG POWDER
PROGRESS
1906
1916
EDMONDS'
BAKING POWDER
TINS SOLD
1906 - 429,780
1907 - 502,548
1908 - 655,668
1909 - 743,796
1910 - 818,772
1911 - 878,268
1912 - 1,077,084
1913 - 1,171,344
1914 - 1,250,000
1915 - 1,300,000
THE NUMBER OF TINS
SOLD IS SUFFICIENT
PROOF OF ITS QUALITY
Scientifically Prepared
and
Manufactured by Machinery
EDMONDS LTD.
CHRISTCHURCH

I was for three years or more studying the problem, during which time various other brands began to creep in. This gave me an impetus in my investigations and enabled me to produce at the end of the period the powder which has become a Dominion favourite and known by one and all as "Edmonds' Sure to Rise," and also resulted in my working out a formula for egg powder, custard powder, and self-raising flour. On completion of the formula, I immediately approached the merchants regarding stocking "Sure to Rise," and succeeded in inducing several of them to place trial orders on their shelves. By this step I considered good fortune had turned my way, and that all I would have to do was to manufacture for the demand.

THE FACTORY AS IT WAS IN 1889

Three months elapsed and no orders arrived from the merchants. Wondering what could be the matter, I at once went to them and was informed that they had never been asked for Edmonds' "Sure to Rise." Realising that it was not known on the market it became necessary to create a demand.

The method adopted was a personal canvass. It was my custom, if people whom I saw would not buy, to leave the powder with them without payment on the understanding that if they did not like it I would take it back next visit.

It is with a certain amount of pride that I look back on these days and remember that never one tin was returned, but instead they asked for more.

Soon after this the business began to grow and necessitated my putting all my time and energy into the manufacture of Edmonds' "Sure to Rise." Enquiries began to come in from all parts of Canterbury, including orders from the merchants, and it was from this point that the business began to

THE FACTORY AS ADVERTISING HAS MADE IT TO-DAY

HOW ADVERTISING HAS HELPED MY BUSINESS

The Interesting Story of Edmonds' Baking Powder—a Product which sells 1,250,000 tins per annum in New Zealand—6½ tins every year to every family in the Dominion

By Mr. T. J. EDMONDS

ON SEPTEMBER 26TH, 1879, I landed in Lyttelton on the ship *Waitangi* after a three months' voyage from London.

Being a married man in my twentieth year, and realising my responsibilities,

MR. T. J. EDMONDS

I at once set about devising means to provide the necessary loaf, and started my business career in a small grocer's shop, with a turnover of about £20 per week.

Finding this was not a very paying concern, I had to look about and find means to increase my income. My business in the grocery line brought me in contact with baking powder, and the idea came to me that if I could manufacture a satisfactory article of this sort there should be a fair sale.

Previous to leaving London I had spent some time in one of the largest confectioner's businesses, that of Messrs. Allen & Sons, and became acquainted with the use and mixing of powders relative to sherbet making.

Having decided to tackle the baking powder business I at once started operations, and one of the chief difficulties that I was confronted with was what name to give it.

Recognising that a good name is an asset, not only to man, but also to an article, long deliberation was indulged in before deciding. One day a lady customer when being persuaded by me to purchase a tin, complained that when using other brands the scones were very flat. I assured her that if she used my brand, her scones would be sure to rise. The name "Sure to Rise" hit me very forcibly, and Edmonds' "Sure to Rise" it has been from that day forward.

My first mixing of baking powder consisted of about 200 tins, which found a ready sale among my own customers, and as time went on the clients would take two or three tins each for friends. Business steadily increased.

Encouraged by the testimonials and enquiries for my baking powder, I decided to concentrate my energy exclusively on the scientific blending of the ingredients that go to make my Edmonds' "Sure to Rise" baking powder.

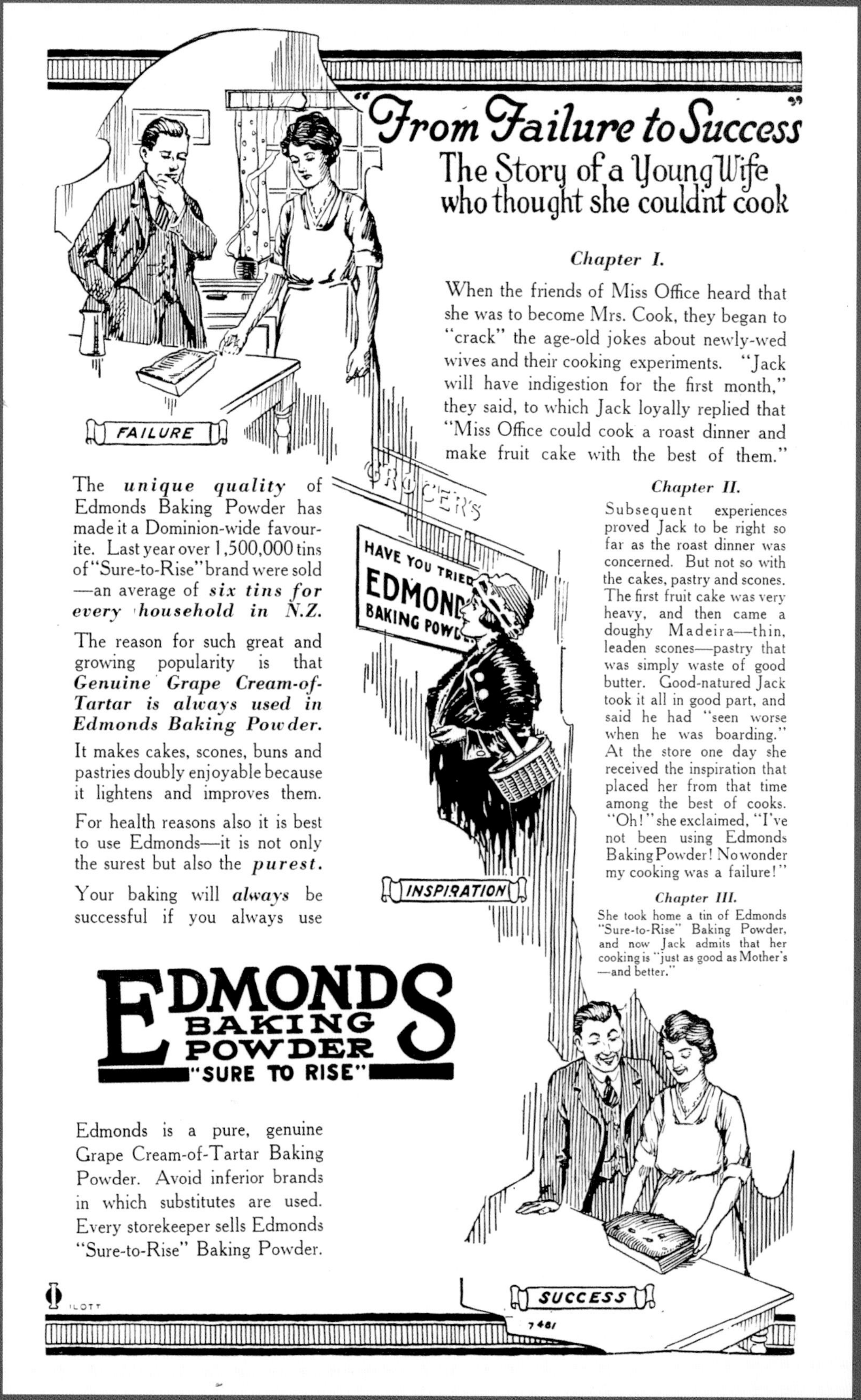

Advertisement from *Mirror* (1922)

Advertisement from *Mirror* (1924)

SOME MORE 6-INCH D.C. DISPLAYS

nine per cent. cream of tartar is the staple ingredient in "Sure to Rise," and during my very early days of manufacturing one ton would perhaps last me twelve months. I now use about 300 tons every twelve months.

During the whole of my business career I have dealt almost exclusively with the merchants, and consequently my cost of distribution has been greatly decreased. It is now an easy line to dispose of, and at the same time enables the merchant to secure a fair working profit.

You could travel every nook and corner of this fair country, and I doubt very much whether you could find a shop that did not stock my lines.

It is quite obvious from the figures already quoted that there is an enormous demand for Edmonds' "Sure to Rise" in New Zealand, and any stoppage of our output would give thousands of housewives a great deal of inconvenience.

To obviate the risk of any such happening, all filling, body forming, mixing and blending machines are duplicated and a large reserve stock of raw materials is always kept on hand, in case a cargo should by any chance go down or be short shipped.

The whole of the office work is done by an accountant and clerk, and this fact bears out the argument previously advanced that dealing in bulk with the merchant greatly reduces the cost of distribution to the manufacturer, and also reduces his chance of bad debts to a minimum.

Some short time ago I opened up trade with the Fiji Islands, and repeat orders indicate that my baking powder has gained a firm footing there. Enquiries from Australia and also for my Cookery Books are of frequent occurrence, and we have several times been approached to place "Sure to Rise" on the market in Tasmania.

assume dimensions which have since grown beyond all expectations.

From 1879 to 1889 the output grew per annum steadily from a few hundred tins to 21,000. From 1889 to 1905 the output grew to 370,600 ; and from 1905 to 1915 1,250,000 for the twelve months.

About June, 1911, when I considered that the limit of our output had been reached, the figures stood at 878,268 tins per annum, I was interviewed on the question of extensive advertising by Ilott's Advertising Agency. For years I had indulged in a mild sort of advertising, but had never looked at it in a very serious light. After listening to the arguments of Mr. J. M. A. Ilott, of the above-mentioned firm, and giving

was selling 878,268 tins per annum, it was my firm belief that the maximum had been reached, but it has gone ahead, and the annual output has grown to just on 1,250,000 tins, or nearly double the amount that was manufactured before advertising was adopted on any scale of note.

I can speak of advertising with a great deal of confidence, and can trace direct results. Since the inauguration of the advertising campaign I adopted a tabulated system covering the whole of New Zealand, and have thereby been able to watch the growth and compare the results each year. This has in itself been exceedingly interesting and has proved to me very conclusively the

A GROUP OF 6-INCH D.C. PRESS ADVERTISEMENTS

the matter very careful thought, I somewhat dubiously decided at least to let them handle my advertising on a somewhat larger scale than usual for a period of twelve months.

That this step was a wise move has been amply illustrated, for during the period that Messrs. Ilott conducted the 1911 campaign, the sales advanced by 200,000 tins, or more than double any increase shown in any particular year in the history of the business. It was this factor that so strongly illustrated to me the benefits of advertising executed by capable hands.

The remarkable success achieved by this first campaign turned me into an ardent believer in advertising.

When the output of " Sure to Rise " great benefits that can be derived from systematic advertising.

Another and very important branch of my advertising consists of the Edmonds' " Sure to Rise " Cookery Book. This production is supplied free on application, and in it are embodied all the best recipes that have been gathered from time to time. The third edition is now in process of circulation, and altogether about 500,000 books, covering the three issues, have been distributed throughout the Dominion. Labels and insets are also another very large item, and our printing and advertising account is heavy.

As illustrating the remarkable growth of the business in another light let me draw attention to this fact. Ninety-

Egg powder was an early Edmonds product, first mentioned in newspaper advertising in 1887. Its main selling point was its reliability compared to the variable quality and unpredictability of real eggs. The bottom label is one of the oldest Edmonds labels known to exist, likely from the early 1890s. It was probably designed by the printer Weeks Ltd. The smaller label details below relate to the evolution of egg powder. All come after 1915 as they refer to the incorporated company, T. J. Edmonds Ltd. The left two labels also carry (on their side panels) the legal disclosure required from 1913: 'This powder is artificially coloured to resemble eggs, but possesses none of their nutritive properties.' The risk that this would put customers off probably led to egg powder being renamed cake powder from 1923.

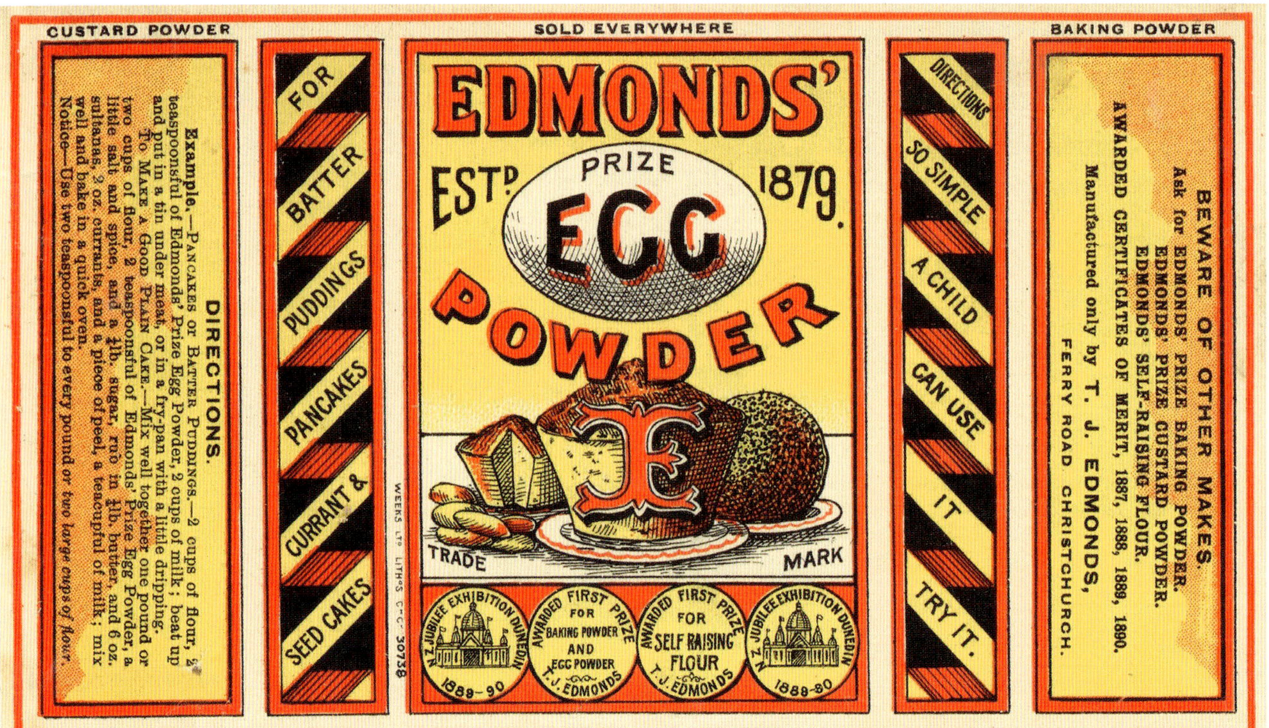

itors to Christchurch can spend a
easant hour or two in our six-storey
ilding. The view from the Roof Gar-
n is beautiful and extensive, while the
cellent cuisine and smart service of
r Tea Room are always appreciated.

LOSSOM DUSTING
R cures chafes and
s. tins, post free.—Ad.
. HAWKINS, George
n.

rimean and Indian War
enduring for half a cen-
ble worry and annoy-
n and continuously dis
wound received in the
. Grace, of Broughton
l, Dunedin, has at last
ely relief but complete
two boxes of SPRING
TMENT.

G BLOSSOM
TMENT

EVERYWHERE.
1s. ONLY 6d and 1s.

NE"—the great Corn,
nion Cure. Price 6d

you suffer from ASTH-
not hesitate, but send
in of—,
INSTANT RELIEF
HMA POWDER.
Influenza, Hay Fever,
ctions and Difficult

and 2s per tin, ser
eceipt of price.
HAWKINS,
CHEMIST
TREET, DUNEDIN.
E:-
ch pleasure in announc-
re the price of "Orange
be reduced to 5s for
eatment.

NERVOUS BREA

METHODIST MINIST

(By Telegraph.—Per P

AUCKLA

The Rev. William
know Methodist Mini
just been relieved from
in the Church on accou
breakdown, was found
Thursday morning in
with a revolver wound
He was 57 years of ag
and died before reachi

He was very much
and saw a doctor last
out for a walk to Ne
Thursday, morning an
after he returned Mrs
shot.

Mr Slade entered
Church of New Zealan
was stationed at Rag
and Port Chalmers
Whilst stationed at P
1886 he offered himsel
mission work and was a
In 1903 he returned to
in New Zealand and w
Onehunga, and for four
placed in charge of the
in Dunedin.

THE MAY QUEEN

The eighth count for
Gala, organised by Mr
in aid of the Westla
was made on Saturday.
The positions were as
No. 10—Fanny Knowl
and white); Rimu

No. 7—Margaret Johns
Kumara

No. 2—Maisie McInto
blue); senior classes
State School

No. 4—Alice Wood, (gr
vent School Hoki

No. 6—Gladys Woolhous
black); ex-scholars
State School

ny doubt. Perhaps
form shown by the
ay leave the stewards
rider's previous guilt,
dealt with the earlier
d at a decision in re-
y cannot well reopen
t, they can do is to
mind and pay special
actions of the parties
"malpractice" would
the appointment of
one with any real
g ever believed. The
s such as I have re-
wever, safely be dis-
is not one practical
on but will admit that
Mahon, Gordon, and
their work we have
and infinitely cleaner
eviously.

Trotting Club will hold
on the Awapuni course
ght harness horse en-
sed an enjoyable day's
intend being present
Jockey Club's fixture
e the opportunity of
Plymouth train as far
rth, seeing the trots,
Wanganui by the train
at 4.50 p.m.

no further withdrawals
ui Cup, and unless
een should occur there
testants. Such a field
proportions—not so
the competitors are
h interference and not
the race of interest.

been engaged to ride
ving Handicap at Wa-
be doubted whether
has been racing over
recently, will be able
opponents during the
journey.

at Gisborne Allegory
essly and returned to
losure on three legs.
from the Wanganui

Parker's colts, Multiply
carry out his Jackson
ts. The former, in
her Davon, may be
nevirke next week, but
to have gone all to
making a noise.

ners are reminded that
Nelson Jockey Club's
Friday next.

FOR WANGANUI CUP

PRESS ASSOCIATION.)
NUI, 24th February.
with the Wanganui
mn meeting, opening
final payments have

Advertisements from *Edmonds Cookery Book* (1923, above) and *Evening Post* (1913)
Following pages: Promotional discs from tins (c.1910–30)

Edmonds'
CUSTARD
is delicious with
STEWED FRUIT

EDMONDS
EDMONDS
EGG
POWDER
EGG POWDER

HAVE YOU TRIED
EDMONDS
CUSTARD
POWDER
ARTIFICIAL
VANILLA
Sold in 4lb and 10oz. Sizes

EDMONDS
CAKE
POWDER
THE
SUN
IS THE
SOURCE OF
LIGHT
THE
SOURCE OF
LIGHTNESS
IN CAKES
IS
SURE TO RISE
EDMONDS'
COLOURED
CAKE POWDER

CAKES LIKE THESE
EASILY MADE
WITH
EDMONDS
EGG POWDER

THE BRITISH BULLDOG
AND
EDMONDS
SELF-RISING
FLOUR
Always
RISE TO THE OCCASION.

THERE'S
ALWAYS
EDMONDS
EGG
POWDER
What's the use!

EDMONDS
EGG
POWDER
EDMONDS
CUSTARD
POWDER
EDMONDS
BAKING
POWDER
EDMONDS'
SELF
RISING
FLOUR
A TRUMP
HAND

Who
Said
EDMONDS'
CUSTARD?

EDMONDS CUSTARD
IS DELIGHTFUL

EDMONDS
Custard with
Rhubarb

EDMONDS' CUSTARD
PURE FRUIT FLAVOUR

ALL MILK PUDDINGS
ARE
EASILY MADE
WITH
EDMONDS
CUSTARD POWDER

EDMONDS
CUSTARD
WITH
TRIFLE
IS JUST
PERFECT

EDMONDS CUSTARDS
DELICIOUS TO THE LAST DROP

Alas! this is
no vision
it is
EDMONDS'
EGG
POWDER

OBTAINED
THROUGHOUT
EDMONDS
ESTD PRIZE
BAKING POWDER
NEW ZEALAND
IN
TINS ONLY

THE
SOURCE
OF
MANY
GOOD
THINGS
EDMONDS' CUSTARD POWDER

EDMONDS'
CUSTARD
WITH STEWED PEACHES
IS DELICIOUS

EDMONDS' CUSTARD
A GOOD
COMBINATION
WITH PINEAPPLE

EDMONDS EGG POWDER
MAKES
CAKES
LIGHT SEED

EDMONDS
CUSTARDS
GOOD FOR
CHILDREN'S
PARTIES

Edmonds'
CUSTARD
With
PEACH
PIE

EDMONDS'
CUSTARD
WITH STRAWBERRIES

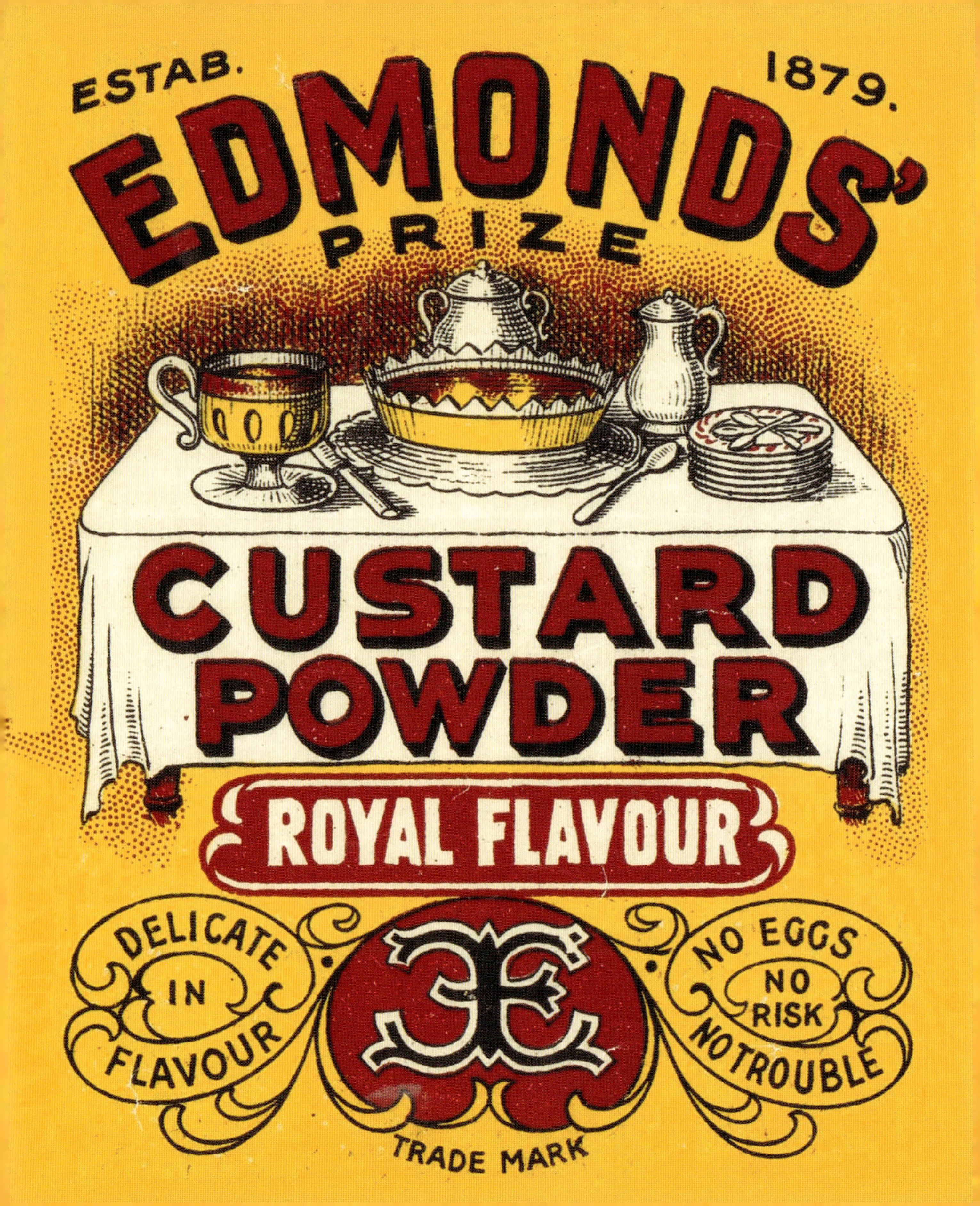
ESTAB. 1879.
EDMONDS'
PRIZE
CUSTARD
POWDER
ROYAL FLAVOUR
DELICATE IN FLAVOUR
NO EGGS NO RISK NO TROUBLE
TRADE MARK

The Christchurch Press Company played an important role in design and printing work for Edmonds in the early 1900s. The immaculate Edmonds sales docket, created in 1907–09, is attributed to designer and lithographer Philip Presants. The photo shows the company's printing presses hard at work in 1905. In the photo on the following pages, Presants is seated on the right, working directly on a lithographic stone, from which labels and advertisements were printed. A sheet of Edmonds labels high on the left wall suggests that Presants or one of his colleagues created (or updated) one or more of Edmonds' early designs.

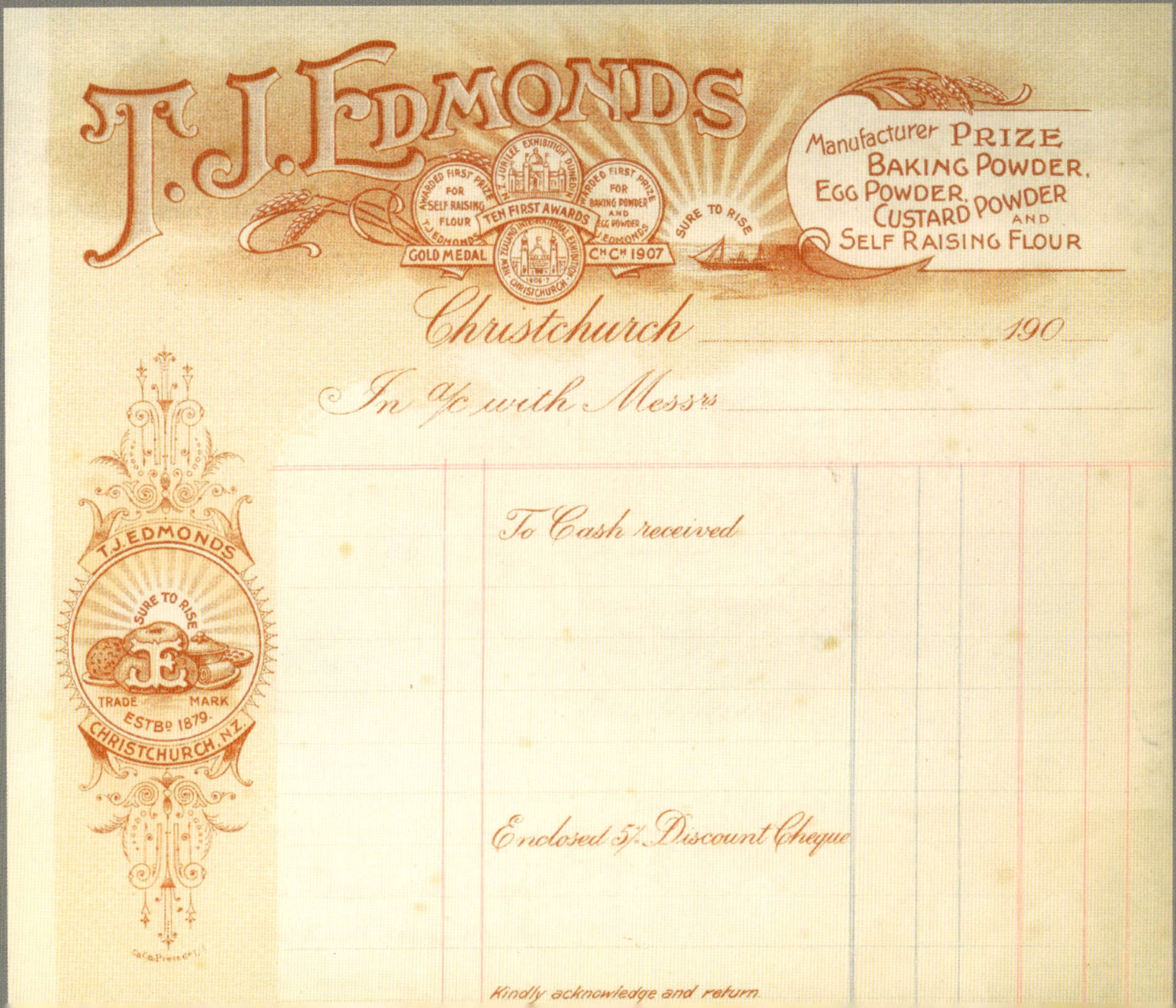

KAIAPOI
ASK FOR THE 'TIGER' BRAND
WEEKLY PRESS
ON SALE HERE
GIBBONS
FARM SEEDS
TREES PLANTS AND BULBS
H.C. GIBBONS & Co.
LAMBTON QUAY WELLINGTON
AULSEBROOK'S BISCUITS
EVERYONE SAYS
K JAM
IS THE PUREST AND BEST
K TOMATO SAUCE
ASK FOR
K MARMALADE
ASK FOR TIGER TEAS
COOLIE & PALM TEA
ON SALE HERE
SOCIETY OF RAILWAY SERVANTS
K TOMATO SAUCE K
FAR EAST
MANN

BALLANTYNE'S
NEW ZEALAND
The Weekly Press
Christmas
K K
S. KIRKPATRICK & Co
K K
THE WEEKLY PRESS
BALLANTYNES
COSTUMIERS
FIRST
CHRISTCHURCH
WEEKLY PRESS
The Weekly Press
JUBILEE INDUSTRIAL EXHIBITION
KAIAPOI
TIGER BRAND
PREMIER
BOOTS & SHOES
K TOMATO SAUCE
TOMATO SAUCE K K MARMALADE

Advertisements from *Mirror* (1927, above) and *Otago Daily Times* (1925)
Following pages: Various newspaper advertisements, 1923–30

evious year, but if we turn to 1919 we d the figure was £23,295, to-day's figure ing an increase of £14,634. Going back other five years to 1914, salaries show £13,202; so that the increase in the e years, 1919-1924, is greater than the al sum payable in 1914. Part of this accounted for by yearly increments, and rt by the fact that in some cases pay- ent by fees has been eliminated, but by the greatest portion is for new appoint- ents, thus giving striking testimony to e development and activities of the Uni- rsity.

STUDENTS' FEES.

A decrease of £919 in students' fees ap- ars large for a decrease of only 13 dents, but this year we lost for the st time the fees for the education class; rthermore, our income from students' fees governed not solely by the number of idents, but by the classes which they ke, there being a considerable variation fees as between the different faculties.

RENTAL FROM RUNS.

The item rent from Otago runs, £12,715, some £8000 in advance of the last year two, this being accounted for by the ayment of back rents from Benmore. It ill be seen that the bank balance debit at 31/12/23 was nearly £5000, and at /12/24 it was reduced to £169; and as appeared desirable to capitalise certain oneys, amounting to £3000, the extra 3000 is thus accounted for. This, of course, oes not mean that we have gone ahead accordance with the above amounts, as is necessary to turn to the arts and eneral account to ascertain the results of e year's working.

ARTS AND GENERAL ACCOUNT.

The arts and general account commenced e year with a debit of £169 11s 2d, and nished with a debit of £1444 14s 11d, thus ppearing to have gone back by £1375 3s . It will be noted, however, that there as a transfer to capital previously men- oned of £3010, so that the net result ould seem to be a gain on the year's work £1734 16s 3d. However, it is sometimes id that the figures are not always what ey appear to be, and such is the case this instance, as owing to the unsettled osition of some of our runs, and the diffi- lty of ascertaining the probable income, e sum taken into account last year as tstanding was £1261 5s 7d less than the nount actually received from this source after all these additions and deducations e result for the year is a gain of £473 s 8d.

The balance sheet needs little comment, e most noticeable feature being the in- ease of £11,410 on the amount invested debentures and inscribed stock.

We now turn to the accounts of the rious schools:—

MEDICAL SCHOOL.

The balances for the past five years e:—1920 (dr.), £3556 8s 9d; 1921 (dr.), 020 9s 9d; 1922 (cr.), £566 14s 2d; 1923 r.), £338 10s 1d; 1924 (dr), £2251 10s. ne debit of £2251 10s is an alarming in- ease over the £338 shown as the debit st year. Students' fees in 1924 have creased by £1012, and the previous year e decrease was £1289, and it appears vious, owing to the decreased number students, that there must be a further minution of fees this year. With this rgely decreased income it is patent that rther grants should be obtained from Hospital Board or as a direct grant from e Government I suggest as the finance the University has a direct bearing on e educational facilities it can furnish that is matter along with others should be ought before the forthcoming Commis- on on University Education.

It is a pleasing fact that the fees from e bacteriology and pathology depart- ents both show an increase, and as I am formed that the number of reports done r the hospital also shows an increase, ere is good ground for the Hospital oard to give a larger grant to the Medi- l School. One great reason for getting e finances of this school on a better basis s in the fact that it is unfair to the rts and General Faculties that such large ains should be made upon their income, us prohibiting desirable increases and tensions by them

MINING SCHOOL.

The balances for the past five years are: 1920 (dr.), £1206 19s 3d; 1921 (dr.), £1374 10d; 1922 (dr.), £1393 3s 2d; 1923 (dr.), 525 2s 6d; 1924 (dr.), £1902 5s 4d.

This school again shows a substantial crease in students' fees and an even eater increase in the debit which this ar stands at £1902. As far as can be as- rtained at the moment there is a slight crease in entrants again this year, and decreased income and increased expen- ture is to continue the finances of this hool will become an increasingly diffi- lt problem, though as I have pointed t previously it is fair to remember at several other faculties benefit from the rvices of Mining School teachers.

HOME SCIENCE SCHOOL.

The balances for the past five years are: 1920 (cr.), £1164 6s 3d; 1921 (cr.), £2637 s 4d; 1922 (cr.), £2289 9s 7d; 1923 (cr.), 357 16s 9d; 1924 (cr.), £2714 6s 7d.

Notwithstanding a slight decrease in idents' fees, the balance to the credit of e account has increased by £356. The lk of the item £749 9s for new work presents the new roof on the school, but is was paid for by Government grant d in turn is responsible for the increase this item.

DENTAL SCHOOL.

The balances for the past five years are: 1920 (dr.), £1873 15s 6d; 1921 (dr.), £1197

Seven years before the great Tarawera Eruption..
A woman in a small store in Christchurch asked for some baking powder. She was requested to try some made by the owner of the store. From that small beginning, 50 years ago, has the fame of Edmonds "Sure to Rise" spread. To-day over 2,500,000 tins go into New Zealand houses each year, making healthier, lighter, better cooking. Over 95% of New Zealand housewives insist on Edmonds, so high has been the standard of 50 years building.
1879
EDMONDS
BAKING POWDER
SURE TO RISE

SURE TO RISE
EDMONDS PRIZE BAKING POWDER
Edmonds Baking Powder stands on the pinnacle of unapproachable quality—and unequalled sales. It has attained this position because every day, in every way, people are recognising that there is only one baking powder recognised by the *whole* of New Zealand to be the best.
In a comparatively few years Edmonds' factory has grown from a small one-roomed establishment to what is the largest factory of its kind in the Southern Hemisphere. Why?
Because Edmonds Baking Powder, with its annual sales of millions of tins, is made with the same care and from the same pure grape cream-of-tartar as when the output was but a few dozen tins a week.
EDMONDS
- BAKING POWDER -
"SURE TO RISE"
199

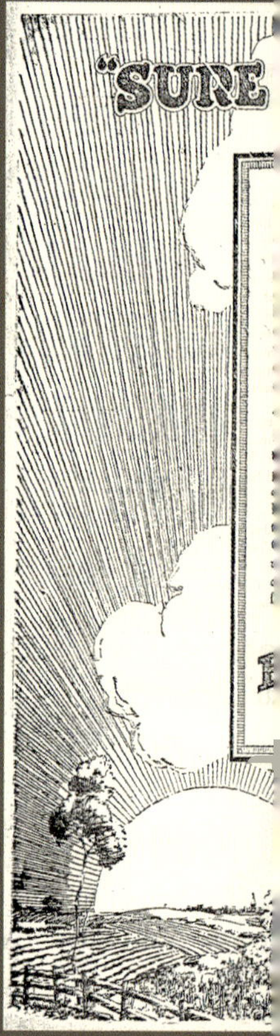
"SURE

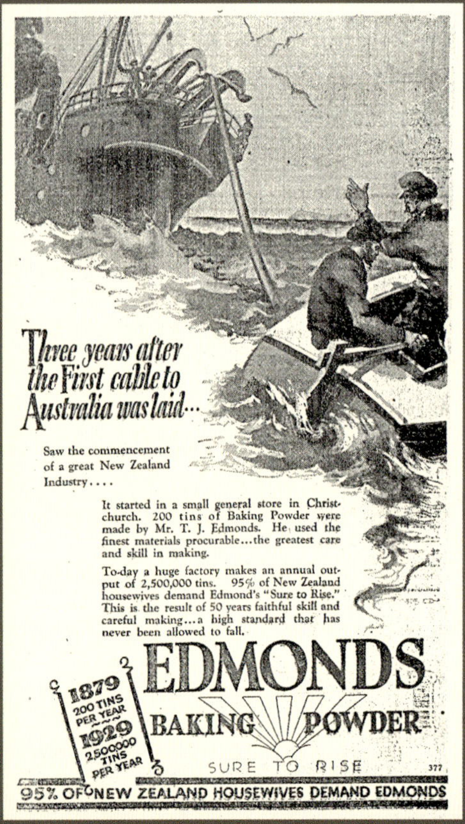
Three years after the First cable to Australia was laid...
Saw the commencement of a great New Zealand Industry....
It started in a small general store in Christchurch. 200 tins of Baking Powder were made by Mr. T. J. Edmonds. He used the finest materials procurable...the greatest care and skill in making.
To-day a huge factory makes an annual output of 2,500,000 tins. 95% of New Zealand housewives demand Edmond's "Sure to Rise." This is the result of 50 years faithful skill and careful making...a high standard that has never been allowed to fall.
1879 200 TINS PER YEAR
1929 2,500,000 TINS PER YEAR
EDMONDS
BAKING POWDER
SURE TO RISE
372
95% OF NEW ZEALAND HOUSEWIVES DEMAND EDMONDS

SURE TO RISE
An Enormous Cake 4,000 Miles High!
If all the Edmonds Baking Powder used in one year were put into one cake then that cake would be 4,000 miles high!
If 1710 mountains the height of Mt. Cook were placed one on top of the other the one would only just reach the top of this stupendous cake.
This reads like a page of Jules Verne but it is absolutely true. Surely a striking tribute to the quality and perpetual goodness of Edmonds.
The secret lies in the fact that only the best grade Cream-of-Tartar is used in its manufacture. Edmond's is a definite assurance against cooking failure. All of New Zealand knows this. *The Cake will be 5,000 miles high next year.*
ILOTT
184
EDMONDS
- BAKING POWDER -
"SURE TO RISE"

ILOTT

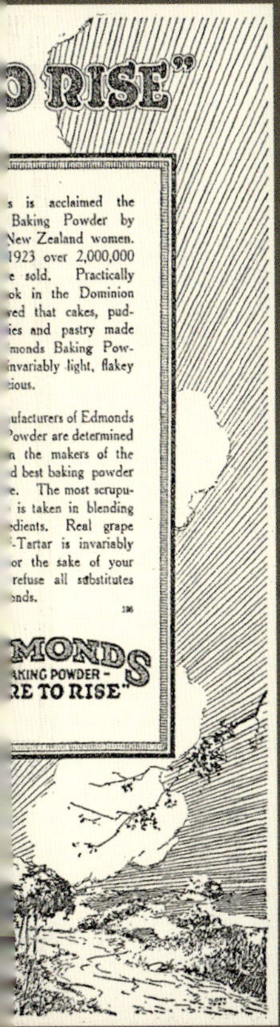
s is acclaimed the Baking Powder by New Zealand women. 1923 over 2,000,000 e sold. Practically ok in the Dominion ved that cakes, pud- ies and pastry made monds Baking Pow- invariably light, flakey ious.
ufacturers of Edmonds Powder are determined n the makers of the d best baking powder e. The most scrupu- is taken in blending dients. Real grape -Tartar is invariably or the sake of your refuse all substitutes onds.
MONDS
AKING POWDER -
RE TO RISE"

Ye Good Old English Xmas Plum Pudding
Plum Pudding!!—as essentially English as the Union Jack. Plum Pudding is possible without Christmas but never Christmas without Plum Pudding.
Ensure your Plum Pudding being a success—use Edmond's Baking Powder. The pure Grape Cream of Tartar makes all the difference.
USE THIS RECOMMENDED RECIPE.
1lb. flour (or 2 heaped breakfast cups), 2 heaped teaspoonfuls Edmonds Baking Powder, 3oz. stale bread crumbs, 1½lbs. suet, 2lbs. raisins, 1lb. currants, 8 eggs, 10oz. brown sugar, 4oz. almonds, ½lb. mixed candied peel; salt and spice to taste. Mix ingredients together well, and add eggs well beaten, and three quarts of milk. Divide into two and boil 8 hours, or four, and boil 6 hours.
ILOTT
177
EDMONDS
- BAKING POWDER -
"SURE TO RISE"

THE ACORN AND THE OAK
SURE TO RISE
In was in a tiny store in Christchurch in 1879 that the first tins of Edmonds Baking Powder were made. It was a venture begun to augment a small business and because the maker real'sed the need in New Zealand for a Baking Powder of good quality, and saw his opportunity.
He started with 200 tins ... to-day 2,500,000 are sold each year.
He started by offering each tin to a se'ected circle of customers and by making personal sales... to-day 95% of New Zealand housewives demand and will take no other than Edmonds. To-day it is sold on its reputation as the purest Baking Powder on the market... a reputation solidly built through 50 years of a consistently h'gh standard of materials and making.
1879
200 TINS PER YEAR
1929
2,500,000 TINS PER YEAR
EDMONDS
BAKING POWDER
SURE TO RISE
95% OF NEW ZEALAND HOUSEWIVES DEMAND EDMONDS

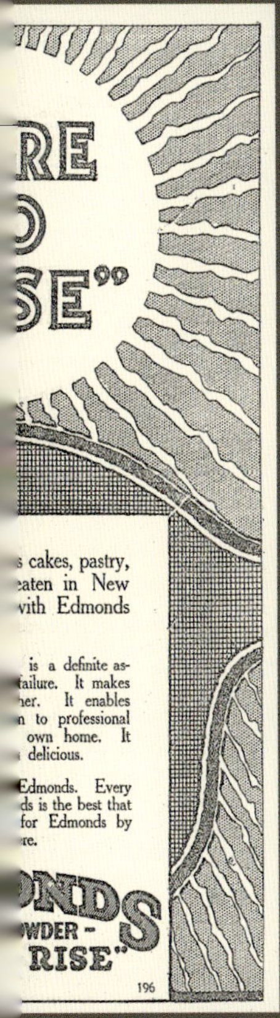
RE
O
SE"
s cakes, pastry, eaten in New with Edmonds
is a definite as- failure. It makes her. It enables n to professional own home. It delicious.
Edmonds. Every ds is the best that for Edmonds by re.
ONDS
WDER -
RISE"
196

SURE TO RISE
This lowly shed formed our humble and unpretentious factory of 1879
TO-DAY
The growth of a Big N.Z. Industry
When you see these pictures you realise the truth of—" from the acorn springs the mighty oak."
And Edmonds growth has been phenomenal! When the founder, Mr. T. J. Edmonds, adopted the slogan, "Sure to Rise," he unwittingly foretold the future of this business.
How is this wonderful expansion accounted for?—give Edmonds Baking Powder a trial and you will understand. It is the pure Grape Cream of Tartar that makes Edmonds Baking Powder preferable to ALL OTHERS.
OVER 2,000,000 TINS OF EDMONDS BAKING POWDER WERE SOLD LAST YEAR.
178
ILOTT
EDMONDS
- BAKING POWDER -
"SURE TO RISE"

As truly New Zealand as this splendid specimen of a fine race is an industry which has begun and developed in New Zealand for New Zealanders.
New Zealanders, both...
50 years of steady and prosperous growth has placed Edmonds "Sure to Rise" Baking Powder in the front rank of New Zealand industries. The first tins were made in New Zealand for New Zealanders.
To-day 2,500,000 tins are sold each year, proof of the splendid and consistent quality of this New-Zealand-Made product.
1879
200 TINS PER YEAR
1929
2500000 TINS PER YEAR
EDMONDS
BAKING POWDER
SURE TO RISE
380
95% OF NEW ZEALAND HOUSEWIVES DEMAND EDMONDS

SURE TO RISE
Life has its many sweetnesses and one of the most delightful in the home are those wonderful cakes we call Mother's-own-make. But *her* secret and that of every other successful housewife resolves itself into one word—'Edmonds.' And that simply because Edmonds is true to its three word motto—"*Sure to Rise.*"
EDMONDS
BAKING POWDER

From early on, Edmonds used different graphical representations of sunbursts in its advertising. The sunburst itself is an ancient symbol, often associated with happiness, optimism and growth. The advertisements shown here were part of a series of five variants published in *Mirror* between 1927 and 1929. The common themes were reliability and quality.

A trusty companion to baking powder, custard powder was advertised by Edmonds in newspapers from 1888. The label at the bottom of the page, which dates from 1913–14, has the legal disclosure about artificial colouring required from 1913. The lack of 'Ltd' in the company name means it pre-dates the 1915 incorporation. The design of the main panel was used until 1928. One of Edmonds' marketing strategies was free samples: the little box dates from 1923–27; the dainty tin was advertised in 1931.

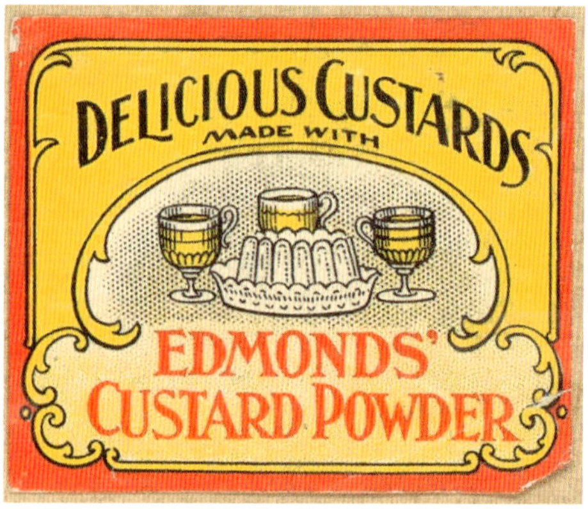

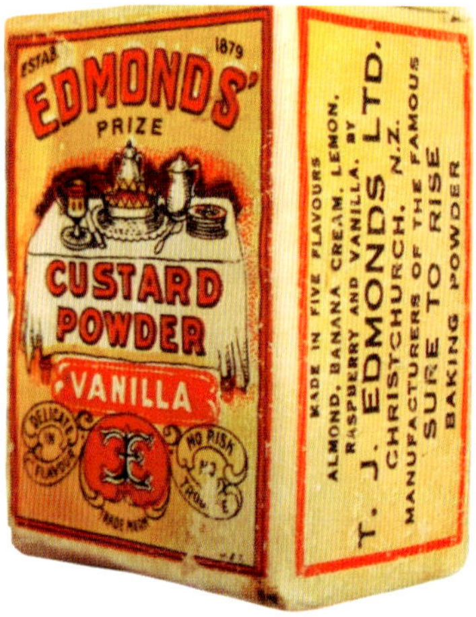

Photo of artists working in Ilott Advertising (c.1930), and an advertisement from *Mirror* (1925)

Grapes featured extensively in Edmonds' baking powder advertisements – they were a symbol of quality because cream of tartar was a by-product of grape fermentation. This original pencil drawing was produced by George Tough at Ilott Advertising around 1935. Tough's grapes appeared in an advertisement during the Second World War with the slogan 'Sure-To-Rise and Sure to return', a reference to the limited supply of cream of tartar. The grape-laden advertisement opposite appeared in 1934.

EDMONDS
Sure-to-Rise
PRODUCTS
BAKING POWDER
SOLD EVERYWHERE
EDMONDS
ESTD PRIZE 1879
BAKING · POWDER
SURE-TO-RISE
(REGISTERED)
CUSTARD POWDER
VANILLA
EDMONDS CUSTARD
EDMONDS
COLOURED CAKE BAKING POWDER
SURE TO RISE
Coloured CAKE BAKING POWDER
CUSTARD FLAVOURS LEMON, ALMOND, RASPBERRY, VANILLA, BANANA & STANDARD.

99 Per Cent PURE GRAPE Cream of Tartar
SOLD EVERYWHERE
EDMONDS
PRIZE
ESTD 1879
BAKING • POWDER
SURE TO RISE
E
TRADE (REGISTERED) MARK
PURITY
PERFECT baking . . . . for flavour, lightness and digestibility, depends almost entirely on the Baking Powder that is used.
By its quality every other ingredient is affected. Perfect Baking Powder must be *pure*. It must be made of Grape Cream of Tartar and no other. Substitutes for Grape Cream of Tartar will only adversely affect other ingredients used in baking, to the detriment of flavour and health-giving properties.
Fifty-two years ago, with the first tins made, Edmonds' Baking Powder established its reputation for purity. It has sustained it, without fluctuation, ever since. Purity is the first consideration in its making. It contains finest Grape Cream of Tartar—made in Edmonds' own factory, and analysis proves it is 99 per cent. pure.
So carefully selected and tested are its ingredients, that to-day 98 per cent. of New Zealand women insist on and will accept no other than Edmonds' Baking Powder. They know that it always gives unfailing satisfaction and perfect results, and that it is always "Sure to Rise."
EDMONDS
'SURE TO RISE' BAKING POWDER

In 1911 Edmonds began its long relationship with Ilott Advertising. The artwork on the wall behind the unknown woman can be seen in the 1925 advertisement below. The other artist is George Tough (1900–83), designing an advertisement to celebrate Edmonds' fifty-seventh year. An immigrant from Scotland, Tough had a short stint at Coulls Somerville Wilkie in Dunedin before working at Ilott's for over 40 years. Tough can also be seen at work on p. 246, second from the rear.

Before computers, the process of producing advertisements was intricate and laborious, as these 1932 photos show. At the top an original artwork is being created. Typically pencil, pen or gouache were used. This required considerable skill, such as drawing lettering to look natural on a curved tin. The artwork would then enter a 'process' phase, in which one or more letterpress printing blocks were engraved (multiple plates were used to layer colours and add textual details). The block above, with its impression opposite, was made after 1931, when the exhibition medals were dropped from the label.

Acknowledged Leader
in the
Baking Powder field
SOLD EVERYWHERE
EDMONDS
PRIZE
BAKING POWDER
SURE TO RISE
Manufacturers:
T. J. EDMONDS LTD.
CHRISTCHURCH.
EDMONDS
Pure Grape Cream of Tartar
"SURE-TO-RISE"
BAKING POWDER

Advertisements from *The Weekly Press* (1928 and 1930)

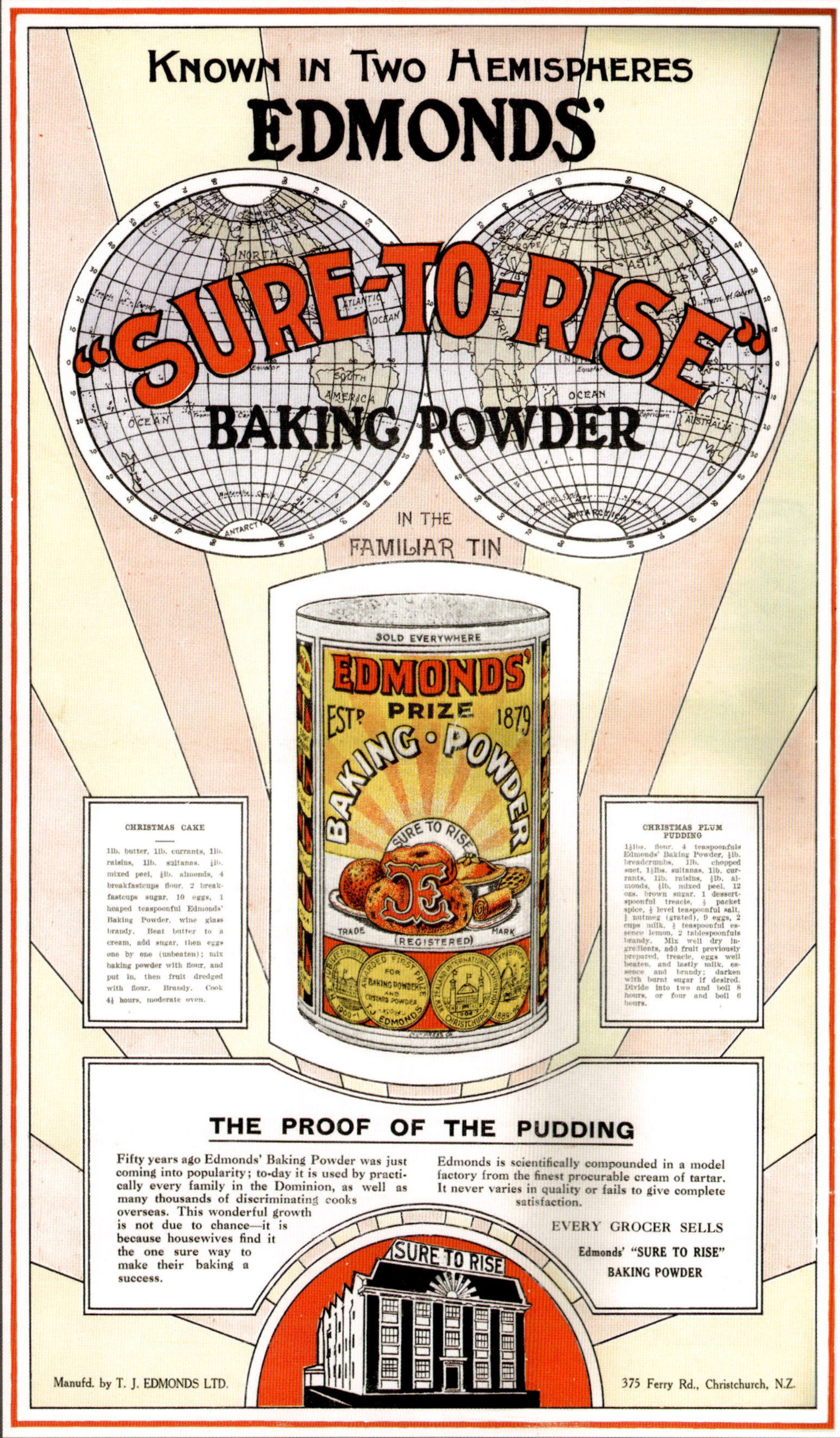
KNOWN IN TWO HEMISPHERES
EDMONDS'
"SURE-TO-RISE"
BAKING POWDER
IN THE
FAMILIAR TIN
SOLD EVERYWHERE
EDMONDS'
ESTD 1879
PRIZE
BAKING · POWDER
SURE TO RISE
TRADE MARK
(REGISTERED)
CHRISTMAS CAKE
1lb. butter, 1lb. currants, 1lb. raisins, 1lb. sultanas, ½lb. mixed peel, ¼lb. almonds, 4 breakfastcups flour, 2 breakfastcups sugar, 10 eggs, 1 heaped teaspoonful Edmonds' Baking Powder, wine glass brandy. Beat butter to a cream, add sugar, then eggs one by one (unbeaten); mix baking powder with flour, and put in, then fruit dredged with flour. Brandy. Cook 4½ hours, moderate oven.
CHRISTMAS PLUM PUDDING
1½lbs. flour, 4 teaspoonfuls Edmonds' Baking Powder, ½lb. breadcrumbs, 1lb. chopped suet, 1½lbs. sultanas, 1lb. currants, 1lb. raisins, ½lb. almonds, ½lb. mixed peel, 12 ozs. brown sugar, 1 dessertspoonful treacle, ½ packet spice, ½ level teaspoonful salt, ½ nutmeg (grated), 9 eggs, 2 cups milk, ½ teaspoonful essence lemon, 2 tablespoonfuls brandy. Mix well dry ingredients, add fruit previously prepared, treacle, eggs well beaten, and lastly milk, essence and brandy; darken with burnt sugar if desired. Divide into two and boil 8 hours, or four and boil 6 hours.
THE PROOF OF THE PUDDING
Fifty years ago Edmonds' Baking Powder was just coming into popularity; to-day it is used by practically every family in the Dominion, as well as many thousands of discriminating cooks overseas. This wonderful growth is not due to chance—it is because housewives find it the one sure way to make their baking a success.
Edmonds is scientifically compounded in a model factory from the finest procurable cream of tartar. It never varies in quality or fails to give complete satisfaction.
EVERY GROCER SELLS
Edmonds' "SURE TO RISE"
BAKING POWDER
SURE TO RISE
Manufd. by T. J. EDMONDS LTD.
375 Ferry Rd., Christchurch, N.Z.

Christmas Cake

CHRISTMAS CAKE

1 lb. butter, 1 lb. sugar, 10 eggs, 1 heaped teaspoon **Edmonds Baking Powder**, 2 lb. flour, 1 lb. currants, 1 lb. sultanas, 1 lb. raisins, 4 oz. mixed peel, 4 oz. almonds (chopped), wine-glass brandy.

Beat butter to a cream, add sugar, then eggs one by one (unbeaten); mix baking powder with flour, and put in, then fruit dredged with flour, lastly brandy. Cook $4\frac{1}{2}$ hours in moderate oven, 350°F.

CHRISTMAS CAKE No. 2

$\frac{3}{4}$ lb. butter, $\frac{3}{4}$ lb. light brown sugar, 4 eggs, $\frac{1}{2}$ cup milk, $\frac{1}{2}$ cup golden syrup (warmed), $1\frac{1}{2}$ lb. flour, 2 teaspoons **Edmonds Baking Powder**, 1 teaspoon each essence vanilla and almond, 2 wine-glasses rum or brandy, 1 lb. seeded raisins, $\frac{1}{2}$ lb. sultanas, $\frac{1}{2}$ lb. currants, $\frac{1}{4}$ lb. cherries, $\frac{1}{2}$ lb. almonds, $\frac{1}{2}$ cup walnuts. Figs, dates and preserved ginger may be added if liked.

Cream butter and sugar, add eggs, then milk and syrup alternately with flour and **Edmonds Baking Powder** mixed. Lastly add essence, rum and fruit (cleaned). Bake in a greased and papered tin for about 4 to 5 hours 350°F.

CHRISTMAS PLUM PUDDING

$1\frac{3}{4}$ lb. flour, 4 teaspoons **Edmonds Baking Powder**. 12 oz. breadcrumbs, $1\frac{1}{2}$ lb. chopped suet, 12 oz. brown sugar, 1 dessertspoon treacle (or more), 9 eggs, $\frac{1}{2}$ teaspoon essence of lemon, 2 cups milk, $1\frac{1}{2}$ lb. sultanas, 1 lb. currants, 1 lb. raisins, 8 oz. almonds (blanched), 8 oz. mixed peel, $\frac{1}{2}$ packet spice, $\frac{1}{2}$ level teaspoon salt, $\frac{1}{2}$ nutmeg (grated), 2 tablespoons brandy.

Mix well dry ingredients, add fruit previously prepared, treacle, eggs well beaten, and lastly milk, essence and brandy. Darken with burnt sugar if desired. Put into scalded and floured pudding cloths or into well greased basins covered with scalded and floured pudding cloths. If divided into two, boil 8 hours; if into four, boil 6 hours. (See next recipe, also Poorman's Xmas Pudding).

CHRISTMAS PUDDING No. 2

9 oz. suet, 4 oz. flour, 6 oz. breadcrumbs, 6 oz. light brown sugar, 6 oz. raisins, 6 oz. sultanas, 6 oz. currants, 6 oz. peel, 3 oz. almonds, 1 teaspoon spice, 1 teaspoon cinnamon, 1 teaspoon **Edmonds Baking Powder**, $\frac{1}{4}$ teaspoon nutmeg, $\frac{1}{4}$ teaspoon salt, grated rind of half a lemon, 2 eggs, tablespoon brandy, $\frac{1}{4}$ pint milk (about).

Prepare fruit, suet, breadcrumbs, etc., add all dry ingredients, mix with beaten eggs, milk and brandy. Put into a well greased basin. Steam or boil 5 or 6 hours.

Christmas Pudding

Recipe feature (1952) and photo from *Edmonds Cookery Book* (1955)

Photo from *Edmonds Cookery Book* (1955, left), and illustration from *The Coronation Plunket Cookery Book* (1937)

Illustration from *Edmonds Cookery Book* (1955)

Illustration from *Edmonds Cookery Book* (1952)

Illustration from *The Coronation Plunket Cookery Book* (1937)

PRESERVING
PRESERVED BEANS
½ lb. Sugar
2½ lbs. Beans (Runner)
1 lb. Salt (not Iodized)
Cut beans finely. Put them into a large basin and cover with salt and sugar. Leave overnight. Next day, fill jars with beans and cover with the liquid. Cover from dust. Store in a dark, dry place.
Note: Beans done this way taste and look like fresh beans.
PRESERVED BEANS OR PEAS
Boil 1 oz. Salt in 1 quart Water for 20 minutes. Put half of this water in a saucepan and when boiling add sufficient peas or beans to fill 2 jars. Boil 5 minutes. Lift out with strainer and fill sterilized jars. Pour over the remainder of the boiling, salted water from the other saucepan. Seal immediately.
Note: The peas and beans must be very young and freshly picked when using this method.
PASSION FRUIT PULP
1 cup Passion Fruit Pulp
1 cup Sugar
Bring passion fruit and sugar to boiling point. Bottle in sterilized bottles and cork. If less sugar is used it is advisable to boil the passion fruit and sugar for 5 minutes before bottling.
TOMATOES
(Whole)
Choose small, firm tomatoes. Pack into sterilized jars. Add 1 teaspoon of salt to each quart jar. Pour over cold water which has been boiled and cooled. Place on rubber ring and lid loosely. Process in the oven at 275°F. for about 30 to 40 minutes. Screw down immediately.
TOMATO PULP
To every 2 lbs. of Tomatoes allow 1 teaspoon Salt.
Wipe and cut up tomatoes, add salt and cook without any liquid till tomatoes are tender. Press through a sieve. Boil pulp about 15 minutes. Put into hot, sterilized jars and seal immediately. Onions, celery, or any other flavouring may be added and boiled in the first process if desired.
(Oven Method)
Wipe tomatoes and cut in half across; put into a baking dish in layers with the cut side up. Sprinkle with a little salt and bake until tender but not broken. Put into sterilized jars with a ladle and pour the juice from the baking dish to overflowing. Screw down
using a sterilized rubber and lid.
N.B.—Do not use water.
TOMATO PULP: 4 lbs. Tomatoes will fill 1 quart jar.
JAM TART
(page 82)

BISCUITS
BISCUITS
CREAM WAFERS
Biscuits
RICE WAFERS
Biscuits
QUALITY BISCUITS
Peek Frean
MAKERS OF FAMOUS BISCUITS
Aulsebrooks
Aulsebrooks
PACKET BISCUITS
GOLD LEAF TEA
GOLD LEAF TEA
GOLD LEAF TEA
THE COLOMBO TEA Co
Bushells
O-Cedar
Edmonds
Pepsodent
GROUND GINGER
COFFEE
WAX CANDLES
WAX CANDLES
KARBOL SOAP
THE 5 in 1 PASTRY SET
BYCROFT'S BISCUITS
PACKETS
WATER CRACKERS
BYCROFT Co AUCKLAND
UNIVERSAL SPRING CLOTHES PEGS
Weet-Bix
PYRAMID TEA
WRIGHT'S
LIFEBUOY
MaXaM
DRINKING STRAWS
National

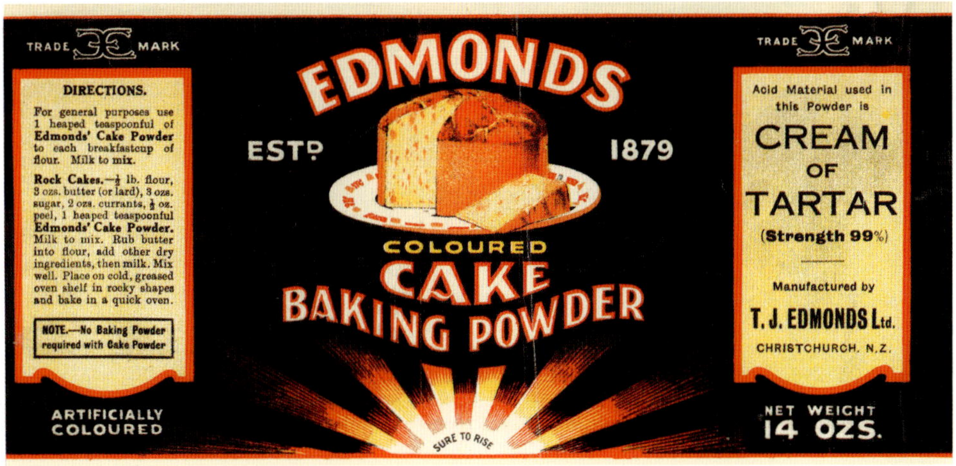

The labels shown here were introduced in 1931, 1939 and 1928 (from top to bottom). Loose labels are relatively rare and, like the tins and packaging seen opposite, have become coveted collectibles and noteworthy pieces of Kiwiana. Following pages: Label detail (1931) and advertisement from *Mirror* (1939).

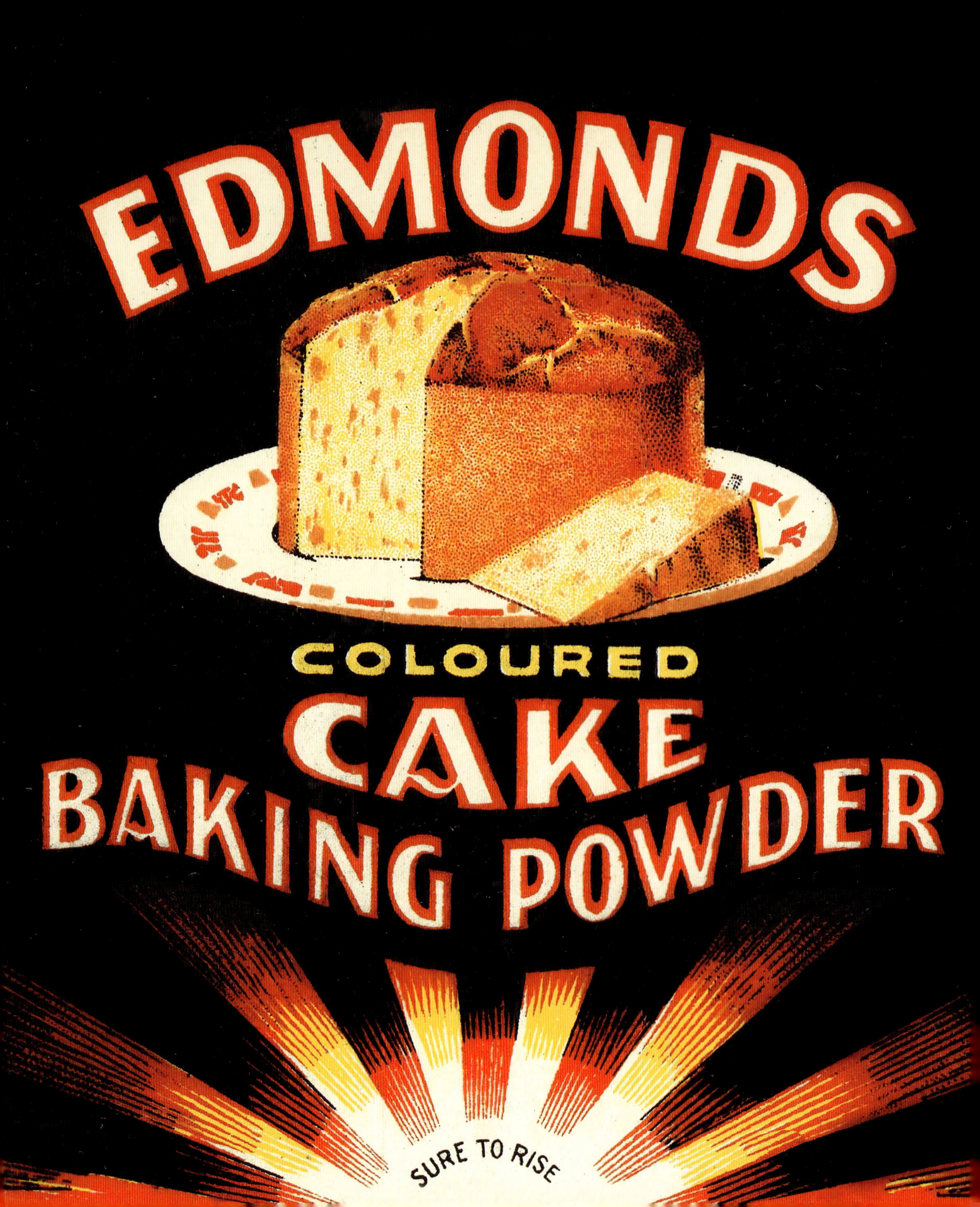
EDMONDS
COLOURED
CAKE
BAKING POWDER
SURE TO RISE

EDMONDS
SURE TO SET
JELLY
RED CURRANT
BANANA
EDMONDS
SURE TO PLEASE
MADE IN
NEW ZEALAND
'SURE-TO-SET' JELLIES
AND
'SURE-TO-PLEASE' CUSTARD
746
Makers also of
Edmonds 'Sure-to-Rise'
Baking Powder

3 entrants last year. The ex- were entered for from schools d as Hillend, Clutha, and Kin- Wakatipu. The school gaining percentage of marks was Ber- t Taieri, the average of each ing 97½, a truly creditable re-

gious education is meant that upply of spiritual food by which ill is strengthened to resist evil around him, and on which the his higher life depends."

DO IT NOW.

are any details of work out- connection with the second term ns, these shall be attended th as they are now long over-

THE FUTURE.

isory Board of the Otago Coun- ies to make arrangements for and remote future. The regular k will be carefully planned and t, and this will carry over into Exhibition enterprise.
are approximately 60 church the city and suburbs and each se should feel that it has a share ght to any benefits accruing from School of Religious Education North and South Community

close this year and face 1925 efforts will be made to have ol represented in the Central at least one.
of institutes will reach the peri- hile through close supervision be done to elevate the general e work.
tudents, and in the case of the rches the Bible Classes will be ake a similar arrangement. This n would give us a school of 100 dents, and there should be 25 ried over from this year.
n authority will be asked to the likeliest people for this task and to see that every- ible is done through lightening in the local church, easing the burden and granting authority rces, to make the most of the v. Those chosen should be at ars of age and have the equiva- high school education. Will the leaders of Dunedin "Take the ien it serves?"
mmunity schools offer opportuni- l—and next year should witness flux of students all keen to be ly furnished."

DAY SCHOOL WORK IN AUSTRALIA.

nter series of teacher training ranged by the United Sunday ouncil of Victoria, has closed. ifficulties prevented as large an as was hoped for, but the sec- ev. David Lewis, has toiled and much good work was done. spondence classes arranged speci- county teachers have been con- l several students have qualified ploma. The council is thoroughly tive, including as it does the chool Committees of the Church d, the Presbyterian Church, the Church, the Congregational the Baptist Church, and the Christ.
ass work shows signs of increase. al years the Presbyterian Welfare has organised most successful women's camps, and the unions much alive. This year the Metho- g People's department followed example, and a most successful p was held, one gratifying result is the formation of a Methodist ble Class League. This, it is believed, will give a great o the adult side of Sunday school o of the organised Bible classes nal gatherings "on their own," ct active evangelistic missions in where the camp is temporarily Members also take services in the ch of their own districts. These il signs.
ralia the annual examinations of chool scholars are great events. odist schools of New South Wales way with 5000 entries annually. in Victoria there has been a try, another sign of interest on f teachers and scholars.

OF RELIGIOUS EDUCATION

iggestions are adopted from the Survey of Religious Education, hey might well be adopted by and Protestantism:—
ocal points in "Better Church programme:
ngs.—"More and better church might become a slogan with us. every church or religious educa- ing should be erected according d.
nsion.—"More pupils, more d more time for religious train-

Advertisements from *Mirror* (1951, above) and *Otago Daily Times* (1924)

CHRISTMAS 1949
1879
Once again
AS FOR OVER 70 YEARS
Edmonds
wish you all
a Very Happy Christmas
SURE TO RISE
1949
EDMONDS
ACTO
BAKING POWDER
EDMONDS
PRIZE
BAKING POWDER
Edmonds
9 FLAVOURS
JELLY CRYSTALS
EDMONDS
SURE TO PLEASE
CUSTARD POWDER
6 FLAVOURS

Christmas, sponge cakes and the factory were all popular themes for Edmonds' advertising. The 'model factory' built in 1922 was a central feature of many advertisements, such as in the 1934 illustration below. The Christmas advertisement opposite combined product promotion with festive greetings, and marked progress from corner grocery store to factory.

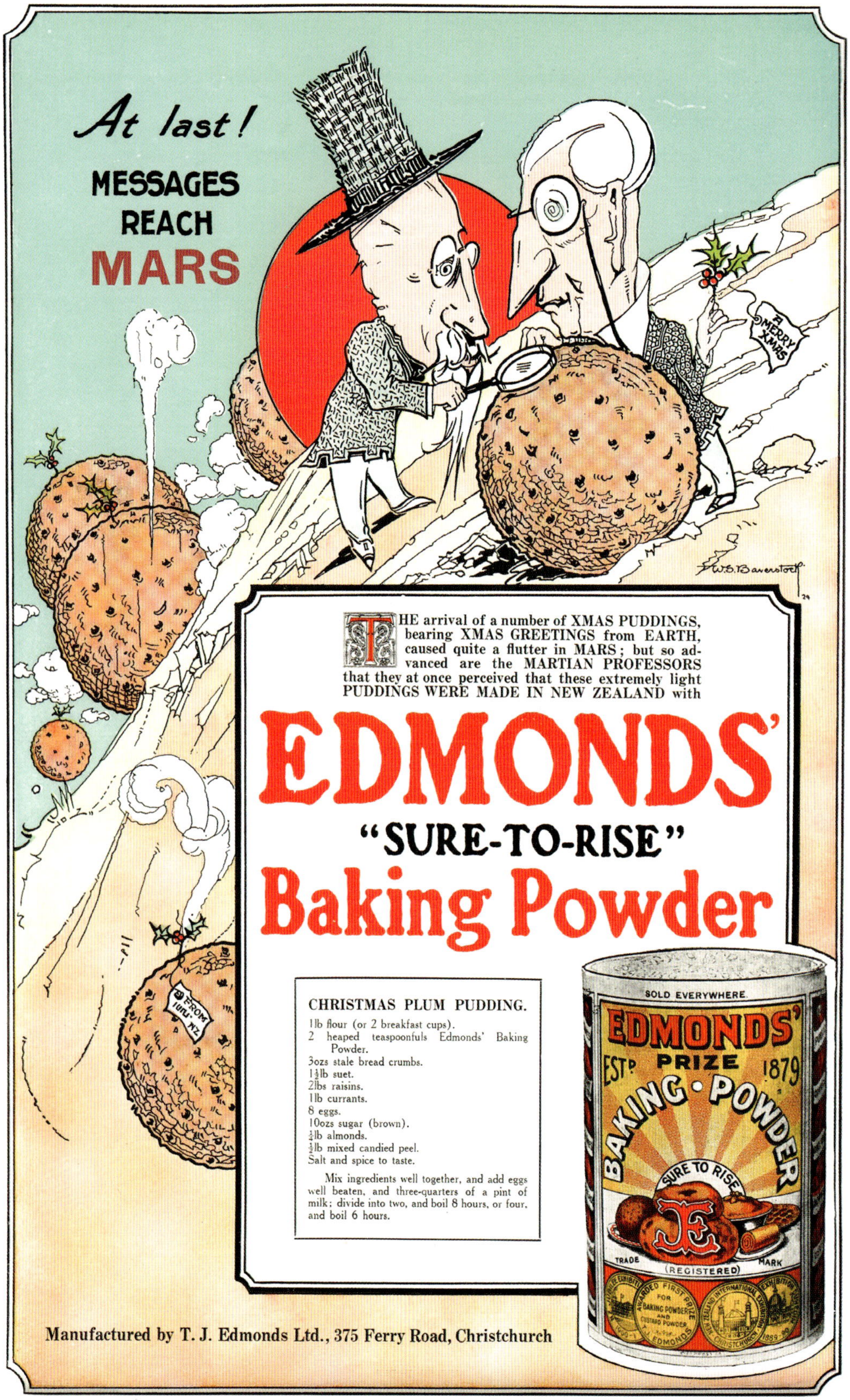

Advertisements from *The Weekly Press* (1924 and 1925, right). The designs were by William S. Baverstock (1893–1975), a caricaturist who worked in the lithographic department of the *Press* from 1910 to 1928. He is now better known as a foundation member of The Group (in 1927), a collection of Christchurch artists who significantly influenced New Zealand art, and as honorary curator (1948) and then inaugural director (1960–68) of Christchurch's Robert McDougall Art Gallery.

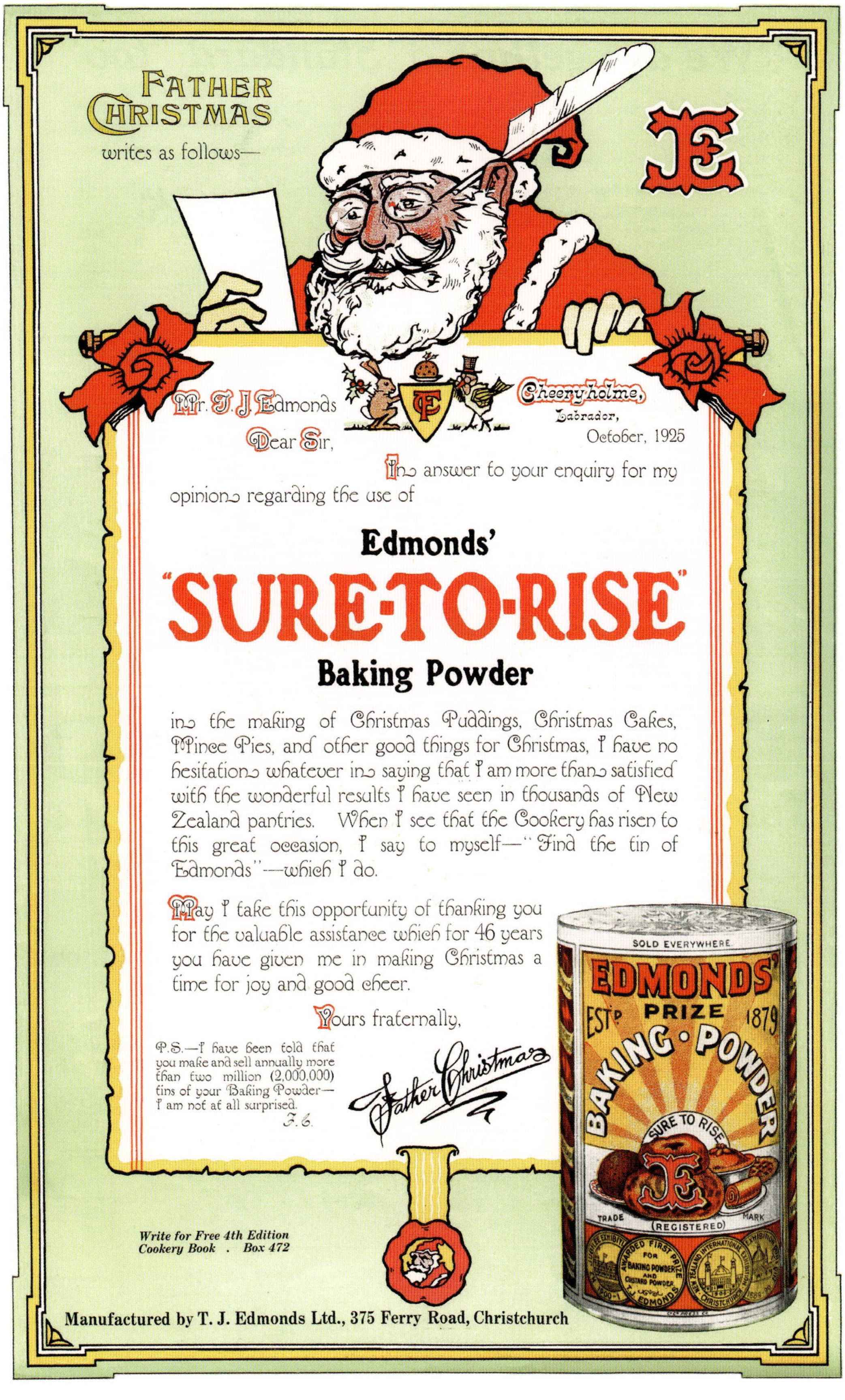

FATHER CHRISTMAS
writes as follows—
Mr. T. J. Edmonds
Cheeryholme,
Labrador,
October, 1925
Dear Sir,
In answer to your enquiry for my opinion regarding the use of
Edmonds'
"SURE-TO-RISE"
Baking Powder
in the making of Christmas Puddings, Christmas Cakes, Mince Pies, and other good things for Christmas, I have no hesitation whatever in saying that I am more than satisfied with the wonderful results I have seen in thousands of New Zealand pantries. When I see that the Cookery has risen to this great occasion, I say to myself—"Find the tin of Edmonds"—which I do.
May I take this opportunity of thanking you for the valuable assistance which for 46 years you have given me in making Christmas a time for joy and good cheer.
Yours fraternally,
Father Christmas
P.S.—I have been told that you make and sell annually more than two million (2,000,000) tins of your Baking Powder—I am not at all surprised.
F. C.
SOLD EVERYWHERE
EDMONDS'
PRIZE
ESTD 1879
BAKING · POWDER
SURE TO RISE
TRADE MARK
(REGISTERED)
Write for Free 4th Edition Cookery Book . Box 472
Manufactured by T. J. Edmonds Ltd., 375 Ferry Road, Christchurch

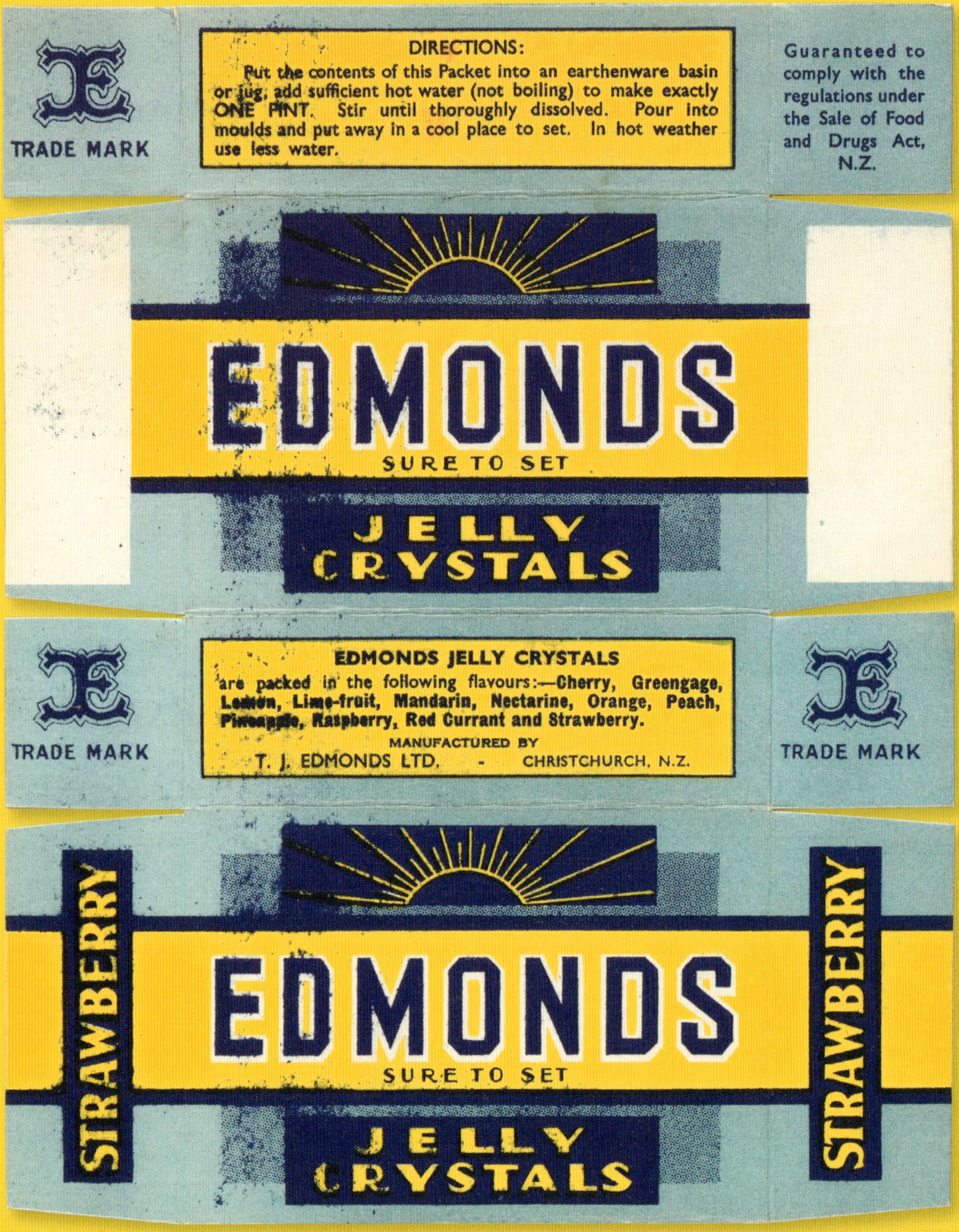
TRADE MARK
DIRECTIONS:
Put the contents of this Packet into an earthenware basin or jug, add sufficient hot water (not boiling) to make exactly ONE PINT. Stir until thoroughly dissolved. Pour into moulds and put away in a cool place to set. In hot weather use less water.
Guaranteed to comply with the regulations under the Sale of Food and Drugs Act, N.Z.
EDMONDS
SURE TO SET
JELLY CRYSTALS
TRADE MARK
EDMONDS JELLY CRYSTALS
are packed in the following flavours:—Cherry, Greengage, Lemon, Lime-fruit, Mandarin, Nectarine, Orange, Peach, Pineapple, Raspberry, Red Currant and Strawberry.
MANUFACTURED BY
T. J. EDMONDS LTD. - CHRISTCHURCH, N.Z.
TRADE MARK
STRAWBERRY
EDMONDS
SURE TO SET
JELLY CRYSTALS
STRAWBERRY

In 1935, Edmonds released 'Sure to Set' jelly crystals in 12 flavours. The attractive packaging (left and shown on the following pages) and the jewel-like jelly colours made for appealing advertisements, such as the beautiful 1935 example, right.

EDMONDS

FRESH FRUIT FLAVOURED

JELLY CRYSTALS

Are Now Ready!

IT is with pride that we now offer EDMONDS "Sure to Set" Jelly Crystals, a line we feel will be accepted as well in keeping with the high standard of Edmonds "Sure to Rise" Baking Powder, Cake Powder, and Custard Powder, which for so many years have been held high in the estimation of the New Zealand housewife.

Edmonds Jelly Crystals are made of the highest-grade ingredients, hygienically wrapped in cellophane to retain the fresh fruit flavours, which we believe cannot be equalled anywhere.

As the slogan indicates, Edmonds Jelly Crystals are guaranteed "Sure to Set" in all weathers. Price, 6d. per packet, 2/9 per half dozen.

For larger users of Jelly Crystals we put up a 1lb. packet which makes a half gallon of jelly. The retail price of the 1lb. size is 1/8 per packet, or 9/- per half dozen

THE HIGHEST STANDARD OF QUALITY & FLAVOUR

PACKED IN 12 FLAVOURS—

2/9 half dozen	Cherry, Greengage, Lemon, Lime-fruit, Mandarin, Nectarine, Orange, Peach, Pineapple, Raspberry, Red Currant and Strawberry.	5/6 dozen

ORDER FROM YOUR GROCER NOW

SUPPORT NEW ZEALAND INDUSTRIES BY BUYING EDMONDS JELLY CRYSTALS WHICH ARE MADE IN NEW ZEALAND

EDMONDS
'SURE-TO-SET' Jellies
IN 12 DELICIOUS FLAVOURS
STRAWBERRY
LEMON
GREENGAGE
ORANGE
RED CURRANT
NECTARINE
LIME FRUIT
RASPBERRY
CHERRY
MANDARIN
PEACH
PINEAPPLE

Original artwork was the beginning of an advertisement's life. The design to promote 12 jelly flavours, by George Tough, coincided with the 1935 introduction of 'Sure to Set' crystals. The designs on this page, produced by Railways Studios, were painted at a small size (25x40cm) so they could be easily held for reference when producing large-scale painted billboards.

A TRADITION

in every New Zealand home

2½ million tins are sold every year –

For over 50 years, ever since the first tins of Edmonds Baking Powder were offered to the public, women have recognised its high purity and quality . . . the reason for its unfailing success. Edmonds is made with 99.9% pure Cream of Tartar and the highest standard of blending. Packed in 4 oz., 14 oz. 5 lb. and 28 lb. tins.

95% of NEW ZEALAND HOUSEWIVES DEMAND – EDMONDS

692

MAKE SURE OF SUCCESS WITH...

EDMONDS

"SURE TO RISE" *Baking Powder*

MAKERS ALSO OF EDMONDS *'Sure-to-Please'* CUSTARD AND *'Sure-to-Set'* JELLIES

Gender stereotypes were once the norm in advertising and these Edmonds' promotions were no exception. The photos are stills from *Cookery Nook*, a 1955 film in which a girl salvages her father's failed baking. The immaculate design below, nurturing the next generation of bakers, has an airbrush finish, and is possibly the work of Bernard Roundhill (1911–2005).

Cornflour was an important part of the Edmonds portfolio. The 1953 advertisement opposite uses recipes, including one for ice cream made with custard powder, to entice consumers to buy a range of products.

Try these New Recipes

SPONGE SANDWICH

3 eggs
4 oz. sugar
1 oz. flour
2 oz. Edmonds Maize Cornflour
1 teaspoon Edmonds Baking Powder ("Sure to Rise" or Acto)
1 oz. melted butter

Method: Beat eggs and sugar until thick and fold in sifted dry ingredients then add melted butter. Put in two sandwich tins (8 inches) which have been greased and floured. Bake 20 minutes in moderate oven (375°F.).

MOCK CREAM FILLING

1½ teaspoons Edmonds Maize Cornflour
2 tablespoons icing sugar
½ cup milk
2 tablespoons butter

Method: Mix Cornflour and milk together into a smooth paste then boil 3 or 4 minutes. Cream butter and sugar and then add Cornflour gradually when cold. Beat well. Flavouring may be added.

ICE CREAM

Make a custard with—

1½ br. cups milk
2 tablespoons sugar
1 heaped tablespoon Edmonds Custard Powder (Vanilla flavour)

Set aside to cool. Beat ¼ pint cream until stiff and fold into cold custard. Whip again and freeze. When still soft remove from refrigerator and beat again.

Edmonds

QUALITY PRODUCTS

Centrefolds were prime advertising space, such as these two examples from 1949–50 (top) and 1955. The advertisement below has strong mid-century features, particularly the atomic design elements presenting 'sure to rise'. By this time, jelly crystals had new packaging, and the inclusion of sponge mix was a hint of the many Edmonds' products that would follow. Both advertisements also reflect the post-war decision to supply both Sure to Rise and Acto baking powders (one cream of tartar, the other phosphate). The advertisment opposite featured Edmonds' most popular products as essential ingredients for festive feasting.

USE
EDMONDS
QUALITY PRODUCTS
Fill up your pantry with good things for Christmas . . . be prepared for additional guests, extra meals . . . You'll need plenty of delicious 'Sure-to-Set' Jellies and 'Sure-to-Please' Custards . . . so easily, quickly made . . . and your tins must be full of cakes and biscuits, crisp and golden brown, and made feather light with Edmonds famous 'Sure-to-Rise' Baking Powder. With tradition behind them, Edmonds Products to-day are unchallenged for quality — unchallenged for value.
EDMONDS 'Sure-to-Set' Jellies, in 12 delicious flavours, in 4-oz. (6d. each and 2/9 half doz.) and 1 lb. (1/8) packets.
EDMONDS 'Sure-to-Please' Custard in six delicious flavours, in 4-oz. (6d.), 10-oz. (1/-), 4-lb. (5/-) and 28-lb. tins.
EDMONDS 'Sure-to-Rise' Baking Powder, in 4-oz. (6d.), 14-oz. (1/4), 5-lb. (6/9) and 28-lb. tins.
All Edmonds Products are sold only in containers bearing the well-known Edmonds labels. Accept no substitute.
Edmonds
Edmonds
SOLD EVERYWHERE
EDMONDS
ESTD 1879
PRIZE
BAKING POWDER
SURE TO RISE
EDMONDS
SURE-TO-SET
JELLY CRYSTALS
Merry Christmas
FOR FESTIVE FARE

REFLECTIONS

I'm willing to bet that a majority of New Zealand homes have what I consider two Bibles, one reached for when they need spiritual guidance and one reached for when they need a hokey pokey recipe. Besides my mother's handwritten notebook, filled with recipes that were shared from numerous afternoon teas and dinner parties, the only cookery book we had on the farm was *Edmonds*. It is still my 'go-to' reference for 'Kiwicentric' recipes that celebrate our past but also make us feel connected and nostalgic in the present. There is something wonderfully comforting and humbling about spying that spiral binding sitting among the modern collections that many home cooks have. Most of these have stunning photography and beautiful design, but the Edmonds has the unique scuffed-up feeling of a reliable old friend, always there and happy to help.
Al Brown

Timing is everything: when I was asked to contribute to this book, I'd just been talking with my partner Katie about the origin story of the Edmonds brand. I have always admired the accessibility of the cookery book and I was fascinated to learn that this has been a hallmark of the Edmonds story for so long. The *Edmonds Cookery Book* is a national culinary taonga. Its impact in the kitchens of Aotearoa is beyond intergenerational and it's inspiring that it remains as loved and relevant as ever. I still use my copy – my go-to recipes are the banana cake and the one-egg chocolate cake.
Monique Fiso

Every home I've lived in has had a copy of the *Edmonds Cookery Book*. In my childhood the pages were crusted together by the splatters from the bubbling pots of tomato sauce or our sticky butter-and-sugar-coated fingers. The recipes were destined to work every time. We were always referring to the weights and measures page and oven temperature conversions for American recipes. To this day I still use the recipes for shortbread and, in the height of summer, an annual batch of tomato relish and sauce.
Sue Fleischl

London is a long way from Sāmoa and New Zealand where I grew up, but thinking about Edmonds takes me right back to the family kitchen. I remember my mum had a tattered copy of the cookery book in the kitchen drawer, and there was always the odd chance of her using it to make afghans and scones. From my memories of growing up in the 1980s and 1990s, and visiting family and friends, I'm also pretty sure every home had a copy of the book. It is lovely to think about and place *Edmonds* within my own journey as a chef.
Monica Galetti

For me, Edmonds is a bit like Tupperware or Glad Wrap – the brand is so well known it defines the product. The minute you think of baking powder, you think of Edmonds and visualise the tin or box; it's the one you reach for straight away. Never once in my life have I thought about comparing baking powders; you just want it to work and do the trick. I'm not even sure I know another baking powder other than Edmonds! The cookery book has also served me well. I immediately think of my extended time working on a superyacht. You can't of course take your library, so the *Edmonds* was the perfect go-to cookbook for inspiration, or to help out in some way for pretty much anything I wanted to cook. And for the crew, scones or a carrot cake would always hit the spot. I'll be hanging on to my worn copy for a long time yet.

Simon Gault

I must have seen my first *Edmonds Cookery Book* when I was four. That's when my mother tells me I made my first cookbook – cutting pages from magazines and pasting them into a scrapbook. Edmonds was as much a part of my 1960s childhood as the various cartoon magazines we read, except I can't recall what any of them were called. I learned to make scones, sponges, cheese sauce, afghan biscuits and the like from the well-worn pages of the family *Edmonds*. When I moved to Melbourne aged 18, and to London in my early twenties, I took copies of the book. During the 31 years I lived in London, I gifted many copies to my non-Kiwi mates as it's a helpful book for any nationality – for first-flatting young folk, or for those who need simple, accessible recipes. I must admit that I do miss the old chicken recipe that had Tang and cornflakes as two ingredients!

Peter Gordon

My mother was not particularly keen on cooking or baking, and so she encouraged me and my two sisters to experiment in the kitchen, hoping we would take over ... We had several community cookbooks, but we always used the *Edmonds Cookery Book* for ginger crunch and scones. When I was asked to rework it in 2015, I discovered how much the recipes had changed through the years. Fashionably drastic reductions in butter and sugar delivered some dismal results and so in the latest version butter and sugar are fully restored. Baking should taste wonderful, not worthy, since baking a special treat is a sure way of showing someone you love them. Happily, the *Edmonds Cookery Book* continues to celebrate and encourage this delightful domestic tradition.

Alexa Johnston

The *Edmonds Cookery Book* was always close at hand for my mum. Fruit sponge pudding was one of her favourite go-to recipes, and undoubtedly shaped my early passion for all things food. We also lived in Malaysia for seven years and I loved how the *Edmonds* gave me a warm feeling of home. It showed me the emotional significance of Kiwiana; it helps speak to who we are. Chocolate coconut rough was our favourite recipe at that time. We'd take it to other homes where it stood out among the Asian treats – and people loved it. I still turn to the *Edmonds*, admittedly more for foundations than flair – like making pastry – but it still really helps me out. It's been great to think back; Edmonds has such a special place in our cooking history.

Nadia Lim

STANDARD
EDMONDS
CUSTARD
POWDER
MARK
1879
POWDER
TO RISE
MARK

OMONDS
CUSTARD
POWDER
VANILLA
EDMOND
SURE TO PLEASE
CUSTAR
POWDE
ARTIFICIAL
RASPBERRY

NOTES

CHAPTER 1: FROM LONDON TO LYTTELTON

1. https://www.theguardian.com/cities/2014/may/15/the-evolution-of-london-the-citys-near-2000-year-history-mapped
2. *London Gazette*, 4 July 1845, p. 2011.
3. *London Gazette*, 29 February 1848, p. 859; 21 May 1852, p. 1462.
4. Alan Palmer, *The East End: Four Centuries of London Life*, John Murray, London, 2004, pp. 38–41; Peter Ackroyd, *London: The Biography*, Vintage, London, 2001, p. 545.
5. https://www.rootschat.com/forum/index.php?topic=750964.0
6. Testimonial, T. J. Edmonds Ltd, to J. Ilott's Ltd, 23 December 1915.
7. https://www.gracesguide.co.uk/Frederick_Allen_and_Sons_(Poplar)
8. Brian Easton, *Not in Narrow Seas: The Economic History of New Zealand*, Victoria University Press, Wellington, 2020, p. 51.
9. http://www.nzlii.org/nz/legis/hist_act/iapwa187033a34v1870n77428/
10. Judith Bassett, 'A Paradise for Working Men', in Judith Binney, Judith Bassett and Erik Olssen (eds), *The People and the Land/Te Tangata me Te Whenua: An Illustrated History of New Zealand 1820–1920*, Allen & Unwin, Wellington, 1990, p. 169.
11. https://nzhistory.govt.nz/files/documents/peopling4.pdf; https://www.parliament.nz/en/pb/research-papers/document/00PLSocRP08011/immigration-chronology-selected-events-1840-2008
12. *Lyttelton Times*, 26 September 1879, p. 4.
13. *Press*, 11 October 1921, p. 7.
14. D. J. Cooper (comp.), Plymouth to Port Chalmers: 'Julia's Story', Dunedin, 2020. Edmonds family members have copies of the original diary.
15. *Kumara Times*, 27 September 1879, p. 1.
16. *Auckland Star*, 20 November 1874, p. 2.
17. David Hastings, *Over the Mountains of the Sea: Life on the Migrant Ships 1870–1885*, Auckland University Press, Auckland, 2006, pp. 27–28.
18. *Globe*, 26 September 1879, p. 2.
19. 'The Stad Haarlem from Plymouth to Lyttelton, Published in Old England & New Zealand, 1879; Extracts from the Author's Diary of his Voyage to New Zealand Accompanied by Five Hundred Emigrants from Kent and Sussex', www.yesteryears.co.nz/shipping/diaries/stadhaarlem1879.html
20. Hastings, *Over the Mountains*, p. 73.
21. Cooper, Plymouth to Port Chalmers. To holystone means to scour with a piece of soft sandstone.
22. Hastings, *Over the Mountains*, p. 76.
23. Cooper, Plymouth to Port Chalmers.
24. Hastings, *Over the Mountains*, p. 173.
25. *Star*, 26 September 1879, p. 2.
26. *Star*, 23 September 1879, p. 2.
27. *Star*, 29 September 1879, p. 2.
28. *Evening Post*, 27 September 1879, p. 2; *Lyttelton Times*, 27 September 1879, p. 3; *Star*, 26 September 1879, p. 2; *Press*, 27 September 1879, p. 2.
29. *Globe*, 26 September 1879, p. 2.
30. *Press*, 26 September 1879, p. 2.

CHAPTER 2: COMING TO CHRISTCHURCH

1. *Press*, 27 September 1929, p. 13.
2. *Lyttelton Times*, 9 August 1872, p. 2.
3. *Press*, 25 September 1879, p. 2.
4. *Appendix to the Journals of the House of Representatives*, 1879, Session II, D-04, p. 2.
5. *Lyttelton Times*, 27 September 1879, p. 6.
6. *Press*, 27 September 1929, p. 13.
7. Geoffrey W. Rice, *Christchurch Changing: An Illustrated History*, Canterbury University Press, Christchurch, 2008, p. 46.
8. *Press*, 27 September 1929, p. 13.
9. Geoffrey W. Rice, *Victoria Square: Cradle of Christchurch*, Canterbury University Press, Christchurch, 2014, pp. 124, 123.
10. Rice, *Christchurch Changing*, pp. 42, 51.
11. *Press*, 26 September 1881, p. 2.
12. https://catalogue.data.govt.nz/dataset/womens-franchise-petitions-1892-and-1893/resource/2e1214d7-c2c0-4da5-9996-99db47eb8903. The 1893 petition also has a signature on sheet 542, by a Mrs E. Edmonds of Olliviers Road: did Sarah sign again, this time using Edwin's initial?
13. Rice, *Christchurch Changing*, p. 53.
14. *Bay of Plenty Times*, 28 October 1879, p. 2.
15. https://www.nzgeo.com/stories/the-canterbury-norwester/
16. *Globe*, 9 September 1880, p. 2.
17. Anna Rogers, *The Shaky Isles: New Zealand Earthquakes*, Grantham House Publishing, Wellington, 2013, pp. 49–51.

CHAPTER 3: A BUSINESS IS BORN

1. Facebook post by John Campbell, https://www.facebook.com/Fiftiys.sixtys.and.seventys/posts/2855811367840867
2. T. J. Edmonds, 'How Advertising Has Helped my Business', *Advertising World* 1915, reprinted in *Profitable Publicity: A Journal for Advertisers*, Vol. 1, No. 1, Wellington, February 1917, p. 1.
3. *The Architectural Heritage of Christchurch: 8. The Legacy of Thomas Edmonds*, Christchurch City Council Environmental Policy & Planning Unit, 1993, http://christchurchcitylibraries.com/Heritage/Publications/ChristchurchCityCouncil/ArchitecturalHeritage/LegacyofThomasEdmonds/, p. 3.
4. *Star*, 2 February 1886, p. 2; *Lyttelton Times*, 10 June 1903, p. 1; 13 June 1903, p. 12.
5. 'Christchurch's Edmonds St name to be finally fixed after typo lasts 124 years', https://www.stuff.co.nz/the-press/news/100996578/christchurch-street-name-to-be-fixed-after-more-than-a-century-in-error
6. *Star*, 5 November 1889, p. 3.
7. *Star*, 11 September 1886, p. 2.
8. *Star*, 11 July 1881, p. 1.
9. *Star*, 20 December 1881, p. 3.
10. Edmonds, 'How Advertising', p. 1.
11. Ibid.
12. Philip Richards, email to Kate Parsonson, 19 February 2021.
13. Edmonds, 'How Advertising', pp. 1–2.
14. *Star*, 25 April 1887, p. 3; Press, 13 April 1888, p. 8.
15. The endorsement, dated 18 November 1887, is in the Edmonds archive of Goodman Fielder.
16. Margaret Parkes, 'The cook and the baking powder mystery: Like father, like son', *New Zealand Genealogist*, April 2014, p. 56; letter from Margaret Parkes, *Listener*, 4 June 1988; Press, 11 October 1889, p. 2.
17. Edmonds, 'How Advertising', p. 2.
18. *Press*, 10 March 1887, p. 1, 23 April 1887, p. 1.
19. *Press*, 17 March 1887, p. 2.
20. *Press*, 11 November 1887, p. 6.
21. *Press*, 17 March 1887, p. 2.
22. C.M. O'Connor, 'Life History: Gertrude Ivy Williams (nee Edmonds), 1891–1987', 17 October 1986, p. 6.
23. *Press*, 5 May 1887, p. 1.
24. *Press*, 30 June 1887, p. 1.
25. For example, *Press*, 7 September 1887, p. 1.
26. *Press*, 11 November 1887, p. 6.
27. *Press*, 19 December 1887, p. 1.
28. *Lyttelton Times*, 22 March 1888, p. 6.
29. *Press*, 4 February 1888, p. 1.
30. *Star*, 2 December 1889, p. 4.
31. Email from Spaans (IPONZ) to Sutherland (researcher). Sutherland was seeking information from IPONZ, New Zealand's trademark registration office, on early Edmonds trademarks related to a historical claim that 'a certain person designed the Edmonds label'. This probably referred to testing whether Philip Presants designed the label, as Sutherland was the author of an unpublished 2004 research note about Presants' life. This note, available from the authors, was held by Julian Heyes, Presants' great-grandson.

CHAPTER 4: BATTLE OF THE BRANDS

1. Banks' Journal, 23 September 1769, http://southseas.nla.gov.au/journals/banks/17690923.html
2. www.sea.museum, information reproduced from Antonia Macarthur, *His Majesty's Bark* Endeavour: *The Story of the Ship and Her People*, Angus & Robertson, Sydney, 1997, courtesy of the author.
3. www.finecooking.com/article/the-science-of-baking-with-yeast-2
4. *Sun*, 18 July 1919, p. 13.
5. Helen Leach (ed.), *From Kai to Kiwi Kitchen: New Zealand Culinary Traditions and Cookbooks*, Otago University Press, Dunedin, 2010, pp. 35–36.
6. *New Zealand Herald and Auckland Gazette*, 8 January 1842, p. 1; *Nelson Examiner and New Zealand Chronicle*, 25 July 1846, p. 84.
7. Charles Royal and Jenny Kaka-Scott, 'Māori foods – kai Māori – Foods introduced by Europeans', Te Ara – the Encyclopedia of New Zealand, http://www.TeAra.govt.nz/en/maori-foods-kai-maori/page-4
8. *New Zealand Gazette and Wellington Spectator*, 21 August 1839, p. 1.
9. *New Zealand Gazette and Wellington Spectator*, 18 April 1840, p. 1.
10. *Daily Southern Cross*, 7 May 1850, p. 2.
11. *New Zealand Spectator and Cook's Strait Guardian*, 28 September 1853, p. 2.
12. http://letslookagain.com/tag/history-of-borwicks-baking-powder/
13. *Nelson Examiner and New Zealand Chronicle*, 26 February 1859, p. 2; 19 May 1860, p. 2.

14. *Nelson Examiner and New Zealand Chronicle*, 27 October 1860, p. 2; *Hawke's Bay Herald*, 11 November 1863, p. 4.
15. *Nelson Examiner and New Zealand Chronicle*, 14 January 1864, p. 2.
16. *New Zealand Spectator and Cook's Strait Guardian, New Zealander, Nelson Examiner and New Zealand Chronicle, Taranaki Herald, Hawke's Bay Herald, Otago Daily Times* and *Lyttelton Times*.
17. *Nelson Examiner and New Zealand Chronicle*, 12 December 1865, p. 10.
18. *Wellington Independent*, 20 July 1867, p. 3.
19. *North Otago Times*, 16 April 1872, p. 3; *Waikato Times*, 29 July 1875, p. 2; *Thames Advertiser*, 14 September 1876, p. 1, 1 December 1883, p. 1.
20. *Daily Southern Cross*, 25 December 1874, supplement, p. 1; *Otago Witness*, 27 February 1875, p. 19.
21. *Press*, 18 October 1878, p. 2.
22. *Oamaru Mail*, 10 August 1889, p. 2.
23. *Thames Star*, 30 December 1891, p. 2; *Taranaki Herald*, 14 July 1892, p. 2; *Star*, 31 January 1895, p. 4.
24. *Hawera & Normanby Star*, 3 October 1881, p. 2.
25. *Taranaki Herald*, 10 January 1882, p. 3, 5 January 1882, p. 2.
26. *Auckland Star*, 20 February 1882, p. 3.
27. *Temuka Leader*, 1 March 1890, p. 3; *Timaru Herald*, 19 November 1890, p. 3; *New Zealand Times*, 25 February 1890, p. 5.
28. The baking powder brands known to have begun advertising in New Zealand in the 1890s included Acme, Bonita, Brooke's, Bruce's, Campbell's, Can't Be Beat, Cardinal, Castle, Cerebos, Champion, Chef, Coronet, Crescent, Crown, Daisy, De Carles, Defiance, Diamond, Dr Price's, Electric, Escott's, Euka, Family Friend, Furness's, Golden Seal, Health, Horsford's Phosphatic, H.O.T., Hygiean, Keating's, Key, Lily, Lion, Maori, Morse's, Nash's, Old Mill, Paris, Peerless, Phoenix, Premier, Rew's, Ricker's, Shield, Ship, Sinclair's, Snow, Snowflake, Southern Cross, Soyer's, Standard, Sunlight, Three Fort, Tuckahoe, Universal, Unxld, Wardell Bros and Windsor.

CHAPTER 5: SURE TO RISE

1. T. J. Edmonds, 'How Advertising Has Helped my Business', Advertising World 1915, reprinted in *Profitable Publicity: A Journal for Advertisers*, Vol. 1, No. 1, Wellington, February 1917, p. 1.
2. *Lyttelton Times*, 19 February 1890, p. 5.
3. *N.Z. Truth*, 29 December 1923, p. 15.
4. *Wairarapa Daily Times*, 17 May 1892; *New Zealand Herald*, 9 April 1902.
5. *Wairarapa Daily Times*, 21 July 1891, p. 2; *Evening Post*, 13 March 1896, p. 3.
6. *Thames Star*, 10 July 1885; *Auckland Star*, 25 October 1887; *Daily Telegraph*, 4 May 1896.
7. *Lyttelton Times*, 8 November 1889, p. 5.
8. Province of Canterbury, New Zealand, New Zealand, List of Sections Purchased to April 30, 1863, London, 1863, p. 3, https://heritage.christchurchcitylibraries.com/Publications/1860s/1863-Sections/Pages/C80732015-001.asp; Certificate of Title 107/229.
9. *Press*, 10 December 1890, p. 1; *Lyttelton Times*, 3 May 1892, p. 1.
10. *Lyttelton Times*, 20 July 1893, p. 6.
11. C. M. O'Connor, 'Life History: Gertrude Ivy Williams (nee Edmonds), 1891–1987', 17 October 1986, p. 2.
12. *Lyttelton Times*, 3 October 1896, p. 3.
13. O'Connor, 'Life History', p. 3.
14. 21 October 1902, Certificate of Title 107/229.
15. *Lyttelton Times*, 9 September 1897, p. 1; *Press*, 25 November 1899, p. 10.
16. O'Connor, 'Life History', p. 3.
17. Ibid.
18. *Lyttelton Times*, 28 September 1900, p. 3.
19. *Taranaki Herald*, 21 January 1892, p. 2; https://www3.stats.govt.nz/historic_publications/1891-census/1891-results-census/1891-results-census.html#d50e376252
20. *Lyttelton Times*, 10 November 1893, p. 5; *Star*, 4 August 1894, p. 6.
21. *Press*, 9 September 1895, pp. 2–3; *Lyttelton Times*, 9 September 1895, p. 2.
22. *Press*, 13 November 1896, p. 5; 12 November 1897, p. 6.
23. *Press*, 13 November 1896, p. 5.
24. *Lyttelton Times*, 22 June 1892, p. 7.
25. *Ashburton Guardian*, 27 April 1901, p. 3.
26. *Taranaki Herald*, 29 August 1901, p. 2; *New Zealand Times*, 26 August 1901, p. 2.
27. *Press*, 5 October 1893, p. 1.
28. *Hawera & Normanby Star*, 13 August 1894; *Evening Post*, 16 October 1894; *New Zealand Herald*, 2 June 1894.
29. *Lyttelton Times*, 22 February 1897, p. 1; 10 March 1897, p. 1; 18 November 1897, p. 1 and 10 April 1899, p. 1; *Star*, 7 December 1898, p. 3; *Press*, 4 June 1900, p. 8; 23 May 1900, p. 2.

CHAPTER 6: A HOUSEHOLD NAME

1. *Evening Post*, 5 May 1900, p. 5; *Ashburton Guardian*, 30 June 1900, p. 3; *Auckland Star*, 30 October 1900, p. 5. Eno's powder contained sodium carbonate, sodium bicarbonate and citric acid, and when mixed with water produced the essential leavening agent, carbon dioxide.
2. *Northern Advocate*, 15 December 1900, p. 2.
3. *New Zealand Herald*, 11 April 1902, p. 1; *Auckland Star*, 15 May 1902, p. 7.
4. *New Zealand Herald*, 17 January 1905, p. 1.
5. *Press*, 19 July 1905, p. 1.
6. *Press*, 8 March 1902, p. 9; 15 April 1902, p. 6; 10 October 1902, p. 6.
7. *Southland Times*, 20 May 1904, p. 3.
8. *New Zealand Times*, 15 November 1906, p. 8; *Press*, 14 November 1906, p. 8; *Lyttelton Times*, 27 February 1907, p. 1.
9. *Press*, 14 November 1906, p. 8.
10. *Evening Post*, 18 January 1907, p. 1; *Lyttelton Times*, 18 June 1907, p. 10.
11. *New Zealand Times*, 15 November 1906, p. 8.
12. *New Zealand Herald*, 2 February 1907, supplement, p. 7.
13. *Lyttelton Times*, 1 March 1907, p. 6; *Otago Daily Times*, 20 August 1907, p. 3; *Manawatu Standard*, 18 August 1908, p. 7.
14. *Otago Daily Times*, 27 May 1910, p. 7.
15. *Wanganui Herald*, 14 July 1909, p. 3; *Star*, 20 August 1910, p. 11; *Nelson Evening Mail*, 15 August 1910, p. 7.
16. *Manawatu Herald*, 29 August 1905, p. 4; *Wairarapa Daily Times*, 9 December 1905, p. 7; *N.Z. Truth*, 6 July 1907, p. 6.
17. *Lyttelton Times*, 3 April 1903, p. 5, 4 April 1903, p. 11.
18. C. T. Ross, 'Constructing the "World's Scenic Wonderland": Photomontage in New Zealand illustrated weekly newspapers, 1900–1930', PhD thesis, University of Otago, 2009. Retrieved from http://hdl.handle.net/10523/323
19. In the photo of the design area of the Christchurch Press Company (see pp. 236-237) (PAColl-8763-3, Alexander Turnbull Library), a sheet of Edmonds baking powder labels is visible high on the left-hand wall. Presants sits on the right; the designer on the left is unknown. Based on the content of four Turnbull photos, particularly the covers and supplements for Christmas editions of *The Weekly Press*, the photo can be dated to 1905.
20. *Colonist*, 9 November 1910, p. 1.
21. *Colonist*, 19 December 1910, p. 4.
22. *Lyttelton Times*, 5 April 1911, p. 10.
23. *Evening Star*, 4 April 1911, p. 2; *New Zealand Times*, 9 January 1912.
24. *King Country Chronicle*, 14 June 1911, p. 4.
25. *Greymouth Evening Star*, 17 July 1911, p. 2. Cumberworth served overseas in the First World War. Some of his sketches and paintings are held in the National Collection of War Art.
26. T. J. Edmonds, 'How Advertising Has Helped My Business', *Advertising World*, November 1915, reprinted in *Profitable Publicity: A Journal for Advertisers*, Vol. 1, No. 1, Wellington, February 1917, pp. 1–3.
27. Jack Ilott, *Creating Customers: The Story of Ilott Advertising New Zealand: 1892–1982*, Ray Richards Publisher, Auckland, 1985, pp. 17, 19, 22, 25.
28. *Lyttelton Times*, 9 September 1911, p. 10.
29. *Greymouth Evening Star*, 4 November 1911, p. 2; *Nelson Evening Mail*, 3 January 1919, p. 3.
30. Edmonds, 'How Advertising', p. xxxiii.
31. Testimonial, 23 December 1915, Ilott Advertising – Record, MS-Papers-3913-13/1. The 'pirated' phrase is from *Henry V*, Act 4, Scene 3: 'But if it be a sin to covet honour, I am the most offending soul alive'.
32. Edmonds, 'How Advertising', pp. 1–3.
33. *Taranaki Herald*, 13 February 1913, p. 8. The number sold was 1,077,084 – 198,816 more than in 1911, and equivalent to five tins for every family in the country over the previous 12 months.
34. Edmonds, 'How Advertising', pp. 1–3; *Greymouth Evening Star*, 4 January 1916, p. 3.
35. *Lyttelton Times*, 29 December 1911, p. 8.
36. *Poverty Bay Herald*, 22 February 1912, p. 7.
37. *Manawatu Times*, 15 July 1912, p. 6.
38. *Poverty Bay Herald*, 31 January 1912, p. 7; *Wairarapa Daily Times*, 29 March, 1915, p. 4.
39. *Auckland Star*, 10 February 1913, p. 10; *Waimate Daily Advertiser*, 1 May 1915, p. 1.
40. For example, *Kai Tiaki*, 1 July 1919, p. vi.
41. *Sun*, 23 September 1914, p. 5.
42. *Wanganui Herald*, 2 September 1912, p. 5.
43. *Evening Star*, 2 May 1911, p. 2.
44. *Lyttelton Times*, 4 May 1911, p. 8.
45. *Wanganui Herald*, 19 December 1916, p. 2.
46. *Appendix to the Journals of the House of Representatives*, 1913, Session I, H-31, p. 3.
47. *Star*, 4 April 1913, p. 1; *Lyttelton Times*, 5 April 1913, p. 12.
48. *Maoriland Worker*, 22 August 1913, p. 4.
49. www.nzlii.org/nz/legis/hist_act/pdata19112gv1911n17367/
50. 'Certificate of Registration of Label Trade-Mark. In the Name of T.J. Edmonds, No. 10823, Patent Office, Wellington', R23394982, Archives New Zealand.
51. https://app.iponz.govt.nz/app/Extra/IP/Mutual/Browse.aspx?sid=637624527689335069; https://www.iponz.govt.nz/about-iponz/history-of-ip-in-new-zealand/

CHAPTER 7: RECIPES FOR SUCCESS

1. See David Veart, *First Catch Your Weka: A Story of New Zealand Cooking*, Auckland University Press, 2008, for interesting coverage of these 'community' cookery books.

2. Veart, *First Catch Your Weka*, p. 56.
3. *New Zealand Herald*, 14 November 1889, p. 7; *Star*, 21 April 1894, p. 5.
4. *Evening Post*, 5 August 1903, p 6; *Nelson Evening Mail*, 18 March 1904, p. 3.
5. Ben Panko, 'The Great Uprising: How a Powder Revolutionized Baking, *Smithsonian Magazine*, 20 June 2017, https://www.smithsonianmag.com/science-nature/great-uprising-how-powder-revolutionized-baking-180963772/
6. Helen Leach, *Culinary Treasures of the Hocken Collections*, Hocken Lecture 3, 2007, Hocken Collections/Uare Taoka o Hākena, University of Otago, 2008, p. 25.
7. For example, Alison Stevenson, 'Iconic Cookbook Online', http://nzetc.blogspot.com/2007/02/iconic-cook-book-online.html; Ann-Marie Kennedy, 'Marketing's Influence on the Food Culture of a Nation: As told through the Edmonds' Cookery Book', Conference on Historical Analysis & Research in Marketing (CHARM) proceedings, Quinnipiac University, 2011. Ron Hooker raised the suggestion of an earlier book in a radio interview http://ketechristchurch.peoplesnetworknz.info/audio/0000/0000/0001/Track_01.mp3. The authors contacted the book's owner, Dawn Barr, and confirmed that it was the fifth edition released in 1933. The addition of a plain red canvas cover may have led to Hooker's theory. David Veart also gives the 1907 date in *First Catch Your Weka*.
8. This letter is held in the Goodman Fielder archive.
9. *Wanganui Herald*, 25 September 1909, p. 2.
10. Leach, *Culinary Treasures*, pp. 29–30.
11. Ibid, p. 30.
12. Duncan Galletly, 'Never Gallop Asparagus: Irene Ballantyne her Cookery Book', *The Aristologist: An Antipodean Journal of Food History*, No. 1, Kōwhiti House, 2011, p. 41.
13. Leach, *Culinary Treasures*, p. 33.
14. Copies are held by Mark Nicholls, an Edmonds descendant: 'The other intriguing thing is that Edmonds factory library had several of the Royal baking books. They looked very similar to the early Edmonds recipe books. I know this because [they have] the TJ Edmonds Factory stamp inside the cover.' Personal communication by Kate Parsonson with Mark Nicholls, August 2019.
15. Leach, *Culinary Treasures*, fn p. 27.
16. C. T. Ross, 'Constructing the "World's Scenic Wonderland": Photomontage in New Zealand illustrated weekly newspapers, 1900–1930', PhD Thesis, University of Otago, 2009. Retrieved from http://hdl.handle.net/10523/323
17. *Press*, 10 February 1910, p. 7.
18. https://edmondscooking.co.nz/cookery-books-history/
19. *Sun*, 18 July 1919, p. 13.
20. *New Zealand Police Gazette*, 17 January 1923, p. 27.
21. A number of original letters to Edmonds requesting a copy of the cookery book, along with testimonials about Edmonds baking powder, are contained in a scrapbook of Edmonds material held in the Goodman Fielder Archive. This content was also used by Ann-Marie Kennedy in her 2011 paper, 'Marketing's Influence on the Food Culture of a Nation: As told through the Edmonds' Cookery Book'.
22. Leach, *Culinary Treasures*, p. 32.
23. Jenny Chamberlain, 'Old Faithfuls: The Best of the Bestsellers', *North & South*, April 1990, p. 92.
24. Chamberlain, 'Old Faithfuls', p. 93.
25. https://edmondscooking.co.nz/cookery-books-history/
26. *Press*, 21 July 1933, p. 6; *Ashburton Guardian*, 12 July 1933, p. 3.
27. Leach, *Culinary Treasures*, p. 31.
28. https://edmondscooking.co.nz/cookery-books-history/; *Thames Star*, 29 October 1936, p. 3.
29. Helen Leach, *The Pavlova Story: A Slice of New Zealand's Culinary History*, Otago University Press, Dunedin, 2008, p. 96.
30. Ibid., p. 31.
31. Ibid.; Leach, *Culinary Treasures*, pp. 27–28.
32. https://edmondscooking.co.nz/cookery-books-history/
33. Leach, *Culinary Treasures*, p. 31.
34. *Mirror*, Vol. 37, No. 1, July 1957, p. 63.
35. Leach, *Culinary Treasures*, p. 30.
36. Ron Hooker, 'The Story of T J Edmonds Cookery Books', 23 October 2009.
37. Ibid
38. https://edmondscooking.co.nz/cookery-books-history/
39. Edmonds Test Kitchen/Laboratory chronology, typewritten sheet, Ron Hooker?, n.d.
40. http://www.fresh.co.nz, 19 September 2016.
41. Leach, *Culinary Treasures*, p. 28.
42. Ibid., pp. 27, 28.
43. Chamberlain, 'Old Faithfuls', p. 92.
44. *Listener*, 5 December 2020, p. 44.
45. Ron Palenski, *Kiwi Milestones: New Zealand's Population Through the Millions*, Hachette, Auckland, 2004, p. 14, quoted in Lorna Piatti-Farnell, 'Sure to Rise: Reading the Edmonds cookery book as a popular icon', in Donna Lee Brien and Adele Wessell (eds), *TEXT Special Issue 24: Cookbooks: writing, reading and publishing culinary literature in Australasia*, October 2013, p. 4.

CHAPTER 8: A FAMILY FLOURISHES

1. *Lyttelton Times*, 13 October 1904, p. 3.
2. *Auckland Star*, 28 January 1905, p. 8.
3. C. M. O'Connor, 'Life History: Gertrude Ivy Williams (nee Edmonds), 1891–1987', 17 October 1986, p. 6.
4. *Lyttelton Times*, 5 June 1907, p. 2; 8 June 1907, p. 3.
5. *Lyttelton Times*, 5 January 1910, p. 12.
6. CH 817/2 1966, 7 July 1908, https://www.ccc.govt.nz/assets/Documents/Culture-Community/Heritage/Archives/CH817Box2CCCBuildingPermits1907-1920.pdf
7. *Star*, 23 September 1933, p. 9.
8. O'Connor, 'Life History', p. 7.
9. *Lyttelton Times*, 26 July 1907, p. 9.
10. *Akaroa Mail and Banks Peninsula Advertiser*, 16 July 1909, p. 2.
11. www.nzherald.co.nz/lifestyle/ipeter-downesi-the-pollards/KBJ7JPMA3TLXDGIMHTOU6CCFTU/, 12 March 2003
12. O'Connor, 'Life History', p. 7.
13. *Lyttelton Times*, 6 January 1909, p. 3.
14. *Sun*, 9 May 1914, p. 11.
15. John and Day Ballantyne, interviewed by Bee Dawson, 9 July 2018.
16. *Star*, 4 November 1919, p. 9.
17. *Lyttelton Times*, 13 December 1904, p. 10.
18. *Star*, 26 April 1906, p. 1.
19. *Lyttelton Times*, 19 September 1912, p. 5.
20. *Lyttelton Times*, 14 August 1902, p. 3.
21. *Lyttelton Times*, 17 December 1902, p. 9.
22. Murray Edmonds, quoted in Paul Smith and Louise Callan, *Our People, Our Century*, Hodder Moa Beckett, Auckland, 1999, p. 106.
23. *Star*, 20 November 1913, p. 7.
24. *Lyttelton Times*, 12 January 1918, p. 2.
25. *Press*, 17 May 1911, p. 6.
26. Philip Richards, email to Kate Parsonson, 19 February 2021.
27. *Lyttelton Times*, 20 November 1901, p. 8; *Press*, 24 December 1901 p. 5; 19 February 1909, p. 7.
28. *Lyttelton Times*, 21 June 1910, p. 2.
29. David Cropp, quoted in Smith and Callan, *Our People*, p. 106.

CHAPTER 9: TRAGEDY & TRAVEL

1. *Press*, 3 August 1914, p. 12.
2. *Sun*, 7 September 1915, p. 10.
3. www.familysearch.org/ark:/61903/3:1:3QSQ-G9KN-QNYT?i=599&cc=1865481
4. www.nzlii.org/nz/legis/hist_act/wpa19112gv1911n16283/
5. *Press*, 12 March 1925, p. 10.
6. David Cropp, quoted in Paul Smith and Louise Callan, *Our People, Our Century*, Hodder Moa Beckett, Auckland, 1999, p. 109.
7. Sir John Ilott, 75th anniversary speech, Ilott Advertising Ltd: Records, MS-Papers-3913-8/15, Alexander Turnbull Library.
8. Certificate of Incorporation, R19909634, Archives New Zealand, Christchurch.
9. *Lyttelton Times*, 24 August 1914, p. 8.
10. *Evening Star*, 15 September 1914, p. 1; *Sun*, 16 September 1914, p. 3.
11. *New Zealand Times*, 10 November 1914, p. 7.
12. *Marlborough Express*, 13 April 1915, p. 2.
13. *Otago Witness*, 2 June 1915, p. 14.
14. *Te Puke Times*, 6 July 1915, p. 2.
15. *Grey River Argus*, 19 July 1915, p. 3.
16. *Greymouth Evening Star*, 30 August 1915, p. 8; *Manawatu Standard*, 4 October 1916, p. 2.
17. *Auckland Star*, 22 January 1917, p. 7; 29 January 1917, p. 8.
18. *Otago Daily Times*, 1 April 1918, p. 2.
19. *Pahiatua Herald*, 7 August 1918, p. 3.
20. *Press*, 19 April 1919, p. 7.
21. *Press*, 11 January 1919, p. 13.
22. *Otago Daily Times*, 22 October 1915, p. 7.
23. *Taranaki Daily News*, 4 December 1915, p. 6.
24. *Evening Star*, 8 February 1916, p. 6.
25. *New Zealand Herald*, 19 October 1916, p. 8.
26. *Lyttelton Times*, 15 August 1914, p. 10; *Star*, 24 August 1914, p. 5; *Star*, 4 June 1915, p. 6.
27. *Star*, 12 April 1916, p. 6; *Sun*, 13 March 1918, p. 4.
28. *Press*, 12 October 1916, p. 7.
29. *Waikato Independent*, 18 May 1918, p. 4.
30. *Sun*, 14 November 1914, p. 1; O'Connor memoir fn 50; *Sun*, 16 October 1915, p. 14.
31. *Lyttelton Times*, 20 June 1917, p. 2.
32. *Lyttelton Times*, 30 October 1914, p. 8.
33. *Star*, 19 June 1918, p. 7.
34. Personnel file 91024, Archives New Zealand; *Sun*, 19 June 1918, p. 3.
35. Personnel file 46658, Archives New Zealand.
36. *Star*, 1 June 1915, p. 6.
37. *N.Z. Truth*, 5 June 1915, p. 9.
38. *Sun*, 8 June 1915, p. 11.
39. Philip Richards, pers. comm., 10 July 2018.
40. C. M. O'Connor, 'Life History: Gertrude Ivy Williams (nee Edmonds), 1891–1987', 17 October 1986, p. 8.
41. Ibid.
42. Jack Carroll & Mosman Historical Society 1953, The Settlement and Growth of Mosman, Mosman Historical Society, Sydney http://mosman1914-1918.net/project/blog/doing-their-share
43. *Mercury*, 6 May 1918, p. 2.
44. O'Connor, 'Life History', p. 9.

45. Geoffrey W. Rice, *Black Flu 1918: The Story of New Zealand's Worst Public Health Disaster*, Canterbury University Press, Christchurch, 2017, p. 45.
46. *Star*, 30 November 1918, p. 8; *Press*, 14 December 1918, p. 10; *Lyttelton Times*, 11 December 1918, p. 7.
47. *Press*, 14 December 1918, p. 7.
48. *Press*, 20 September 1919, p. 2; *Star*, 6 November 1919, p. 3.
49. *Star*, 18 January 1919, p. 10.
50. *Press*, 2 December 1920, p. 2.

CHAPTER 10: A LANDMARK FACTORY

1. *Otago Witness*, 10 February 1920, p. 55.
2. *Grey River Argus*, 1 May 1920, p. 2.
3. *Southland Times*, 5 January 1920, p. 6.
4. *Sun*, 18 July 1919, p. 13.
5. CH 817/2 1643, 21 November 1907, CH 817/2 1965, 17 July 1908, www.ccc.govt.nz/assets/Documents/Culture-Community/Heritage/Archives/CH-817Box2CCCBuildingPermits1907-1920.pdf; CH 817/2 2662, 4 February 1910, CH 817/2 4177, 1 May 1913, CH 817/2 6583, www.ccc.govt.nz/assets/Documents/Culture-Community/Heritage/Archives/CH817Box2CCCBuildingPermits1907-1920.pdf
6. For example, *Sun*, 10 July 1920, p. 10; *The Architectural Heritage of Christchurch: 8. The Legacy of Thomas Edmonds*, Christchurch City Council Environmental Policy & Planning Unit, 1993, p. 6, http://christchurchcitylibraries.com/Heritage/Publications/ChristchurchCityCouncil/ArchitecturalHeritage/LegacyofThomasEdmonds/
7. CH 817/2 6583, 27 October 2910, https://www.ccc.govt.nz/assets/Documents/Culture-Community/Heritage/Archives/CH817Box2CCCBuildingPermits1907-1920.pdf
8. Certificate of title 12910, Chronology of Development - Edmonds Factory Gardens, Appendix 1, Edmonds Factory Garden: Conservation and Development Proposals 1992, Landscape Section, Design Services Unit, Christchurch City Council.
9. *Through the Changing Years*: History of T.J. Edmonds Ltd. in its jubilee year, *1879–1929*, printed by Whitcombe & Tombs Ltd, Christchurch, 1929, quoted in *The Architectural Heritage of Christchurch: 8*, p. 5.
10. 'Where Magic Baking Powder and Other Gillett Products are Made', booklet, n.d, Collection of Peter Alsop.
11. *Press*, 20 February 1922, p. 7.
12. R19909634, Archives New Zealand.
13. *Press*, 20 February 1922, p. 7.
14. The certificate is held in the Goodman Fielder Archive.
15. *Press*, 24 August 1937, p. 18.
16. *Press*, 4 December 1937, p. 3.
17. *Manawatu Times*, 10 February 1923, p. 7.
18. *Evening Post*, 9 August 1927, p. 12; *Auckland Star*, 11 October 1927, p. 4.
19. *Press*, 13 December 1928, p. 4.
20. Donald T. Brash, *American Investment in Australian Industry*, Harvard University Press, 1966, p. 312.
21. *Press*, 13 December 1928, p. 4.
22. *Hastings Standard*, 2 January 1920, p. 3.
23. *Southland Times*, 25 February 1920, p. 7.
24. *Bay of Plenty Times*, 7 May 1920, p. 3; 24 May 1920, p. 4.
25. A 1911 Steffano Webb photograph shows the party, with people representing named Christchurch firms, 1/1-009250-G, Alexander Turnbull Library; *Hawera & Normanby Star*, 19 July 1920, p. 8.
26. *Lake Wakatip Mail*, 28 September 1920 p. 3.
27. *Wairarapa Daily Times*, 11 March 1935, p. 3.
28. *Taranaki Daily News*, 4 November 1920, p. 2.
29. *Franklin Times*, 23 February 1931, p. 6.
30. *Auckland Star*, 13 September 1921, p. 9. Since then, the peak, now known as Aoraki/Mt Cook, has been reduced in height to 12,218 feet (3724 metres).
31. *Manawatu Times*, 5 March 1924, p. 10.
32. No. 1, *Bay of Plenty Times*, 27 July 1928, p. 4; No. 2, *Otago Daily Times*, 21 July 1928, p. 21; No. 3, *Stratford Evening Post*, 11 October 1928, p. 8; No. 4, *Poverty Bay Herald*, 12 December 1928, p. 4; No. 5, *Hawera Star*, 4 January 1929, p. 8; No. 6, *Evening Star*, 31 December 1928, p. 4.
33. *The Ladies' Mirror*, 1 July 1922, p. 23.
34. *Press*, 29 June 1925, p. 4.
35. *Western Star*, 5 November 1920, p. 2; *Ashburton Guardian*, 15 June 1921, p. 6.
36. *Evening Star*, 23 April 1931, p. 17. The book had an alternative title inside on the title page: *The Edmonds Story & Painting Book*. Valentine Studios was possibly the first design studio in New Zealand to be established by a woman, Gladys Valentine Howey (1901–1985).
37. *Press*, 17 October 1927, p. 10.

CHAPTER 11: BENEFACTORS & BELIEVERS

1. *Press*, 27 September 1929 p. 13, and following quotes.
2. *Star*, 27 September 1929, p. 3.
3. *Telegraph* (Brisbane), 25 November 1929, p. 24.
4. *Press*, 12 November 1929, p. 10.
5. *Telegraph*, 25 November 1929, p. 24.
6. *Star*, 12 December 1932, p. 2.
7. *Star*, 5 March 1898, p. 6.
8. Nancy Swarbrick, 'Harris, Jane Elizabeth', *Dictionary of New Zealand Biography*, first published in 1993. Te Ara - the Encyclopedia of New Zealand, https://teara.govt.nz/en/biographies/2h16/harris-jane-elizabeth
9. *Press*, 30 December 1899, p. 12.
10. *Press*, 19 May 1894, p. 9.
11. *Press*, 13 September 1997, p. 5; Geoffrey W. Rice, *Christchurch Changing: An Illustrated History*, Canterbury University Press, Christchurch, 2008, p. 56; *Press*, 27 September 1897, p. 4.
12. https://www.theosophical.org/about/theosophy
13. *Press*, 26 June 1893, p. 5.
14. *Sun*, 22 November 1919, p. 10.
15. *Who's Who in New Zealand*, International Press Service, Wellington, 1933, p. 433.
16. *The Architectural Heritage of Christchurch: 8. The Legacy of Thomas Edmonds*, Christchurch City Council Environmental Policy & Planning Unit, 1993, p. 8, http://christchurchcitylibraries.com/Heritage/Publications/ChristchurchCityCouncil/ArchitecturalHeritage/LegacyofThomasEdmonds/
17. https://canterburystories.nz/exhibitions/places-christchurch-buildings/theosophical-society-hall
18. *Press*, 3 July 1929, p. 2.
19. https://nzhistory.govt.nz/culture/radiant-living/herbert-sutcliffe
20. *Press*, 21 January 1929, p. 2.
21. *Star*, 22 February 1929, p. 14.
22. *Press*, 5 April 1929, p. 16.
23. *Press*, 6 June 1929, p. 6.
24. *Press*, 14 November 1929, p. 2.
25. *Press*, 16 December 1930, p. 10.
26. Rice, *Christchurch Changing*, pp. 53, 55.
27. H.N. Parton, 'Bickerton, Alexander William', *Dictionary of New Zealand Biography*, first published in 1993. Te Ara - the Encyclopedia of New Zealand, https://teara.govt.nz/en/biographies/2b23/bickerton-alexander-william
28. https://christchurchartgallery.org.nz/collection/90-9/petrus-van-der-velden/professor-alexander-william-bickerton
29. Kay Forrester, 'Eccentric prof. recalled', undated *Press* clipping; C. M. O'Connor, 'Life History: Gertrude Ivy Williams (nee Edmonds), 1891–1987', 17 October 1986, p. 5.

CHAPTER 12: FAREWELL TO THE FOUNDER

1. *Poverty Bay Herald*, 5 February 1930, p. 9.
2. *Evening Star*, 23 January 1930, p. 17; 21 April 1930, p. 16.
3. *Through the Changing Years*: History of T.J. Edmonds Ltd. in its jubilee year, *1879–1929*, printed by Whitcombe & Tombs Ltd, Christchurch, 1929. See also Ann-Marie Kennedy, 'Marketing's Influence on the Food Culture of a Nation: As told through the Edmonds' Cookery Book', Conference on Historical Analysis & Research in Marketing (CHARM) proceedings, Quinnipiac University, 2011, p. 100.
4. *Wairarapa Daily Times*, 17 May 1932, p. 3.
5. *New Zealand Herald*, 8 November 1935, p. 5.
6. *Auckland Star*, 24 September 1929, p. 4.
7. *Otago Daily Times*, 31 October 1931, p. 2.
8. *Evening Star*, 30 December 1933, p. 16.
9. *Press*, 22 June 1935, p. 12.
10. *Evening Star*, 10 July 1931, p. 10.
11. *Manawatu Standard*, 17 August 1933, p. 12.
12. *Otago Daily Times*, 15 November 1932, p. 12; *Northern Advocate*, 2 May 1934, p. 2.
13. *Farmcraft: Hundreds of hints for saving time, labour and money on the farm: selected from Handy Andy's column in 'The Weekly News'*, Vol. 2, Wilson & Horton, Auckland, 1937.
14. *Press*, 29 June 1934, p. 5.
15. Quoted in Paul Smith and Louise Callan, *Our People, Our Century*, Hodder Moa Beckett, Auckland, 1999, p. 110.
16. *Evening Post*, 24 March 1931, p. 2.
17. Ibid., p. 4; *Press*, 3 December 1932, p. 16; *Evening Star*, 22 December 1932, p. 2.
18. *New Zealand Herald*, 24 March 1931, p. 3.
19. *Poverty Bay Herald*, 17 December 1931, p. 8; *Star*, 23 November 1931, p. 7; *Star*, 31 December 1931, p. 9.
20. *New Zealand Herald*, 29 April 1932, p. 13.
21. *Manawatu Standard*, 14 October 1932, p. 10.
22. *Star*, 19 April 1932, p. 7.
23. *Press*, 20 April 1932, p. 13.
24. *Press*, 3 June 1932, p. 16.
25. *Star*, 3 June 1932, p. 4.
26. *Star*, 4 June 1932, p. 9.
27. *Press*, 6 June 1932, p. 3.
28. Will of Thomas John Edmonds, R20185297, Archives New Zealand.
29. *Star*, 20 March 1933, p. 2.
30. Food and Drugs Act, Part 2 - baking powder, 142/3, H1 Box 1315, Archives New Zealand; *Waipawa Mail*, 26 September 1932, p. 3.
31. *Star*, 30 March 1935, p. 14.
32. *Press*, 8 May 1935, p. 10.
33. T. J. Edmonds Ltd, R19909634, Archives New Zealand; Memorandum of Association of T. J. Edmonds Limited signed 6 August 1935 (included as part of the Memorandum and Articles of Association of T. J. Edmonds Ltd. reprinted February 1964, source unknown, available from the authors). The change technically applied from 1 April 1935.
34. https://teara.govt.nz/en/weekends/page-3
35. *Thames Star*, 5 November 1935, p. 3.
36. Quoted in Smith and Callan, *Our People*, p. 110.
37. Ian Kinley, interviewed by Bee Dawson, 21 November 2018.

38. *Press*, 11 February 1936, p. 10.
39. http://ketechristchurch.peoplesnetworknz.info/site/images/show/715-edmonds s#.XXDGGi2U
40. Staff memories from Ron Hooker, 24 January 2001.
41. *Press*, 13 October 1933, p. 13; *Star*, 13 October 1933, p. 9.
42. *Press*, 23 September 1933, p. 22.
43. *Press*, 25 May 1938, p. 5.
44. Quoted in Smith and Callan, *Our People*, p. 106.
45. Philip Richards, email to Kate Parsonson, 10 September 2021.

CHAPTER 13: WAR & PEACE

1. *Otaki Mail*, 27 September 1939, p. 3.
2. *Auckland Star*, 20 October 1939, p. 3.
3. *Evening Star*, 8 November 1939, p. 8.
4. *Ashburton Guardian*, 7 March 1940, p. 7.
5. *Evening Star*, 29 November 1939, p. 8; *Otago Daily Times*, 30 November 1939, p. 10.
6. *Press*, 4 October 1940, p. 12; 15 February 1941, p. 2.
7. *New Zealand Herald*, 23 August 1941, p. 10.
8. *Ashburton Guardian*, 2 November 1939, p. 4; *Patea Mail*, 1 May 1940, p. 1.
9. *Waikato Independent*, 19 May 1941, p. 5; *Northern Advocate*, 28 April 1942, p. 2.
10. Photograph by Eileen Deste, Registration no. 0302/4/183, The Fletcher Trust Archives.
11. *Gisborne Herald*, 25 January 1940, p. 13.
12. *Press*, 16 July 1941, p. 4.
13. O.N. Gillespie, *Railways Magazine*, 1 November 1939, pp. 12–13.
14. *Evening Post*, 19 October 1940, p. 13; *Press*, 30 December 1940, p. 4.
15. Staff memories from Ron Hooker, 24 January 2001.
16. *Ashburton Guardian*, 15 January 1941, p. 7.
17. *New Zealand Herald*, 1 February 1941, p. 12.
18. *Otago Daily Times*, 7 April 1941, p. 11; *Press*, 29 March 1941, p. 7.
19. *Otago Daily Times*, 1 June 1932, p. 15.
20. *Press*, 21 July 1944, p. 2.
21. *Evening Post*, 22 March 1944, p. 4.
22. *Evening Star*, 13 October 1945, p. 11.
23. *Evening Star*, 12 July 1946, p. 10.
24. *Gisborne Herald*, 30 November 1946, p. 3.
25. *Otago Daily Times*, 16 January 1947, p. 7.
26. 'Ian Kinley – Memories of the Edmonds Factory', interviewed by Bee Dawson, 21 November 2018.
27. Megan Watson, '"Of course you had to keep the cake tins full": Pakeha women and afternoon tea from 1930–50', MPhil thesis, Massey University, 2011, p. 15.
28. T. J. Edmonds Ltd, *Your Visit to Edmonds*, c.1949.
29. *The New Zealand Grocer's Review*, 7 February 1952, p. 508.
30. 'Ian Kinley – Memories'.
31. Ibid.
32. John O'Shea, in Jonathan Dennis and Jan Bieringa (eds), *A Charmed Life: Fragments of Memory, Film in Aotearoa New Zealand*, Victoria University Press, Wellington, 1996, https://www.filmsocietywellington.net.nz/db/screeningdetail.php?id=402&sr=1
33. *Cookery Nook*, Ngā Taonga Sound & Vision, Film and Video Collection, F9146.
34. Ron Hooker, draft of article, undated, c.2004.
35. G.A. Tait (ed.), *Manufacturing in New Zealand*, Cranwell Publishing Co. Ltd, Auckland, 1959, 'Preface' (unpaginated) and B16-17.

CHAPTER 14: A NEW ERA

1. Frank Bennett, 'Frank Bennett on Finance / T. J. Edmonds in the Dough', unsourced newspaper clipping.
2. 'Fond memories Ron's sure to prize', *Christchurch Mail*, 13 May 2009.
3. 'A Second Presentation to the Shareholders of Henry Berry Ltd from the Directors of T.J. Edmonds Ltd', T.J. Edmonds Ltd, 1969.
4. This and following company information from annual reports.
5. *Asburton Guardian*, 1 May 1979.
6. 'Governor's export award for Edmonds', *Press*, 12 June 1979, part of R17239784, Archives New Zealand, records of the application by T.J. Edmonds Ltd, along with the decision and announcement.
7. R17239784, award speech of Governor-General Keith Holyoake.
8. 'Edmonds' Coup', *Christchurch Star*, 24 March 1979.
9. 'Here's What I'm Told: On Tape With the Editor/ Opportunities, Not Problems, The T.J. Edmonds Philosophy', *The New Zealand Company Director & Executive*, March 1978, p. 32.
10. 'Recommended Offer by H.W. Smith Ltd for all the issued capital of T.J. Edmonds Ltd, January 1982'; Bunting & Co. Ltd, *Annual Report*, 1982.
11. Bert and Ron Fuller, interviewed by Bee Dawson, 21 November 2018.
12. Bunting & Co. Ltd, *Annual Report*, 1983.

CHAPTER 15: THE NEXT GENERATION

1. John and Day Ballantyne, interviewed by Bee Dawson, 9 July 2018.
2. *Press*, 24 September 1954.
3. *N.Z. Truth*, 10 April 1920, p. 5.
4. *Star*, 10 April 1933, p. 8.
5. *Press*, 28 January 1924, p. 2.
6. *Press*, 13 July 1935, p. 3.
7. John and Day Ballantyne interview.
8. *Press*, 6 October 1936, p. 2.
9. Murray Edmonds, quoted in Paul Smith and Louise Callan, *Our People, Our Century*, Hodder Moa Beckett, Auckland, 1999, p. 108.
10. Memories of Cassandra Philpot, email to Kate Parsonson, 12 July 2021.
11. C.M. O'Connor, 'Life History: Gertrude Ivy Williams (nee Edmonds), 1891–1987', 17 October 1986, p. 14.
12. Undated newspaper clipping, November 1995.
13. http://honesthistory.net.au/wp/beatrice-jauncey/
14. Jane Lee, email to Kate Parsonson, December 2014.
15. Duncan Galletly, 'Never Gallop Asparagus: Irene Ballantyne her Cookery Book', *The Aristologist: An Antipodean Journal of Food History*, No. 1, Kōwhiti House, 2011.
16. Philip Richards, emails to Kate Parsonson, 27 and 28 July 2021.

CHAPTER 16: A FAMOUS GARDEN

1. *Press*, 4 December 1937, p. 3.
2. *Press*, 11 March 1924, p. 3.
3. *Press*, 27 February 1925, p. 15.
4. Chronology of Development – Edmonds Factory Gardens, Appendix 1, Edmonds Factory Garden: Conservation and Development Proposals 1992, Landscape Section, Design Services Unit, Christchurch City Council. Paddock bought 6 November 1924 (certificate of title 13276). First section of 511m^2 bought 4 May 1925 (certificate of title 13319). Second section of 339m^2 bought 9 July 1925 (certificate of title 13341).
5. Bert and Ron Fuller, interviewed by Bee Dawson, 21 November 2018.
6. *Press*, 22 May 1931, p. 7.
7. *Press*, 31 March 1936, p. 18.
8. Murray Edmonds, quoted in Paul Smith and Louise Callan, *Our People, Our Century*, Hodder Moa Beckett, Auckland, 1999, p. 107.
9. *Press*, 29 April 1939, p. 9.
10. 'Kindergartens in New Zealand 1889–1975', www.kindergartenhistory.org.nz/media/1687/kindergartens-in-new-zealand-1889-1975-lockhart-pm-varcoe-pm-ryan-m.pdf, pp. 21, 23.
11. Thelma Strongman, 'Garden Goes Too When Factory Demolished', *New Zealand Historic Places*, 33, June 1991, p. 8.
12. Jenny and John Hoskin, conversation, 20 August 2018.
13. Strongman, 'Garden Goes Too', p. 8.
14. Ibid.
15. *Edmonds Factory Garden: Conservation and Development Proposals*, pp. 13–16; Ron Hooker, 'History of the Gardeners', undated; Thelma Strongman, 'Garden Goes Too', p. 8.
16. Winton Cassels, 'Sure to rise again …', *Southern Skies*, July 1994.
17. Bruce Ansley, 'The Going Down of the Sun', *Listener*, 12–18 November 1990, p. 20.
18. Strongman, 'Garden Goes Too', p. 9.
19. Cassels, 'Sure to rise again …'.
20. Hoskin conversation.
21. Adrienne Rewi, 'Prized gardens to return', *NZ Gardener*, February 1993, p. 38.
22. District Plan – Listed Heritage Place / Heritage Assessment – Statement of Significance / Heritage Item Number 193 / Edmonds Factory Garden – 357, 365 Ferry Road, 72 Ryan Street, Christchurch', Christchurch City Council, 12 February 2015, p. 2.
23. Hoskin coversation; www.cinch.org.nz/categories/a-z/f/311/entries/4379

EPILOGUE

1. *Press*, 18 November 2020, p. 15.
2. *Press*, 10 April 2021, p. A8.
3. https://nzhistory.govt.nz/culture/tv-history/history
4. http://www.businesshalloffame.co.nz/past-laureates/
5. 'Edmonds stamp', nzhistory.govt.nz/media/photo/edmonds-stamp, (Ministry for Culture and Heritage), updated 13 January 2016.
6. https://collections.tepapa.govt.nz/object/1285567. Rebecca Lovell-Smith's tea towel is in the collection of the Museum of New Zealand Te Papa Tongarewa.

IMAGE CREDITS

2. T.J. Edmonds, c.1931, H.H. Clifford (photographer), Canterbury Museum, 1980.175.23793. Digitally coloured by Brendan Graham.
4–5. Window display of Remuera grocer L.O. Thomas, 1938, Collection of Rosemary Edmonds. Digitally coloured by Brendan Graham.
6. Edmonds tin, 1923, illustration from *Edmonds Cookery Book* fourth edition, Collection of Peter Alsop.
8. Thomas and Jane Edmonds, c.1920, Photographer unknown, Collection of Cassandra Philpot.
11. Edmonds factory, c.1906, Photographer unknown, Collection of Philip Richards.
12. Map, LSE Library, London School of Economics and Political Science, BOOTH/E/11, 1898-99.
15. 'F. Allen & Sons Cocoa Chocolate and Confectionery Works', c.1880, Evanion Collection, Evan.6343, © British Library Board.
16. (Left) Thomas Edmonds, c.1878, Photographer unknown, Collection of Philip Richards. (Right) Jane Edmonds, c.1878, Photographer unknown, Collection of Dianne Gallagher.
17. London docks, c.1875, Photographer unknown, Alamy stock photo, M8H64F.
18. *Clipper Ship 'Waitangi'*, Date unknown, Richard Ball Spencer (1812–97), Oil on canvas, 58 x 94cm, Collection of Waimate Museum & Archives, 2012-011-001.
19. Montage of sketches depicting life on board an emigrant ship, *The Illustrated New Zealand Herald*, 9 April 1875; reproduced in *Making New Zealand*, 1940, Alexander Turnbull Library, MNZ-0661-1/4-F.
21. Landing Immigrants at Lyttelton, N.Z., *Illustrated Australian News*, 23 January 1878, Alexander Turnbull Library, PUBL-0119-1878-13.
22–23. *Lyttelton Harbour, N.Z. Inside the Breakwater*, 1886, John Gibb (1831–1909), Oil on canvas, 1080 x 1590mm, Christchurch Art Gallery Te Puna o Waiwhetū, 89/209, Presented by the Lyttelton Harbour Board 1989.
24. Colombo Street, from the album 'Panorama of Christchurch from Cathedral Tower', 1881, Wheeler & Son (photographer), Te Papa Tongarewa, O.043691.
25. *Addington Station*, 1879 (20 July, inscribed on painting), George Turner (1841–1910), Oil on canvas, 595 x 440mm, Canterbury Museum, GT.20.
26. *The First Four Ships, Lyttelton Harbour, December 1850*, printed and published by James Clunie Wilkin for the *Lyttelton Times*, Supplement to *Canterbury Times* Jubilee Number, 16 December 1900, Collection of Peter Alsop.
27. *The River Avon: Christchurch N.Z.*, 1887 (20 March), Artist unknown, Watercolour, Collection of Hawke's Bay Museums Trust, Ruawharo Tā-ū-rangi, 6426.
28. Interior of the Cathedral shown while under construction, 1879, *The Weekly Press*, 9 February 1898, p. 9. Christchurch City Libraries, File Reference: CCL-KPCD06-0087, Obtained from the collection, and used with permission, of Christchurch City Libraries. http://christchurchcitylibraries.com/
29. Christchurch scenes taken from the Cathedral Tower, 1881, E. Wheeler & Son (photographer), Te Papa Tongarewa, O.043690 and O.043685.
30. Covers of Special and Christmas Number editions, Collections of Barry Hancox (left) and Alexander Turnbull Library.
31. Advertising poster for Aulsebrook & Co, c.1882, Alexander Turnbull Library, Eph-C-FOOD-1880s-01.
32. 'The Acorn and the Oak', 1930 (5 February), *Otago Daily Times*.
33. Photo of Jane and William, 1880, Photographer unknown, Collection of Philip Richards.
34. (Top) *Through the Changing Years*, 1929, History of T.J. Edmonds Ltd. in its jubilee year, 1879–1929, Alexander Turnbull Library, unnumbered item. (Bottom) Edmond Street, Map 'Part of City of Christchurch', 1926, Christchurch City Libraries Tūranga, CCLMaps 365579.
35. Plan of town of Ashbourne in c.1883, Alexander Turnbull Library, MapColl-834.4492gbbd/[ca.1883?]/Acc.3235.
36. *Carte de visite* of Edmonds family, c.1883, J. Spiller (photographer), Collection of Philip Richards.
37. Horse and cart, c.1885, Photographer unknown, Image courtesy of Kete Christchurch.
38. (Top) Newspaper classifieds, 1887 (5 May), *Press*. (Bottom) 'Edmonds' Prize Baking Powder', 1888 (7 June), *Press*.
39. Edmonds horse and cart, c.1906 (original photo), Reproduced in the *Press* on 29 January 2000.
40–41: Detail of the front cover of the Jubilee Number of *The Weekly Press*, 1900, Alexander Turnbull Library.
42. 'The Premier Baking Powder of New Zealand', Empire Packing Co., Wellington, Alexander Turnbull Library, Eph-B-FOOD-1918-01. The library's dating of this item (c.1918) is likely significantly too late. The design style is older and Papers Past suggests the company's baking powder advertising had all but ceased by 1904.
43. Miss Grimstone representing Hudson's baking powder at the Auckland Floral Fete, 1907 (12 December), *Auckland Weekly News*, Auckland Libraries, AWNS-19071212-10-4.
44. Interior of a grocer's store, 1903, Christmas Number of the *Auckland Weekly News*, Collection of Peter Alsop.
45. (Top) Illustration from a Borwick's advertising booklet, c.1890, Collection of Peter Alsop. (Bottom) Hudson's advertisement, c.1895, cropped from advertising poster, Supplement to the *New Zealand Herald* and *Auckland Weekly News*, Collection of Peter Alsop.
46. Hudson's 'Balloon' Brand Baking Powder Exhibit, Featured in *Scenes in and about the Auckland Exhibition 1913–1914*, Collection of Peter Alsop.
47. Details of baking powder labels, Archives New Zealand, R20955213.
48–49. Miscellaneous baking powder tins, Collections of Peter Alsop, Allan Paterson, Barry & Adrienne Stephens, and Elsie Wolfe Decorative Antiques.
50. 'Sure to Rise Edmonds Prize Baking Powder', 1890 (15 November), *Lyttelton Times*.
51. Sunrise cordial label, undated, H. Louis Gallien (manufacturer), Dunedin, Collection of Peter Alsop.
52. The factory as it was in 1889, 'How Advertising Has Helped My Business', Mr T.J. Edmonds, *The Advertising World*, N.Z. Supplement, November 1915. Digitisation courtesy of University of Chicago Library.
53. (Top) Photo of Jane's mother, Granny Allchin, with Gertrude, Beatrice and Irene, c. 1899, Photographer unknown, Collection of Philip Richards. (Bottom) Works 1900, Part of 'The Romance of Baking Powder', 1925 (16 December), *Lyttelton Times*, Image courtesy of Christchurch City Libraries Tūranga.
54–55. Edmonds factory photo, c.1906, Kete Christchurch, Collection of Burnside Family.
56. Edmonds family lounge, 1898, F.W. Dutch (photographer), Kete Christchurch.
57. Advertisement for Patty Pan baking powder, 1901, Christmas Number of *The Weekly Press*, Collection of Peter Alsop.
58–59. Inside the Edmonds factory, c.1908, Photographer unknown, Kete Christchurch, Collection of Burnside Family.
60. Detail of Edmonds baking powder label, c.1890–95 (thought to be used soon after the 1889–90 New Zealand & South Seas Exhibition), Goodman Fielder Archive.
62. Details of custard and egg powder labels, Goodman Fielder Archive.
63. (Top) Medal from the 1906–07 International Exhibition, Image courtesy The Purple Penny, Australia. (Bottom) Advertisement for Edmonds tin recipes, 1907 (24 August), *Otago Daily Times*.
64–65. Recipe and promotional discs included in Edmonds tins, Collection of Peter Alsop and Goodman Fielder Archive.
66. Trade flyer for Exhibition First Prize Baking Powder, 1907, Goodman Fielder Archive.
67. Illustration for paper bag for self-raising flour, c.1907–09, Philip Presants (attributed artist), Collection of Barry & Adrienne Stephens.
68. 'Edmonds Baking Powder, Try It Next Time You Bake', 1910 (1 December), *Nelson Evening Mail*.
69. 'The Hand that does the Cooking has a Finger in the Pie', 1911 (6 April), *Mataura Ensign*.
70. 'Sure to Rise' (ploughing field), 1923 (October), *The Ladies' Mirror*, Alexander Turnbull Library, S-L-1661-47.
71. (Left) Art & Business, Promotional booklet, Ilott Studios, c.1920, Alexander Turnbull Library, MSPapers-3913 4/1. (Right) 'As Light as a Fairy', 1911 (29 December), *Lyttelton Times*.
73. 'After the hard work of the shearing & harvesting camps', 1913 (20 February), *The Feilding Star*.
74. 'One 1/- tin of Edmonds Egg Powder equals 30 eggs', 1911 (22 May), *Evening Star*.
75. Edmonds application for a label trademark, 1912 (1 November), Archives New Zealand, R23394982. The trademark itself was issued in 1913 and thereafter dated to that year.
76–77. Edmonds factory, 1912, Photographer unknown (photo manipulation also undertaken), Christmas Number of *The Weekly Press*, Collection of Peter Alsop. The photo also appeared in the third edition of *Edmonds Cookery Book*.
78. Edmonds cookery books with baking, 2021, Hazel Redmond (photographer), Scene and ephemera courtesy of Barry & Adrienne Stephens.
79. Advertisement for free cookery book, 1908 (29 October), *Manawatu Standard*.
80. *Edmonds Cookery Book* first edition, 1908, Smith & Anthony Ltd (printer), Collection of Allan Paterson.
81. International and domestic cookery books, Collection of Peter Alsop.
82. Lilian, Alice and David Cropp, c.1916, Collection

of Dianne Gallagher.
83. (Top) Photos of Rene, c.1904, and Rita, c.1911, Collection of Philip Richards. (Bottom) Edmonds tin, 1908, Back cover of *Edmonds Cookery Book* first edition, Collection of Allan Paterson.
84–86 (fold-out). Covers of the second, third and fourth editions of the *Edmonds Cookery Book*, Collections of Peter Alsop, Allan Paterson and Barry & Adrienne Stephens.
86 (fold-out). 'This Free Book is invaluable', 1914 (17 July), *Patea Mail*.
87. Letter to Mr Edmonds, 1910 (28 May), Goodman Fielder Archive.
88. Illustration of festive table setting, 1955, De Luxe edition of *Edmonds Cookery Book*, Collection of Kate Parsonson.
89. *Edmonds Cookery Book* fifth edition, 1933, Collection of Peter Alsop.
90. 'A Perfect Carnival Cake', 1936, *Edmonds Cookery Book* sixth edition, Collection of Peter Alsop.
91. 'Edmonds Famous Quality Products', and 'Delicious Desserts with Edmonds', 1936, *Edmonds Cookery Book* sixth edition, Collection of Peter Alsop.
92. 'make friends with this wonderful Banana Cake!', 1960 (11 April), *The New Zealand Woman's Weekly*, Alexander Turnbull Library.
93. Illustration detail from the 1977 De Luxe edition of *Edmonds Cookery Book*, Collection of Peter Alsop.
94. Illustration detail from the 1955 De Luxe edition of *Edmonds Cookery Book*, Collection of Peter Alsop.
95. Recipe leaflet, c.1960, Alexander Turnbull Library.
96. Spread from the 1955 De Luxe edition of *Edmonds Cookery Book*, Collection of Peter Alsop.
97. Various covers of *Edmonds Cookery Book*, Collection of Peter Alsop.
98–99. Miscellaneous recipes from various editions of *Edmonds Cookery Book*, Collection of Kate Parsonson.
100. Beatrice and Rene, c.1908, Collection of Philip Richards.
102. Will, Alice, Nelma and Rita Edmonds, c.1908, Collection of Grace Hart.
103. Lilian and Bert Cropp, c.1917, Collection of Dianne Gallagher.
105. Milburn Light Electric, Model 27L, c.1921, Collection of Philip Richards.
106. Beatrice, Gertrude, Thomas and Irene at Hanmer Springs, c.1908, Collection of Michael Williams.
107. Thomas and Jane with Bert and David Cropp at Taronga Zoo, c.1916, Collection of Dianne Gallagher.
108–109. The extended family, 1901, Collection of Dianne Gallagher.
110–111. James Edmonds with Ginger, Collection of Cassandra Philpot. Thomas and Jane with Irene, c.1912, Collection of Dianne Gallagher. Irene and Alice Edmonds (née Hart), c.1913, Collection of Dianne Gallagher. Ernest Edmonds, Woolston Primary School, c.1887, Collection of Susan Park. Julia Blackwood, née Edmonds, 1892, author of a *Shipboard Diary* (1884), Deirdre Cooper Photo Collection, Published in *Plymouth to Port Chalmers: Julia's Story*, Contains Original Shipboard Diary, ISBN 978-0-473-53537-7. Edwin and Sarah Edmonds (née Irvine), and family, c.1901, Collection of Rosemary Edmonds. Edwin Edmonds (Thomas's brother) in later life, Collection of Marie Edmonds. Ernest Edmonds with family, c.1920, Collection of Susan Park. Thomas and Jane, c.1915, Collection of Michael Williams. Crab hunting at Castle Rock, Sydney, Australia, c.1918, Collection of Michael Williams. Outside the wooden factory, c.1918, Collection of Rosemary Edmonds. Will Edmonds in his 1912 Mitchell (Touring), Collection of Michael Williams.
112–113. 'On the beach at Waikiki'. Irene, Thomas and Jane, with Gertrude and Beatrice, c.1916. 'Bathing at Waikiki' with Diamond Head in the distance, c.1916. Irene in Waikiki, Hawaii, c.1916. 'Our guide, and Rene expecting to lose her life any minute', Glacier Point, Yosemite National Park, USA, c.1916. Beatrice, Irene and Gertrude with friend. Beatrice, on the voyage to Hobart to perform with the Cheer-Ohs, c.1917. Gertrude with her camera, c.1917. Beatrice, Irene and Gertrude with the ship's captain and Mrs Bennett White, Cheer-Ohs director, c.1917. 'The fashion of 1916': in costume, Gertrude in the centre and Beatrice on the right, with fellow Cheer-Oh Girl on the left. Beatrice and ukelele, Hawaii, c.1917. Gertrude and ukelele, Hawaii, c.1917. Beatrice and her Cheer-Oh Kewpie doll, c.1917. Beatrice, Gertrude and Irene, c.1917. Cheer-Oh Girls, c.1918. All photos from Collection of Michael Williams.
114–115. Keith Edmonds and David Cropp, overlooking Auckland Zoo, c.1924, Collection of Dianne Gallagher. Eileen and Edna Edmonds, c.1920, Collection of Susan Park. George and Clara Edmonds' children, Nola, Thelma, Jack and Ray, c.1920, Collection of John Edmonds Family. James and Edith Edmonds' daughter, Marijean, c.1923, Collection of Cassandra Philpot. Eileen Edmonds with sister Edna and cousin David in the barrow, c.1916, Collection of Dianne Gallagher. Thomas and Jane at their daughter Beatrice's wedding, Sydney 1920, Collection of Michael Williams. Thomas and Jane Edmonds with granddaughter Pamela, c.1922, Collection of Dianne Gallagher. Lilian with son David, c.1917, Collection of Dianne Gallagher. The four Edmonds sisters with David Cropp, c.1917, Collection of Dianne Gallagher. Thomas with Will's widow Alice (née Hart) and their two youngest children, Keith and Brenda, and some of the Hart clan, c.1918, Collection of Dianne Gallagher. Lilian and Jane Edmonds, c.1920, Collection of Dianne Gallagher. Ernest and family, c.1914, Collection of Susan Park. Brenda and Keith Edmonds and David Cropp, c.1918, Collection of Dianne Gallagher. Family group, c.1922, Collection of Dianne Gallagher.
116. Will Edmonds, c.1904, Collection of Grace Hart.
118. Bert Cropp, Collection of Dianne Gallagher.
119. Certificate of Incorporation and Shareholders, 1915, Files of T.J. Edmonds Ltd, Archives New Zealand (Christchurch), R19909634.
120. 'Absolutely Free from Substitutes!', 1916 (16 February), *Grey River Argus*.
121. (Top) Jim Edmonds, Collection of Cassandra Philpot. (Bottom) 'No rival but the sun–', 1920, Christmas Number of *The Weekly Press*, Collection of Peter Alsop.
122. (Top) Ernest and Ethel Edmonds with Lily and Edna, c.1915, Collection of Susan Park. (Bottom) Irene with violin, c.1915, Collection of Philip Richards.
123. Jane and Thomas in Portland, c.1916, Collection of Dianne Gallagher.
124. 'The Cheero Girls', 1918 (31 March), *Sun* (Sydney), Image courtesy State Library of NSW. Names as credited: (Back row) Miss Edith Dickerson, Miss Dorrie Ward, Mrs Bennnett White, Miss Beatrice Edmonds, Miss Jack Neill, (Middle row) Miss Joan Walford, Mrs Morse, Miss Amy Bice, (Seated) Miss Gertrude Edmonds, Miss Thora Wood.
125. Gertrude and Harry Williams on their wedding day in 1921, Collection of Michael Williams.
126. Cover photo from *Your Visit to Edmonds*, 1949–50, V.C. Browne (photographer), Collection of Peter Alsop.
127. Invitation for tenders to build new factory and office buildings, 1920 (10 July), *Sun*.
128. Edmonds factory on Ferry Road, 1923, R.P. Moore (photographer), Alexander Turnbull Library, Pan-0215-F.
129. 'The Largest Baking Powder Factory South of the Line', 1922, Christmas Number of *The Weekly Press*, Collection of Peter Alsop.
130–131. The old and new Edmonds factories, c.1922–23, G.H. (George) Edmonds (photographer), Collection of John & Jenny Hoskin. George worked at Edmonds and kept up an interest in photography, including placement of photographic studies in Christchurch papers between 1922 and 1924.
132. Edmonds factory and offices, 1923, *Edmonds Cookery Book* fourth edition, Collection of Peter Alsop.
133. Photo of 'The Present Executive', *Printed in Through the Changing Years*, 1929, Alexander Turnbull Library.
134. 'Further Extensions …', 1937 (11 December), *Auckland Star*, Image courtesy Auckland Libraries.
135. Photo of a diorama of the Edmonds factory complex after alterations, c.1938 (visible in Edmonds' display at the 1939–40 Centennial), Christine Umbach (photographer), Collection of Friends of Edmonds Factory Garden.
136. 'Where Our Principal Materials and Supplies Come From', *Your Visit to Edmonds*, 1949–50, Collection of Peter Alsop.
137. Factory scene, Still from *Cookery Nook*, 1955, 35mm, B&W, sd, Frame enlargement, Stills collection, Ngā Taonga Sound & Vision, Courtesy Pacific Films Ltd and the Aotearoa/New Zealand Film Heritage Trust – Te Puna Ataata.
138–139. Edmonds factory and gardens, 1952, *Edmonds Cookery Book* seventh edition, Collection of Peter Alsop.
140. Tin labelling, Still from *Cookery Nook*, 1955, Ngā Taonga Sound & Vision.
141. 'A Column of Tins 733,333 Feet High', 1921 (10 September), *Press*.
142. (Left) Edmonds colouring competition entry, c.1950, Goodman Fielder Archive. (Right) *The Edmonds Custard Fairy Book*, 1931, Valentine Studios (designer), Unknown collection.
143. 'Mama's Favourite', 1914, Christmas Number of the *Canterbury Times*, Collection of Peter Alsop.
144–145. Tin production, c.1950, Goodman Fielder Archive (left) and Collection of Peter Alsop (right). Tin making, c.1950, Collection of Peter Alsop. Packing sponge mix, c.1950, Goodman Fielder Archive. Factory floor, 1922, Collection of Peter Alsop. Filling room floor, 1923, *Edmonds Cookery Book* sixth edition, Collection of Peter Alsop. Engineers' workshop, Collection of Peter Alsop. Case-making department, c.1950, Collection of Peter Alsop (left) and Goodman Fielder Archive (right). 75th anniversary celebrations, 1954, Edmonds Family Collection. Staff receiving awards for 25+ years of service, 1951, Edmonds Family Collection. Colin Hart in the laboratory, *Edmonds Cookery Book* sixth edition, Collection of Peter Alsop. Rosa Stern, scientist, 1955, and Dr Stern & colleague, Stills from *Cookery Nook*, 1955, Ngā Taonga Sound & Vision. Packing jelly crystals, c.1950, Collection of Peter Alsop. Staff, 1950s, Collection of Peter Alsop. Staff of T.J. Edmonds Ltd, March 1937, Goodman Fielder Archive.

The photo of staff receiving awards for 25+ years of service was taken in 1951 on the occasion of P.J. Smith, factory manager, retiring after 50 years

of unbroken service. There were 16 employees who qualified for awards, with 503 years total combined service. Back row: G. Hart (26 years), A. Clarke (31), A. Fuller (31), R. Everest (26), F. Kinley (36) and G. Fisk (27). Front: F.S. Taylor (25), P.J. Smith (50), C. Stemmer (31), E. Lowe (25), J. Penn (30), G. Webber (27), A. Smith (31), G.C. Cox (25+), B.S. Yuill (29). C. Parry (45 years) was absent. In the copy of the photo viewed for the book, the original photo was referenced to the Parry Family. It was also noted that C.G. Cox (Tiny) went on to stay at Edmonds for over 50 years, passing P.J. Smith's previous record.
146. Edmonds Band Rotunda, 1932 (30 August), Photographer unknown, Stuff Limited, 622956481. Digitally coloured by Brendan Graham.
147. 'A Half Century Celebrated', 1929 (27 September), *Star.*
148. Invitation to the Official Opening of Poplar Crescent, 1929 (11 November, event date), Collection of John & Jenny Hoskin.
149. Pages from *Through the Changing Years* (separate pages joined for display), 1929, Alexander Turnbull Library.
150. Temple of Truth, c.1895, Photographer unknown, Hocken Collections, Asset ID 8292.
151. Edmonds clock tower, 2019, Michal Klajban, Wikimedia, CC-BY-SA 4.0.
152. Theosophical Society Building, Photographer and source unknown.
153. Repertory Theatre (originally Radiant Hall), 1984 (December), P.R. Wilson (photographer), Published in the N.Z. Historic Places Trust Buildings Record Form.
154. Alexander William Bickerton, c.1905, Photographer unknown, Alexander Turnbull Library, 1/2-038594-F.
155. Wainoni Park Entrance, Christchurch, c.1908, L.B. Quartermain collection, Canterbury Museum, Ref: Postcard 745.
156–157. Hand-coloured photograph of the Edmonds Band Rotunda with the Clock Tower in the background, c.1930 (likely soon after the rotunda's completion), J.P. Drewitt (photographer), Collection of Peter Alsop (originally owned by T.J. Edmonds (inscription on the back)).
158. Thomas Edmonds, 'My Jubilee', 1908, Photographer unknown, Collection of Cassandra Philpot.
159. Illuminated certificate gifted to T.J. Edmonds by employees, 1929, Artist unknown, Auctioned in 2009 (website image) by Watsons Auctions Christchurch.
160. 'Save 11D', 1933 (July), *Mirror*, Collection of Peter Alsop.
161. *Through the Changing Years*, 1929, Alexander Turnbull Library.
162. Sure to Rise (illuminated factory with levitating tin), 1933, *Brett's Christmas Annual*, Collection of Peter Alsop.
163. Cathedral Square (detail from cover), 1931, Christmas annual of the *Star*, Collection of Bill Main.
164. 'Grocer Manufacturer Philanthropist', 1932 (July), Obituary for T.J. Edmonds, *The N.Z. Bakers' & Grocers' Review*, Goodman Fielder Archive.
166. T.J. Edmonds, Date unknown, Archibald Nicoll (1886–1953), Oil on canvas, 915 x 712mm, Canterbury Museum, 1986.259.1.
167. (Top) Newspaper clippings, 1932 (26 September), *Waipawa Mail* and 1932 (24 November), *Ashburton Guardian*. (Bottom) Acto label, 1932–c.1940, Goodman Fielder Archive.
168. 'Vacancies for Girls & Youths', Leaflet advertising employment benefits, c.1947 ('nearly 70 years' since the founding), Goodman Fielder Archive.
169. The staff of T.J. Edmonds Ltd, 1929 (26 September), Official jubilee photograph, Green & Hahn (photographer), Collection of Michael Williams. Names as credited: (Back row) A. Clifford, R.D. Overend, C.G. Cox, A.J. Cockburn, A.E.B. Clarke, E.W. Lowe, B.S. Yuill, G.W.J. Fisk, W.I. Davey, (Third row) G.R. Hart, P.E. Ewart, A.W. Smith, W. Paton, J.W. Penn, F.B.P. Kinley, C. Parry, G.A. Melrose, H. Field, W.H. Round, (Second row) C. Hart, J.D. Edmonds, R.J. Murly, A.L. Cropp (Managing Director), T.J. Edmonds (Chairman Director), G.H. Edmonds (Director), Miss V.G. Coton, F.S. Taylor, (Front Row) J.A. Lanyon, N.A. McCready, F.G. Webber, C.C. Stemmer, A.W. Everest, A.E. Fuller, H.W. Brown, (Absent) P.J. Smith, C. Webster.
170 & 171. Jane Edmonds, c.1903 and c.1930, Photographers unknown, Collection of Philip Richards.
172. Edmonds tin, 1939 (June), *Mirror*, Collection of Peter Alsop.
174. Edmonds display at the 1939–40 New Zealand Centennial Exhibition, Eileen Deste (1908–86, photographer), Fletcher Trust Archives, 0302-4 183.
175. Photos of factory activity, *Edmonds Cookery Book* sixth edition, Collection of Peter Alsop.
176. (Left) Acto label, c.1945, Goodman Fielder Archive. (Right) 'Edmonds "Sure-to-Rise" Baking Powder', 1945 (15 October), *Evening Post.*
177. 'Above All Others', 1945 (December), Artist unknown, *Mirror*, Collection of Peter Alsop.
178. 'For Successful Cooking', 1946 (December), *Mirror*, Collection of Peter Alsop.
179. (Top) 'Mrs. Active Acto', 1946 (1 November), *Otago Daily Times.* (Bottom) 'Both the Peak of Perfection', 1947 (16 January), *Otago Daily Times.*
180. (Top) 'The Important Human Factor', Page from *Your Visit to Edmonds*, 1949–50, Collection of Peter Alsop. (Bottom) Edmonds truck driver Fred Kinley, late 1940s, Photographer unknown, Collection of Ian Kinley.
181. Man baking, Still from *Cookery Nook*, 1955, Ngā Taonga Sound & Vision.
182–183. 'Milestones – T.J. Edmonds Ltd.', 1950, 1850–1950 Centennial Number of *Star-Sun.*
184. Advertisement for Edmonds Tang (detail), Date unknown (c.1975), Railways Studios, Original billboard design, Collection of Graham Winter.
185. T.J. Edmonds Ltd Annual Report, 1981, Collection of Philip Richards.
186. (Top) Ron Hooker (right) and lab technicians, Photographer unknown, Unknown collection. (Bottom) T.J. Edmonds Ltd Annual Report, 1981, Collection of Philip Richards.
187. (Left) Governor-General's export award, T.J. Edmonds Ltd Annual Report, 1979, Collection of Philip Richards. (Right) Edmonds of New Zealand – food exporters to the world, Promotional booklet, c.1978, Archives New Zealand, R17239784.
188. (Top and bottom) T.J. Edmonds Ltd Annual Report, 1975, Collection of Philip Richards.
189. (Logos) Back cover of Edmonds Prīma cook book (top), c.1970, Collection of Peter Alsop; T.J. Edmonds Ltd Annual Report (bottom), 1972, Collection of Philip Richards. (Tins) Collection of Barry & Adrienne Stephens.
190. Siblings together, Collection of Michael Williams.
191. Ernest with Eileen and Edna, c.1905, Collection of Susan Park.
192. (Top) Lilian with Elaine and David, c.1927, Collection of Dianne Gallagher. (Bottom) The four sisters in younger years, Collection of Michael Williams.
193. The four sisters in later life, Collection of Michael Williams.
194. The wedding of Irene and Kenneth Ballantyne, 1925, Collection of Philip Richards.
195. Studio portrait of Irene, c.1935, Collection of Philip Richards.
196. Edmonds gardeners Ray Leech and Norm Griggs, 1984 (14 September), Christchurch City Libraries. CCL-StarP-04994A, with permission from *Christchurch Star.* Digitally coloured by Brendan Graham.
197. Introductory statement in *Your Visit to Edmonds*, 1949–50, Collection of Peter Alsop.
198 & 199. Women from the Rangiora Housewives Association (left) and Edmonds staff (right), Stills from *Cookery Nook*, 1955, Ngā Taonga Sound & Vision.
200–201. Edmonds factory and gardens, c.1948, V.C. Browne (photographer); the photo was included in an advertisement inviting visitors that appeared in *Mirror* in December 1950, Collection of Peter Alsop.
202. Sketch of Edmonds factory and gardens, front of Edmonds Christmas card, Date unknown, Marmaduke Matthews (artist, 1886–1949), Collection of Mark Nicholls.
203. The Edmonds gardens (clockwise from top left) in 1978, 1970, 1970 and 1974, Photographers unknown, Images courtesy of Neiel Drain, Collection of the Canterbury Horticultural Society.
204. 'Owners see no merit in Edmonds buildings', 1990 (21 September), *Press*, Image courtesy of Christchurch City Libraries Tūranga.
205. Jack Hislop and Joe Smart of Carlyle Demolition, 1990 (29 October), Photographer unknown, Stuff Limited, 645012642. Digitally coloured by Brendan Graham.
206. (Top) Tickler box, Christine Umbach (photographer), Collection of John & Jenny Hoskin. (Bottom) Commemorative plaque donated by Brierly Investments Ltd in 1991, Photographer and source unknown.
207. Jenny and John Hoskin, founders of Friends of Edmonds Factory Garden, 2022, Christine Umbach (photographer).
208. Display of Edmonds tins, 2020, Peter Alsop (photographer), Collection of Peter Alsop.
209. John Edmonds celebrating the reinstatement of Edmonds Street, *Star*, 22 November 2017, Photographer unknown, Collection of John Edmonds.
210. 'A to Z of New Zealand', Stamp series, 2008, New Zealand Post, Collection of Peter Alsop.
211. (Left) 'Aunt Daisy!', Poster for Peter Hawes' play, performed at Downstage Theatre, Wellington, 1989, Source unknown. (Right) 'Sure to Rise' (tea towel, postcard and print design), 2011 (April), Rebecca Lovell-Smith (artist), Image courtesy of the artist.
214–215. Photograph of the newly restored Edmonds Band Rotunda, 2021 (20 August), Stuff Limited, 644540895.
216. Custard powder tin, 1923, *Edmonds Cookery Book* fourth edition, Collection of Peter Alsop.
218. (Top) 28 August 1890 (earliest) *Lyttelton Times.* (Bottom) 28 January 1891 (earliest) *Star.*
219. (Bottom) Label, c.1895, Goodman Fielder Archive.
220 & 221. (Custard Bay) Panel of baking powder label, 1906, Goodman Fielder Archive. (Medals) Period labels, Goodman Fielder Archive. (Banners) Label details, Goodman Fielder Archive. (Lids)

Collections of Peter Alsop and Kate Parsonson.
222. Various Edmonds tins, Collections of Peter Alsop, Allan Paterson, Barry & Adrienne Stephens and Museum of Everyday (Courtesy of Christine Fernyhough).
223. Tin production in the Edmonds factory, Still from *Cookery Nook*, 1955, Ngā Taonga Sound & Vision.
224–225 (fold-out). 1916 baking powder label, Goodman Fielder Archive.
225–228 (fold-out). 'From Failure to Success', 1922 (July), and 'Can you imagine anything nicer for a summer day', 1924 (November), Ilott Advertising (artist), *Mirror*, Collection of Peter Alsop. 'How Advertising Has Helped My Business', Mr T.J. Edmonds, *The Advertising World*, N.Z. Supplement, November 1915. Digitisation courtesy of University of Chicago Library.
228 (fold-out). (Labels) Egg and cake powder labels, Goodman Fielder Archive. (Illustration) 'Cakes Without Eggs', 1908, *Edmonds Cookery Book* first edition, Collection of Allan Paterson.
229. 'You can't pick out the bad egg from the good one', 1916 (April), Ilott Advertising (artist), *West Coast Times*.
230. 'They've Broken the Record this year', 1913 (25 February), Ilott Advertising (artist), *Evening Post*.
231. 'Friends Past Present Future', 1923, *Edmonds Cookery Book* fourth edition, Collection of Peter Alsop.
232–233. Promotional discs included in Edmonds tins, Goodman Fielder Archive.
234. Custard powder label (detail), 1913–14 (includes disclosure required by law from 1913 and pre-dates the company's incorporation), Goodman Fielder Archive.
235. (Top) Photo of printing presses in the offices of the Christchurch Press Company, 1905 (or shortly after), Alexander Turnbull Library, PACoII-8763. (Bottom) Invoice/docket of T.J. Edmonds, 1907–09, Philip Presants (1867–1942, attributed artist based on style), Goodman Fielder Archive.
236–237. Photo of Philip Presants (right) and an unknown artist in a design studio of the Christchurch Press Company, 1905 (or shortly after), Alexander Turnbull Library, PACoII-8763. Advice from Julian Heyes, Presants' great-grandson, is gratefully acknowledged.
238. 'Edmonds Baking Powder "Sure to Rise"', 1927 (July), Ilott Advertising (artist), *Mirror*, Collection of Peter Alsop.
239. 'Next time you visit Mr. Grocer', 1925 (22 April), Ilott Advertising (artist), *Otago Daily Times*.
240–241. Various newspaper advertisements by Ilott Advertising (1–10, clockwise from top left): (1) 1930 (28 April), *New Zealand Herald*; (2) 1926 (20 January), *Evening Post*; (3) 1924 (18 March), *Poverty Bay Herald*; (4) 1923 (1 December), *Waikato Times*; (5) 1930 (5 February), *Otago Daily Times*; (6) 1930 (1 May), *Evening Star*; (7) 1923 (29 December), *Waikato Times*; (8) 1924 (28 June), *Nelson Evening Mail*; (9) 1924 (8 March), *Waikato Times*; (10) 1930 (25 January), *Poverty Bay Herald*.
242 & 243. Edmonds sunburst advertisements (left to right): 1927 (September); 1927 (November); 1929 (January), *Mirror*, Collection of Peter Alsop.
244. (Sample box) 1923–27, Collection of Irene & Roger Devlin. (Sample tin) 1931 (see, for example, the *Evening Star* on 13 August), Collection of Barry & Adrienne Stephens. (Small promotional item) Delicious Custards, c.1915, Goodman Fielder Archive. (Label) Custard powder 'Royal' flavour label, 1913–14, Goodman Fielder Archive.
245. Photo of meringues and other baking, 1955 De Luxe edition of *Edmonds Cookery Book*, Collection of Peter Alsop.
246. Photo of artists working in Ilott Advertising, c.1930, Ilott Collection, Alexander Turnbull Library, MS-Papers-3913. Digitally coloured by Brendan Graham. George Tough is the artist second from rear, the other artists are unknown.
247. 'The happy hostess', 1925 (August), Ilott Advertising (artist), *Mirror*, Collection of Peter Alsop.
248. Original pencil drawing of grapes produced for Ilott Advertising, c.1935, George Tough, Collection of Peter Alsop.
249. 'Edmonds Sure-to-Rise Products', 1934, Christmas Number of *New Zealand Illustrated*, Collection of Peter Alsop.
250. 'Edmonds "Sure-to-Rise" Baking Powder', 1931, Christmas Number of *New Zealand Illustrated*, Collection of Peter Alsop.
251. (Top left) Photo of unknown woman working in Ilott Advertising, c.1925 (the advertisement on the wall was published in 1925 in *Mirror*), Ilott Collection, Alexander Turnbull Library, MS-Papers-3913. (Bottom left) 'Are you proud of your cakes & pastry?', 1925 (February), *Mirror*, Collection of Peter Alsop. (Top right) '57 Years of Progress', 1936, *Tui's Annual – N.Z. Exporter Annual Inc.*, George Tough (attributed artist based on Tough working on a similar composition in the accompanying photo), Wellington Publishing Co., Hocken Collections, Uare Taoka o Hākena, University of Otago, S19-560a. (Bottom right) Photo of George Tough working at Ilott Advertising, 1936, Collection of Antony Stariha.
252 & 253. (Printing plate and associated print) 'Acknowledged Leader in the Baking Powder field', c.1935, Collection of Kate Parsonson. (Top left) The Artist at Work, 1932 (March), Walter J. Thompson (photographer), *Mirror*, Collection of Peter Alsop. (Bottom left) The Etcher at Work, 1932 (November), J.D.G. Drought (photographer), *Mirror*, Collection of Peter Alsop.
254. 'Sure to Rise and to make a safe landing in every corner of New Zealand', 1928, Christmas Number of *The Weekly Press*, Collection of Peter Alsop.
255. 'Known in Two Hemispheres', 1930, Christmas Number of *The Weekly Press*, Collection of Peter Alsop.
256. 'Christmas Cake – Christmas Pudding', 1952, *Edmonds Cookery Book* seventh edition, Collection of Peter Alsop.
257. Photo of baking, 1955, De Luxe edition of *Edmonds Cookery Book*, Collection of Peter Alsop.
258. Photo of baking, 1955, De Luxe edition of *Edmonds Cookery Book*, Collection of Peter Alsop.
259. 'Edmonds', 1937, *The Coronation Plunket Cookery Book*, Invercargill City Libraries & Archives, Support from Amanda Hunter and Katherine Rich is gratefully acknowledged.
260. 'Edmonds Famous Quality Products', 1955, *Edmonds Cookery Book* economy edition, Collection of Peter Alsop.
261. 'Edmonds Famous Quality Products', 1952, *Edmonds Cookery Book* seventh edition, Collection of Peter Alsop.
262. 'Edmonds Custard', 1937, *The Coronation Plunket Cookery Book*, Invercargill City Libraries & Archives.
263. Photo of Adrienne Stephens' baking, 2021, Hazel Redmond (photographer), Image courtesy of Barry & Adrienne Stephens.
264. Photo of the collecting room of Barry and Adrienne Stephens, 2021, Hazel Redmond (photographer), Image courtesy of Barry & Adrienne Stephens.
265. Cake and custard powder labels, 1931, 1939 and 1928 (top to bottom), Goodman Fielder Archive.
266. Coloured cake baking powder label (detail), 1931 (coloured cake powder was advertised from this time), Goodman Fielder Archive.
267. 'Jellies and Custard', 1939 (April), *Mirror*, Collection of Peter Alsop.
268. 'A Merry Xmas to All', 1924 (13 December), *Otago Daily Times*.
269. 'The Big Three in Christmas Cooking', 1951 (December), *Mirror*, Collection of Peter Alsop.
270. 'Once again as for over 70 years Edmonds wish you all a Very Happy Christmas', 1949 (December), *Mirror*, Collection of Peter Alsop.
271. (Top left) 'Happier Baking days', 1934 (November), *Mirror*, Collection of Peter Alsop. (Bottom left) 'Edmonds "Sure to Rise" Baking Powder', 1934 (October), *Mirror*, Collection of Peter Alsop. (Right) Photo of sponge cake with flowers (detail, image flipped), 1955, De Luxe edition of *Edmonds Cookery Book*, Collection of Peter Alsop.
272 & 273. 'At Last! Messages Reach Mars' (1924) and 'Father Christmas writes as follows–, (1925), W. Baverstock (artist), Christmas Numbers of *The Weekly Press*, Collection of Peter Alsop.
274. Sure to Set jelly crystals packaging, 1935 (introduced from this year), Goodman Fielder Archive.
275. (Newspaper advertisements) 'for Perfect Jellies' (top), 1935 (20 November), *Manawatu Standard* and 'Edmonds "Sure-to-Set" Jellies' (bottom), 1942 (19 February), *Evening Star*. (Promotional disc) 'Announcing Edmonds Jelly Crystals', 1935 (introduced from this year), Goodman Fielder Archive. (Right) 'A Wonderful New Jelly', 1935, Christmas Number of *New Zealand Illustrated*, Image courtesy of Stuff Ltd.
276–277. 'Edmonds Fresh Fruit Flavoured Jelly Crystals Are Now Ready!', 1935 (introduced from this year), Goodman Fielder Archive.
278. 'Edmonds "Sure-to-Set" Jellies', c.1936 (advertised as a new product line from 1935), Original artwork by George Tough, Collection of Peter Alsop.
279. 'choose Edmonds Jellies they are Sure-To-Set!', 'Custard Makes it Better', 'Edmonds Full Flavour Jellies', c.1950, Original artworks by Railways Studios, Archives New Zealand (ABIN W3806, first two designs) and Collection of Peter Alsop.
280. 'A Tradition in every New Zealand home', 1937 (16 October), *Evening Star*.
281. (Photos) Table setting and baking scenes, Stills from *Cookery Nook*, 1955, Ngā Taonga Sound & Vision. The woman in the right-hand image is Ethne Mahoney. (Bottom) 'Edmonds Makes Cooking a Pleasure', 1955, De Luxe edition of *Edmonds Cookery Book*, Collection of Peter Alsop.
282. (Advertisement) 'Recipes with Edmonds Maize Cornflour', 1955, *Edmonds Cookery Book* economy edition, Collection of Peter Alsop. (Box) Wheat cornflour box, Collection of Peter Alsop.
283. 'try these New Recipes', 1953 (March), *Mirror*, Collection of Peter Alsop.
284. (Top) 'Favourites in Every Home', 1949–50, *Your Visit to Edmonds* (booklet for visitors to the factory), Collection of Peter Alsop. (Bottom) 'Edmonds ... Quality Products', 1955, *Edmonds Cookery Book* economy edition, Collection of Peter Alsop.
285. 'Use Edmonds Quality Products', 1937 (December), *Mirror*, Collection of Peter Alsop.
286–287. Reflections, Images supplied. Al Brown was photographed by Alex McVinnie.
288–289. Edmonds tins and box, 2021, Hazel Redmond (photographer), Image courtesy of Barry & Adrienne Stephens.

INDEX

Page numbers in **bold** refer to illustrations.

ACKNOWLEDGEMENTS

We would like to recognise Goodman Fielder's ownership of the Edmonds brand and thank their New Zealand CEO, Bernard Duignan. Special thanks go to the following people who made significant contributions to this book: Catherine Montgomery and Katrina McCallum of Canterbury University Press; Anna Rogers for invaluable writing and editorial support; Gillian Tewsley for editing; Gary Stewart for design and production work and long-running goodwill; Kaye van Grunsven, Christchurch City Libraries, for research support; and Bee Dawson for early research and writing.

This book would not have been possible without the enthusiasm and support of the Edmonds family. A special thanks to Philip Richards and Mark Nichols, but also to other descendants: Day Ballantyne, Deb Ballantyne, John Ballantyne, Kay Ballantyne, Robert Ballantyne, John Edmonds, Rosemary Edmonds & Chrissy West, Dianne Gallagher, Jacqui Griffith & Beverley Edmonds, Grace Hart, Kerry Nicholls, Susie & Daryll Park, Cassandra Philpot, Jane Williams, Michael Williams, and Genevieve & James Willoughby. Also, descendants and family of Edwin & Sarah Edmonds and Henry & Fanny Edmonds: Marie Edmonds, Jen Edmonds and Deidre Cooper.

Appreciation is also extended to people and organisations who supported the book in various ways (with apologies to anyone missed): Fiona Allison, Amy Ryan & Rosalind Stewart (Christchurch City Libraries); Max Alsop; Samuel Ardell, Gillian Headifen, Graeme Shaw, Alicia Tolley & Claire Viskovic (Alexander Turnbull Library); Roger Barclay; Alison Barnett & Courtney Seefeldt (Micrographics); Julia Barron & Keith Giles (Auckland Libraries); Shahn Bastow; Lydia Baxendell & Erin Kimber (Macmillan Brown Library); Claudia Bell; Nicolas Boigelot, Abbey Foster, Neill Phillips & Anthony Wright (Canterbury Museum); Bill Bryce; Fi Brinble (Sauce Communications); British Library; Will Britton & Elsie Wolfe (Wondrous Antiques); Angus Brow; James Brow; Mal Brow; Nadine Burnett; Barry Clarke (Star Media); Jo Carter (Carterworks digitisation); Steve Costello; Irene & Roger Devlin; Peter & Joan Duncan; Freya Elmer & Emily Hames (MOTAT); Andrew Fenwick, Karen Gonzaga, Katherine Jensen & Angela Monk (Goodman Fielder); Christine Fernyhough & Kathrine Sullivan (Museum of Everyday); Steve Flora; Bert Fuller; Ron Fuller; Jessie Garland; Lucy Glausiuss; Sally Goldsmith; Bill Goldsworthy; Elizabeth Goodall (MTG Hawke's Bay); Brendan Graham; Ken Hall & Tim Jones (Christchurch Art Gallery); Kevin Hannah (Richmond Antiques); Natasha Harris (NZ On Screen); Jennifer Hart (University of Chicago); Sandra Hart; Matthew Hayes (AJ Park); Julian Heyes; Judith Holloway (IPONZ); Gillian Hooker; Paula Hooker; Sandra Hooker; Kristin Hoskin; Amanda Hunter (Invercargill City Libraries & Archives); Irene Joseph; Sam Kay; Ann-Marie Kennedy; Ian Kinley; Laila Lambert; Michael Lawson; Helen Leach; Nicola Legat (Te Papa Press); Rebecca Lovell-Smith; Trevor Marechal; Katherine Milburn & Baylee Smith (Hocken Library); Terry Moyle (Contour Creations); Lindsay Neill (AUT); New South Wales Library; Adrienne Olsen; Justine Olsen; Claire Orbell (Toitū Otago Settlers Museum); Allan Paterson; Anthony Rackstraw; Hazel Redmond Photographer (and the team at The Photo Shop, Ashburton); Sheree Reid; Katherine Rich; Zoe Richardson & Susan Tolich (Auckland War Memorial Museum); Steve Russell (Ngā Taonga Sound & Vision); Richard Sheaff; Alison Shucksmith (Hachette Publishing); Julian Smith (Dunedin City Library); Antony Stahira; Barry & Adrienne Stephens; Isabel Sutherland (Fletcher Archives); Dan Tait-Jamieson; Dennis Taylor; Jude Tewnion (Stuff Ltd); Hamish Thompson; Mike Todd; David Tossman; Dr Christine Umbach; David Veart; and Darian Zam.

Thanks to John and Jenny Hoskin for their wide-ranging support. We would like to acknowledge too all who were involved in the community effort to salvage and retain the Edmonds gardens, particularly John & Jenny.

Lastly we would like to acknowledge Gertrude Edmonds (1891–1997). Her memory and stories of Edmonds life were a rich source of fascinating detail for this book, and her photographs provided insight into the lives of Thomas and Jane Edmonds and their children and grandchildren.

AUTHORS

Peter Alsop is a senior executive who has worked across the public and private sectors. He is a keen collector of New Zealand art and design, including vintage ephemera and hand-coloured photography – interests that have underpinned his spare-time passion for publishing. He is the author and co-author of 10 previous books, including *Selling the Dream*, *Mauri Ora – Wisdom from the Māori World* and *Hand-Coloured New Zealand*.

Kate Parsonson is a great-great-granddaughter of Thomas and Jane Edmonds and a descendant of their eldest son, William. Kate began researching for this book in 2018, curious to discover more about her family history and keen to document the Edmonds story, especially the story around the iconic *Edmonds Cookery Book*. Kate has a love of literature and a strong interest in the visual arts. This is her first book.

Richard Wolfe is an art, design and cultural historian who has a PhD in Art History from the University of Auckland and a BFA from the Elam School of Fine Arts. He was Curator of Display at Auckland War Memorial Museum (1977–1997), and has written or co-authored 41 previous books, most recently *Footprints on the Land: How Humans Changed New Zealand*. He has also written a large number of articles, covering diverse aspects of New Zealand art, history and popular culture.

UC
UNIVERSITY OF
CANTERBURY
Te Whare Wānanga o Waitaha
CHRISTCHURCH NEW ZEALAND

First published in 2023 by
CANTERBURY UNIVERSITY PRESS
University of Canterbury
Private Bag 4800, Christchurch
NEW ZEALAND
www.canterbury.ac.nz/engage/cup

ISBN 978-1-98-850331-8

A catalogue record for this book is available
from the National Library of New Zealand.

Design: Peter Alsop & The Gas Project
Production: The Gas Project
Index: Diane Lowther

Front cover. 'Above All Others', 1945 (December), Artist unknown, *Mirror*, Mirror Publishing Company, Collection of Peter Alsop. Brendan Graham has superimposed a Sure to Rise baking powder label over the Acto original.

Back cover. Edmonds factory photo, c.1906, Kete Christchurch, Collection of Burnside Family.

Printed in China through Asia Pacific Offset